*Sidney Sussex College
Cambridge*

HISTORICAL ESSAYS
IN COMMEMORATION OF THE QUATERCENTENARY

Lady Frances Sidney, Countess of Sussex, Foundress of the College, attributed to Steven van der Meulen, c.1565

Sidney Sussex College Cambridge

HISTORICAL ESSAYS
IN COMMEMORATION OF THE QUATERCENTENARY

Edited by D. E. D. BEALES *and* H. B. NISBET

THE BOYDELL PRESS

© Contributors 1996

All Rights Reserved. Except as permitted under current legislation no part of this work may be photocopied, stored in a retrieval system, published, performed in public, adapted, broadcast, transmitted, recorded or reproduced in any form or by any means, without the prior permission of the copyright owner

First published 1996
The Boydell Press, Woodbridge

ISBN 0 85115 629 0

The Boydell Press is an imprint of Boydell & Brewer Ltd
PO Box 9, Woodbridge, Suffolk IP12 3DF, UK
and of Boydell & Brewer Inc.
PO Box 41026, Rochester, NY 14604–4126, USA

British Library Cataloguing-in-Publication Data
Sidney Sussex College, Cambridge:
Historical Essays in Commemoration of the
Quatercentenary
I. Beales, Derek II. Nisbet, H. B.
378.4265909
ISBN 0–85115–629–0

This publication is printed on acid-free paper

Printed in Great Britain by
St Edmundsbury Press Ltd, Bury St Edmunds, Suffolk

CONTENTS

List of Plates	vii
Notes on Contributors and Editors	ix
Foreword THE RIGHT HONOURABLE THE VISCOUNT DE L'ISLE, M.B.E., VISITOR OF THE COLLEGE	xi
Editors' Preface	xii
Sidney before the College PETER SALWAY	3
Sir Philip Sidney THE LATE VISCOUNT DE L'ISLE, V.C., K.G.	35
The Building and Endowment of the College T. S. WYATT	43
'Sovereignty and Counsel': The Patron, the Poet, and Penshurst C. E. PRESTON	55
The Early History of Sidney Sussex College Library NICHOLAS ROGERS	75
Sidney's 'Errand into the Wilderness': The American Careers of Sidney Men in the Pre-Commonwealth Era KARL S. GUTHKE	89
The Posthumous History of Oliver Cromwell's Head CHRISTOPHER PARISH	105
Joshua Basset, Popery and Revolution MARK GOLDIE	111
Dictionary Johnson amidst the Dons of Sidney: A Chapter in Eighteenth-Century Cambridge History JAMES BASKER	131
William Chafy and the Architectural Transformation of Sidney Sussex College, 1813–37 PETER SALT	145
The Growth of Cleethorpes and the Prosperity of Sidney, 1616–1968 R. W. AMBLER and ALAN DOWLING	177
The Sidney College Laboratory A. L. GREER	195

George Ralph Mines (1886–1914) and the Electrophysiology of Sudden   223
Cardiac Death
   REGIS A. DE SILVA

The New Chapel of Sidney Sussex College, Cambridge   235
   C. S. B. PYKE

Index   249

PLATES

Colour plates

Frontispiece. Lady Frances Sidney, Countess of Sussex, Foundress of the College, attributed to Steven van der Meulen, c.1565

between pages 18 and 19, and 50 and 51

I   Stained glass from the Franciscan church
II   Stained glass from the Franciscan church
III   Aquatint of Hall Court, artist unknown, published by W. Mason, Cambridge, 1822

Black-and-white plates, between pages 114 and 115

1   Portrait of Ralph Simons, *reproduced from the portrait at Emmanuel College by kind permission of the Master and Fellows*
2   View of Sidney Sussex College, from David Loggan, *Cantabrigia illustrata*
3   View of Penshurst Place, engraved by George Vertue, 1747
4   Wooden box containing incrusted skull, presented by Captain William Stevens in 1627
5a   A selection of volumes by Suarez from the College Library, showing titling across the head of the book
5b   Gabriel Vasquez, *Paraphrasis et compendiaria explicatio ad nonnullas Pauli epistolas* (Ingolstadt, 1613), binding with Willmer arms
6   Two views of Cromwell's head
7   Canon Horace Wilkinson holding Cromwell's head. *Photo: Dr Ann Silver*
8a   The west front of the College immediately prior to Wyatville's remodelling
8b   The west front of the College, showing the façade of the Hall and Master's Lodge as built to Wyatville's designs, 1822–4, and the proposals for the second phase, 22 October 1824
      The two photographs for Plate 8 are reproduced by permission of the Royal Commission on Historical Monuments (England) and are Crown copyright
9   Portrait of William Chafy, artist unknown
10   The 1820s houses on the north side of Sussex Street in 1936
11a The New Cleethorpes area from the air. *Photograph by courtesy of the Grimsby Evening Telegraph*
11b Fellows on their annual visit to Cleethorpes, c.1959

LIST OF PLATES

- 12a   Portrait of Charles Thomas Heycock (1858–1931)
- 12b   Portrait of Francis Henry Neville (1847–1915)
- 13a   Interior view of the main laboratory
- 13b   Exterior view of laboratory buildings
- 14   Portrait of George Ralph Mines (1886–1914)
- 15a   J.L. Pearson's plans for a new Chapel: exterior from Jesus Lane
- 15b   J.L. Pearson's plans for a new Chapel: interior section, showing stalls
- 16a   The old College Chapel, *by permission of the Royal Commission on Historical Monuments (England) (Crown copyright)*
- 16b   The rebuilt Chapel

NOTES ON CONTRIBUTORS AND EDITORS

Contributors

R.W. Ambler is Senior Lecturer in History at the University of Hull. He is an economic historian, one of whose research interests for many years has been the history of Cleethorpes.

James Basker is Professor of English at Columbia University, New York, and a former Visiting Fellow of Sidney Sussex College. His publications include works on Tobias Smollett and on eighteenth-century periodicals.

The late Viscount De L'Isle, V.C., K.G., as head of the Sidney family, was Visitor of the College from 1945 to 1991. He took a special interest in his kinsman, Sir Philip Sidney, raised funds for a memorial to him in St Paul's Cathedral, which was unveiled in 1985, and came to the College two years later to read to the Confraternitas Historica the paper which is here published.

His son, the Right Honourable the Viscount De L'Isle, M.B.E., who succeeded him as Visitor, contributes the Foreword.

Alan Dowling is Warden of the Centre for Continuing Education, Development and Training at the University of Hull. His research concerns institutional landowners and their attitude to estate development in the nineteenth century.

Mark Goldie is Vice-Master of Churchill College and Assistant Lecturer in the Faculty of History. He has written extensively on British political and religious controversies between the Restoration and the French Revolution.

A.L. Greer is a Fellow of Sidney Sussex and Graduate Tutor, and University Lecturer in Materials Science.

Karl S. Guthke is Kuno Francke Professor of German Art and Culture at Harvard University and a former Visiting Fellow of Sidney Sussex College. He has published numerous books on German literature of the eighteenth and nineteenth centuries and on many other topics.

Christopher Parish, Emeritus Fellow of the College, is Keeper of the Muniments and Co-Editor of the *College Annual*. He was formerly a Consultant Surgeon at Addenbrooke's Hospital.

C.E. Preston is a Fellow of Sidney Sussex and College Lecturer in English. Her publications deal chiefly with the literature of the English Renaissance, including Sir Philip Sidney and Sir Thomas Browne.

C.S.B. Pyke, having read History at Sidney from 1989 to 1992, is an Assistant Master at Lancing College.

NOTES ON CONTRIBUTORS

Nicholas Rogers is the Archivist of Sidney Sussex, and has done much work on the restoration and cataloguing of the College's rare books and manuscripts.

Peter Salt, formerly a Fellow of Sidney Sussex, is one of the co-ordinators of the Royal Historical Society British Bibliographies Project. He has published on seventeenth-century British history as well as on the College's architectural development.

Peter Salway, formerly Research Fellow of Sidney Sussex and Fellow of All Souls College, Oxford, is Professor Emeritus of Archaeology and the History of Roman Britain at the Open University.

Regis A. de Silva is Assistant Professor of Medicine at the Harvard Medical School and Consultant in the Division of Cardiology at Deaconess Hospital.

T.S. Wyatt, Emeritus Fellow of the College, was formerly Director of Studies in Modern Languages and Secretary of the Local Examinations Syndicate of the University of Cambridge.

Editors

D.E.D. Beales is a Fellow of Sidney Sussex and Professor of Modern History in the University. His publications relate to eighteenth- and nineteenth-century British and Continental history.

H.B. Nisbet is Fellow and Vice-Master of Sidney Sussex, and Professor of Modern Languages (German) in the University. He has published mainly on eighteenth-century literature and thought.

FOREWORD

It is with the greatest pleasure that I introduce this collection of essays in commemoration of the quatercentenary of Sidney Sussex College.

What strikes me most about them is how much has grown from modest beginnings; and how much *can* be grown when people are minded to take a long-term view. In our own age when the short-term perspective overwhelms so much day-to-day endeavour and obscures our Island history, the celebration of a quatercentenary reminds us we can only be the guardians of our future by proper husbandry of our past.

These essays celebrate stewardship on many fronts. The honouring of fine minds in scholarship appears delightfully side-by-side with anecdotes of Johnson's riotous weekend at Cambridge as well as an account of the preservation of Cromwell's head. My father would have been proud at the editors' inclusion of his essay on Sir Philip Sidney, while I am equally delighted to see the connections made with North America, where my ancestor Algernon Sidney's republican thoughts still reverberate.

In the diversity of the essays is a reminder of how much College history there is still to be known and recorded. The Quatercentenary lets us turn our minds also to how much of the future there is still to be made. Sidney Sussex is, I believe, at as strong a point in its life as it has ever been and has the vigour to engage with its future in a way that its Foundress could only applaud. Her original bequest is also our obligation for the future.

As hereditary Visitor I am proud that my family's connection with the College which bears our name is still maintained. I remind myself, however, that we are at the start of the next four hundred years. This volume marks the start in celebrating the past, and I commend it to you.

Easter Day 1995   De L'Isle
                                                                                                               Visitor

EDITORS' PREFACE

The purpose of this volume of essays is to commemorate the quatercentenary of Sidney Sussex College, which falls on 14 February 1996. The contributors include two successive Visitors of the College, Fellows and members of Sidney, and other scholars who have studied aspects of its history. Their essays discuss the Franciscan friary that preceded the College on its central site, the Foundress's family, the foundation and buildings of the College, its estates, its library, some notable episodes in its history, and the achievements of some of its Fellows and members.

Though two admirable short histories of Sidney exist, by G.M. Edwards (1899) and C.W. Scott-Giles (1951), there is obviously scope for a fuller account, which could, among other things, do greater justice to the part played by the College and its members in the history of education and scholarship and in the life of Britain and the English-speaking world. Thanks to the work of the late Dr R.C. Smail and the subsequent appointment of Mr Nicholas Rogers as College Archivist, the extensive archives preserved in the Muniment Room have recently become much more accessible, and it has become evident that many aspects of the story of the College have hardly been investigated at all. Before a new and comprehensive history can be contemplated, however, basic research on many of these areas is plainly necessary.

The forthcoming quatercentenary seemed an ideal opportunity to commission an appropriate collection of essays, and with the permission and support of the College Council we invited contributors to present the results of their research on some of the neglected themes in the College's history (and prehistory) over the entire period from the Middle Ages to the present century. We wish we could have covered an even wider range of topics, and we particularly regret that the death of Sir Austin Robinson deprived us of an account of Sidney during the Second World War. But, while we believe that the resulting essays include much of the necessary groundwork for a new history of the College, we are also confident that they make up a lively and stimulating volume in their own right, fully accessible to the general reader as well as to specialists.

We owe thanks to the Visitor for permission to publish his late father's paper on Sir Philip Sidney, to the Master and Fellows of Sidney for generous financial support, to Mr N. Rogers for dealing with numerous archival enquiries, to Dr R. Hyam and Mrs C. Linehan for helpful advice, to Dr Paul Scott and Dr John Longley for assistance with computer problems, and to the College secretaries, especially to Mrs Jean Herdman and Mrs Tricia Brooks, for typing some of the articles.

D.E.D. BEALES
H.B. NISBET

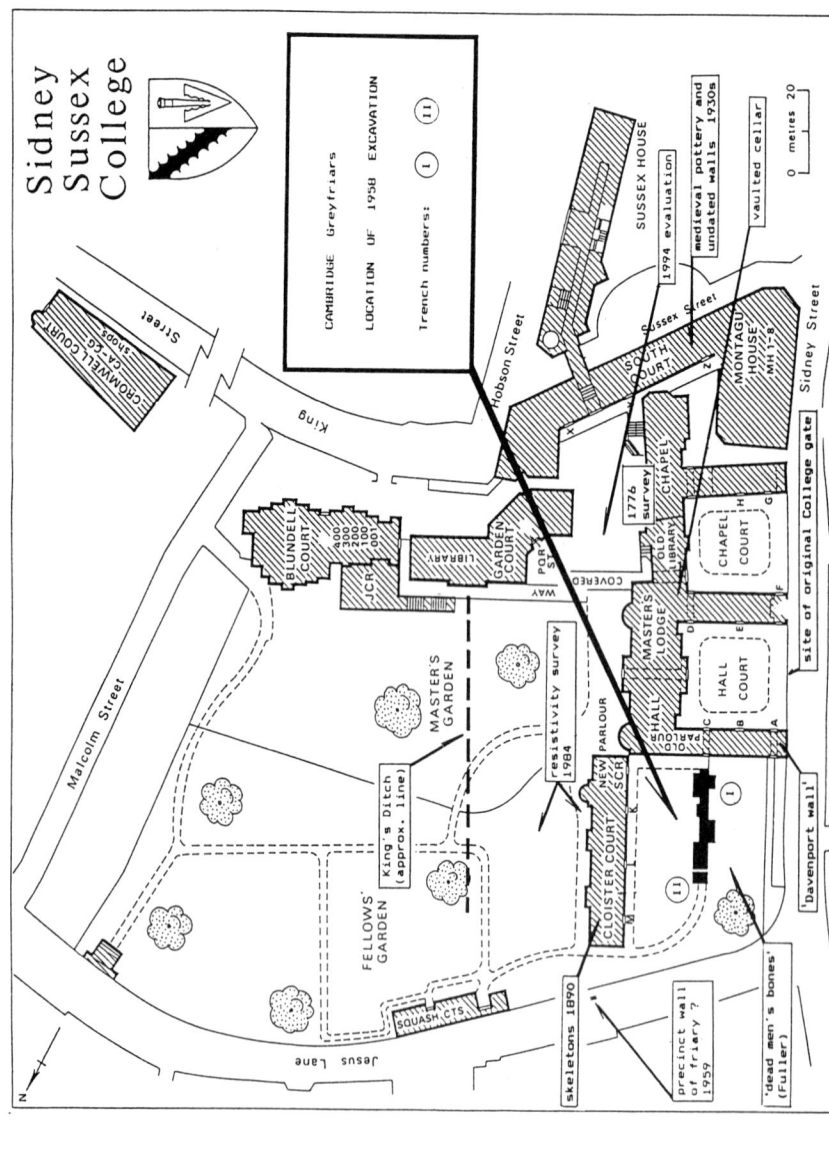

Figure 1 Plan of Sidney Sussex College, showing present buildings and sites of archaeological investigation

Sidney before the College

PETER SALWAY

Archaeology often proceeds by analogy: the understanding of one site is unexpectedly illuminated by discoveries on another. This is particularly true of urban sites that have been in continuous occupation to the present day. On these the opportunities to observe the physical remains beneath the ground or concealed in standing buildings are few. It is sometimes the case that the accumulation of separate pieces of information – whether from small-scale archaeological investigations or from chance observations during building works – makes it possible to form some general hypotheses about the history of a site and its layout at different periods in the past. However, where the character of present-day use makes extensive excavation impractical – as in a college – it can be difficult to be very confident of any interpretation, particularly where there are few close parallels to the sort of site being excavated. In the case of the 'prehistory' of Sidney, the fortunate accident of large-scale archaeological operations on analogous sites elsewhere can provide just the sort of illumination needed to make better sense of the scatter of evidence already acquired. For the friary of the Franciscans that preceded Sidney this illumination from elsewhere has principally been provided by the definitive publication in 1991 of the excavation of the Oxford Greyfriars between 1968 and 1976, and by excavation in 1994 – not yet published – on the site of Rewley Abbey, Oxford, both by the Oxford Archaeological Unit.

The layout of Franciscan friaries followed the general pattern of monastic houses in Western Europe, but with certain peculiarities, particularly in the plan of the church. However, in Britain almost all the visible surviving remains are in towns and are fragmentary. The only unencumbered site with substantial standing structures is at Walsingham, in Norfolk (fig.2). Walsingham was a relatively small settlement, where the founders of the friary are likely to have been comparatively unconstrained by surrounding buildings (though, of course, subject to the usual necessities of acquiring sufficient land from existing owners). It can therefore be assumed that what the Franciscans laid out at Walsingham was broadly the ideal

Acknowledgements. It is a considerable pleasure to have an opportunity to acknowledge the support of the Master and Fellows for the 1958 excavation and their sustained interest ever since, and also the generous provision of information and assistance by many individuals without which this enquiry into the 'prehistory' of Sidney would not have reached its present point.

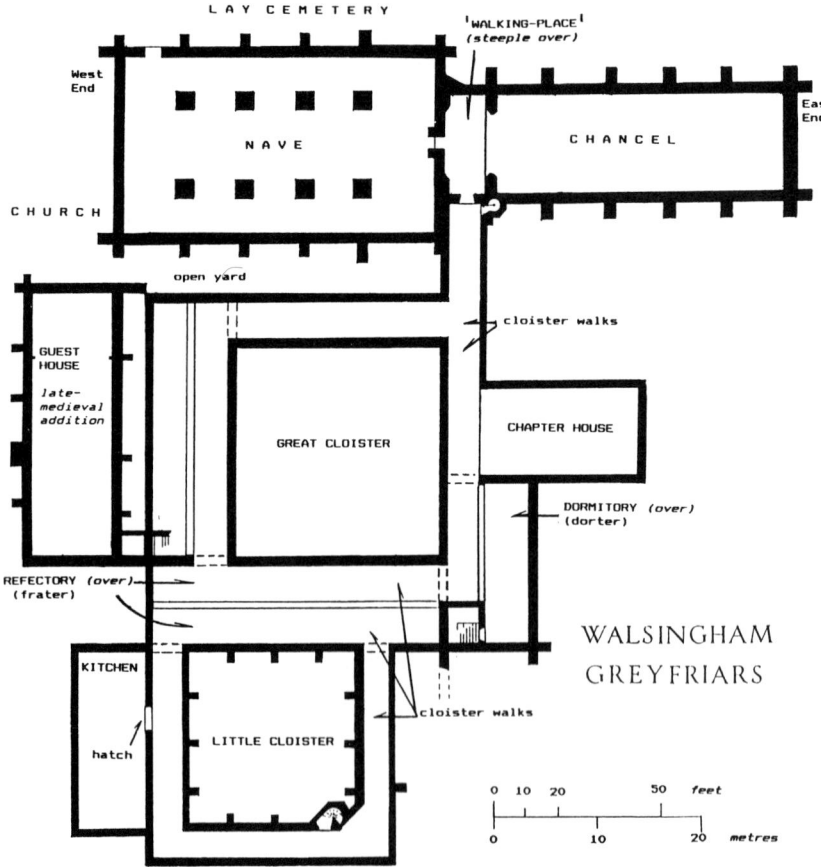

Figure 2

pattern that they would aim at wherever possible. The excavation of the Oxford friary suggested how much of that 'ideal' plan the Franciscans felt it necessary to try to reproduce on a town site. It was, moreover, in a city where the friars were late-comers, having to acquire property from existing owners, and in a period – the thirteenth century – when pressure on urban space was mounting towards its medieval peak.

The appropriateness of the Oxford excavations for providing information useful in interpreting the Cambridge site is, of course, strengthened by the fact that in Oxford and Cambridge the Franciscans had a function that they did not have elsewhere in England. In both they became an important element in the rise of the respective universities, in which the early role of the friars as teachers and thinkers is well-recognized. The thirteenth-century philosopher Duns Scotus was a resident member of both the Cambridge and the Oxford Greyfriars houses at different stages in his peripatetic career; Roger Bacon's ideas were thought so dangerously unsettling at Oxford that he was transferred to the Franciscan house in Paris to silence him; and William of Ockham's lectures at Oxford early in the following century were enormously influential in the debates over free will and predestination.

The first small party of Grey Friars entered England in September 1224, and dispersed to various destinations. While it is not certain that they appeared in Cambridge in 1224 itself, it seems likely. The town authorities had acquired, either in that year or before, two adjacent Jewish properties, one a house that included a disused synagogue, the other providing buildings that they put to use as a gaol. On arrival the friars were given the former property as their first convent. At this stage their structural ambitions were modest, and it is reported that their chapel was constructed by a carpenter in a single day, using twenty-eight pieces of timber. At Oxford the first two friars were initially accommodated in 1224 by the Dominicans, subsequently renting a house in St Ebbe's. When the Oxford community increased in 1225 they took another house, and by 1236 had acquired more. There are uncertainties about the position of these properties and of the exact line of Oxford's town wall in this period, but it seems reasonably certain that the land the friars now held was adjacent to the defences. It is likely that they established at least a temporary chapel immediately. They were certainly constructing one in 1232 – either an enlargement of whatever was done in 1225, or a new building – when Henry III granted thirty baulks of timber towards the chapel works then under way (interestingly almost the same number as used at Cambridge), and encouraged others to match his gift. Other buildings seem also to have been going up. Henry gave another ten trees in 1240, and the best of their buildings in this early period is said, significantly, to have been the 'schoolhouse' (in the early university sense of 'school', meaning a place in which undergraduate teaching was undertaken, as in 'Old Schools'). From 1229 to 1235 the Oxford friars' lecturer in theology was the remarkable Robert Grosseteste, who played a very important part both intellectually and politically in the early development of that university. Soon after 1200 – at the latest – both Oxford and Cambridge had emerged as universities, and there was much interchange of personnel with centres of study abroad, especially with Paris. The first chancellor of Oxford (in the medieval period the executive head of the university) is recorded in 1224 but the first college not till 1249, by which time the Franciscans had been established in the city for a quarter of a century. Grosseteste himself became chancellor of Oxford and bishop of the enormous medieval diocese of Lincoln, and to the end of his life remained a powerful friend of the Franciscans. It is clear that by the early 1240s the Oxford Franciscan community had so prospered that there was severe pressure on its facilities, and space for expansion was being sought. What then happened is surprising (fig. 3). They did not move to another site. Instead, Henry not only gave them permission in 1244 to stop up a street, but allowed them to make a long breach in the town wall. This opened the way to the creation of a much larger precinct – extending on both sides of the wall – by the acquisition of more property, stage by stage between 1245 and 1278. To

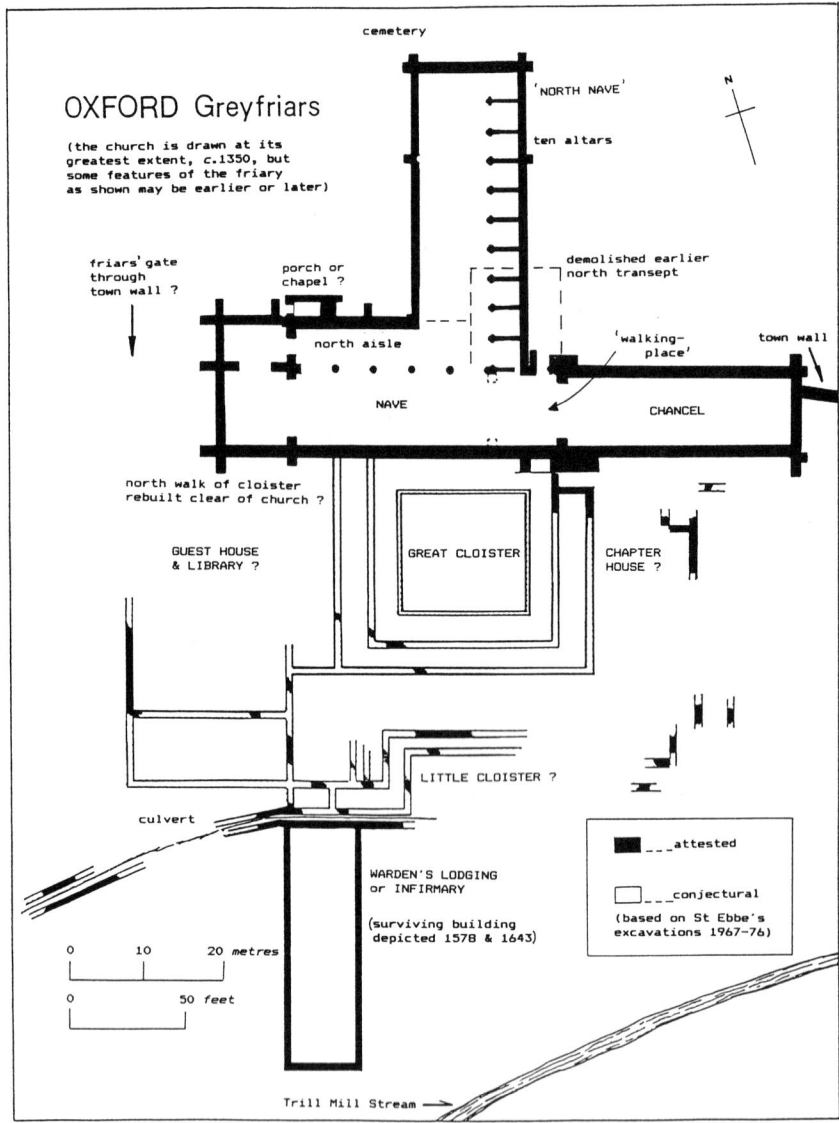

Figure 3

repair the gap in the defences the king at first intended that the friars should build a new crenellated wall ('to match the existing wall') all the way round the part of the precinct that extended forward of the old line. The friars' purposes, the king recognized, required conventual quiet and domestic security. Before this had been done, however, they had achieved the same end by a further extension, by gift of the king, across a stream. Henry now, in 1248, changed his instructions, ordering that the north side of the friars' church then under construction should form part of the town wall. The rest of the gap that had been made should be closed up, but the friars would be allowed access from one part of their expanded site to the other by means of a postern gate.

What, then, did the Oxford friars want to do with this much enlarged plot? The answer may be very significant for understanding the situation in Cambridge, for it seems that the latter friary, too, was expanding, also with help from Henry III. The desire for tranquillity seems to have been just as active here as in Oxford, for the necessity to use a common entrance with the prison caused them considerable discomfort. Like the Oxford friars, they were also looking for more space, as their site was becoming too small. Moving the gaol and granting the friars 'the house of Benjamin the Jew' by royal permission temporarily alleviated their problems. The location of these properties – and therefore of the original Franciscan habitation – remains uncertain: currently the balance of opinion is that the friars were not yet on the Sidney site.

By 1325 the Franciscans were certainly on the present site, and it is very likely that the plot of something over six acres where a Hundred Rolls reference for 1274 states that they live and have their church is the same land. If that is correct, then Henry III's grant of large building timber in 1267 is almost certain to have been for construction on the Sidney land. It was not, however, a 'green-field' site, for the Hundred Roll also tells us that there had been a substantial number of dwellings on it (*diversae . . . mansiones in quibus multi inhabitabant*) which had previously paid local taxes. Moreover, the town ditch (the King's Ditch) ran across the middle of the new site, from north to south. Just as in Oxford, we find Henry III showing concern for the security of the town (in Cambridge by enlarging the King's Ditch) but it would seem at the same time permitting the Franciscans to extend on both sides of the defences. The parallels continue. In Oxford the Grey Friars went on acquiring properties well into the following century, certainly till 1321, with a possible final addition in 1376. In 1328 the Cambridge friars were permitted to incorporate a lane into their property 'to the east of the orchard', and in 1353 they added two more plots. They had already added greatly to the amenities of their site by laying a new conduit in 1327 to bring water from a source west of the Observatory on Madingley Road. Two years earlier they had bought seventeen strips of land two feet wide, a total length of 5,510 feet (nearly 1.7 km). An inquiry in 1434 described the conduit as a lead pipe running in a trench. This pipe was taken under the river, a considerable feat of engineering, and confirms the impression of considerable prosperity in the early fourteenth century. This conforms to a general pattern observed in the English houses of the Franciscan Order, in which there was a surge of rebuilding and extension in the fifty years or so from about 1270. It is not, perhaps, a surprise that the first half of the fourteenth century saw substantial disputes developing at Cambridge between the authorities of the University and the friars over issues of independence and admission of students.

The first probable reference to the new church of the Cambridge Franciscans is an incident in 1267 when a chaplain of Barnwell took refuge there. Its formal consecration in 1349 – in the Middle Ages often long after use of the building had commenced – suggests that it had been substantially completed, but continuing work on the buildings in the middle of the fourteenth century is indicated by a benefaction in 1355 *pur lour overaigne* from the immensely wealthy Elizabeth de Clare, granddaughter of Edward I. She refounded Clare College in 1338 and assisted a number of religious houses in the Cambridge region. At Oxford, it is thought probable that the Greyfriars' church had reached its greatest extent – and the friars themselves their greatest influence in the university – by the time the Black Death arrived in 1348. So extravagant was their enthusiasm for construction that the ghost of a friar is said to have appeared to warn that if they 'were not damned for their excesses in building, they would at any rate be severely punished'.

There is both archaeological and documentary evidence to suggest that by the early sixteenth century the Oxford friary was in serious need of repair. Despite a recorded bequest of money for the fabric in 1535, the commissioners who inspected the friary at its dissolution in 1538 reported that it was 'a great hoge howce conteynyng moche ruinose bylding'. This reflected the decline in the importance of the friars in the university. In the middle of the previous century it was reported that the friary had two libraries, one the friary library proper, the other for the students. By the time John Leland visited it on his great tour before the Dissolution of the Monasteries describing the state of the realm for his master Henry VIII, he had to report that 'there are cobwebs in the library, and moths and bookworms; more than this – whatever others may boast – nothing if you have regard to learned books. For I, in spite of the opposition of all the friars, carefully examined all the bookcases in the library'. Archaeologically this decline is reflected by blocking-off of a substantial part of the church (the 'north nave', discussed below) which was left disused and ruinous. At Cambridge the condition of the church at least seems to have been rather better. References in wills of 1508 and 1533 indicate that it was still a functioning church for laymen as well as friars (one will refers to 'the south aisle'). In addition, the University was making use of it for ceremonies. In 1507–8 the University paid for the transport of stages to the friars' church and back to the Schools, and to repair windows in the church broken in consequence. In 1523 it decided to pay an annual fee to the friary for the hire of the church for the 'Commencement' ceremony, and for storing the staging. It is significant that when the friary was surrendered to the king in 1538 there were still twenty-four friars and their warden, which allows us to assume that the complex of buildings remained substantially in use. This is confirmed by the fact that from 1540 the University was very anxious to obtain the whole friary as well as retaining use of the church. The scholar Roger Ascham, who was an official letter-writer for the University, described the Franciscan house both as a worthy ornament of the university (*decus atque ornamentum*), and as offering excellent facilities for the holding of meetings and the carrying out of all sorts of university business. University use continued for a little while (there are accounts for the cleaning of benches in 1539/40 and of the church itself in 1541), but the campaign failed, and at the end of 1546 the site formally became the property of Trinity. Demolition had already started, as a valuation earlier in the year reported that 'the church and cloysters with all the other houses thereupon builded, bine defaced and taken towards the bilding of the king's majesties new college in Cambridge, and therefore valued . . . nothing'. The only items of worth were the soil itself, plus 'the orchard, brewhouse, malthouse, millhouse, and garner, within the wallis thereof'. These structures must have been what remained usable as buildings. However, it is not safe to assume that all the other buildings – the main buildings of the friary – had already been totally demolished, as the Trinity bursary records (for access to which in the 1950s the present writer is indebted to Trinity) show regular transport of materials from the site for the construction of Trinity throughout the period 1548–57.

The Sidney College histories by G.M. Edwards (1899) and C.W. Scott-Giles (1951) conveniently summarize most of what was known or deduced from documents and from observation on the College site before any modern archaeological work was undertaken. Scott-Giles noted that 'In their final state, early in the sixteenth century . . . [*the buildings*] comprised a church with a belfry, cloisters, lodgings for the Warden and friars, a schoolhouse and a refectory . . . also such necessaries as a malthouse, brewhouse, millhouse and dovecote. The property was surrounded by a high wall pierced by an archway in much the position of the main gate of the present College. From a spring in a field near the Madingley Road . . . the friars brought water to their house by a conduit . . . coming to the surface within the western wall of the convent.' To Scott-Giles' summary we need to add the barn ('garner') mentioned above, a 'little house by the orchard gate', and a cemetery mentioned in the Trinity bursary records and elsewhere. It is also probably necessary to correct the conjecture about the position of the gate. The maps made before the foundation of the College (especially Braun's map of 1575) tend to suggest a position further north than the seventeenth-century College gate. Both Edwards and Scott-Giles rightly placed great emphasis on the observations of Thomas Fuller, whose association with the College began in 1629. Fuller acutely noted in his 1655 *History of the University of Cambridge* that 'The area of this church is easily visible in Sidney College garden, where the depression and subsidence of their bowling green east and west, present the dimensions, and I have oft found dead men's bones thereabouts.' The location of the bowling green – running across the present Cloister Court parallel to A, B, and C staircases and into the Fellows' Garden as far as the dip in the ground that marks the line of the King's Ditch – is shown clearly on Loggan's 1688 perspective drawing of the College and on his map of Cambridge. G.M. Edwards reports the discovery of skeletons during the building of Cloister Court (Scott-Giles adds fragments of stained glass), observing that this was in line with Thomas Fuller's note of 'dead men's bones thereabouts', and seemed to put the cemetery between the presumed site of the church and Jesus Lane.

Other minor discoveries added detail. Undated walls were discovered and noted on a plan at the time of the construction of South Court and Montagu House, and medieval pottery discovered then and during the extension of the Chapel in the 1930s is preserved in College and its findspots recorded. This area must have been very heavily disturbed when the surviving medieval structures – thought to have been the minor domestic buildings of the friary mentioned above – were replaced. At the other end of the College, the late Major Davenport, formerly Bursar, reported orally that substantial foundations were found when inserting a lavatory at the foot of A Staircase, which he thought could well have been part of the church. However, what appeared to be the footings of the northern precinct wall of the friary was seen by the present writer in 1959 as a foundation three feet thick (0.9 m) in a contractor's trench in Jesus Lane, and it is quite likely that the A Staircase structure was part of the western stretch of the circuit. Nothing is known on the ground of the southern boundary wall, but the stone core of the brick-faced wall between the College gardens and the houses of Malcolm Street has long been thought to survive from the eastern side of the precinct wall, and is recorded as probably that in the Royal Commission survey of Cambridge (see Bibliography below).

A further detail of the site has been deduced by some of those who have written on the subject from the fact that the University's draft petition to the king mentioned 'the whole church' (*totam ecclesiam*) but listed the belfry separately (*campanile cum campanis*). This has suggested that the belfry was a detached bell-tower rather than a steeple over the junction of nave and choir, which was the more normal Franciscan arrangement. Fifteenth-century examples of such towers include King's, Cambridge (subsequently demolished), and All Souls, Oxford (projected but not built), while an earlier instance has been found at Abingdon Abbey (excavation report forthcoming). A reference in the Trinity records, however, casts some uncertainty over this deduction. It refers to 'the corner of the cloyster next to the steple'. The site for the projected bell-tower at All Souls was just outside the cloister, at one of the corners furthest away from the chapel, and it may be that the Trinity reference denotes a similar arrangement. However, it would also be consistent with a bell-tower or steeple over the west end or centre of the church. A reasonably substantial structure is certainly implied by documentary evidence that there were three bells still remaining at the Cambridge Greyfriars after the Dissolution.

G.M. Edwards noted that 2,950 loads of stone were carried to Trinity in a single year as late as 1557. He inferred that it was because not all the site had been cleared that Trinity put off till 1562 the renting out of a part of the land alongside Jesus Lane 'butting on the east side a diche commonly called the kynges diche ... on the west side the kynges highe way called the conduit street [*Sidney Street*]'. These years between the acquisition by Trinity and the handover to Sidney are reflected in three important old maps of Cambridge. The two earlier show a largely empty site, except for a causeway or bridge across the King's Ditch and a single substantial building lying on a north-south orientation in the south-west part of the site. There seems little doubt that the latter was the building adapted for use as the original College Chapel and drawn by the architect James Essex before being demolished in 1776 to make way for its replacement. As this building had to be thatched for immediate use, it was presumably not in good order when the College acquired the site. The third map, by John Hamond, was issued in 1592 shortly before the Lady Francis's executors began negotiating for the site. It rather surprisingly shows considerably more buildings than the slightly earlier maps. It is possible that some of these buildings appear on Hamond's map because they had been erected by the sixteenth-century tenants after the first two maps were drawn. However, to assume this without question ignores the likely conditions of Tudor map-making. It is perfectly possible that only Hamond managed to get inside the old friary precinct wall – or cared to record more than a token building. On the other hand, it also cannot be assumed that his final map was totally up-to-date with the state of the Sidney site at the moment of issue, as collection of cartographic information for the whole city must have proceeded over quite a long period of time. Some of the buildings shown by him are more likely than not to have been former elements of the friary. While it is difficult to be confident about using the details of specific buildings as depicted by Hamond in distinguishing between surviving friary buildings and structures put up after the Dissolution, his map does show not only what is clearly the building demolished in 1776 but another at right-angles to it, extending towards Sidney Street approximately on the line of the present south side of Chapel Court and about half the length. It is drawn as a two-storey building, with a large Gothic window in the east end looking convincingly medieval.

The other large building shown by Hamond also lies at a right angle to Sidney Street. Without a fixed point, it is difficult to be sure where this lay, but it looks as if it was roughly where the north side of Hall Court now stands. Unlike the previous building, however, none of the detail suggests anything medieval. It is possible that it is the 'greet store house' leased in 1562 to one Hedley with the northern part of the site. This may, of course, have been a surviving friary building used by Trinity to store materials recovered from the ruins (though this would be no evidence that it was a storehouse before the Dissolution). However it may equally have been erected by Trinity when the site came into their possession, and cannot with any confidence be included in a conjectural restoration of the monastic layout.

Whatever the correct identifications of the buildings shown on the Tudor maps, it is worth noting at this point that the commonly repeated story that Trinity had effectively exhausted the site as a quarry when Sidney was founded is difficult to uphold. The Master and Fellows of Trinity were probably inflating the value of the site to some extent when they claimed to Archbishop Whitgift that they deserved 'some proporcion of monie answerable to the buildings and other comodities of stone and stuffe, as well within as above the ground, which by estimacion of workemen being of great valew we are content to leaue behinde us'. Indeed, Whitgift, at the end of July 1595, noted the claim but refused to regard as more than a minor matter what – if anything – should be paid to Trinity

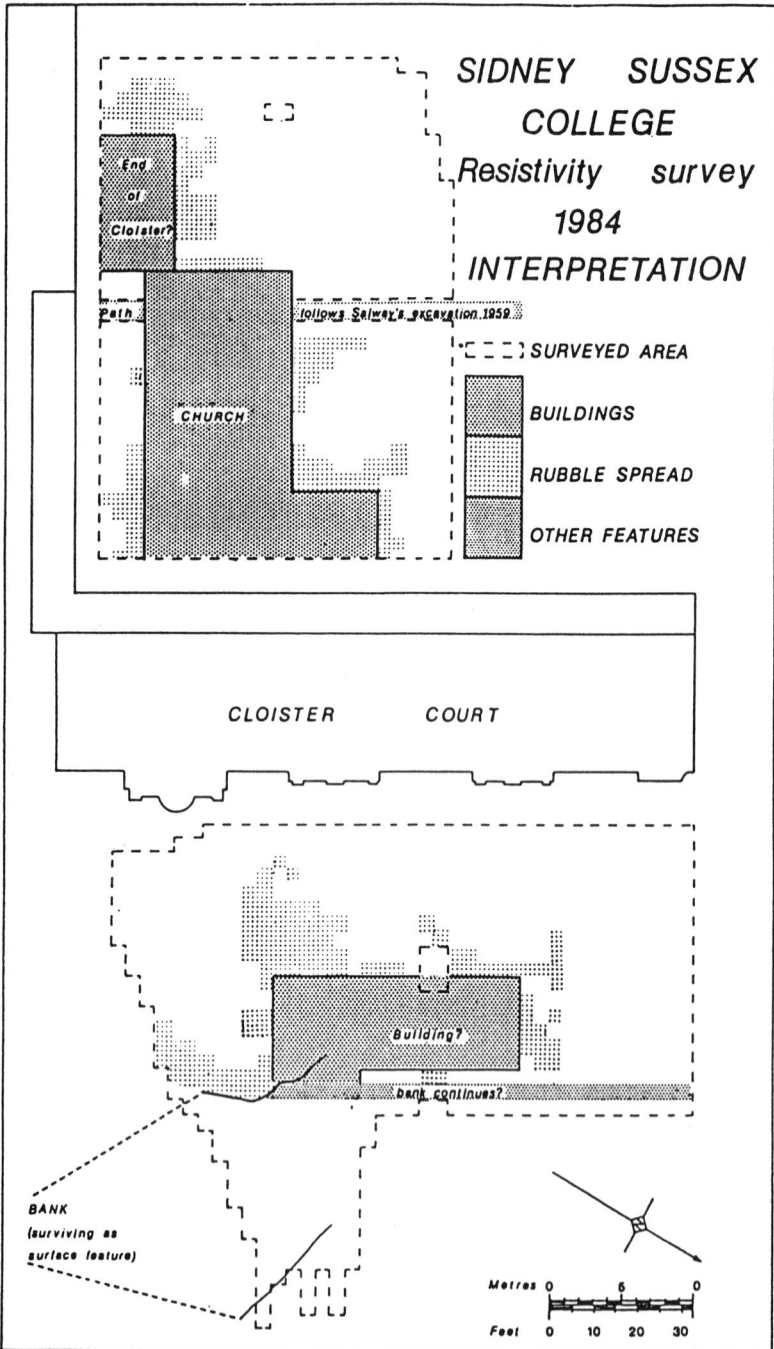

Figure 4. Courtesy of Dr Kenneth Dark

'for an olde buylding standing within the wall of the Grey-Fryers now used for a malting-howsse'. Yet soon after work on the College had begun – but before the site was finally conveyed by Trinity in September 1595 – the first Master of Sidney wrote that 'in provision of stuffe the grounde of it selfe hath ben very liberall, in affordinge boeth free stonne and whit stonne and ragge, and other necessaries of sand and gravell so good a store as will serve for the layinge of all the foundations and bringinge up of the walles above the water table . . .'. It is therefore clear that, even if Trinity had more or less extracted all they immediately needed from the site by 1562, nevertheless from 1595 Sidney's workmen were engaged in large-scale grubbing-up of what remained below ground and the winning of sand and gravel on site.

James Essex's drawing of the building he demolished is the only architectural record of a standing building of the Greyfriars that we have (fig. 9), and phrases from his accompanying notes have often been quoted. His acute observations deserve to be reproduced in full (see Appendix, below). Essex's identification of the structure as the friars' refectory *(frater)* was based on architectural details observed by him during the 1776 demolition and on small finds discovered at that time. He rightly rejected Thomas Fuller's speculation that it had been the dormitory *(dorter)*, but the identification as the frater has caused great difficulties in subsequent attempts to deduce the plan of the friary as a whole. To this we shall return. Essex also observed the foundations of other structures immediately to the south, which he thought had been added and probably served as butteries, and also stated that 'the cellars and other offices were ranged to the south next Walls Lane'.

To understand what we might expect on an English Franciscan site, it is helpful to turn back to Walsingham. The Grey Friars' house there, being of late foundation (1347), represents the developed Franciscan plan. Broadly speaking it follows general monastic practice, but with certain of the principal Franciscan idiosyncrasies. These include the physical separation of the chancel of the church from the nave by a 'walking-place' in the form of a narrow corridor, instead of an open crossing. The side walls of this corridor effectively cut the church into two halls, one for the private monastic services, the other for the lay public. The construction of belfries had been forbidden by a General Chapter of the Order in 1260, but this seems not to have been enforced. Early belfries had often been of timber over an open walking-place, but the introduction of heavy stone versions seems to have been made possible by the blocking of chancel arches and walling up the corresponding opening into the nave. The nave itself was commonly large in friaries, and reflects their use as halls in which to practise the friars' vocation as preachers to the population at large. The chapter-house range at Walsingham lacks the parlour and sacristy of other orders, perhaps due to the fact that the members were meant to be out in the world much of their time. Other Franciscan friaries often display enlarged transepts and, as here, separation of the church from the cloister by an open alley or court. At Oxford the north walk of the main cloister seems originally to have adjoined the south wall of the church, but when

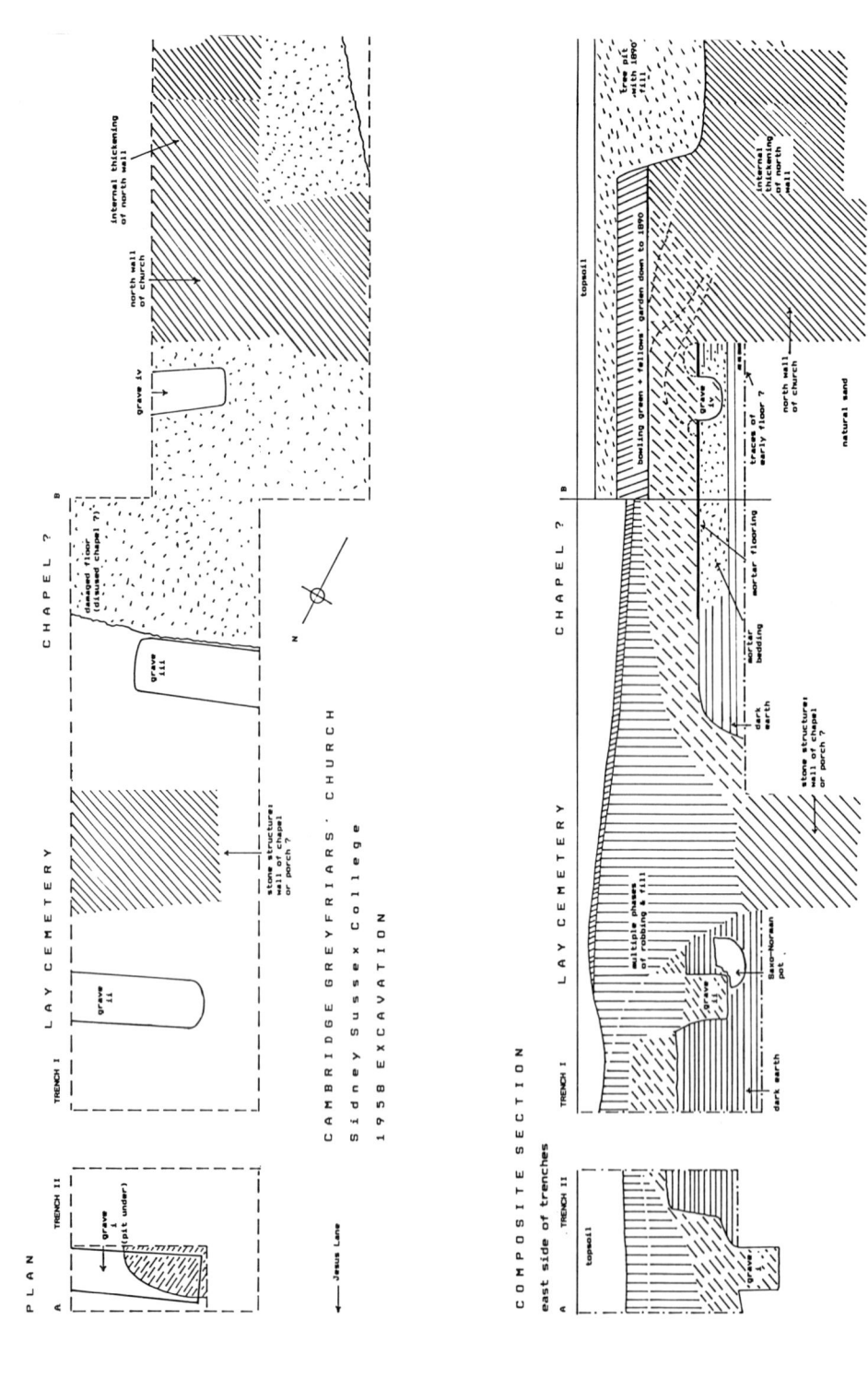

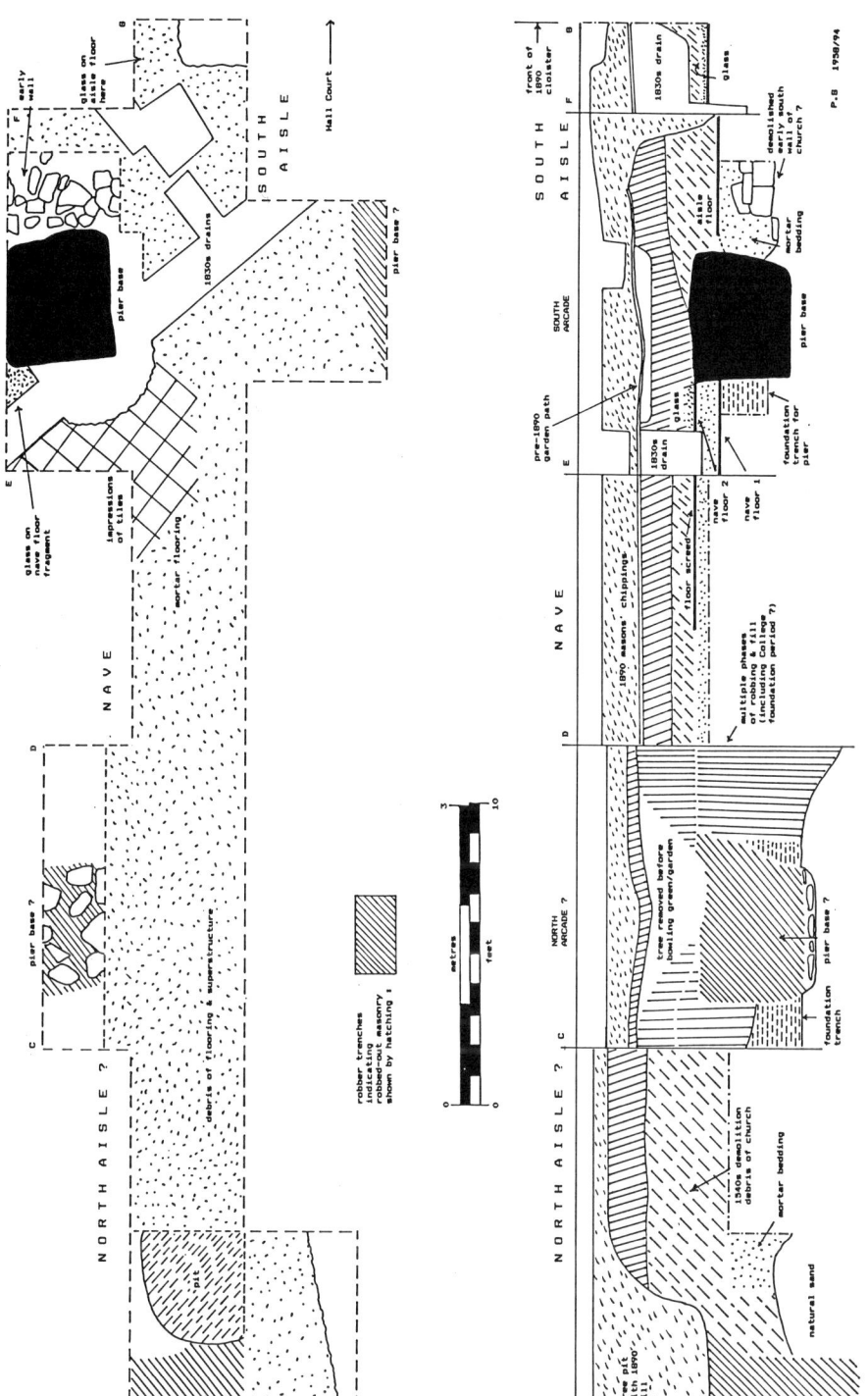

Figure 5

subsequently rebuilt was moved clear of it. At Walsingham, it is interesting to note the presence of *two* enclosed cloisters. These do not follow the regular monastic pattern with four walks under lean-to roofs constructed against the principal buildings. Instead, the Walsingham cloisters have the main apartments on the first floor extending out over the walks themselves. The friars' dormitory lay over the east walk of the great cloister, and their refectory integrated the two cloisters structurally by spanning the south walk of the main cloister and the north of the little cloister. At the pilgrimage centre of Walsingham it is not surprising to find an exceptionally large guest-house, here occupying the west side of the great cloister; but one might conjecture that something similar would be needed in the university towns to accommodate visitors.

Walsingham displays a compact plan, making efficient use of space, unlike the sprawling layouts observable on many monastic sites belonging to other orders. It has been argued that, in view of its relatively late date, the compactness reflects solutions that had been reached on much tighter urban sites. At first sight, however, it is difficult to believe that in most towns Franciscans would have attempted the luxury of setting out two formal cloister-courts – however ingenious their architects – when it meant working so hard to assemble sufficient land. It is therefore a surprise to find that the investigations in Oxford provided good – if not 100 per cent certain – evidence that those friars achieved just that architectural scheme as they spanned the town wall and piece by piece extended their property.

In 1952 J.R.H. Moorman included a conjectural plan of the friary in his history of the Franciscans in Cambridge. It was partly to test this plan that, when an opportunity for excavation was offered in 1958 by the proposed relaying of the path across Cloister Court parallel to Sidney Street, it was taken by the present writer on behalf of the College (fig. 5). In the jargon of the 1990s this would be called an 'evaluation': an excavation undertaken to establish what of archaeological significance survives on a site, in the light of which decisions, at the time or in the future, can be taken. Such archaeological investigations are nowadays mostly undertaken when owners are applying for permission to develop a site or alter a listed historic building. This has become particularly true since the issue in 1990 by the Department of the Environment of much stronger guidance on handling the archaeological implications of development ('PPG 16'). Most Planning Authorities regularly require the developer to provide an independent professional archaeological assessment of the effect of their proposals if carried out. There are, however, still enlightened owners who simply wish to know whether archaeology could tell more about the history of their properties, whether out of intellectual curiosity or to manage them better, and who make use voluntarily of the same methods of archaeological enquiry. The 1958 excavation would nowadays fall into the latter category, and was similar in scale to much current evaluation. The cost of the excavation was borne by the College, and was carried out with paid labour from the College's usual contractors and by volunteers from Cambridge and elsewhere whose energy and enthusiasm was much appreciated.

The method of investigation was straightforward excavation of the whole of the limited area originally available, plus some minor extensions. The dig succeeded in its primary objective of testing for the extent of survival of archaeological deposits, and confirmed the suspected location of the friary church and cemetery. The excavation, however, being in effect a transect north-south across the church and into the graveyard beyond, did not provide firm evidence for the length or precise alignment of the church (which has always, rightly, been assumed to lie east-west in the conventional manner), and uncertainties remained about its width. This led in 1984 to a further stage of evaluation, using a resistivity meter, one of the techniques of remote-sensing that permit 'non-invasive' investigation of archaeological sites and have been much developed in the years since the 1958 excavation was carried out (and, indeed, further in the decade since the survey described below was carried out). These methods are particularly appropriate where the ground is relatively unencumbered but excavation is deemed undesirable, such as college lawns. Such surveys are certainly often difficult to interpret, and rarely give precise outlines of buried features, but are particularly helpful when they can be used to extend or modify information provided by excavation or standing structures. In 1984 Kenneth Dark, then a Sidney research student, executed a resistivity survey of the open areas of Hall Court and the southern half of Cloister Court, and also of the part of the garden that lies immediately to the east of the Cloister Court range, between it and the depression that is believed to mark the line of the medieval King's Ditch (fig. 4).

The 1958 excavation was initially planned as a trench along the line of the north-south path across the centre of Cloister Court, starting immediately beyond the nineteenth-century cloister walk at the end of the passage between Hall and Cloister Courts. It was to be confined to the existing width of the path to cause minimum disturbance. This restricted the initial breadth of the excavation to 1.22 metres (4 ft). In the course of digging it became necessary for safety to widen this trench (Trench I) outwards at certain points into the lawns, in order to explore the deepest features encountered which extended down into the natural gravel to a maximum of 3.20 metres (10ft 6ins). As predicted – against strongly-expressed scepticism – the grass in Cloister Court recovered very rapidly ! One further addition was a small trench (Trench II) of path width beyond the Jesus Lane end of the original excavation. Taken together, these trenches represented a section of just over 29 metres (96 ft) across the traditional site of the Franciscan church.

In an archaeological report the excavation would normally be described from the bottom upwards, but it will be convenient here to list what was found from the top down, starting from the present appearance of Cloister Court, more or less as left by its architect Pearson in the late nineteenth century and familiar to members of the College, thus proceeding in stages – via the periods represented by the Wyatt alterations and the Loggan print – from the known to the unknown. Immediately under the present garden topsoil, a thick layer of masons' chippings was encountered in 1958 throughout most of the length of the excavation and appeared to be building debris from the construction of Cloister Court in the 1890s. It did not, however, appear in the section at the northern end where the excavation had been extended sideways into the lawn. It seems probable, therefore, that the builders' debris had been used to make up the path, rather than simply dumped at random. At the southernmost end of Trench I a series of blocked drains were encountered under this layer, which must have been associated with the Senior Combination Room that was added to the back of the Hall Court range at a late stage in the Wyatt alterations. This Combination Room was demolished when Cloister Court was constructed in 1890–1 and this area ceased to be part of the Fellows' Garden. Just beyond the drains, a path was found running east-west, cut slightly into a layer of humus. A plan of the College dated 1868 shows just such a path skirting the Combination Room of that period. The same humus layer appeared throughout almost the whole length of the excavation trench, varying in thickness but only cut through at one point, by a large pit that probably represents the removal of a tree during the construction works of 1890. The 1868 plan indicates that the Fellows' Garden had at that time a number of irregularly shaped beds containing shrubs and trees. It was not possible to distinguish any subsidiary layering within the humus, and it must represent both the informal garden of the nineteenth century and the seventeenth-century bowling green. Another tree-pit was visible approximately a third of the way along the section, but under the humus layer and cutting into the back-fill of a robber trench. This must have been caused by the removal of a tree before the laying-out of the bowling green.

In archaeological parlance 'robber trenches' are the disturbances produced by digging to salvage stone from the below-ground remains of a demolished building. They often preserve the form of a structure in 'ghost' or negative form. It will be seen from the drawn section that a thick layer of demolition debris (it was mostly scraps of stone) was present below the humus layer. Towards the northern end of Trench I and near the middle it extended down to fill rectangular trenches. These certainly represent stone structures, cleanly dug out and immediately backfilled before any silting occurred. The robber-trench under the seventeenth-century tree-pit showed a rather more complicated sequence, to which we shall return. The most dramatic survival under the demolition debris, however, appeared at the southern end. Here a single solid square mortared footing for a pier had survived intact. The pier had been cut off at floor level, but fortunately a substantial patch of floor-screed survived. Though almost severed by one of the Combination Room drains, a small portion of this remained attached to the pier-base, proving that the two were associated. This bedding retained very clearly the impressions of nine-inch tiles laid in a pattern diagonal to the pier. On the mortar surface itself was found a very large number of fragments of medieval stained window-glass and pieces of window-lead. Under this floor there were remains of an earlier floor, also associated with the pier, indicating that the building had been re-floored at least once. Brick and plaster fragments came from the debris, which also included Collyweston roofing slates and a ridge tile

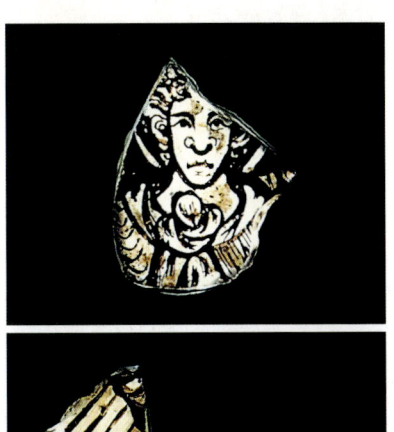

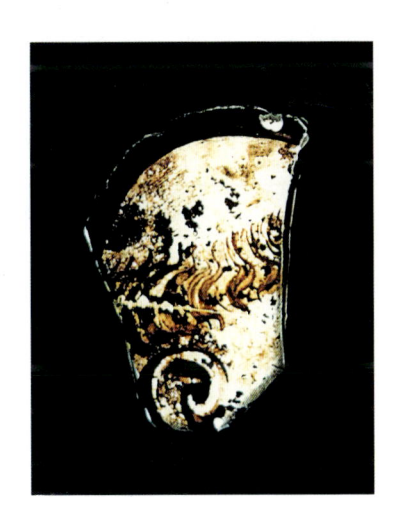

Plate I Stained glass from the Franciscan church;
(top left) head, wings and feet of a seraph: *(bottom left)* tonsured friar;
(top right) male head; *(centre right)* lion; *(bottom right)* bearded prophet

Plate II Stained glass from the Franciscan church: *(top)* architectural detail, probably framing a figure; *(centre)* Annunciation: Archangel Gabriel, *left;* scroll, *right,* representing spoken message: . . . *plen/a d(omi)n(u)s tecum; (bottom left)* monkey with tambourine; *(bottom right)* devil

Figure 6. Glass: *(left)* Crucifixion; *(right)* female saint

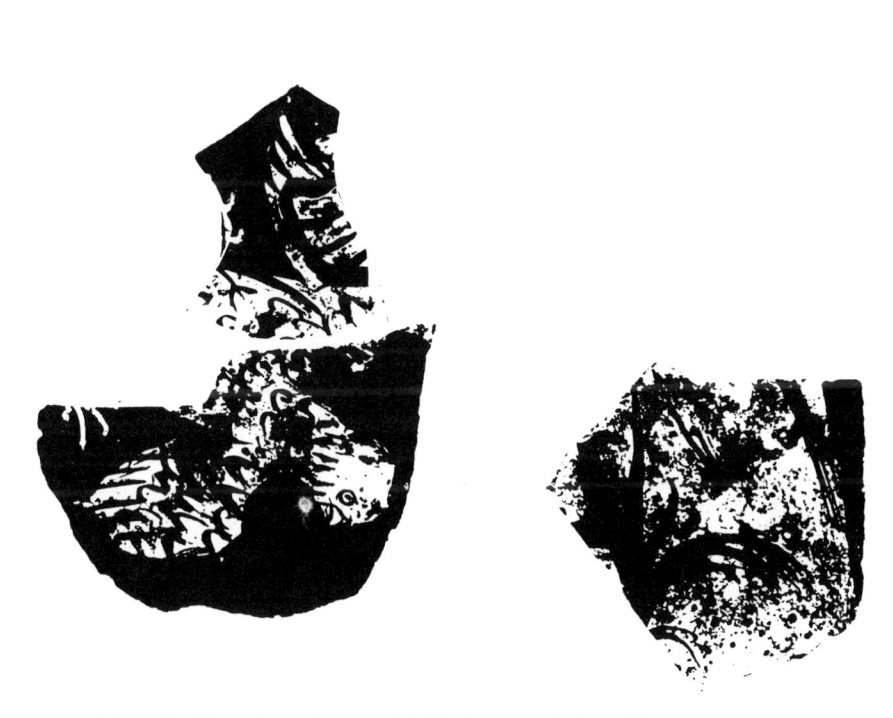

Figure 7. Glass: from a group of child Christ in the lap of the Virgin Mary (child clothed and holding a bird)

decorated with coloured spots. An extension of the excavation trench westwards just caught the edge of robber trench or pit, possibly marking the extraction of another pier-base. If so, it would suggest an arcade with a distance between columns of perhaps 3–3.5 metres (around 9 to 12 ft). Immediately to the south of the surviving pier were footings of limestone rubble packed with gravel. These were not accompanied by any datable material but were structurally earlier than the pier and its associated floors.

The glass was examined by the late Peter Newton, then of the Courtauld Institute, University of London. A few of the figured pieces are illustrated in plates I–II and figures 6–7. It dated largely from the second half of the fourteenth century. The basic material was in four colours – green, blue, ruby, and white – varying considerably in shade (the white, for example, from nearly-clear to amber). The green and blue were dyed in the mass, the ruby composed of a thin sheet of red flashed onto white. Painting of details was done in a red-brown pigment with a brush onto the surface of the glass, which was then fired in an oven. This pigment appears black when held against the light. The work of several different painters is represented in the Sidney glass, and they are likely to have worked on site, painting onto coloured sheet glass manufactured elsewhere. Very little glass is known for certain to have come from other Franciscan sites in England. The Oxford friary church produced in excavation a much smaller amount – about ninety fragments, ranging in date from the thirteenth to the fifteenth century. It is thought probable that a panel of late thirteenth-century date now in the Burrell Collection in Glasgow came from the same site, as it shows Beatrice van Valkenburg, who was married to Richard, Earl of Cornwall, a political figure of European importance in his period. She was interred in the church in 1277 – where her husband's heart was also buried – indicating the social level of patronage that might be behind the embellishing of the Franciscan churches in the English universities.

Returning to the robber-trench under the seventeenth-century tree-pit, it now becomes possible to disentangle the sequence. The tree-pit had disturbed the demolition debris, but enough debris had survived at the sides untouched to be clear that there was another, straight-sided pit below it. This went down through a dark fill, and right at the bottom there were limestone rubble footings similar to those found at the south end of the excavation. The dark fill looked as if it had been cultivated soil used to pack the original construction trench of the limestone feature, but might have been the remains of the contents of a soakaway or cesspit. In a more recent excavation environmental analysis would have followed, which might have settled the point: enough probably remains *in situ* to allow future sampling and testing if desired. The pit itself was unlike the other robber-trenches that were full of undifferentiated demolition debris, as it had been carefully filled with horizontal layers of tipped material, including a few pieces of limestone that seemed to have come from the rubble footings. The fill strongly suggested that this feature had been robbed out at a different date from the rest, perhaps most likely at the foundation of the college. It is more likely to have been the base of one pier of an arcade dividing the nave from a north aisle than anything else, but more piers need to be located before there can be any certainty.

The next feature northwards was a pit that had penetrated the garden humus layer but not right through the demolition debris below it. It was filled with 1890 masons' chippings, and probably represents a tree from the nineteenth-century garden removed at the time of the construction of Cloister Court. Below it was a clean-cut robber trench filled with demolition debris, representing a linear stone feature approximately 3 metres wide across which the excavation had cut. Immediately to the north of this, a substantial layer of dark earth – almost certainly the product of human activity rather than natural action – appeared at the bottom of the excavation, cut by the robber trench just described and sealed by the demolition debris. This dark earth ran consistently from this point to the north end of the excavation. The earliest pottery was of the late first century AD to the fourth, coming from Roman pits into the natural gravel at the bottom of the excavation, the rest medieval. Cut into the dark earth were four graves. The graves, orientated east-west, contained skeletons laid out on their backs in an extended position. There were no grave goods, but the presence of nails and fragments of wood indicated that there had been coffins. Presence of demolition debris in the graves indicated that they had been opened at the time of the demolition, but the skeletons left in place. In one grave (no. i) the large bones of the left leg had clearly been disturbed accidentally, as they had been replaced across the shoulders. North of the linear feature mentioned, another straight-sided robber trench appeared, not extending westwards for the full width of the excavation but square-ended. Presence of parts of a fifth skeleton here at first suggested that it might have been a stone-built burial vault, though a structural part of the main building is more likely, as there were remains of a floor running out towards it from the very large robber-trench to the south. This floor was itself cut by one of the graves (no. iv). A wide pit had been dug down to the square-ended feature, right through the demolition debris and sealed by only a relatively thin layer of old garden humus below the modern topsoil. A single grave was discovered on each side of it, dug into the dark earth (nos. ii and iii). The northern of these two graves (no. ii) had been reached from above for the second time by a small trench through the demolition debris, earlier than the large pit that cut it but with very similar fill. By a fortunate accident, the original grave-digger had encountered a very large Saxo-Norman Thetford Ware storage jar lodged in the dark soil into which he was digging, but had clearly decided it was easier to break part of it off than to spoil his neat hole by grubbing it out. Finally, in Trench II, one last grave was found (no. i), the fill of which was demolition material, into which had been dug a shallow pit containing similar material to the fill under the garden humus in Trench I, but with no garden humus itself visible under the modern topsoil. It is possible that here the excavation had reached beyond the site of the bowling green into the area between it and Jesus Lane shown on Loggan's print occupied by a walk and then a grove.

The skeletal material was deposited in the Duckworth Laboratory, Cambridge,

CAMBRIDGE GREYFRIARS

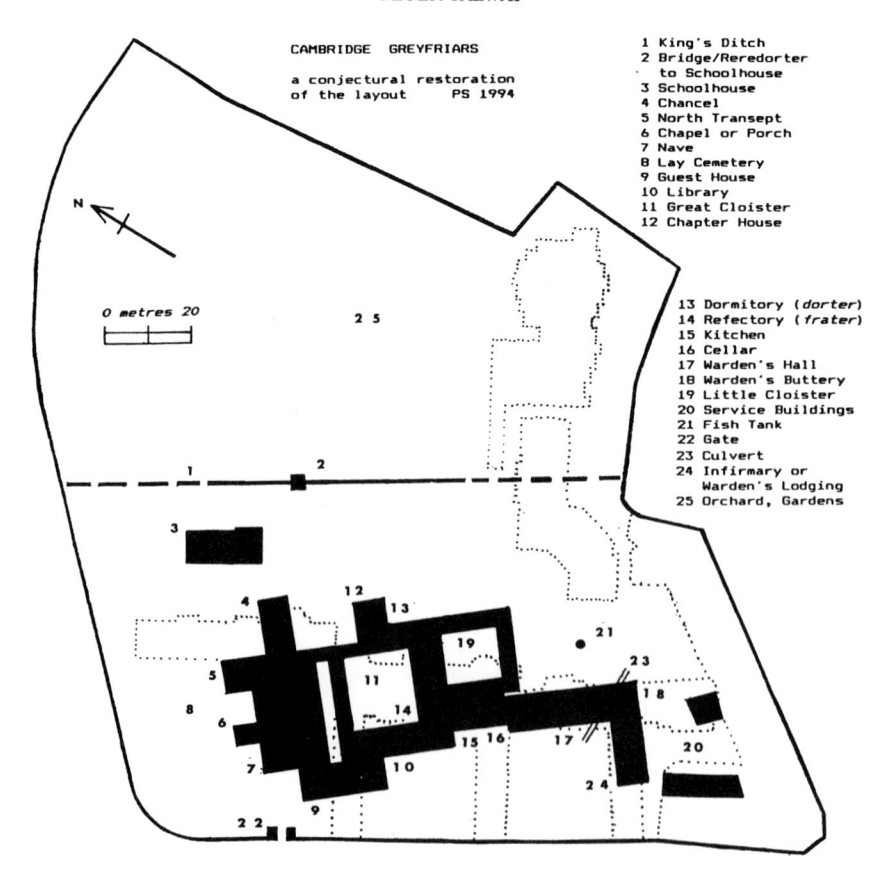

a conjectural restoration
of the layout   PS 1994

1 King's Ditch
2 Bridge/Reredorter to Schoolhouse
3 Schoolhouse
4 Chancel
5 North Transept
6 Chapel or Porch
7 Nave
8 Lay Cemetery
9 Guest House
10 Library
11 Great Cloister
12 Chapter House
13 Dormitory (*dorter*)
14 Refectory (*frater*)
15 Kitchen
16 Cellar
17 Warden's Hall
18 Warden's Buttery
19 Little Cloister
20 Service Buildings
21 Fish Tank
22 Gate
23 Culvert
24 Infirmary or Warden's Lodging
25 Orchard, Gardens

Figure 8

which examined and reported on it. The remains were (*1*: in grave i) female, aged around 50, height approximately 5 feet (1.52 m); (*2*: grave ii) female, around 45, 5 feet 1¾ inches (1.59 m), with very considerable osteo-arthritis and extremely severe dental decay; (*3*: grave iii) male, perhaps around 40, 5 feet 6½ inches (1.69 m), also with some osteo-arthritis; (*4*: grave iv) the skull only of a child, possibly female, aged 7–8; (*5*: from the robber trench nearest to the north end of Trench I) the skull and a few post-cranial bones of a male, around 60, estimated at 5 feet 7½ inches (1.71 m), with serious osteo-arthritis in the surviving vertebrae and a (healed) depressed fracture of the skull.

We can now begin to put the excavation into context. Figure 8 is an attempt to combine the fragments of information about the friary from all the different sources and to see how these might be accommodated within the pattern of a Franciscan house. The most critical elements are the size and position of the church, and the general alignment of the principal elements of the monastic layout. In this reconstruction the church is derived from the 1958 excavation and the 1984 resistivity survey, and the alignment from Essex's plan. It cannot be emphasized too much that this is an exercise in controlled speculation, and that the evidence for different parts of the plan varies enormously, from the certainty about the physical size and shape of James Essex's building and the stratigraphic detail from the 1958 and 1994 excavations, through the positive and negative indications of the 1984 resistivity survey, down to guesses at the existence and location of elements such as the chapter house which are based solely on analogy from elsewhere. The plan is very much subject to correction as fresh discoveries are made.

The earliest datable material from the site was Roman, and the pits of that period strongly suggest that it was associated with occupation nearby rather than casual deposition due to agricultural activity such as manuring. It is thought that the principal road from the south to the Roman town that lay northwards across the river ran along Sidney Street, heading for a gate in the town's defences somewhere in the neighbourhood of St Giles' Church. The subsequent dark occupation material in the northern part of the excavation probably represents the back yards and gardens of medieval houses facing onto Sidney Street, demolished before or at the time the friars took possession of the land.

There does not seem to be any reason to doubt that the principal structure encountered was indeed the Franciscan church destroyed in the 1540s, and earlier theories that there was a cemetery between it and Jesus Lane were confirmed, but not that it was the friars' own graveyard. The presence of women and a child make it highly probable that this was a lay cemetery. Burial in the precincts of religious houses was a privilege sought after, and the presence of such a cemetery outside the north wall of the church is not uncommon.

The surviving pier-base locates the arcade between the main body of the church and the south aisle (for which there is documentary evidence) and fragments of whose floor remained in place. The remains of earlier limestone walling found immediately south of the pier cannot be interpreted for certain, but might well represent an original solid south wall to the nave, demolished to allow the addition of a south aisle. However, secondary or not, there undoubtedly was an aisle extending south from the pier. This seems at first sight to contradict one of the apparent results of Dr Dark's resistivity survey, which appeared to show the south side of the church clear of the present southern walk of Cloister Court. The answer almost certainly must be that the construction of Wyatt's Combination Room and its subsequent demolition in 1890 destroyed practically all the relatively fragile remains of the aisle floor, whose existence the 1958 excavation was very fortunate to detect. The southern edge of the anomaly revealed by the resistivity meter will then represent the nave arcade.

The uncertainty about the presence of a corresponding arcade on the opposite side of the nave has already been noted, and it remains possible that the Cambridge church had (like the Oxford one) only one aisle. On the whole, however, the probability of a north aisle remains strong. Beyond that putative

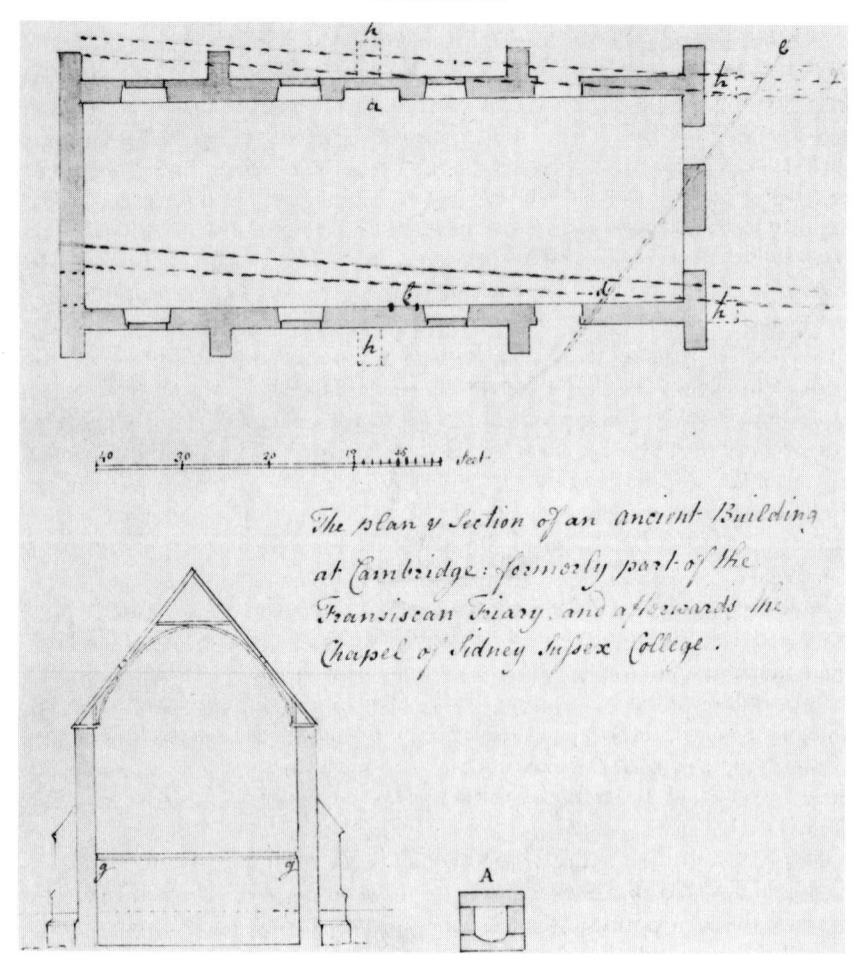

Figure 9

north arcade the very large robber-trench must indicate the main north wall of the church, at this point apparently with some thickening or attached feature on its inner side. This may well have corresponded with whatever external structure was represented in the excavation by the square-ended feature seen to the north as a robber-trench. The floor extending out towards it from the north wall of the church suggests this space had at some time been under cover. However, the fact that this floor had been cut by one of the graves – and that this contained the burial of a child, unlikely to have been a benefactor or other person with special claim to be buried inside the church – strongly suggests that it had gone out of use before the end of the friary. A smaller feature in this position at Oxford has been interpreted as a porch, or as a chantry chapel intended for praying for the soul of a benefactor.

The existence of a north transept was clearly indicated by the resistivity survey, lying much closer to the present Cloister Court building than the excavation trench and probably not to be associated with the structure just described. It seems very likely that, as in Oxford, the Cambridge friars' church had a single transept in this position. At Oxford, however, that transept was replaced by a 'north nave' (called such by William Worcestre in 1480), which was extended in stages to accommodate no fewer than ten chapels. At one point during the Oxford excavations it was suggested that this was the lecture hall, which would raise the question why Cambridge seems to have no such feature. It became clear, however, as the excavation progressed that the structure represented a multiplication of small chapels – exactly as William Worcestre measured and described – not an open hall. The reason, one might speculate, was that Oxford had the advantage of a saint's shrine on the premises (St Agnellus of Pisa, leader of the original Franciscan mission to England). We have no evidence for such a proliferation of chapels at Cambridge: the available documents record only the high altar, an altar in the south aisle, and one in an unspecified position dedicated to St Barbara. It is intriguing that before the end of the Oxford house the extravagant north nave had fallen out of use and was blocked off.

We have no direct evidence for the size or shape of the chancel of the Cambridge church, but the negative evidence of the resistivity survey suggests that it did not reach much beyond the present Cloister Court building into the Fellows' Garden. There is sufficient space on the plan, however, to postulate a simple choir without aisles or separate presbytery in reasonable proportion with the other dimensions of the church. At Oxford a chancel of this sort was proved by excavation to be the earliest part of the structure, and seems to have served for some time alone as the friars' church.

Dr Dark took the absence of structures revealed by resistivity under the grass plot in Hall Court to support the traditional location of the Franciscan cloister in much the same position as the present court. However, figure 8 demonstrates that, if the west end of the church came where the resistivity survey suggested and the overall alignment was the same as the building recorded by Essex, then the empty space in the centre of Hall Court is more likely to have been part of a yard reached from the main gate of the friary. The latter would have permitted the public access to the nave of the church and the lay cemetery without passing through the conventual buildings. The survey did indicate a substantial structure in the south-west corner of Cloister Court. The resistivity plot shows it partially overlapping the west end of the church. That would make it unlikely to have been part of the cloister – as conjectured by Dark – even if the alignment of the church was as previously thought. It is much more likely to have been the guest house, as at Walsingham where it was added not long before the Dissolution. At Cambridge the number of visitors to the friary generated by the presence of the University is likely to have caused a requirement for guest accommodation of unusual size, perhaps explaining why the building encroached on the west front of the church. The overlap is also more likely to have occurred with an added building than as part of an early plan. Access to it, too, would have been directly from the gate to the street.

The eastern range of the main cloister should have lain under the Master's Lodge, and it is possible that a chapter house on the pattern of Walsingham may sometime be detected projecting into the Master's Garden (which was not subjected to the resistivity survey), though it may be that a Franciscan house could dispense with a chapter house, as with a parlour and a sacristy, since many of the friars would have been on the road at any one time. The friars' dormitory would have lain in this range above the cloister walk, possibly extending southwards beyond it. A western range – which has been conjectured elsewhere to have held the library – can be more or less accommodated under the entrance to the Hall and Lodge and the paving along that side of Hall Court.

The understanding of the plan of the friary as a whole and the cloister in particular has long been bedevilled by Essex's identification of the building he replaced as the friar's refectory (*frater*). Such a refectory would normally be expected to lie along the south side of the cloister and parallel to it, and (being Franciscan) probably partially over it. The present writer tried in 1958 to explain the anomaly by assuming adoption by the Franciscans at Cambridge – for no obvious reason – of the Cistercian practice of placing the refectory at right-angles to the cloister walk. This implied an extraordinarily large cloister, only believable before Dr Dark established with greater accuracy the size of the church. The problems disappear if one accepts the convincing suggestion in the Royal Commission's *City of Cambridge* inventory that it was not the general refectory of the friars but the hall of the Franciscan warden's lodging. Essex was certainly right in identifying it as a dining hall. Quite apart from the small finds he describes, the plan is precisely that of a medieval domestic great hall (preserved and still working in many of the college halls of Oxford and Cambridge). At the south end there was a screens passage through the building, with twin buttery openings where one would expect them. Around the north end, Essex noted a decorative moulding high up on the wall, reaching down the sides only as far as the first windows. The probability of a dais and high table in this position is strong. Essex also noted and drew a culvert crossing under the screens end and supplying a basin there. It is probable that it was fed from the main conduit serving the friary from the west, and drained eastwards into the King's Ditch, via a yard. At Oxford the one building that survived the Dissolution was similarly identified as either an infirmary or the warden's lodging. At the Canterbury Greyfriars a building believed to be the warden's lodging was similarly adjacent to running water. Conduits in monastic houses commonly provided fresh water for the kitchens, drainage for sculleries, and flushing of latrines.

The existence of a substantial building in this position raises the strong possibility that – as at Walsingham and almost certainly Oxford – there was a second cloister. It would be possible to fit such a cloister into the area now occupied by the College Kitchens and the garden immediately in front of the Master's Lodge, particularly if the Walsingham arrangement is adopted, where the refectory oversails the walks of both great and little cloisters. South of this secondary cloister one would expect the service buildings of the friary, and this is precisely where the minor buildings that survived the Dissolution seem to have been located. Essex, it will be remembered, reported structures that he thought served kitchen and buttery purposes south of the building now identified as the warden's hall: early domestic buildings survived till reconstruction of the area in the angle between Sidney Street and Sussex Street; and medieval pottery preserved in College came from various locations during the construction of South Court and Montagu House in the 1930s. Hamond's map shows houses along Sussex Street, but also a scatter of minor structures which, though they cannot be very exactly matched with what survived till relatively recent times, probably do record minor friary service buildings. More important is the larger building mentioned earlier that Hamond shows at 90 degrees to Essex's building. Though it is not clear how it related to the buttery identified by Essex, it does seem likely that it was associated with the 'refectory', most probably being the private rooms of the warden.

There is one further feature that may have been part of the same complex. A small vaulted cellar, once part of the Master's Lodge but now absorbed into the College Kitchens, was thought by Knox-Shaw, former Master, to be the only surviving part of the friary. What is now visible internally is approximately 5.32 metres (17 feet 5 ins) long. Its structure is at present concealed by smooth modern plaster, and its original depth is impossible to establish without digging because of modern flooring, but its shape in cross-section would be consistent with its being half of a medieval undercroft. Its precise relationship with the buildings above remains to be established, but it might well have served either the dais of the warden's hall or kitchens supplying the main refectory and conveniently located at this point. At Warkworth Castle in Northumberland a private cellar communicated directly (and only) with the high-table end of the fifteenth-century great hall, and was quite separate from a beer cellar that served the rest. Essex's observation that the structures immediately south of the hall itself had been additions is not entirely surprising if the identification as part of the warden's lodging is correct, as the development of increasingly elaborate separate facilities for the heads of houses is a feature of late medieval monasticism.

East of the putative warden's hall, between the present Chapel and Garden Court, is an area that might be expected to produce evidence of the most domestic activities of the friary – the likely site of a back yard between the lesser cloister and the King's Ditch. In 1994 the proposal to build a new hall to improve lecture and dining facilities in College led to a small evaluation excavation in the centre of this area by the Cambridge Archaeological Unit. The results support the Unit's judgment that this was such a service area, for the dig revealed a clay-lined pit containing pottery dating from the thirteenth century to the fifteenth, almost certainly a fish-tank. The likelihood that further excavation in this area would provide extensive evidence of the environment and diet of the friary from pits and other minor features undisturbed by major structures seems high. In that friars were a group of people who lived under special rules that set them aside from the general population, it would historically be particularly interesting to observe whether there were differences in the environmental evidence from that encountered on other sites in Cambridge, and whether there were signs of change in diet in the course of the three centuries of Franciscan life on the site.

The 1984 resistivity survey located one other large structure, at the opposite end of the site. This lay in the Fellows' Garden, just inside the King's Ditch, north-east of the Franciscan church and at right angles to it. Dr Dark must be right in dismissing it as an early church, but it is not necessary to assume a pre-Franciscan date. This is not an unlikely location on a monastic site for a storehouse or other service building, but excavation in 1994 on the site of Rewley Abbey in Oxford emboldens one to make a different suggestion. Rewley was founded in 1281 by Edmund of Cornwall, using endowment left by his father Richard, whose heart we have already met being buried in the church of the Oxford Greyfriars. Richard had intended a chantry of secular priests on the Rewley site to pray for his own soul, but what has always intrigued historians of Oxford is that Edmund diverted the funds to found a Cistercian abbey with a *studium* (or 'school'), which for a century attracted significant numbers of students. If the *studium* could be identified on the ground, much might be learnt about prototypes of college buildings. The first tentative results suggest that the *studium* lay north of the abbey church, against the outer precinct wall beyond which ran an artificial moat. The building or buildings appear to have formed an L-shape, quite unlike a normal monastic cloister. Julian Munby, of the Oxford Archaeological Unit, has pointed out to the writer that the earliest surviving college court at either university (Mob Quad, Merton) was not a quadrangle in its original phase (first half of the fourteenth century) but two separate buildings at a right angle to one another. At Rewley Abbey, these similar buildings were provided with a reredorter (latrine block) out over the moat. It is tempting to suggest that this was a student area deliberately sited away from the abbey's domestic buildings (not yet located, but likely to have been on the opposite side of the church). By the 1370s this teaching establishment had failed, and the buildings were incorporated into the abbey proper. Ironically, they continued to stand after the rest was demolished, surviving into the nineteenth century, while the remains of their reredorter were used as a bridge.

The relevance of the discoveries at Rewley Abbey to the Cambridge Franciscans is more than just a matter of general interest in the form of early university buildings. It seems extremely likely that when planning Rewley the founder or his advisers will have looked at the Oxford Greyfriars, with which his father and stepmother had such a close association and which by now had half a century of success as a leading institution of learning. This probability allows us to take a shot at filling the gap left by the failure of the investigations on the Oxford Greyfriars site to provide direct evidence of what Franciscan teaching facilities were like. It seems almost too convenient to be true that the building located by Dark in the Fellows' Garden lies in more or less the same relationship to the church as the presumed *studium* at Rewley Abbey, tucked away in the northern part of the precinct. There is even an adjacent structure spanning the King's Ditch – certainly in use as a bridge after the Dissolution – to complete the pattern. If it was indeed the school, then the absence of a building shown on any of the early maps in this relationship to the bridge is consistent with the documentary evidence, for the Trinity accounts record payment in 1553–4 'for taking downe of the scholehouse at the freres'. And another Trinity document – an inventory dated not earlier than the end of 1547 – gives us one valuable detail about that building, for by listing 'hewen stone . . . for [*from*] the turrett under the scole howse' it implies that it was a structure of at least two storeys or a hall with an undercroft. Written references to the bridge itself in the sixteenth-century sources are lacking, unless it was the 'little house by the orchard gate', which , if as at Rewley Abbey it had been a small but substantial building rather than an open bridge, it just might have been. The schoolhouse identification can be no more than a tantalizing hypothesis in the absence of further excavation at Sidney, but the chances of testing it are perhaps better on this site than at either the Oxford Greyfriars or Rewley Abbey.

The same inventory also gives us a glimpse of one other building. The inventory included 'a roofe of tymbre wch [*was*] ouer the hall at [*the*] freres lying in a storehouse next to Laings [*tenant of part of the site from 1547*]'. This presumably came from the main refectory, not from the building later converted into the first Sidney chapel, since the latter still had its medieval roof timbers when Essex drew it. It may have been reused at Trinity, just as the medieval roof of the dissolved St Mary's College in Oxford was reused for the chapel of Brasenose.

The fate of the Cambridge friars' conduit raises some interesting questions. At Oxford just before the Dissolution the friars – in serious financial difficulties – had been trying to raise money by selling off what they could. A report to Thomas Cromwell in 1538 stated that 'they have taken vppe the pypes of ther condytt lately and haue cast them in sowys [*pigs of lead*] to the nombre lxxij, whereof xij be sold for the costes in taking vppe of the pypes, as the warden saith. The residew we haue putt in safe garde. Butt we haue nott yet weyde them. An ther is yett in the erthe remaynyng much of the condytt nott taken yppe.' This dismantling of the Oxford conduit *before* the Dissolution leads one to wonder whether the Cambridge example was still working to the end of the friary. The western part was certainly usable in 1601–2, when it was made to serve the fountain in Trinity Great Court. Quite apart from Henry VIII's grant of the full length to his new college, the friars had lost their exclusive right to it since the investigation in the reign of Henry VI, thenceforth holding it jointly with King's Hall, the most important of the earlier colleges incorporated into Trinity and through which the conduit ran. It is therefore not possible to assume without question that the sector beyond the site of King's Hall (i.e. beyond Trinity Street) remained in operation to the end of the friary. Certainly no sign of it has yet been found in Sidney, though if encountered by chance its course might be detectable archaeologically, however early it was dismantled.

The Trinity documents represent the contemporary paperwork of the demolition of the buildings of the friary. In the case of the church, the 1958 excavation added some vivid traces on site of the gangs in action. The floor-tiles had been ripped up, using crowbars to lever out those that resisted. Then the windows were removed, the glass knocked out and the spider's web of lead 'cames' crumpled ready for the melting-pot. The roof was stripped of slabs and tiles, and the walls demolished by men standing on the top, emptying the rubble core and hooking out the facing stones. Some of the stone was burnt on the spot for lime – no carved pieces were found and one may assume that some such were considered too awkward for reuse. In the cemetery stone covers were removed from the graves, though care was taken to rebury bones disturbed in the process. An inventory in the possession of Trinity dated not earlier than 1547 matches very neatly with the archaeological evidence, recording 'three sowes of lede of which one lieth where the church stode . . . and two in the corner of the cloyster next to the steple and lyme kylne . . .'. However, the stratification also indicates that not all the robbing of the monastic site was carried out in the first phase, and confirms what was deduced earlier from the documentary evidence. Since it is clear from the inventory just quoted that the church had already been demolished by the time it was written, there was probably *less* remaining by the 1590s in the area of the 1958 excavation than elsewhere on the site. Nevertheless signs of renewed robbing did appear, most obviously in the cemetery area towards the northern end of the excavation, where the original demolition debris of the church was cut through to at least one of the graves.

The accumulation of knowledge about the archaeology of the site before Sidney has been slow, but we now have enough of a framework that quantitatively quite small future investigations ought to add qualitatively significant information. There is no doubt that even the smallest holes dug for whatever purpose should be observed archaeologically and recorded. Much more could be learnt about the layout of the Franciscan establishment, the hints of Roman activity followed up, and possibly even something important added to the much too obscure history of early medieval Cambridge, perhaps most promisingly by testing the origins of the King's Ditch. It may be possible to confirm quite closely the dating of the phases encountered in 1958 by further examination of the finds recovered in the excavation, especially in the light of the great advances in knowledge of medieval ceramics in the intervening years. Improvements in remote sensing methods would make it worth while to repeat the 1984 resistivity survey, and undertake magnetometer and ground-penetrating radar scans of the unencumbered areas of the site (the last being particularly effective in cemeteries). And perhaps most revealing of all, it is now possible – as it was not in 1958 – to employ the advanced techniques of environmental archaeology (as mentioned above in connection with the 1994 evaluation) to learn a great deal – even from quite small excavations – about the conditions in which the people who preceded us on the site lived out their daily lives.

Appendix

James Essex's plan of the medieval building that had been re-used as the original College Chapel is accompanied in the British Library by his manuscript notes (Add. MS 6761). The text of these was transcribed in 1925 by Gordon Pringle, whose typescript is preserved in the Sidney College archives:

OBSERVATIONS ON THE OLD CHAPEL OF SIDNEY COLLEGE
IN CAMBRIDGE

The Franciscan Friary of which thie [*sic*, typescript] building was a part, was founded in the time of Edward the 1st.[1] The site of it was very extensive before the Dissolution, and the Church which stood on the ground that is now the College Bowling Green, was one of the largest in the Town, and generally used for Commencement Acts and other Publick exercises by the University so late as the year 1507 when the Commencement was held ther tho' during the time that St. Mary's Church was building, they used the Church of the Augustins for their Sermons.

This Church being so commodious for the University they apply'd for it to King Henry 8 at the Dissolution of the monastery, but he gave it to Trinity College, who pulled it down and imployed the best of the materials in building their College.

The site of the Monastery was purchased of Trinity College, by the executors of Lady Francis Sidney and with it the remains of the old Church, and this building with some other out buildings on the South Side next walls lane.

Mr. Fuller in Hist. of Cam speaking of this Chapel says some have reported that it formerly was a Stable, which is not improbable, though he will not admit it to be true, for we cannot say what uses it might have been apply'd to, between the time of the dissolution of the Monaster [*sic*, typescript] and the time of its being converted into a Chapel, but within that interval of time, about twenty feet at the south end, was separated from the rest by a wall, and used to lay coals in, as plainly appeared when the foundations were digging for ye new Chapel, and the other end might have been used for a stable for ought he knew to the contrary, tho' it certainly was not built for that purpose.

This building consisted of one room 69 ft. 6 in. long 23 ft. 8 in. wide between the walls, and 25 ft. high to the setting on of the Roof, which formed a ceiling with arched principals, and the intermediate spaces flat in the middle and sloped on the sides, as represented in the section. There were three windows and a door on the West side; on the East there were the same number of windows and a door with a chimney at (a) seven feet wide, placed near the midle [*sic*, typescript], on

---

[1] The Grey Friary was founded in the year 1224 by Henry the 3, in an old Synagague [*sic*] near the Common prison (which was made of a house belonging to one Benjamin, a Jew) and afterwards was removed to this place in the time of Edward 1st. (Tann [?Tanner] Note)

the west side nearly opposite the Chimhey [*sic*, typescript] (at b.) two holes appear in the wall, which being too low for a table or sideboard, and too high for a seat, might receive timbers to support the floor of a pulpit or desk, where the Lecturer read the scriptures to the Friars while they were at meals – about ten feet from the South west angle near the side of the South door (at d.) are some marks in the wall by which it appears that a Cistern or a Laver had been fixed there; under this, about a foot lower than the loor [*sic*, typescript] of the room, was a neat stone drain, about one foot square in the form of fig. A. which running obliquely in the direction d e. under the South end of the room, conveyed the water from this place into the Kings ditch, and served likewise to convey other waste water from some other part of the Monastery, or from the Conduit belonging to it, which was served from the spring in the fields near Madingly road before it was given to Trinity College who cut it off the pipe and retained the spring for their own use, when they sold the site of the Monastery.

At the south end of the room there were two doors 4 ft. wide leading into an adjoining building, the foundations of which may be partly traced as at f and f.

The floor of this room was made of plaister, or common mortar mixt with clay (not unlike those used in malt houses) and lay'd four feet below the level of the Chapel floor; at the upper end (which was to the north) ten feet above the floor; [*sic*, typescript] there was a moulding or cornice (g g) which runs across that end, but not round the room there was neither doors nor windows at that end unless the entrance into the Chapel had been a door enlarged. (a).

From these particulars in the plan, and from the quantity of small bones of fowls and rabbits and other animals with pieces of spoons etc. which were found among the rubbish when this building was pulled down, we must conclude that it was originally the refectory of the Fransiscans [*sic*, typescript], (b) and not the ancient dormitory, as Mr Fuller would prove from the concavities in the walls which being no other than the windows and doors, could not serve as places for their several repousre and as there is no appearance of any timber floor within the height of this building except that of the Library which was made when it was converted into a Chapel, it is probable the Dormitory was not over the Refectory but in some other part of the Monastery.

The buildings which adjoined to the south end of this, I suppose were the Butteries into which the doors at that end open'd (a) the other offices were ranged on the south next walls lane; where the Warden and Friars appartment were situate cannot be traced; but as the church stood about fifty yards north of this building it is probable they were ranged somewhere between them; in an old plan of

a. which is not improbable for the principal appartments were not on that side, but did not join this building.
b. The theatre for ye commencement was built *in Edibus Friciscanorum* [*sic*, typescript] anno 1549. (Hist Univ. p. 155. 29.)

Cambridge other buildings appear to have joined this, running from it towards the street where now the south wing of the College stands.

According to Mr. Fullers account this Building was not converted into a Chapel until some years after the first founding of the College, the first stone of which was laid the 20th day of May. 1596, but it certainly was intended to be so when the plan of the College was made, tho' it might not be in their power to do it at the same time for want of money, which according to his account was raised by subscription some years after.

The situation of this chapel is nearly North and South and the same as the old Chapel of Emanuel College now their Library, they were both built by the same Architect *Rodolph Simons* who ingeniously contrived to convert the Chapel of the Dominican Friars, into a *Refectory* and the Refectory of the Franciscans into a Chapel.

This building being greatly decayed was taken down in the month of August 1776 and on the first day of October at noon, the first stone of a new Chapel was laid in the south east angle of the Foundation, about five feet below the surface of the ground; the head of the stone which is eleven inches square, lieth towards the east and projects two inches before the range of the wall; the date of the year 1776 is cut deep in figures two inches long and on the lower surface this ┼ is cut with a chisel.

The Master and Fellows being at that time engaged at the College Audit, none was present but the Master Bricklayer and a Labourer who assisted me laying it.

The situation of the new Chapel is little different from the old, but not upon the old Foundations the dotted lines in the plan show the variation. The Butteries L.L.L. represented with dotted lines were not part of the original building but added afterwards.

a. The floors of the Butteries were higher than the floor of the Refectory two steps, which being made of clunch were much worn.

James Essex.

Select Bibliography

Clark, J.W., and Gray, A., *Old Plans of Cambridge 1574–1798* (Cambridge, 1921).

Dark, K.R., 'Archaeological survey at Sidney Sussex College, Cambridge, 1984', *Proceedings of The Cambridge Antiquarian Society,* 74, 1985 (1987), 81–4.

Edwards, G.M., *Sidney Sussex College,* University of Cambridge College Histories (London, 1889).

Hassall, T.G., Halpin, C.E., and Mellor, M., 'Excavations in St. Ebbe's, Oxford, 1967–1976: Part 1', *Oxoniensia,* 54, 1989 (1991), 72–277.

Hind, D., Marsden, I., and Evans, C., *Archaeological Investigations at Sidney Sussex College, Cambridge (The Dining Hall Site) 1994,* Cambridge Archaeological Unit Report 109, July 1994 [*PPG 16 evaluation report, not intended for publication*].

Martin, A.R., *Franciscan Architecture in England,* British Society of Franciscan Studies, 18 (Manchester, 1937).

Moorman, J.R.H., *The Grey Friars in Cambridge, 1225–1538* (Cambridge, 1952).

Royal Commission on Historical Monuments, England, *Inventory: City of Cambridge* (London, 1959).

Thornely, J.W.A., and Parish, C., eds., *Sidney Sussex College Annual 1993* (Cambridge, 1993) [*colour plates: glass mounted in Old Library; p. 35: presentation of a panel of glass to the Chancellor (Duke of Edinburgh)*].

Willis, R., and Clark, J.W., *The Architectural History of the University of Cambridge and of the Colleges of Cambridge and Eton,* vol. 2 (Cambridge, 1886).

Sir Philip Sidney

A Paper Read by
THE LATE VISCOUNT DE L'ISLE, V.C., K.G.
to the Confraternitas Historica at Sidney Sussex College, 22 April 1987

> The differences which I have found between times, and consequently the changes of life into which their natural vicissitudes do violently carry men, as they make deep furrows of impressions into my heart, so the same heavy wheels cause me to retire my thoughts from free traffic with the world and rather seek comfortable ease or employment in the safe memory of dead men, than disquiet in a doubtful conversation among the living.

Thus Philip Sidney's first biographer, Fulke Greville, Lord Brooke, who goes on ' – Which I ingenuously confess to be one chief motive of dedicating these exercises of my youth to that worthy Sir Philip Sidney, so long since departed'; he proceeds: 'But besides this selfrespect of dedication, the debt I acknowledge to that gentleman is far greater; as with whom I shall ever account it honour to have been brought up.'[1]

Fulke Greville's devotion to his long-departed friend still stands writ in marble on his own tomb in St Mary's Church, Warwick, where he described himself as 'Servant to Queen Elizabeth, Counsellor to King James and friend to Sir Philip Sidney'. The 'deep furrows of impressions' which troubled Greville when considering 'the differences . . . between times' and 'the changes of life' which 'do violently carry men' through their 'natural vicissitudes' must ever be a challenge to historians and literary critics too. For historians and literary critics have to assess the motives of men and women who have stood out amongst their fellows. They have, as well, to try to understand and measure the power of the personalities which gave their subjects so much influence over their own contemporaries.

The modern scientific approach to history has stripped layers of romantic wrapping from the past. Although the assembly, from records, of masses of detailed information can be valuable in removing errors and in drawing attention to actual material circumstances of existence at the times described, this method

---

[1] *A Dedication to Sir Philip Sidney* [1652], in *The Prose Works of Fulke Greville, Lord Brooke*, edited by John Gouws (Oxford, 1986), p. 3.

cannot of itself create 'the safe memory of dead men'. This 'memory' must ever fascinate us when we try to connect the past with the present to create a coherent and intelligible synthesis, from which to form judgements about the human characteristics of 'dead men' who were once as much alive and actual as we are ourselves. Imagination be our guide. For in the final analysis, imagination must be the bridge which allows us to cross the 'deep furrows' which divide us from the past. It is especially only imagination which allows us to enter into the feelings of great creative spirits of the past and sift the gold of original thought from the dross of imitative mediocrity.

The problem of recovering and reviving character and personality is nowhere greater than in the case of poets, and I mean poets recognised as great. Sometimes the contradictions are striking between the beauty of their creative work and the ordinariness, even the meanness, of their lives and social relations. In such instances the biographer's and the critic's task is simplified. The contrast between light and shade makes delineation sharper. With Philip Sidney the difficulty lies in the fact that the symmetry of his life and his work, his character and achievements is almost too complete to be true. In *English Literature of the Sixteenth Century*, C.S. Lewis wrote:

> Even at this great distance Sidney is dazzling. He is that rare thing, the aristocrat in whom the aristocratic ideal is really embodied. Leicester's nephew, Pembroke's brother-in-law, an eligible parti for a princess, painted by Veronese, poet and patron of poets, statesman, Knight, Captain – Fate has dealt such hands before but seldom have they been so well played.[2]

Though a great deal has been written about Philip, no better biography has so far appeared than that of a Canadian and Professor of English at University College, Toronto, written as long ago as 1915. In the postscript to his work, Malcolm Wallace summed up his subject when he wrote: 'Personal charm or magnetism can never be made to yield up its mystery by enumerating its ingredients.' And he went on:

> In Sidney's case it was not due to any perfection or lack of faults. Of his faults we could sum up a formidable list were it worthwhile doing so. He was foolishly extravagant in the spending of money, and was sometimes forced to seek to improve his financial position by means which were at least not dignified. He was somewhat arrogant and hot-headed. He was inclined to be egotistical.

But he goes on: 'But all these tell nothing about the man.'[3]

Nevertheless it is comforting, for me at least, to read about the shortcomings

---

[2] C.S. Lewis, *English Literature of the Sixteenth Century, Excluding Drama* (Oxford, 1954), p. 324.
[3] M.W. Wallace, *The Life of Sir Philip Sidney* (Cambridge, 1915), pp. 400f.

of a man upon whom for so long, by so many people, so much praise has been bestowed: from James VI of Scotland, immediately following his death, to the words of C.S Lewis which I have just quoted. The shortcomings make him more human and comprehensible. Indeed, to portray Philip Sidney as a saint in a stained-glass window cannot be a fate fitting for a vigorous, athletic, sexually aware and probably sexually active man, who was a brave soldier and a man of affairs, and for whom literature was, on his own profession, no more than a 'toyful' pursuit.

May I remark in passing that it is a curiosity of literature that the best biographical work on Sidney, and the best literary criticism and editorship, all come from foreign pens. Wallace I have noted. The editor of the first complete edition of Philip's work, including the *Arcadia*, was a Frenchman, Albert Feuillerat, Professor of English Literature in the University of Rennes; and it remained for Professor William Ringler of Washington University, St Louis, USA, to produce the complete critical edition of Philip's poetry which was published by Oxford University Press in 1962.

We live in a Britain which has contrived to shrug off its Empire and most of its other worldwide responsibilities. Now in our sophisticated, rather weary world-view, we believe we can afford to patronise the empire-builders of the past. Through the television screens the present generation is more aware of General Dyer's 'Massacre at Amritsar' than Wolfe's capture of Quebec. So it is easier for it to appreciate Sidney's sonnets than his combative Protestantism and deep interest in colonial expansion. In our mood of reductionism we may even suspect his patriotic fervour. These aspects of his character and career, together with his learning and his patronage of the arts, were ones which aroused such a deep sense of loss and such a public display of grief at his death. In an age of confident self-assertion Philip was a representative Englishman and a national hero.

The 'deep furrows' which Greville experienced have deepened, the more effectively to divide our present from our past. The hero has been supplanted by the anti-hero. Other-worldliness has been replaced by man's ability to pull himself upward by his bootstraps. The only world we can know, it is said, is the world of senses powered by science, though our confidence in a boundless future has to be mitigated by the fear that 'stupidity' (note 'stupidity', rather than moral obliquity) will end life in a nuclear winter.

Our rationality may or may not be greater than the rationality of the Elizabethans. It is certainly a different sort of rationality. They believed in witchcraft and sea serpents, they believed in the Devil as well as God. They believed that men and women have immortal souls and are individually answerable for them. We have been taught to place our faith in the inevitability of progress, the implicit benevolence of the collective mass of mankind when purposefully guided by abstract and objective scientific truth. However a society so 'enlightened' may be administered, we are apt to ignore evidence supplied by such incidents as Hitler's Holocaust or Pol Pot's genocide in Campuchea, both of which were justified by 'scientific' certainties.

In considering Philip's career and his place in history, whether as a man of affairs or as a writer, we are not compelled to judge between the values and norms of conduct and belief then and now. We have merely to note differences the better to understand the ideas which furnished his mind and stimulated his ambitions and actions. Once due allowance has been made for the 'natural vicissitudes' which have altered circumstances, we shall, I think, find we have more in common with Philip than is apparent at first, as the creature of his times as we are of ours.

The England of Elizabeth lived in continual fear of infiltration of foreign agents and alien ideas. It faced constant threat of invasion, later made actual when the Spanish Armada sailed. The balance of power was shifting and uncertain. The persecution of the Protestants in France and the invasion of the Protestant Netherlands by Spain were further evidence of the fate which awaited English Protestants should either France or Spain become the successful agents for the restoration of Catholicism here. We can recognise the recurrence of many of the same threats to our modern Britain, though in different guises, and we can appreciate the longing of a remarkably intelligent, politically aware and socially well-placed youth to face the challenge and to train himself to become, under his sovereign Queen, a leading figure in the councils of the nation.

We can understand how important was the moral support he received from devoted parents. His mother, who was born a Dudley, had seen her father and one of her brothers and her sister-in-law fall victims of the headsman's axe, not to mention her paternal grandfather, who met a similar fate. She must have longed to see her own son rise to an assured position of authority through his intelligence, force of character and superior judgement. As to his father, Sir Henry Sidney, one of the Queen's ablest administrators, he must have hoped that his devoted but largely unrecognised services in Ireland and Wales would finally be rewarded through his eldest son.

What is more difficult for us to comprehend is the intensity of Philip's concentration and the rapidity with which he absorbed all that he was taught or read. Men and women of those days had a far shorter life expectancy, and so had a great incentive to complete life's business within a limited span. Even for the well-off the physical conditions in which they lived were exacting – indifferent diet, lack of warmth, long dark winters, immensely long journeys over bad roads on horseback in all weathers; all these they had to contend with as a matters of course. Even so, Philip's achievements in less than thirty-two years are remarkable judged by the standards of his time.

Philip was born at Penshurst on 30 November 1554, some nine months after his grandfather, Sir William Sidney, had died there. The house and estates had been granted to Sir William by Edward VI in a deed dated March 1552. The house of which the Sidneys were then possessed must have seemed large, bare, and inhospitable. Apart from a small early Tudor addition, Penshurst would have then constituted a fourteenth-century manor house, that is, a vast hall, two great chambers, kitchens and offices, to which had been added another hall in 1430 built by John of Lancaster, Duke of Bedford.

There is evidence, partly based on tradition, that the family occupied one or more of the eight towers, which together with the curtain walls that joined them formed the medieval defensive system. It took Sir Henry, Philip's father, more than thirty years gradually to extend the house he had inherited and provide a series of smaller and more commodious lodgings for his growing family, for his friends and, no doubt, for his correspondingly enlarged household. The time which he took to complete his building work must have been partly due to his official responsibilities. He was constantly travelling. The burden of governing Ireland was especially heavy and involved him in more than one arduous military campaign. So Philip would have become accustomed to separation from his parents and to a family life often divided by distance; but despite this he was not denied affection. The whole family seems to have enjoyed happy relationships.

Life at Shrewsbury School where Philip was educated from the age of ten was no doubt uncomfortable physically, yet the standard of scholarship was high. As President of the Marches of Wales Sir Henry had his headquarters in Ludlow, within easy reach of the school. This must have contributed to Philip's sense of security and his self-confidence. After four years at Shrewsbury, at the age of fourteen, he was entered at Christ Church, Oxford. He remained there for some three years. Just short of his seventeenth year Philip was on his travels in Europe. He was to be three years abroad. He left Paris immediately after the horrifying massacre of St Bartholomew's Eve in 1572 and never set foot in France again. He travelled on through Germany, Austria and Italy whence he made an expedition into Hungary. He met many of the leading figures of Europe and some leading poets and artists. Perhaps most important for his education, he came under the influence of Hubert Languet, a Protestant Frenchman and scholar who had been a disciple of Melanchthon. Languet became Philip's mentor, politically and doctrinally, and they entered a long and serious correspondence. This throws much light on the development of Philip's ideas and world view.

He reached Penshurst again, in August 1574. The same year he went to Ireland with his father, who was then Lord Deputy. The rest of Philip's short life, a mere eleven years, was a record of frustrated hopes for a position and responsibility at Court in the royal service, and of fruitful private activity both as a patron of letters and as a serious writer himself. He was intent on raising the prevailing standards of literature in England.

As Cupbearer to the Queen his duties were formal and took him occasionally to Court; but he seems to have spent a great deal of time either at Penshurst or with his sister Mary at Wilton. He was sent abroad again in 1576 as ambassador to the Emperor Rudolph, and the opportunity was provided to canvass assiduously for support for the formation of a Protestant League of princes to oppose Catholic powers. On his return journey through the Netherlands he met William, Prince of Orange, and made a deep impression on that Prince.

The Queen determinedly pursued her policy of non-intervention in European wars. Philip made no secret of his impatience with the royal policy. Moreover, on the question of the Queen's marriage to the French Prince, the Duc d'Alençon, he became the mouthpiece of the opposition to the marriage by a strongly Protestant section of the Council. He wrote to his sovereign a long reasoned memorial setting out the objections to this marriage. It was a dangerous initiative, but his position in the hierarchy was strong enough to save him from more than royal displeasure. Not for the first or the last time, Philip's independence of spirit cost him the possibility of advancement.

His strong desire for active service continued, together with his great interest in colonial expansion. This interest prompted him to arrange with Francis Drake that he should secretly embark at Plymouth in Drake's ship and sail with that great adventurer on his West Indies expedition. But his plans were revealed to the Queen and she peremptorily summoned the discomfited Philip back to Court.

Plans had early been made for him to marry Lord Burghley's daughter and a marriage agreement was actually drawn up; but the project was allowed to drop. Philip's ultimate financial prospects were good. He was for a time heir to his two Dudley uncles, the Earls of Warwick and Leicester. But Philip's actual financial position remained embarrassed. Moreover, his hopes of promotion were continually blighted. In 1575 the Earl of Essex, who was devoted to Philip, wanted him to be betrothed to his elder daughter, Lady Penelope Devereux. The Earl died, and in the event Penelope's guardian married her to Lord Rich in 1580. In 1581 Philip was betrothed to Frances, daughter of Sir Francis Walsingham, a political alliance rather than a financially advantageous one. Philip and Frances were married in 1583. He was knighted in the same year.

The romantic element in Philip's great sonnet sequence *Astrophel and Stella*, in which the author is 'Astrophel' and Penelope (who became Lady Rich) 'Stella', has inevitably aroused more interest and comment than has his *Arcadia* and the rest of his considerable literary output. The notion of his frustrated love for a married woman expressed in poetry of great passion has tended to divert attention from the less romantic aspect of this, perhaps Philip's most serious contribution to English poetry. The sequence was formally addressed to 'Stella', though she was not the recipient of the sonnets. With feeling, it represents an internal discussion between the writer and his perception of his own emotions, and so becomes a personal account of the struggle between passion and reason within one heart and mind. Yet we do not have to suppose that Philip's passion had not been aroused by Penelope and that the sonnets are no more than a brilliant imaginative and intellectual exercise.

Malcolm Wallace writes: 'In spite of his deep moral earnestness there was nothing of the Puritan in Sidney'; and he adds that he 'had no enthusiasm for special prohibitions and constraints' and that 'his melancholy . . . was not akin to the Puritan's melancholy which was a recrudescence of the ideals of the mediaeval Church, and which condemned as evil in themselves the desires and passions of the natural man'.[4] It is comforting to me to be sure that Philip was

---

[4] Wallace, *Life of Sidney*, p. 237.

such a natural man. One can read his poetry with all the more enjoyment, expressing as he does in memorable language the passionate feelings, and bitter disappointments, in which we all can share. But as with all great poetry, our response is deepened in proportion as the emotional tension is raised by the skill of the writer, who has learned to master his craft through intense application as well as through natural genius.

I have to admit I find *Arcadia* hard going. It takes a great deal of concentration to extract the author's meaning from the elaborations of verbiage; still greater effort to disentangle from these elaborations the thread of order and purpose which can be discovered by those who have soaked themselves in Elizabethan thought and imagery. But I find great satisfaction in Philip's description of the landscape of Arcadia.

In the *Arcadia*, 'nature', as C.S. Lewis writes, 'is a nature thoroughly humanised. The romantic poet wishes to be absorbed into nature, the Elizabethans absorb her.'[5] I am moved when I read in *Arcadia*, Book One, a description of Kalander's house:

> They perceived he was not willing to open himself further, and therefore without further questioning brought him to the house; about which they might see (with fit consideration both of the air, the prospect, and the nature of the ground) all such necessarie additions to a great house as well might show that Kalander knew that provision is the foundation of hospitality, and thrift the fuel of magnificence.
>
> The House itself was built of fair and strong stone, not affecting so much any extraordinary kind of fineness as an honourable representing of a firm stateliness. The lights, doors, stairs rather directed to the use of the guest than to the eye of the artificer; and yet as the one chiefly heeded, so the other not neglected; each place handsome without curiosity and homely without loathsomeness; not so dainty as not to be trod on, nor yet slubbered up with good fellowship; all more lasting than beautiful; but that consideration of the exceeding lastingness made the eye believe it was exceeding beautiful.[6]

Philip can have had in mind no other house than Penshurst as it stood as he first remembered it, and later with the 'necessarie additions to a great house' which his father was engaged in making when Philip was writing *Arcadia*. It is true, if I may say so, that 'exceeding lastingness' still makes the eye believe that Penshurst is 'exceeding beautiful'.

There is a still more evocative description of the 'backside of the house' which

> was neither field, garden nor orchard; or rather it was both field, garden and orchard; for as soon as the descending of the stairs had delivered them down, they came into a place cunningly set with trees of the most taste-pleasing

---

[5] Lewis, *English Literature of the Sixteenth Century*, p. 341.
[6] Sir Philip Sidney, *The Countess of Pembroke's Arcadia*, edited by Albert Feuillerat (Cambridge, 1912), Book I, Chapter 2, p. 15.

fruits; but scarcely they had taken that into their consideration but that they were suddenly stepped into a delicate green, of each side of the green a thicket: behind the thickets again new beds of flowers, which being under the trees, the trees were to them a pavilion, and they to the trees a mosaical floor; so that it seemed that art therein would needs be delightful by counterfeiting his enemy error, and making order in confusion.[7]

This would not be exactly a *Country Life* description of our garden as it is today, but it is not too far off. Sir Henry's stairs still deliver the visitor down to the garden which he created, with its walls and terraces, delicate greens and new beds of flowers, as well as most taste-pleasing fruit – features no doubt differently disposed but still occurring in the garden as it is now. I confess that our Kentish countryside with alternations of woods and fields, 'silvery streams, greens and thickets', remains to me truly arcadian. And who shall say that the inspiration of our poet has not continued to prevail here as a restraining influence in a world subject to vicissitudes 'violently carried'?

In 1585, in Philip's thirty-second year, the opportunity for which he yearned at last came. He became Governor of Flushing under his uncle Leicester. He raised a regiment and played his part with distinction in the expeditionary force which the Queen reluctantly sent to support the Protestant cause in the Netherlands, in a rebellion against Spain.

The fatal wounding of a shining chivalric figure in an ill-considered skirmish outside the walled town of Zutphen, and his death three weeks later, have the dramatic quality of Greek tragedy, just as if the event had been foretold. Tragic, too, was the depth of grief displayed on his demise: as if all the posthumous tributes showered on the dead knight had been delivered by an Athenian Chorus. The melancholy note of mourning voices is in the falling cadence of his own most moving sonnet:

> Leave me, O Love, that reachest but to dust,
> And thou, my mind, aspire to higher things;
> Grow rich in that which never taketh rust;
> What ever fades, but fading pleasure brings.[8]

The hero dies and is buried, though not forgotten. Philip's voice peals to us across the centuries. It tells us that in the never-ending struggle between passion and reason (of which we are all aware ourselves), its resolution is to be looked for not in time but across the frontier to an eternal 'other world' to which his verse points the way.

---

[7] Sidney, *Arcadia*, ed. Feuillerat, Book I, Chapter 3, p. 17.
[8] Sidney, *Certain Sonnets* (1598); reproduced in many anthologies, including the *Oxford Book of English Verse* (new edition, 1939), p. 144.

The Building and Endowment of the College

T. S. WYATT

When our widowed Foundress died on 9 March 1589 her will directed her executors to employ the sum of £5,000, together with all her goods not otherwise bequeathed, in the erection of a new college in Cambridge to be called the 'Lady Frances Sidney Sussex College' and in the purchase of some competent lands for maintaining a Master, ten Fellows and twenty Scholars; but, if in their opinion these means should appear insufficient for the purpose, to use them for the benefit of Clare Hall, the title of which would be changed to 'Clare and Lady Frances Sidney Sussex College'. She constituted her good friend the Archbishop of Canterbury John Whitgift, formerly Master of Trinity, as supervisor of the will, Henry Gray, Earl of Kent, as her chief and principal executor, and five other executors including her sister's son Sir John Harington.[1] It was with the consent of the other executors that Kent and Harington undertook the task of putting her pious intentions into effect.

In his *History of the University of Cambridge* published in 1655, that loyal son of Sidney, the worthy Dr Thomas Fuller, described the College as 'so low, so lean and little at the birth thereof. Alas! what is 5000 l. to buy the scite, build and endow a Colledge therewith? As for her unbequeathed goods they answered not expectation . . .'.[2] We can agree with him when we compare this small pittance with the £26,470 at the disposal of Wadham College at Oxford, which was founded some fourteen years later,[3] and even more emphatically when, as will be seen later, we know (which Fuller did not) that the sum actually available to the executors proved to be only £4,027 8s 10d, of which £700 remained to be paid in satisfaction of two outstanding legacies. Kent and Harington must have pondered hard and long but finally decided that, with the strictest economy, it would be possible to proceed with the foundation of the college of Lady Frances. The site which they selected was that of the former Franciscan convent

---

[1] Sidney Sussex Muniments [hereafter SSM], Box 19/9. (My grateful thanks to Nicholas Rogers must be recorded here for his help, so freely given, in the deciphering of difficult passages in Montagu's handwriting and the elucidation of certain references.)
[2] Thomas Fuller, 'The History of the University of Cambridge, since the Conquest', in *The Church-History of Britain* (London, 1655), p. 154.
[3] H.B. Wells, 'Wadham College', in *The Victoria History of the County of Oxford*, III (London, 1954), p. 279.

surrendered to Henry VIII in 1538 at the dissolution of the monasteries and in 1546 conveyed by him to his new foundation of Trinity College. It was a desirable one, coveted in vain by the University and the Mayor and Corporation of Cambridge, but which according to an Act of the last Parliament of Queen Mary might be sold or let for the erecting of a new college. The land was bisected by the King's Ditch, an ancient watercourse serving originally as the town boundary and also for defence, which had been recut and modified by order of Henry III from whom it derived its name, but was now little more than an open sewer. From 1556 onwards the old home of the Grey Friars was used by Trinity as a quarry for the stone of good quality (rare in Cambridge) needed for the construction of its new Chapel, to such effect that only one significant building remained standing when the property was acquired by the executors. Another valuable asset, the conduit constructed by the Friars, which brought pure water from a spring near the foot of Madingley Rise, was also appropriated by Trinity and used to feed the fountain in Great Court, as it does to this day. The land was leased piecemeal between 1547 and 1562 to three tenants from the town who used it for their various purposes.[4]

There is no need to rehearse here the negotiations over the transfer of the site between the executors and the Master and Fellows of Trinity, which proved difficult and protracted since these latter took their stand on their Statutes which prohibited any alienation of their property – despite the beforementioned Act of Parliament of Queen Mary's time. Suffice it to say that another Act promoted by Kent and Harington in 1593 and the intervention of Archbishop Whitgift and Queen Elizabeth herself were needed to press matters forward, until, in July 1594, Elizabeth could issue her letters patent authorizing the executors to found their intended college, which they did formally on 14 February 1596, giving possession of the site to its representatives six days later. The formal conveyance of the land from Trinity to the executors had not been signed and sealed until 10 September 1595.[5] Meanwhile the executors had been considering the appointment of a prospective Master and of an architect. For the former they chose James Montagu, a nephew of Harington and a grand-nephew of the Foundress, a young Fellow-Commoner of Christ's, a man of great ability and energy who was destined for future eminence in the Church and as a favourite of James I. Before confirming their decision they took the precaution of sounding out opinion in the University, no doubt because Montagu was at the most twenty-four years old and had not yet taken the D.D. degree. In reply to an enquiry by Harington, the Vice-Chancellor and nine other heads of houses expressed their cautious approval in a letter containing the interesting statement that Harington had informed them that 'it was in the minde of the honorable foundresse to have an especiall regarde

---

[4] Robert Willis and John Willis Clark, *The Architectural History of the Uiversity of Cambridge*, 4 vols (Cambridge, 1886), II, pp. 723–731.
[5] Ibid., II, pp. 731–736.

[to] those of her owne kindred'.[6] The decision having been taken, Harington became responsible for channelling to Montagu funds needed for the construction of the College, while Montagu, to whom he gave his power of attorney, took charge of the day-to-day business from his convenient base in Christ's. The 170 pages of the latter's detailed account of money received from Harington and the corresponding expenditure constitute the principal record of our early building history.[7]

The architect selected was Ralph Simons, freemason of Berkhamsted and later of Westminster, who came to Cambridge in 1584 to assist in converting the former Dominican priory for collegiate use by Emmanuel, for which service he was highly commended. Thereafter he left his permanent mark on the architecture of Cambridge also by the building of Sidney and the second court of St. John's, while being employed, sometimes concurrently with his other commissions, by Thomas Nevile, the Master of Trinity, on the creation of that college's Great Court from about 1586 to 1605. His design for the hall of Trinity shows what Sidney might have possessed had the necessary funds been available. His portrait in Emmanuel credits him also with several other distinguished buildings which as yet have not been identified. We also once had our own portrait of him but, sadly, this had disappeared from our inventories by 1760. Some authorities give his surname as Symons, but he himself signed his receipts in Montagu's book in the phonetic spelling of the time as RAFE SIMONS, SIMANS or SIMENS with the N inverted and with three letters combined in one by a baroque fantasy to produce a kind of monogram.[8]

The older colleges had been modelled on the great country houses of their founders, containing the essential features of medieval communal life in a dining hall and adjoining parlour, a kitchen and a buttery separated from the hall by a screens passage running through the building, a house for the master and his family, and a chapel. The lodgings for the staff opened off independent staircases around courtyards surrounded by buildings on all sides, and the main entrance, which usually was not in the centre of the side on which it was situated, was sometimes surmounted by an impressive tower – a fashion which persisted well into the sixteenth century as at Christ's, St John's and Trinity.

At Emmanuel Simons had to convert the medieval priory for collegiate use, and at both St John's and Trinity had to make his plans harmonise with older work; but at Sidney he had an almost clear site on which he could develop his own ideas, constrained only by the financial considerations which made it necessary to use the surviving Franciscan building as the Chapel and to deprive the Master of a ground floor in his Lodge, which was placed over the kitchen and buttery. His design is illustrated faithfully in the engraving by Loggan (Plate 2),

---

[6] SSM, Box 1/17.
[7] SSM, MR.29.
[8] Willis and Clark, *Architectural History*, I, p. 555, II, pp 248–259, 475, 477, 490, 517, 693, 736, 775; SSM, MR.31D, 7, 14, 20, 26, 32, 38, 47. See Plate 1.

published in 1690 (in which Sir Francis Clerke's south wing of about 1628 in Chapel Court is to be ignored). If studied in detail, the aquatint of 1822 (Plate III) shows changes made by that time, notably in the uppermost storey of the south range and the entrance to the Hall; but it emphasizes better the picturesque appearance of the Hall and the Master's Lodge. In this design Simons appears to be thoroughly a man of his time, in some respects even ahead of it, conversant with medieval practice and also with the newer concepts of order, regularity and symmetry. Like the college architects of former years he took the large country house as his model, but now the house of his own day. His plan for the single court which his employers could afford is thus essentially that of the E-shaped Elizabethan manor in its landscape of gardens, but with the two outer arms extended to provide two ranges of lodgings linked at the east end by the Hall and Master's Lodge and on the west by a low screen wall along the street. The concept has been compared with that of Burton Agnes and Burton Constable in Yorkshire, both, like our Hall Court, built of red brick with white stone quoins and dressings. At the latter, a medieval building was adapted in the second half of the sixteenth century to form a court open to the east, with projecting wings joined by a central range with three towers, occupied entirely by the hall, an arrangement not so tidy as that of Simons since the entrance had to be placed near one end with the adjacent kitchen in the south wing. The design of a three-sided court familiar in French country houses was introduced to Cambridge colleges by Dr John Caius who, when he gave his new court to Gonville's college in 1565, enjoined that for reasons of hygiene the south side should never be obstructed by any building, an example followed later at Emmanuel and Sidney.

Modern, too, was the axial composition, noted by Mr M.R. Noutch, in which a walkway led straight from the entrance gate, now placed centrally in its wall, to the entrance to the Hall and thence through the screens passage and the gardens to a crossing over the King's Ditch and so to the meadow beyond.[9] The two ranges of chambers followed a traditional design of three floors, of which the uppermost was a half-storey with some small attics in the roof and dormer windows capped with characteristic stone ornaments at the angles and crowns of their gables. The form of these dormers, in which the front was carried up in continuation of the wall, had been introduced in Cambridge at Caius in 1565 and at Corpus Christi later, but haphazardly in both cases; and it was Simons who, in his work for colleges, arranged them symmetrically at equal distances along the whole building. His windows at Emmanuel and Sidney were modern in the rectangular shape of their lights, contrasting with the older arch-headed openings which were still popular in the second half of the century. On the western face of the central range were two small staircase towers in the corners of the court, that to the south giving access to the Master's Lodge and its companion to the north containing the entrance to the Fellows' Parlour, with a more prominent tower in the centre over

---

[9] Unpublished lecture.

the porch leading to the Hall. The pattern of the gables on this side of the building had its counterpart on the eastern face, where at each end there were also two large bay windows, for the Hall and the Master's Lodge respectively. The gables, the bay windows, the regularity of the rest of the fenestration, the vertical emphasis given by the three towers, the handsome lantern over the south end of the Hall which contained the College bell, the high weather vane over the gate, and the prestigiously tall chimneys were all characteristics of contemporary country houses. The only signs of classical influence were to be found in the columns of the gateway and the porch of the Hall, both of which were good examples of Renaissance architecture, but Mr Peter Salt has pointed out that the curved gable over the central tower, most clearly visible in the aquatint, would have been a very advanced feature in the 1590s and that the two small oval windows shown by Loggan over the lowest row of conventional windows, repeated on the other face of the building, came into fashion only forty years later.[10] There was no great tower over the gate, and in general the external appearance was plain and relatively simple, perhaps not surprisingly domestic rather than grand, relieved only by the shields of arms of the Foundress over the gate, of Kent on the central tower and of Harington beneath the oriel windows at the ends of the north and south ranges; but, when new, the court had its admirers. When the Bohemian Baron Waldstein visited Cambridge in the summer of 1600 he listed fifteen colleges with the following notes, translated from the original Latin by G.W. Groos in his edition of Waldstein's diary: 'In addition to these there is the new college – or palace rather – of Sidney' and again after inspecting Magdalene 'We then visited the new college called "Sidney", which is very fine, with a very splendid hall.'[11] And Giles Fletcher in his Latin poem on the colleges published in 1633 paid a tribute which can be rendered as:

> Soon you shall see these buildings rising in the midst,
> Bright with their snow-white pinnacles and rose-red walls,
> A noble lady will consecrate them to the Muses . . .[12]

There is no information in Montagu's accounts concerning the internal arrangements except in the case of the Hall, which had a plain hammerbeam roof like that at Emmanuel, like it still in place above the present ceiling, although the lower end of both has been mutilated in order to accommodate the latter. The accounts show that the lower part of the walls was covered with wainscot, with mouldings, to which may refer payments on 11 March and 30 May 1598 for the setting up of 500 deal boards and then for the painting of boards in the Hall and

---

[10] Peter Salt, 'Wyatville's Remodelling and Refurbishment of Sidney Sussex College, 1820–1837', *Proceedings of the Cambridge Antiquarian Society*, 81 (1992), p. 135 n. 111.
[11] *The Diary of Baron Waldstein: A Traveller in Elizabethan England*, trans. G.W. Gross (London, 1981), pp. 91, 105.
[12] Giles Fletcher the elder, *De literis antiquae Britanniae, regibus praesertim qui doctrina claruerunt, quique collegia Cantabrigiae fundarunt* (Cambridge, 1633), p. 16.

the Master's chamber. Painted deal would be used as a substitute for oak, which could not be afforded. At the south end there was a wooden screen with two doors giving access to the kitchen and buttery across the passage. Reference to the making of stairs suggests that there was a cellar beneath the building, as now. Round the walls were fixed seats and elsewhere a large table and forms. The building must have appeared much loftier than now, being open to the roof, more spacious since there was then no gallery, and far better lighted in true Elizabethan fashion with the large window at the north end and the tall bay on the east as at present, and also with three rows each of three windows on the east side and three rows each of two windows on the west; only three of these latter fifteen windows, of the middle tier on the east, have survived later modifications and additions, for although the present east face copies the original fenestration the remainder are dummies. The arrangements in the lodgings must be a matter for surmise but it can be guessed that life in them was not comfortable by modern standards. Despite the tall painted chimneys, fires were allowed only in the Hall, the kitchen, the Master's Lodge and the Fellows' Parlour. According to the Statutes handed down by Kent and Harington, scholars were to sleep four to a chamber, where each may have had a small study partitioned off in a corner of the room, and every tutor must have two or more of his own pupils sleeping in his own chamber. Even so the popularity of the new college was such that it must have been overcrowded during its first thirty years before the erection of Sir Francis Clerke's range in Chapel Court. Students were not the only ones affected, since according to the College accounts seven Fellows in succession had to sleep in their Parlour between about 1612 and 1620 'for want of chambers'[13] and others seem to have been accommodated in the Master's Lodge.

Montagu's book of accounts lists the regular transfer to him of funds from Harington, together with expenditure in minute detail, ranging from payment for a consignment of 40,000 bricks to 4d spent on the repair of a wheelbarrow, remuneration to the molecatcher who claimed half a dozen victims, the purchase of Spanish black and red ochre to be 'tempered with broken beere' for colouring the chimneys, of baskets for the kitchen and buttery, and of two books for the manciple. Although Montagu does not by any means always record the names of the recipients of his payments, he provides evidence which could be the basis for the compilation of a short directory of the men active in the thriving building trade in Cambridge at the time. Prominent among these was Gilbert Wigge, freemason, of Histon who was the partner of Simons in the construction of Sidney and the second court of St. John's, supplied stone for the paving of the Hall of Trinity and, after Simons had left Cambridge about 1605, built a range in Walnut Court in Queens'.[14] The contractor John Atkinson, who provided timber to Sidney, went on to be associated with Simons and Wigge at St John's and to work

---

[13] SSM, MR.41, note on flyleaf.
[14] Willis and Clark, *Architectural History*, II, pp. 19, 250–259, 491.

on new buildings at St Catharine's, Christ's, Caius, and again on the Chapel of Christ's until 1637.[15] Andrew Chapman the joiner, who made the wainscot, the screen, and some of the furniture in our Hall, subsequently moved to Trinity where he worked on the pulpit and organ case in the chapel and on the wainscot in the hall before being employed by King's on the organ case in the chapel and by Queens' on the library there.[16] Richard Thorpe the stonecarver made the shields of arms which decorated the exterior of Hall Court and executed the delicate carving on the superstructure of the gate which resembles that on the fountain in Trinity's Great Court, on which he also worked in 1601–02.[17] Others who by the recurrence of their names become familiar acquaintances of the readers of Montagu are Richard Loe, who made the benches in the Hall, Clements, another joiner and carpenter, the plasterers Matthews and Edward Meeres, John Plasterer, Richard Brasher the smith and John Simon the gardener.

As has already been noted, the conveyance of the site to the executors of Lady Frances was not signed and sealed until 10 September 1595, but some informal agreement must have been reached before then since Montagu's first entry records the receipt on 28 January of that year of £200 from Harington, of which £100 was Harington's own money, and on 23 March the first payment of £20 to Simons, presumably for the plans which he must have been making for some time previously. On 23 March also the first load of stone was purchased from Barrington, indicating that building was about to begin, on 5 April the interest of one of Trinity's tenants on the site was bought out, and one-and-a-half year's rent was paid to Trinity for his garden plot. The foundation stone was laid by Montagu on 20 May and thereafter building continued actively for three years and three months, except for the customary breaks between October and March when new work was protected against frost. Building materials were obtained from many sources since Montagu made bargains as opportunity served. Many bricks were shipped from Ely, one consignment of 10,000 came from Burrough Green, and for the most part their origins, which are not identified, were probably not far from Cambridge; deliveries varied in size from large quantities to as few as 300 items. Some of the stone was the soft white clunch brought mainly from Barrington and also from Haslingfield. Since heavy and bulky materials coming from a distance had to be transported by water, many loads of these were brought from the area around Peterborough close to the stone of superior quality from Northamptonshire and to timber probably from Rockingham Forest, and with easy access to the network of Fenland waterways. Thus large quantities of freestone, paving-stone and slates and also of timber were shipped from Gunworth Ferry on the Nene near Castor, five miles west of Peterborough, and a former monastic establishment was robbed of stone since we find that George Write of Yaxley made several deliveries from 'the abbey', which was presumably

[15] Ibid., I, pp. 186–187, 204–208, II, pp. 90, 200, 207, 258.
[16] Ibid., I. p. 519, II, pp. 50, 491, 492, 574, 575.
[17] Ibid. II. p. 628.

the Benedictine foundation at Ramsey – already plundered by Trinity – or the Cistercian house at Sawtry. Lime was mainly brought up the Cam from Reach. These cargoes were usually landed in Cambridge at the quay opposite Magdalene near the Great Bridge, commemorated by the name Quayside, where on one occasion a watchman was paid for keeping guard over them, but from time to time further down the river at Barnwell Pool, Chesterton and Ditton. Occasionally small items such as boards, slats and nails were bought locally at Stourbridge Fair. Ironically (in view of the previous history of the site), nine loads mainly of stone, but including also lime and mortar, were purchased from Trinity.

During the summer of 1598 work was in hand on the provision of some vital services. On 28 July payment was made for the digging of a well to make good the loss of the Franciscan conduit to Trinity, and by 3 August two pumps for it had been made, one of which (or its successor) is shown by Loggan placed for public use in an alcove in the wall along the street and so possibly perpetuating an arrangement made by the Friars, the thoroughfare having been known as Conduit Street in former days. The other, for the benefit of the College, was on the inner face of the wall in the small enclosure, also clearly visible in Loggan's plate, adjoining the north side of the north range. Sanitary arrangements were provided in a wooden 'house of office' somewhere in the grounds, where a supplement to the menus could be obtained from an old dovehouse which had been repaired in November 1595. In the third week of August a labourer was paid for cleaning the chambers in readiness for their occupation, and the issue of commons to Fellows and Scholars on 25 August (noted in the College accounts) indicates that our communal life began on that day, two senior members having even moved in before building had quite finished. We cannot be certain of the precise dates of the events chronicled by Montagu, because we do not know by how much his payments lagged behind the execution of the operations, but it seems that, although essential services had been installed in time for the occupation of the court, expenditure continued until 1602 on minor works such as the completion of the lantern over the Hall and the superstructure of the gate, the building of a wall and pavement round the pump, the finishing of the coats of arms and the repair of wainscot in the Hall.

The land occupied by Trinity's remaining tenants having been acquired on 10 August 1597, the development of the grounds began in the spring of 1599, to continue for the next three years. John Simon the gardener was employed on levelling the ground and planting while soil, sand and 'moulds' (compost) were brought in for the plots and walls were built. The area west of the King's Ditch was divided between the Master's garden on the south and that of the Fellows on the north, each containing an orchard. As depicted by Loggan, each also had a pleasure garden and the Fellows had a large lawn which was used as a bowling green. Both are now much smaller than then, the Fellows having lost the western portion of theirs to Cloister Court a century ago, and the Master the whole of the southern side of his more recently to Garden Court and Blundell Court. The sluggish and odorous King's Ditch required constant scouring until 1607, when

Plate III Aquatint of Hall Court, by unknown artist, published by W. Mason, Cambridge, 1822

Montagu diverted a clear running stream into it at his own expense. In the same year Mr Peck, probably the father of William, a pensioner admitted in June 1606, improved the appearance of this part of the grounds by purchasing from London a number of sycamores to be planted alongside the Ditch. These trees, which were brought to Cambridge by Hobson the famous carrier, proved to be remarkably long-lived, being illustrated in their prime by Loggan and the last of them surviving until 25 January 1935 when it was brought down by a gale.[18] Ancillary buildings needed by the establishment were put up elsewhere in the grounds in succeeding years, probably in the area behind the Chapel and towards Walls Lane (the present Sussex Street): there is mention in the records of a rush house, a College order of 7 December 1619 decreed that the Steward should have an allowance of twelve pence weekly 'for his paines about the Bakehouse', apparently then new, and another of 15 January 1620 recorded that by agreement between the Master and Fellows 'there should be allowed out of the profitts of the Bakehouse at Christenmas 13s 4d for wyne att Christenmas.' The reason for this was: 'because before ye coll. had a bakehouse, the baker, yt was, gave the Mr & ffellowes wine, as ye brewer gave the brawne'.[19]

It had been decided from the outset that the surviving Franciscan building should become the Chapel, since it is so named in an entry by Montagu in early November 1595 and the new court was erected adjoining it. Occupying almost the same site as the northern part of the present Chapel and the extension to the south side of the Master's Lodge which was added much later, it was not orientated and lay approximately north and south like that at Emmanuel, which also had been adapted from a medieval building (an arrangement which was criticized by High Churchmen but defended by Puritans). Having been possibly the hall of the lodging of the Warden of the Friary, it had become a malting-house used by one of Trinity's tenants, a plain, somewhat dilapidated structure open to the roof, with a floor of plaster or common mortar mixed with clay, and a cellar beneath. It was cleared of rubble and essential repairs were carried out in the autumn of 1595, and although it was not consecrated and so remained throughout its life (another subject of controversy) services are said to have been held in this makeshift accommodation from the time when the first students were admitted in August 1598. Thereafter there is no further mention of it until 22 March 1601, when an entry in a manuscript chronology of significant events reads 'Chapel begun' and Simons was paid £10, probably for his plans.[20] This long delay in the resumption of work may be attributed to the need to accumulate sufficient funds. The walls were now built up and buttressed and the interior was divided into two floors, the lower containing the Chapel and ante-Chapel and the upper a 'chapel chamber' and the College Library, and the walls and ceiling were plastered by our acquaintances Matthews and Meeres. The general impression of the Chapel must

---

[18] *Sidney Sussex College Annual*, 1935, p. 14
[19] SSM, MR.1 pp. 1, 13.
[20] SSM, Box 1.

have been one of simplicity, but not of completely unrelieved austerity, since the royal arms were displayed in the great window at the south end and outpayments show that the ceiling was decorated in the Elizabethan fashion with plaster pendants, as was that of the drawing room of the Master's Lodge in Trinity, which was also the work of Simons. The floor remained unpaved until 1612 when Harington gave the necessary stone and Montagu, now Bishop of Bath and Wells, provided wainscot for the south end surmounted by the arms of his see impaling his own.[21] A picture of the interior can be built up from an inventory of the College goods made in 1639 and other contemporary sources. There was no altar decorated with crucifix and candlesticks, nor altar steps, but a communion table round which the congregation sat stood elsewhere in the room. No other furniture is mentioned save a pulpit and three desks, one for the Bible and two 'for the use of them that read common places'.[22] However the Earl of Kent had presented his splendid parcel-gilt communion service made in 1611 and suitable coverings for the communion table had been acquired by 1639. Simons' contract terminated in October 1601, after which Montagu became responsible for finishing the project. Payment to glaziers on 24 June 1602 indicates that the work on the Chapel was nearing completion and Montagu's last entry on 3 August signals the end of the College's first building programme, which from first to last had occupied seven years and four months. The deed of conveyance of the property contained a covenant according to which, if the College to be erected by the will of the Countess be not built within the seven years next ensuing, then the indentures and everything therein contained were to be 'vtterlie voyde and of none effect'. The wording might have been open to more than one interpretation by eager lawyers but, by beginning his work well before the conveyance was signed, Montagu had left no room for argument.

Harington's regular transfers of funds to Montagu noted by the latter amounted to £2,267 13s 4d, including £100 of his own money, of which approximately (because some entries are ambiguous) £771 15s was paid to Simons, who was both builder and architect. Further details of the financial situation are given in a document dated 10 December 1601 and entitled 'State of the Foundress' Will', which records that her estate was valued at £12,813 2s 2d and that, after payment of funeral charges and debts and the satisfaction of almost all legacies, the residue was £4,027 8s 10d, as has been mentioned previously. Expenditure to date was £3,312 17s 4d, including £2,616 4s on building, £230 on other expenses incidental to the foundation, £400 on the purchase for the endowment of a rent-charge out of the manor of Bagington in Warwickshire, and £66 13s 4d on rent to Trinity. There remained £713 14s 4d towards the finishing of the Chapel, the payment of outstanding debts and extraordinary items, £200 for the foundation of a perpetual lectureship in

---

[21] SSM, Box 1/17/8, 1/18a, 1/18b, 1/18c.
[22] SSM, MR.31D, ff. 1–2.

Westminster Abbey and £500 for buying a cupboard of plate for Harington, both of these last being bequests from Lady Frances, a total of £1,140.[23] We do not know whether Westminster Abbey received its bequest or Harington claimed his silver, but taking into account his great generosity towards the College we may surmise that he renounced it. If he did so, income and expenditure were nicely balanced, a nearly-run thing, and all concerned could be congratulated on finishing their enterprise within their budget, a result not always attained in building projects.

The rent charge on Bagington was, however, the only contribution yet made to endowment, and though in 1608 Harington gave to the College his manor of Saleby in Lincolnshire, it was necessary in 1612 to reduce the number of Foundation Fellows from the ten envisaged by Lady Frances to seven until matters should improve.[24] Numerous other benefactions were received in the years following the foundation, but nearly all of these were directed to specific purposes such as the creation of additional Fellowships and Scholarships, or in one case a new building, and were not available for the general funds of the College, with the consequence that the upkeep and alteration of the fabric had to be financed in the seventeenth century by the sale of silver donated by Fellow-Commoners, and in the eighteenth by leaving Fellowships vacant for a time. In 1602 this deficiency in endowment was a concern for the future, which it was hoped would make better provision, as eventually it did (although very much later). Those who were concerned at the time did all that was possible with the limited funds available to them and, as we celebrate our quatercentenary, we should acknowledge our debt not only to the Foundress, but also to Kent and Harington for their decision to strive to achieve her prime objective instead of taking the easier course of transferring her bequest to Clare Hall and for their general oversight of their scheme, to Montagu for his daily control of the building operation, and to him and again to Harington for their benefactions, which in the case of the latter were acknowledged by the College as amounting to at least as great a sum as that bequeathed by Lady Frances. To Simons we owe the creation of a court which was thoroughly Elizabethan in character, and the core of which stands to this day beneath all the changes both external and internal made by subsequent generations.

---

[23] SSM, Box 19/11.
[24] SSM, Box 1/14/1.

'Sovereignty and Counsel':
The Patron, the Poet, and Penshurst

C. E. PRESTON

In his life of Philip Sidney, Fulke Greville describes his hero as 'the true friend without hire and common rendezvous of worth in his time',[1] a phrase which expresses the twin virtues – selflessness and bounty – of the ideal patron. Philip Sidney was by no means, however, the only champion of the arts and learning in his family; many Sidney relations, who joined their glamour, wit, taste, and talent to advantageous marriages, were celebrated patrons. The Foundress of Sidney Sussex College was merely one of many Sidney and Dudley cousins (mostly women) who wielded great political and cultural power in the form of influence and remuneration. An account of their cultural patronage would include associations with virtually every English humanist and poet, and with many of the dramatists of the period, as well as with numerous Continental *literati*. Some member of Sidney's immediate family, circle of cousins, or near descendants was connected in one way or another with the literary production of Edmund Spenser, William Shakespeare, William Camden, Fulke Greville, Abraham Fraunce, Samuel Daniel, Thomas Nashe, Gabriel Harvey, John Donne, Francis Meres, Ben Jonson, Edward Dyer, John Harington, John Hoskins, Giordano Bruno, Robert Greene, George Chapman, George Buchanan, Walter Raleigh, Geoffrey Whitney, George Herbert, John Florio, Michael Drayton, Thomas Kyd, John Davies, Henri Estienne, Théophile de Banos, and Hubert Languet. This is a remarkable list, and it is not complete. What follows is a brief examination of the nature of literary patronage in this period; of the patronage practised by several members of this extended family; and of the condition of dependence on the Sidney circle, and the effect of that dependence, on the imagination of one of their most famous clients, Ben Jonson.

---

[1] *A Dedication to Sir Philip Sidney* in *The Prose Works of Fulke Greville, Lord Brooke*, ed. John Gouws (Oxford, 1986), p. 21.

A Definition of Patronage

Recent scholarship has clarified the concept of patronage.[2] First, it has distinguished the reality of artistic benefactions (which were generally irregular and insufficient to support the writer) from the myth of patronage. This myth (to be described presently) was initially promulgated by the benefit-seeking poets of this period, but taken at face value by later scholars, who proposed a monolithic notion of 'English culture' as promoted by the leading patrons of the day such as Leicester, Queen Elizabeth, and families like the Sidneys.[3] Second, modern research reminds us that the term 'patronage' cannot do justice to the variety of relationships which are comprehended under it.[4] In the Elizabethan period, patronage was often not financial, but rather inspirational, influential, or hospitable. Patrons were persons of important social position whose attention, once attracted by a writer, *may* have been expressed by remuneration of one kind or another, but might more frequently have been characterised by help or encouragement in other forms. These other forms – housing or entertaining men of letters (perhaps in exchange for tutorial services), advancing them in Court circles, in the Church, or in government positions, merely corresponding with them, or acting, as Sidney appears to have done, as ringleader of a group of literary friends of his social circle – are difficult to quantify and delimit, but they remain as important, if not more so, than the remunerative arrangement usually meant by 'patronage'. Even more difficult to assess, but of primary importance to any literary discussion, is the role of inspiration or generalised influence of patrons on writers. The relationship of the second Earl of Pembroke, Henry Herbert (Mary Sidney's husband), to the Earl of Pembroke's Men (the dramatic company to which Shakespeare may have belonged in the early 1590s)[5] was a relatively straightforward political matter; the role of his son, William, the third Earl (Sidney's nephew) as 'only begetter' of the Sonnets (if, indeed, he is one day proven to have been 'Mr W.H.') can be a matter of speculation only, but may well have been of this other, more purely inspirational, kind.

The assessment of literary patronage is especially difficult in the case of men

---

[2] See, for example, Cedric C. Brown (ed.), *Patronage, Politics, and Literary Traditions in England, 1558–1658* (Detroit, 1991); Guy Fitch Lytle and Stephen Orgel (eds), *Patronage in the Renaissance* (Princeton, 1981); Robert C. Evans, *Ben Jonson and the Poetics of Patronage* (Lewisburg, Ohio, 1989); Michael G. Brennan, *Literary Patronage in the Renaissance: the Pembroke Family* (London, 1988); David Norbrook, *Poetry and Politics in the English Renaissance* (London, 1984); Annabel Patterson, *Censorship and Interpretation: The Conditions of Writing and Reading in Early Modern England* (Madison, 1984).

[3] See M.D. Jardine, 'New Historicism for Old: New Conservatism for Old?: The Politics of Patronage in the Renaissance', in Brown, pp. 291–309; and John Buxton, *Sir Philip Sidney and the English Renaissance*, third edition (London, 1987).

[4] Mary Ellen Lamb, 'The Countess of Pembroke's Patronage', *English Literary Renaissance*, 12 (1982), 162–179.

[5] Brennan, pp. 94–95; and Buxton, p. 242.

such as John Donne: he did not attempt or care to make a living by writing; in fact, he would have scorned such a proceeding. He wished to advance in political circles, and seems partly to have courted attention from such as the Countess of Bedford through his writing because he wished to gain preferment. Can such a relationship, which may have *inspired* some of his finest writing, be said to be literary patronage?[6] Arthur Marotti has wisely observed that literary, social, and political patronage are quite indistinguishable from one another in this period, that all Renaissance literature is the literature of patronage.[7]

Because most writers had no official or regular connection to a patron, they attached dedications to their work in a prospective fashion.[8] An able and interested aristocrat might try to remunerate such compliments at a set and modest rate;[9] other dedicatees (maybe most) did nothing. Dedications and addresses might also have solicited preferment or favours other than cash. It is also possible that dedications, verse epistles, and the like, expressed genuine allegiances, sympathy, and admiration, instead of financial and political need. There are few records of any of these transactions.[10] All we can confidently say about the real nature of literary patronage is that patrons and poets generally had little claim, control, or influence on each other, and that as a source of income patronage in any form was unreliable and usually paltry.

Our view of patronage is occluded also by the existence of professional writers. The very notion of the *professional* literary writer (the playwright, translator, pamphleteer, masque-writer, or paid rhymer in royal or civic employ – anyone, in essence, who expected his principal income from commissioned or printed writing) was quite new in the late sixteenth century.[11] With the steep rise in literacy, and the availability of university (or excellent grammar-school) education for the ambitious sons of the middle classes and skilled labourers, London enjoyed a quarrelsome, talented population of writers, all angling for custom, or patronage; all peculiarly placed socially in being well educated and possibly in communication with the Court and government, yet not usually gentry themselves; wishing to be paid for their labours, yet disdaining to lump themselves with other trades; forming no 'Worshipful Company' for themselves, yet proposing their work as commodity. Because writers of the period probably could not expect to

---

[6] Arthur F. Marotti, 'John Donne and the Rewards of Patronage', in Lytle and Orgel, p. 231.

[7] Marotti, p. 207.

[8] Spenser attached seventeen dedicatory sonnets to *The Faerie Queene* (1590), including one to the Countess of Pembroke in honour of her brother; Geoffrey Whitney's *A Choice of Emblems* (1586) had ninety dedications.

[9] About two or three pounds per dedication (Brennan, p. 13).

[10] The exception is the case of the dramatic companies, which could only operate legally if under the protection of a lord; and these arrangements were matters of convenience for both parties, not acts of patronage.

[11] Edwin H. Miller, *The Professional Writer in Elizabethan England: A Study of Nondramatic Literature* (Cambridge, Mass., 1959).

make a living by patronage connexions alone, virtually every non-aristocratic writer of the period had to pursue his livelihood in the marketplace and with the coterie; and there were too many 'professional' writers chasing too few benefits.

Dedications to members of the Sidney circle probably reflect their cultured reputation as much as their wealth and influence. Philip Sidney's uncle Robert, Earl of Leicester, was, along with William Cecil and the Queen, one of the foremost dedicatees of printed books in the early part of Elizabeth's reign;[12] Lucy Harington, Countess of Bedford (a first cousin once removed), had more dramatic dedications than any other woman of the period;[13] most notably, Sidney's sister Mary Herbert, Countess of Pembroke, was patron, poet, and translator, and recipient of some of the most distinguished dedications of the time, including her brother's *Arcadia*.[14] But Mary Ellen Lamb, in her admonitory article on the Countess of Pembroke's patronage, stresses that dedications (in past investigations, used as a reckoning of patronage activities) are not reliable indicators of anything; they may be suggestive or hortatory, or bold advertisements to persons of power or wealth, or outright solicitations of support;[15] but they do not even prove connexion between writer and patron, much less transaction.

In assigning influence, the Sidney family presents unique difficulties: with the immense prestige of Philip, both before, but especially after, his death, and the rise of his cult, many writers who never knew him make a ritual genuflection to his memory, or to the assumed poetic sympathies of his relations. The amazing potency of Sidney as a mythic hero-figure for late-Elizabethan and Jacobean England can merely be noted within the scope of this essay.[16] We must bear it in mind, however, since that myth was itself a kind of inspirational patron to the literary output of the early seventeenth century, and attracted the hopes of writers to the surviving members of the family.

Philip's aunts and uncles on both his parents' sides had already established themselves as important patrons: on the Sidney side his aunt Frances and her husband, the Earl of Sussex, had between them ten dedications, including that of a translation of Apuleius and a number of religious and improving works;[17] and in her widowhood, Frances' principal act of intellectual patronage was the

---

[12] Jan van Dorsten, 'Literary Patronage in Elizabethan England: The Early Phase', in Lytle and Orgel, p. 194 (hereafter cited as van Dorsten 1981).

[13] David Bergeron, 'Women as Patrons of English Drama', in Lytle and Orgel, p. 283.

[14] For more on the Countess of Pembroke's patronage, see Lamb; and Margaret Hannay, ' "Doo What Men May Sing": Mary Sidney and the Tradition of Admonitory Dedication', in *Silent But For the Word: Tudor Women as Patrons, Translators, and Writers of Religious Works* (Kent, Ohio, 1985), pp. 149–165.

[15] Lamb, p. 162.

[16] See, for example, Jan van Dorsten, *Poets, Patrons, and Professors: Sir Philip Sidney, Daniel Rogers, and the Leiden Humanists* (Leiden and Oxford, 1962), pp. 152–166.

[17] See Franklin B. Williams, Jr., *Index of Dedications and Commendatory Verses in English Books before 1641* (London, 1962).

provision of funds for the Cambridge college which bears her family names. On Sidney's mother's side, among the Dudleys, were found some of the most culturally powerful men and women in the realm. His own mother, Mary, gave money to Geffrey Fenton, the translator of Bandello, who dedicated this work to her.[18] Her brother, the Earl of Leicester, was associated with Gabriel Harvey and Edmund Spenser; with Arthur Golding, the translator of Ovid; the chroniclers John Stow and Ralph Holinshed; George Gascoigne, the poet; Geoffrey Whitney, the first English emblematist; John Florio, translator of Montaigne; and the playwright, Robert Greene.[19] In addition, Leicester assembled the most spectacular art collection in England before the time of Charles I. Her sister-in-law, Anne, Countess of Warwick, and Anne's husband Ambrose Dudley, were dedicatees of many works, Anne of some twenty in her own right.[20]

In his brief lifetime Sidney became the rendezvous of poets in England. As heir to the Earls of Leicester and Warwick, and potentially also of Sussex and Huntingdon, and as son of the distinguished governor of Wales and of Ireland, Sidney would naturally interest favour-seekers, even though he himself had little money and less power in fact; he and his sister entertained a group which included Dyer, Spenser, Greville, and Harvey at Wilton, where they may have discussed their various metrical experiments and received the unmatchable encouragement of the wealthy Countess and her poet-brother. Although the most celebrated products of this remarkable literary fraternity were *Arcadia* and *The Faerie Queene*, the 'areopagus', or college of poets at Wilton to which Spenser playfully referred, never existed formally or even regularly.[21] Little English aristocratic patronage before the 1580s supported purely literary endeavours. William Cecil's house, for instance, was full of men of letters, and their dedications and addresses reflect this; but their works were religious, historical, or philosophical.[22] Jan van Dorsten has rightly described Sidney as 'the single patron of poets' in his time.[23] Only Leicester promoted poets before his nephew did.[24]

Sidney inspired fellow-poets of his own generation; and he endowed his family with an unparalleled literary reputation for succeeding generations. His daughter

---

[18] Katherine Duncan-Jones, *Sir Philip Sidney, Courtier Poet* (London, 1991), p. 6.
[19] For the extent of Leicester's vast patronage, see Eleanor Rosenberg, *Leicester, Patron of Letters* (New York, 1955); and Henry Woudhuysen, 'Leicester's Literary Patronage', unpublished D.Phil. thesis, Oxford University, 1982.
[20] Duncan-Jones, p. 12.
[21] Spenser's remark appears in 'Letters from Spenser (Immerito) to Gabriel Harvey' in *The Works of Gabriel Harvey, D.C.L.*, 3 vols (privately printed, 1884; facsimile reprint, New York, 1966) I, 7. Buxton remarks that 'In England, academies, which were innumerable in Italy and France, never existed. The Areopagus was a joke.' (p. 253)
[22] van Dorsten 1981, pp. 197–198.
[23] van Dorsten 1981, p. 200. We must assume his patronage to have been more substantially hospitable and inspirational than financial, although he did remunerate dedications when he could, and signally assisted Spenser, who dedicated his *Shepherds' Calendar* to him.
[24] van Dorsten 1981, p. 200; Rosenberg, Chapter 9 (pp. 323–353).

Elizabeth and his younger cousin Lucy Harington, the Countesses of Rutland and Bedford, and their cousin John Harington, the translator of Ariosto, were to make marks for themselves as patrons and as writers. His nephew William Herbert, the son of his sister Mary, became one of the most important patrons of James' Court and supported Shakespeare.[25] The other nephew of this connexion, Philip (the fourth Earl of Pembroke), was a patron in his own right, and his remarkable second wife Anne Clifford was a patroness to rival the reputation of her mother-in-law, Mary Herbert. Sidney's niece, Lady Mary Wroth, the daughter of his brother (also a poet), produced *The Countess of Montgomery's Urania* (the most important of the many imitations of the *Arcadia*), and was one of the earliest women fiction-writers of whom we have record.[26] Sidney and other poetically gifted members of his family were writers by inclination rather than necessity; their example, however, as poet-patrons, encouraged others to look to them for sympathy and support of all kinds.

But Sidney, like Donne, considered poetry ('fiction') to be an 'unelected vocation'. In the *Defence of Poetry* he claims with Castiglionian insouciance not to know 'by what mischance, in these my not old years and idlest times' he has 'slipped into the title of a poet',[27] a 'mischance' which befell him during periods of enforced political inactivity. The period 1577–79, during which he retired from Court, mainly to the Pembroke estate at Wilton, and wrote the first version of his *Arcadia*, was the time during which his reputation as a patron of poetry gathered force. It was also the time of his greatest frustration, as he waited to be given some important task to perform for Queen and country. Sidney's delight in and respect for poetry never obscured his primary ambition, which was to help establish England as the radical Protestant power leading the fight in Europe against Rome and Spain.

Not quite by accident, therefore, but through unlooked-for political inactivity, Sidney was responsible in large part, and in the main by his own example, for the magnificence of the Elizabethan literary renaissance, whose central and distinctive voice is captured in his *Defence of Poetry*, probably its most important document. The vigorous and graceful case it makes for the English vernacular as a language of art is a 'defence' made playfully, almost arrogantly; it is an argument the writer knows is already won. It is the manifesto of a national literary culture joyfully arriving at the pinnacle of European accomplishment, and Sidney's own incomplete revision of the *Arcadia* as an epic romance gloriously confirms the justice

---

[25] See Samuel Schoenbaum, *William Shakespeare: A Documentary Life* (New York and London, 1975), p. 125; Brennan, pp. 141–142, 94–95; E.K. Chambers, *William Shakespeare: A Study of Facts and Problems*, 2 vols (Oxford, 1930), I, 45–54; E.A. Honigmann, *Shakespeare: The 'Lost' Years* (Manchester, 1985), pp. 60–64; Dennis Kay, *Shakespeare: His Life, Work, and Era* (New York, 1992), p. 153.

[26] See Barbara Kiefer Lewalski on Wroth's work and patronage in *Writing Women in Jacobean England* (Cambridge, Mass., 1992), pp. 243–307.

[27] *A Defence of Poetry*, in *The Miscellaneous Prose of Sir Philip Sidney*, edited by Katherine Duncan-Jones and Jan van Dorsten (Oxford, 1973), p. 77.

of that arrogance.[28] The *Defence*'s central, audacious claim was the establishment of the poet at the confluence of divine wisdom and earthly power.

The Mendicant Poet: Ben Jonson

That there had been a remote age which honoured poetry and the rhetorical arts was one of the enduring humanist patronage myths.[29] Ben Jonson, writing about the Sidneys in poems and dramatic dedications, best expressed the ideal of the humanist patron-client relationship.[30] 'Tofore, great men were glad of poets', he remarks wistfully to the Earl of Salisbury (*Epigrams*, 43); in that wiser age, the Horatian poet provided 'free and wholesome sharpness, which pleaseth Caesar more than servile fawns'.[31]

This nostalgia for an invented past is acute in Jonson, who straddled uncomfortably the fence which separated the gentlemen from the players. The step-son of a bricklayer but classically educated under Camden at Westminster, he was obsessed with his standing among poets and patrons. Not, by his reckoning, one of the hacks of the theatre like Shakespeare, Marlowe, Kyd, and Beaumont and Fletcher, he constantly tried to separate himself from that common herd; and he was able to do this partly through the patronage of King James, who pensioned him in 1616 in recognition of his poetic services to the Court. Although not officially recognised as such, his most successful strategies were to style himself a 'poet-laureate',[32] a classically-inspired conceit specifically distinct from patronage or professional poets; and to become the first 'textual' poet in the language: that

---

[28] The detailed history of Sidney's place in English letters cannot be given here; let it be summarised in the following facts: *Arcadia* was a bestseller for a century after its publication in 1590; it inspired a host of continuations and imitations; and it was the first work of English fiction to be translated into other languages. See Buxton; Kenneth Myrick, *Sir Philip Sidney as a Literary Craftsman* (Cambridge, Mass., 1935); Dorothy Connell, *Sir Philip Sidney: The Maker's Mind* (Oxford, 1977); John Danby, *Poets on Fortune's Hill* (London, 1952); Forrest G. Robinson, *The Shape of Things Known: Sidney's Apology in its Philosophical Tradition* (Cambridge, Mass., 1972); Andrew D. Weiner, *Sir Philip Sidney and the Poetics of Protestantism: A Study of Contexts* (Minneapolis, 1978).

[29] Daniel Javitch, *Poetry and Courtliness in Renaissance England* (Princeton, 1978), pp. 160–61; Lauro Martines, *Society and History in English Renaissance Verse* (Oxford, 1985), pp. 53–72; Graham Parry, *The Golden Age Restor'd: The Culture of the Stuart Court, 1603–42* (New York, 1981), pp. 165–183.

[30] *Cynthia's Revels* (1601) was offered to Lucy, Countess of Bedford; *Catiline* (1611) to William Herbert; and *The Alchemist* (1612) to Mary Wroth.

[31] *Poetaster*, V.i.94–95 in *The Complete Works of Ben Jonson*, IV, edited by C.H. Herford and P. Simpson (Oxford, 1932), p. 292.

[32] Richard Helgerson, *Self-Crowned Laureates: Spenser, Jonson, Milton, and the Literary System* (Berkeley, 1983), pp. 21–54, and 104–122; Katharine Eisaman Maus, *Ben Jonson and the Roman Frame of Mind* (Princeton, 1984), pp. 134–138; Javitch, pp. 160–161; Robert Wiltenberg, ' "What need hast thou of me? or of my *Muse*?": Jonson, Cecil, Politician and Poet' in *'The Muses Common-Weale': Poetry and Politics in the Seventeenth Century*, edited by

is, unlike the 'toyful' productions of the courtly writers (in Sidney's phrase), or the professional drama, he envisaged his complete *oeuvre* as a discrete and authorially determined work in print. He saw the publication of his works in Folio (1616) through the press in a manner unprecedented at the time, carefully excising what he considered unworthy pieces, rewriting where necessary, and adorning it in many places with an obsessively pedantic critical apparatus; shaping, in short, his literary remains during his life with an eye to posterity.

No age was more smitten with the idea of poetic immortality than the late Renaissance, but in contrast to Jonson, writers like Shakespeare (one of the 'hacks') and Donne (a gentleman) were far more careless of their finished product. Shakespeare's profit came not from publication, but from performance; the quartos were merely a pragmatic forstalling of pirate productions by rival companies, and consequently often sloppily produced. Donne, on the other hand, like Sidney, was socially inclined to *sprezzatura*, an assumed posture of indifference to his creative output. Gentlemen and women simply did not traffic with print; and the Italian fashion for casual and nonchalant brilliance forbade them to seem too engrossed in their poetry.[33] Both Donne and Sidney were published only posthumously. Jonson, however, staked a middle ground by claiming both the social status of the humanist whose learning and wisdom make him indispensable to the powerful, *and* the legitimacy of print publication which acknowledges the gravity and importance of his labour and his product. For him, poetry conferred status, and print maintained it.[34]

To sustain this aggrandised definition of poethood, Jonson and the humanists required a model patron whose own power would give an ethical imprimatur to the poet, and whose financial backing would free him from the enforcements of the market. In the patron of classical antiquity, they found their model. The antique patron supposedly supported the poet, who was his counsellor, historian, critic, eulogist, and moral arbiter. 'Learning needs rest: sovereignty gives it', says Jonson. 'Sovereignty needs counsel: learning affords it'.[35] It is a role almost indistinguishable from that of the civic humanist: the poet is both useful and ornamental, an embodiment of the Horatian *utile et dulce*, a proof of the taste, discrimination, and power of the patron. In return for financial and other forms of support of Jonson and his Muse, the patron is advised, celebrated, and immortalised, as Jonson claims in *The Forest*:

Claude J. Summers and Ted-Larry Pebworth (Columbia, Mo., 1988), pp. 34–47; George Parfitt, *Ben Jonson, Public Poet and Private Man* (London, 1976), pp. 28–30.

[33] See Sidney's epistle dedicatory to his sister in *Arcadia*, in which he professes to disown the work altogether, and describes its desultory generation as a kind of scribbling game played to amuse her friends.

[34] Don E. Wayne, *Penshurst: The Semiotics of Place and the Poetics of History* (Madison, 1984), p. 156.

[35] *Timber, or Discoveries*, in *The Complete Works of Ben Jonson*, VIII, edited by C.H. Herford and P. and E. Simpson (Oxford, 1947), p. 565.

> It is the Muse, alone, can raise to heaven ...
> ... when they were born, they died,
> That had no Muse to make their fame abide.   (*The Forest*, 12)

It is to Sidney's daughter, the Countess of Rutland, that these lines are addressed. An even more complicated and self-reflexive thought to the Countess of Bedford figures Jonson's ideal patron:

> If works (not th'authors) their own grace should look,*
> Whose poems would not wish to be your book?
> But these, desired by you, the maker's ends
> Crown with their own. Rare poems ask rare friends.
>   (*Epigrams*, 94)

'Rare poems ask rare friends': this is an elegant summary of the reciprocal nature of the patron-client relationship imagined by Jonson, and which he takes such care to propose to current and prospective benefactors, whose rareness is best discovered and advertised by rare poems. To support this rose-coloured rendition of literary patronage he must establish the difference between true praise and self-interested obsequiousness. His poems are as 'free from servile flattery (common poets' shame) as thou stand'st clear of the necessity', he tells Salisbury (*Epigrams*, 43). Salisbury's greatness requires no aid from Jonson's pen; therefore, Jonson's poem can *only* be disinterested. The simplicity of this pronouncement is confused, however, by the sounding final word 'necessity', which discomfits us with Jonson's own need; the poem itself is a servile act of self-abnegation. Indeed, many of Jonson's patronage poems end with, or metrically highlight, the central vocabulary of payment, payment which the poet purports to give *to* the patron, but which he must subtly demand *from* him: 'I know no abler way to thank my benefits: which is, to *pay*', he concludes in Epigram 127; 'you reckon nothing, me owe all' (*Underwood*, 15); or, most bluntly and desperately from his sickbed, he urges Charles I

> ... to make all the Muses debtors
> To his bounty; by extension of a free poetic pension,
> A large hundred marks annuity,
> To be given me in gratuity ...   (*Underwood*, 78)

The stickiness of having to ask for benefits while insisting that poets are objects outside the drossy commercial network of hack writing, that they are representatives instead of some notional republic of letters whose only purpose is to add to the gaiety of nations, requires canny literary stratagems which carry subliminal messages of request below a panegyric, epideictic surface. Fortunately, female patrons lend themselves to Muse-hood, and this proves a convenient trope for Jonson in addressing Lucy Harington:

---

* 'be responsible for'

> I thought to form unto my zealous Muse,
> What kind of creature I could most desire,
> To honour, serve, and love; as poets use.*
>
> (*Epigrams*, 76, lines 1–3)

His created patroness will be high-born, beautiful, virtuous, and wise, and equipped with 'a learned, and a manly soul', a combination of traits which makes her infinitely praisable, and also ensures that she will justly appreciate Jonson's style of poetry (which is manly, and not, as he says in *The Forest*, 1, 'of love'). In the end, his Muse bids him ' "Bedford" write, and that was she'. This poem is particularly interesting because it shows us Jonson at his most cunning. The 'unto' of the first line makes it radically unclear whether Jonson is proposing to feign an idealised figure *for* the benefit of his Muse (he often speaks of his Muse as a kind of spouse or partner);[36] or whether the created figure is to *be* his Muse. It is a telling ambiguity. Either Bedford is an object of desire, as he says in line 3, though hastily qualified in the next line by the terms of clientage; or she is the bestower of poetic inspiration, a thought which chimes with the ideals of patronage, and exonerates him from the suspicion of loving her only for her money. By blurring the distinction, Jonson can compliment the patroness as his Muse; and he can introduce the Petrarchan paradigm of the unattainable woman who lives more in the poet's fancy than in his reality, the poetic broadcasting of whose desirability would flatter her vanity. Either effect, or both, may prompt her to reward him.

Jonson's Rutland Epistle

> Madam,
> Whil'st that for which all virtue now is sold
> And almost every vice, almighty gold;
> That which, to boot with hell, is thought worth heaven,
> And for it life, conscience, yea souls, are given;
> 5   Toils by grave custom up and down the court
> To every squire or groom that will report
> Well or ill only, all the following year,
> Just to the weight their this day's presents bear;
> While it makes ushers serviceable men,
> 10 And someone apteth to be trusted then,
> Though never after; whiles it gains the voice
> Of some grand peer, whose air doth make rejoice
> The fool that gave it, who will want and weep
> When his proud patron's favours are asleep;

---

[36] For instance, 'How full of want, how swallowed up, how dead/ I, and this Muse had been, if thou hadst not/ Lent timely succours.' (Epigram 127, 'To Esme, Lord 'Aubigny'). See also 'Epistle to My Lady Covell' (*Underwood*, 56).

* 'as poets traditionally do'

15 While thus it buys great grace and hunts poor fame,
    Runs between man and man, 'tween dame and dame;
    Solders cracked friendship, makes love last a day
    Or perhaps less: whilst gold bears all this sway,
    I, that have none to send you, send you verse.

The signal Jonsonian example of all these patronal concerns and strategies is his 'Epistle to Elizabeth, Countess of Rutland', part of his collection *The Forest*, itself a document of Jonson's theory of poethood. The poem begins with a direct address to the Countess ('Madam'). Unlike any other poem of direct address by Jonson, 'Madam' is here prosodically distinguished and set apart, reminding us that this is not a deferential or disengaged epigram on, but a verse letter to, the Countess. There is a certain temerity here: Jonson presumes to write to her as an equal and makes no apology for it. The notion of the poet as the peer of aristocrats (and indeed, of monarchs) by virtue of his vatic power is essential to Jonson's definition of poethood. It is a view inherited directly from Martial, Cicero, Seneca, Quintilian, and above all, Horace; and from Sidney, the Countess' father, whose recuperation of poetry and of poets was founded on a doctrine of their necessity in the moral life of mankind, a function of their divine ability to present useful wisdom in delightful form. As Jonson says in *Timber*:

> I could never think the study of wisdom confined only to the philosopher; or of piety to the divine; or of state to the politic. But that he which can feign a commonwealth (which is the poet) can govern it with counsels, strengthen it with laws, correct it with judgements, inform it with religion and morals, is all these.[37]

This distinctly Sidneian statement locates the poet at the regal centre of earthly power.

The Rutland epistle properly opens with an extraordinary grammatical construction, a dependent clause ('Whil'st', followed by a list of conditions) which does not resolve itself for nineteen lines. The burden of these nineteen lines, that gold bears sway over all virtues, is situated (in the word 'whil'st') specifically in the present, fallen world. The suspense generated by the deferred grammatical resolution of the opening is satisfied at last by the sudden intervention of the poet, who, amid the gilded corruption he describes, sends poetry, not gold: 'I that have none to send you, send you verse'. This announces that the poet, too, is a giver; it establishes his parity with the patron. The siting of the poet and his gift at the critical closure of the nineteen-line structure highlights both, and gives 'verse' a value equal to, if not higher than, gold.

The argument of the Rutland epistle goes on to invoke an 'elder' time, when poetry was 'of more esteem' (line 30), a golden age of remote antiquity; but Jonson

---

[37] *Timber*, p. 595.

quickly shifts this conception onto a much more recent past, that of the Countess's father:

> With you, I know, my off'ring will find grace.
> For what a sin 'gainst your great father's spirit
> Were it, to think that you should not inherit
> His love unto the Muses . . . (lines 30–33)

The oscillation between an antique time of poetic honour and glory and the ruder present, and again, between the present and the recent past of the Sidney family, is uneasy; and the uneasiness arises from the inherently disabling nature of the patronage idea. The poet must blow his own trumpet in order to attract the interest and admiration of the patron, but must temper self-advertisement with an assumed humility which denigrates the skill of the poet in favour of the greatness or beauty or skill of the patron in order to flatter his or her vanity ('What need hast thou of me . . .?' he asks Salisbury; 'whose actions so themselves do celebrate?' (*Epigrams*, 43)). In the Rutland epistle he must profess contempt for 'this dross' while reminding the Countess to give him some. The fact of late-Renaissance patronage was inherently shameful to the poet for, in writing patronage poems, he sacrifices his autonomy to his necessity. Only by proposing a model patron, content with the glory of supporting poets but indifferent to flattery, can Jonson write his way out of this dilemma.

Jonson has got to praise his patronesses and simultaneously remind them to encourage his genius. The difficulty is particularly acute in the Rutland epistle because the concurrent derogation of gold and celebration of the Countess delicately skirts the fact that her husband was one of the richest men in England. Her access to gold is, ironically, the very reason he is applying to her in verse. He touches on her actual wealth only once, when he makes her inherited poetic skill a dowry 'worth an estate, treble to what you have' (line 36). No sooner has this glancing allusion been made than he must veer away from it into the more seemly pronouncement that beauty, blood, and wealth are not the guarantors of fame that poetry is; and this is couched in the invocation of her father's name and poethood, as if that can take the nastiness out of the pressing question of funds.

This troubled poem was left unfinished because the platitude with which Jonson tried to conclude it, wishing her a son, became inappropriate after the Earl's impotence was generally known. But its nervous journey between gold and virtue may also have proved too disturbing, since it emphatically recreates the dilemma of the patronage poet who wishes to assert his intellectual freedom from and equality with those who finance his production, and the rather more pragmatic necessity of getting a living by poems which elicit that finance. The fiction of the Good Patron of antiquity is not only a myth; it is a myth which the poet alone must somehow promulgate to his prospective benefactors. Poets, having devised the ideal patron, they are obliged to be the whippers-in, instilling respect for poetry in their benefactors and keeping poetry as an object of commodity ever before their eyes. Their poems must help their patrons invent their own need to fund them.

Jonson was, we know, habitually dismayed by the conditions of poethood: his comical doggerel verse to Master John Burges (*Underwood*, 59) acknowledges that a minor clerk of the Exchequer, though useful in procuring wine and food, is hardly a 'rare friend' of poetry; his dramatic works, he would have us believe, were written under duress, purely as money-making exercises, and almost the only plays he could own without shame were either court masques, or Senecan tragedies which had no popular audience and made no money.[38] The 'loathed stage', as he described it, could never win him acclaim from those whose opinion most mattered. Thomas Carew chidingly questioned Jonson's 'immodest rage' in satirising the foibles of the time 'when thine own tongue proclaims thy itch of praise';[39] and Jonson's poetic pathology indicates that the longed-for appeasement of his literary anxiety would be unasked patronage in the form of praise and support from a benefactor whose own standing was secure enough not to require the blandishments of epideictic poetry.

'To Penshurst'

Thou art not, Penshurst, built to envious show
Of touch, or marble, nor canst boast a row
Of polished pillars, or a roof of gold;
Thou hast no lantern whereof tales are told,
Or stair, or courts; but stand'st an ancient pile,
And, these grudged at, art reverenced the while.
Thou joy'st in better marks of soil, of air,
Of wood, of water: therein thou art fair.
Thou hast thy walks for health as well as sport:
10   Thy Mount to which the dryads do resort,
Where Pan and Bacchus their high feasts have made
Beneath the broad beech and the chestnut shade;
That taller tree, which of a nut was set
At his great birth, where all the Muses met.
There, in the writhed bark, are cut the names
Of many a sylvan taken with his flames;

---

[38] Jonas Barish, *The Anti-Theatrical Prejudice* (Berkeley, 1981), pp. 132–154; David Riggs, *Ben Jonson: A Life* (Cambridge, Mass., 1989), pp. 178–179.
[39] 'To Ben Jonson upon the occasion of his Ode of defiance annexed to his play of The New Inn' (line 26), in *The Poems of Thomas Carew*, edited by Rhodes Dunlap (Oxford, 1949), pp. 64–65; also cited by Isabel Rivers, *The Poetry of Conservatism, 1600–1745: A Study of Poets and Public Affairs from Jonson to Pope* (Cambridge, 1973), p. 24.

And thence the ruddy satyrs oft provoke
The lighter fauns to reach thy lady's oak.
Thy copse, too, named of Gamage, thou hast there,
20   That never fails to serve thee seasoned deer
When thou wouldst feast, or exercise thy friends.
The lower land, that to the river bends,
Thy sheep, thy bullocks, kine and calves do feed;
The middle grounds thy mares and horses breed.
Each bank doth yield thee conies, and the tops,
Fertile of wood, Ashour and Sidney's copse,
To crown thy open table, doth provide
The purple pheasant with the speckled side;
The painted partridge lies in every field,
30   And, for thy mess, is willing to be killed.
And if the high-swoll'n Medway fail thy dish,
Thou hast thy ponds that pay thee tribute fish:
Fat, aged carps that run into thy net;
And pikes, now weary their own kind to eat,
As loath the second draught or cast to stay,
Officiously, at first, themselves betray;
Bright eels, that emulate them, and leap on land
Before the fisher, or into his hand.
Then hath thy orchard fruit, thy garden flowers,
40   Fresh as the air and new as are the hours:
The early cherry, with the later plum,
Fig, grape, and quince, each in his time doth come;
The blushing apricot and woolly peach
Hang on thy walls, that every child may reach.
And though thy walls be of the country stone,
They're reared with no man's ruin, no man's groan;
There's none that dwell about them wish them down,
But all come in, the farmer and the clown,
And no one empty-handed, to salute
50   Thy lord and lady, though they have no suit.
Some bring a capon, some a rural cake,
Some nuts, some apples; some that think they make
The better cheeses, bring 'em; or else send
By their ripe daughters, whom they would commend
This way to husbands; and whose baskets bear
An emblem of themselves in plum or pear.
But what can this (more than express their love)
Add to thy free provisions, far above
The need of such? Whose liberal board doth flow
60   With all that hospitality doth know!
Where comes no guest but is allowed to eat
Without his fear, and of thy lord's own meat;
Where the same beer and bread and self-same wine

> That is his lordship's shall be also mine;
> And I not fain to sit (as some this day
> At great men's tables) and yet dine away.
> Here no man tells my cups, nor, standing by,
> A waiter, doth my gluttony envy,
> But gives me what I call, and lets me eat;
> 70 He knows below he shall find plenty of meat,
> Thy tables hoard not up for the next day.
> Nor, when I take my lodging, need I pray
> For fire or lights or livery: all is there,
> As if thou then wert mine, or I reigned here.
> There's nothing I can wish for which I stay.
> That found King James, when, hunting late this way
> With his brave son the Prince, they saw thy fires
> Shine bright on every hearth, as the desires
> Of thy penates had been set on flame
> 80 To entertain them; or the country came
> With all their zeal to warm their welcome here.
> What – 'great', I will not say, but – sudden cheer
> Did'st thou then make 'em! and what praise was heaped
> On thy good lady then! who therein reaped
> The just reward of her high huswifery:
> To have her linen, plate, and all things nigh
> When she was far; and not a room but dressed
> As if it had expected such a guest!
> These, Penshurst, are thy praise, and yet not all.
> 90 Thy lady's noble, fruitful, chaste withal;
> His children thy great lord may call his own,
> A fortune in this age but rarely known.
> They are and have been taught religion; thence
> Their gentler spirits have sucked innocence.
> Each morn and even they are taught to pray
> With the whole household, and may every day
> Read in their virtuous parents' noble parts
> The mysteries of manners, arms, and arts.
> Now, Penshurst, they that will proportion thee
> 100 With other edifices, when they see
> Those proud, ambitious heaps, and nothing else,
> May say their lords have built, but thy lord dwells.

Penshurst Place in West Kent was the family seat of the Sidneys, and remains in the hands of their descendants today (see Plate 3). Contrary to the implication of 'To Penshurst', the estate had been in the family only since 1552, a scant sixty years before Jonson's visit. The Sidneys were prominent, but not 'old money'; in fact, they were successful minor gentry who had risen through hard work; they had little spare cash, and the virtues of old-fashioned architecture celebrated in the poem were necessary ones, since Sir Henry Sidney had not been able to afford to restyle his Gothic house as his son-in-law William Herbert and his brother Philip were to do at Wilton. Although wealthy grandees like Cecil and Thynne were building the prodigious Burghley House and Longleat, houses characterised by extravagantly inessential form, and by lavish use of glass (and consequently rather fragile-looking in comparison with earlier buildings), Jonson praises Robert Sidney for maintaining a functional 'ancient pile' which has been made to last. His is the usual snobbery about arrivistes, who buy their furniture and their houses because they have none to inherit. But of course the Sidneys were themselves a fine example of this type: Penshurst was given to Sidney's grandfather by Edward VI in return for service, and their subsequent prominence came about through employment by Elizabeth, and marriage into the Dudley, Herbert, Hastings, and Radcliffe families. The factual antiquity of Sidney grandeur and habitation at Penshurst is spurious.

Part of Jonson's intention in the poem may be to supply this deficiency by couching his celebration of the house in the terms of the classical country-house poem. Such an amelioration would be exactly within the poet's brief as glorifier of wise patrons. This form, which he resurrected from Martial, Horace, Juvenal, and Ausonius, equates the wholesomeness of country life with ethical soundness;[40] and as Jonson brilliantly realised, it was the ideal form in which to praise potential patrons, since by definition they were the owners of such houses.[41] 'To Penshurst' was the first country-house poem in English.

Such a poem may also have assuaged the fragile sense of social standing in the aristocracy: under Elizabeth, 'old' money and blood were often disregarded in favour of clever young men from nowhere who were the foundation of her civil service – Burghley is an example. Under James, the combination of a previously absent Scottish aristocracy which arrived on the scene with him, and his habits of selling titles and ennobling favourites, meant that nothing could be taken for granted by the entrenched groups.[42] 'To Penshurst' reconfirms the innate worth of established families.

Like the Rutland epistle, 'To Penshurst' documents Jonson's attitude toward the patronage system. Like the epistle, it proposes two extremes of cultural

---

[40] William A. McClung, *The Country House in English Renaissance Poetry* (Berkeley, 1977); G.R. Hibbard, 'The Country House Poem of the Seventeenth Century', *Journal of the Warburg and Courtauld Institutes*, 19 (1956), 159–174; James Turner, *The Politics of Landscape: Rural Scenery and Society in English Poetry, 1630–1660* (Oxford, 1979). The similarities between Jonson's description of Penshurst and Sidney's of Kalander's house in Arcadia (*Arcadia*, I.2) has been noted many times; Sidney may have been using his own home as the model for Kalander's, and there is little doubt that Jonson was paying homage to that Arcadian episode.

[41] The adaptation of the classical tradition by Jonson is doubly brilliant when we remember that Martial, Ausonius, and Horace celebrate simple dwellings, family farms, comfortable, but not ostentatious, country villas, often the possession of a friend of the poet or even the poet himself.

[42] See Lawrence Stone, *The Crisis of the Aristocracy, 1558–1641* (Oxford, 1965), pp. 21–128.

production. In the Rutland epistle, the two poles are, broadly, poetic virtuosity and the necessities of subsistence, and these antithetical terms engender an unfinished poem full of touchiness, unable to settle, and a poet, therefore, in some sense disabled by the act of writing. But 'To Penshurst', also a poetic address, discovers in the country estate and its family an extreme which by contrast soothes rather than disables him.

'To Penshurst' fluctuates between the past and the present, in the humanist nostalgic tradition, but because the present that Jonson observes in and around the ancestral home of the Sidneys is consonant with its past and with his vision of an ideal present, the poem has many fewer inherent poetic anxieties. This does not claim for it any extraordinary stasis: such stability would be almost inconceivable in a work of Jonson's; and the poem is full of internal structural polarities such as house/home, nature/society, and natural/artificial, which maintain a characteristically Jonsonian febrility.[43] What 'To Penshurst' accomplishes, however surreally, is the laying to rest of Jonson's deeply felt unease in the patron-client pattern by which he must live. 'To Penshurst' is a poet's fantasy, where the mythical antique past and its intuitive reverence for poetry, a past conflated with a prelapsarian golden age, is preserved in the family and acres of the Sidneys. Penshurst is a place full of old-fashioned virtues: there, Jonson's cherished rules of plainness, hospitality, and liberality remain inviolate.

In Epigram 84, a minor but memorable poem, Jonson tells the Countess of Bedford how, having asked for and been denied the gift of a buck from some patron-lord, he was instead given one by the Countess:

> . . . ere I could ask you, I was prevented:
> For your most noble offer had supplied me.   (lines 3–4)

The telling expression here is 'prevention' – that is, anticipation: the Countess offered Jonson a buck before she was asked for one. This happy vignette of prevention, or 'anteriority', is a key element in Jonson's idealised version of patronage in 'To Penshurst'. If the poet's disappointment – that is, the despair of the true poet who, like Jonson, finds the world less ready spontaneously to honour his art than he would wish – is best summarised by the constant requirement to ask for support, to invent the need and its benefits, usually through poetry; and if the act of making such poetic requests necessarily disables or deforms the poet's voice, then the ideal patron would be one who did not need asking, who anticipated the poet's needs and left him free to write as he chose and not as he must. Anteriority becomes emblematic of the golden age. This quality of Penshurst enables the liberty which allows the patronised poet to write non-patronage poems.

At Penshurst anteriority is appealing but improbable. In Andrew Marvell's

---

[43] Wayne, Chapters 2–3 (pp. 22–80).

poetry, where it is even more apparent, anteriority is connected with an Edenic, infantile condition of utter passivity (a condition which may reflect his anxieties about taking sides in the Civil War); in 'The Garden' he imagines that 'the nectarine and curious peach,/ Into my hands themselves do reach',[44] the unusual reflexive construction which has fruit 'reaching itself' enacts the fantasy of complete satisfaction, a condition associated in the poem with prelapsarian man. George Herbert uses a similar syntactical device to propose predestined salvation in 'Redemption': the sinner-tenant, who has been searching for the great landlord (Christ) to whom he owes fealty in order to convert his old lease into a new one (the New Covenant), discovers him at last in the final line; before the sinner can make his request, however, Christ '. . . straight, "Your suit is granted", said, and died'.[45] The interruption of the speech ascription seems to recapitulate the condition of election or grace, which cannot be received simply because it is requested, which is given before it *can* be requested. The anteriority of these poems is connected with heavenly grace; it may be significant that Jonson applies the anteriority of Christian grace to his patrons, and ascribes prelapsarian acts of 'prevention' to their lands.

The Edenic copses and fields 'provide' partridges and pheasants, as if the landscape itself were sentient of man's needs, and benevolent; but more amazingly, these partridges are 'willing to be killed', and the carp, pike, and eels 'run into the net' and leap into the hand of the fisherman. The local peasants, too, spontaneously offer up the fruits of their labours ('though they have no suit'), as well as the fruits of their loins, in the form of 'ripe' daughters. Despite the fact that this fabulous and contented hierarchy of 'natural' social relationships can never have existed, it was thought to be breaking down in the late-Elizabethan and Jacobean era.[46]

The land and the house at Penshurst display equal bounty, equal anteriority. The owner-patrons are present for much of the poem only by implication; it is the house's liberal board which 'doth flow with all that hospitality doth know', the house whose guest is allowed to eat in comfort and to satiety, 'without his fear, and *of thy lord's own meat*' (my emphasis).[47] It is at this point, about two-thirds of the way into the poem, and before any real notice is taken of the Sidneys themselves, that Jonson asserts his own presence, a surprising appearance similar to the 'I' of line 19 in the Rutland epistle. The moment of sudden authorial entrance is offered in a dinnertime vignette:

---

[44] *The Poems and Letters of Andrew Marvell*, edited by H.M. Margoliouth, 2 vols, third edition, revised by Pierre Legouis and E.E. Duncan-Jones (Oxford, 1971), p. 51.
[45] *The English Poems of George Herbert* edited by C.A. Patrides (London, 1974), p. 60.
[46] Rivers, p. 21.
[47] The hint of unequal dining provisions at other tables may arise from an incident involving Lord Salisbury, who offered his guests a meal less sumptuous than his own.

> Where the same beer and bread and self-same wine
> That is his lordship's shall be also mine.
> And I not fain to sit (as some, this day,
> At great men's tables) and yet dine away. (lines 63–66)

That the casual and bountiful equality of rank at Penshurst should be particularised in its food is both charming and pathetic: this is a poet who probably *does* remember the menu of the last good meal he had; the experience of hunger has made him almost as sybaritic as his creature Sir Epicure Mammon in *The Alchemist* in his need to describe food. Like other forms of abundance at Penshurst, the provision of food is anterior. It is an anteriority identical to Bedford's in the buck incident of Epigram 84:

> Nor when I take my lodging, need I pray
> For fire, or lights, or livery: all is there;
> As if thou, then, wert mine, or I reigned here:
> There's nothing I can wish, for which I stay. (lines 72–75)

The apotheosis of this extraordinary anteriority is the final vignette of the poem, in which Lady Sidney 'reaped the just reward of her high huswifery' when during her absence King James happened to come into the area on a hunting expedition:

> ... and not a room but dressed
> As if it had expected such a guest! (lines 87–88)

When Jonson claims in an epigram 'That poets are far rarer birth than kings' (*Epigrams*, 79),[48] he asserts his superiority to the masters of the earth; it is a belief which can neither be proven nor honoured in the commonplace world, where patrons have got to be persuaded to part with cash and favours. In the idealised climate of Penshurst, however, Jonson imagines the practical consequences of this assertion, and lives (in the coincidence of his shared guesthood there with James) the experience of equality with his sovereign. All guests are kings at Penshurst, or in any case, poets are treated as they deserve. Penshurst allays all the anxieties of the needy poet, who finally, in this vision, is relieved of his begging.

In a poem to King James, Jonson likens laurels and sceptres, an equation of ceremonial metonyms which asserts the likeness of poets and monarchs (*Epigrams*, 4). Jonson did receive benefits from James; but he outlived him, and he fared less well with his son Charles, whose apparent indifference reduced Jonson to frank begging. The slide into the chaos of mid-century seems almost uncannily

---

[48] Jonson concludes his 'Panegyre on the Happy Entrance of James ... to His First High Session of Parliament ... 1603' with the words of the Latin poet Florus: '*Solus Rex et poeta non quotannis nascitur*' ('The King alone, and the poet, is not born every year'). For a history of this idea, see Michael McCanles, *Jonsonian Discriminations: The Humanist Poet and the Praise of True Nobility* (Toronto, 1992), pp. 46–83.

apprehended in 'To Penshurst', a poem which attempts to halt the decline by a retrograde imaginative relocation into the age of gold, instanced in the brief candescence of Philip Sidney and his family, and sited in their own English paradise.

The Early History of Sidney Sussex College Library

NICHOLAS ROGERS

This account of the early growth of the College Library covers the period prior to the compilation of the first surviving library catalogue in 1674. The chief source for the accessions during the first three-quarters of a century is MS 91, the donors' register, which covers the period up to 1618 and, more patchily, from the early 1630s onwards. In addition, evidence about the stocking and furnishing of the library can be gleaned from College accounts, and from the 1639 Master's inventory. Last, but definitely not least, there is the evidence of the books themselves. The compilation of an on-line catalogue has led to several significant discoveries about the provenance of the collection now housed in the Muniment Room.

When the College began to function in August 1598 it is likely that the decision had already been taken to house the library over the chapel in a refurbished former Franciscan hall or frater. The position was a good one, high up, and thus well away from damp and mice.[1] It can be seen clearly on the Loggan print (Pl. 2), lit on each side by four dormer windows. This view can be supplemented by the account of the German scholar Zacharias Conrad von Uffenbach, who visited Cambridge in 1710:

> In the afternoon we went to Sidney-Sussex college, an old but still tolerably fine building. The library of this college is indeed high up, under the very roof of the chapel, but yet tolerably good and well-lighted; the books, too, though not numerous, are still in a good state.[2]

That the building required substantial repairs is indicated by the rather worrying earliest specific references to the library, in the accounts for Lady Day 1604:

> Item for lyme and sande for repaireinge of the gable end of the lybrarie and buildinge the buttres in our Masters garden   xijs. iiijd.

---

[1] On the position of libraries see Robert Willis and John Willis Clark, *The Architectural History of the University of Cambridge* (4 vols, Cambridge, 1886), III, pp. 416–17. Between 1579 and 1823 the Corpus Christi library was in a room in the roof of the chapel (ibid., I, pp. 262–3). At Magdalene the books were kept over the chapel until 1733 (ibid., II, p. 382).
[2] *Cambridge under Queen Anne*, ed. J.E.B. Mayor (Cambridge, 1911), p. 159.

> Item for buildeinge up the end of the library which fell downe xvs. viijd.
> Item to the glasiers for mendinge the library window which fell downe and other woorke about the colledge xijs.[3]

By 1639 all the paraphernalia of a Renaissance library had been acquired; the inventory taken that year conjures up a picture of a miniature version of the University Library at Leiden.[4] There were four tables and four stools for readers, who could use desks which were placed on two of the tables. Two of the stools had been provided in 1607 at a cost of 3s 4d.[5] For larger books there was a 'turning deske upon a frame'. Uffenbach provides a fuller description of this piece of furniture:

> We noticed here also an old desk and book-stand, the only peculiarity of which was that you could raise and lower it by a long screw, passing through the desk; within it was fitted with drawers. It rested on a cross, which wanted however a firm stand, especially for writing.[6]

Lying around, perhaps on one of the tables, were a few scientific instruments: a small brass sphere, a terrestrial globe made in 1593 by Emery Molyneux, under a green serge cover,[7] and 'Mr Outreds instrument mathematicall in brasse with a lether case, & a little book belonging to it', most probably the double horizontal dial of which William Oughtred published a description in 1632.[8] Both the globe and the 'instrument mathematicall' were given by Paul Micklethwaite, an early Fellow of Sidney. To these was added, between 1679 and 1688, the Earl of Castlemaine's terrestrial globe, with its accompanying manual, in a fir box.[9]

On the walls were a half-length portrait of the foundress, protected by a green silk curtain,[10] an equestrian portrait of the second Lord Harington, now only

---

[3] Sidney Sussex Muniments [hereafter SSM], MR.61, p. 40.
[4] SSM, MR.31D, f. 4.
[5] SSM, MR.61, p. 54.
[6] *Cambridge under Queen Anne*, p. 163.
[7] The date given in MR.31D either indicates an unknown version of Molyneux's globe, or is a misreading of the date on a 1592 globe (cf. Elly Dekker and Peter van der Krogt, *Globes from the Western World* (London, 1993), p. 36, fig. 15). The only surviving example of the 1592 terrestrial globe is at Petworth.
[8] A.W. Pollard and G.R. Redgrave, *A Short-Title Catalogue of Books Printed in England, Scotland and Ireland and of English Books Printed Abroad 1475–1640*, second edition, 3 vols (London, 1976–1991) [hereafter STC] 18899c.5; Augustus de Morgan, *Arithmetical Books from the Invention of Printing to the Present Time* (London, 1847), p. 38. The instrument was an early form of slide rule.
[9] SSM, MR.31D, f. 15.
[10] A deleted entry on f. 6 of MR.31D indicates that the portrait was transferred from the Great Chamber of the Master's Lodge after 5 July 1639, during the compilation of the inventory.

known from a seventeenth-century engraving,[11] and three tables compiled by John Scot the elder, two of them charting the foundation of the Universities of Oxford and Cambridge, acquired in 1634, and one, purchased for 10 shillings in 1633, listing the chancellors, vice-chancellors, and other officials. These were later supplemented by two chronological tables, and two further pictures, briefly described as 'ye Presentation of our Saviour: & a Temple'. These two, possibly relics of Joshua Basset's mastership, recur in every inventory down to 1760, but were probably discarded when the old library and chapel were demolished in 1776.

In a cupboard were kept curiosities, for which a college library was the natural repository before the development of museums. Still in the carved wooden box in which it was presented to the College in 1627 by Captain Stevens of Rotherhithe (Pl. 4) is the skull of a child, incrusted with carbonate of lime, found ten yards underground during the digging of a well near Candia in Crete. This was borrowed by William Harvey, who wrote on returning it after having shown it to Charles I:

> Mr Doctor Ward I have showed to his Majesty this scull incrustated with stone, which I receyved from you, & his Majesty wondered att it & look'd content to see soe rare a thinge. I doe now with thanks retorne to you and your Colledg the same with the key of the case & the memoriall you sent me inclosed heare in thinking it a kinde of sacriledg not to have retorned it to that place where it may for the instruction of men heare after be conserved.[12]

As early as the time of Uffenbach's visit, Harvey's note, which confirms Aubrey's comments about the badness of his handwriting, had become as much an exhibit as the skull itself. Also shown to Uffenbach were various cylinder pictures, including one of Charles II on horseback.[13] Between 1639 and 1688 the College acquired a remarkable chronicle starting from the Creation, in roll form, printed in Paris in 1521. This survives in a Jacobean cabinet which would have been a prominent feature of the furnishing of the library.[14]

Despite Uffenbach's comment about the number of books, at a rough estimate there were some 2500 in 1674. These were in bookcases arranged in twenty-six classes lettered A–Z and Gamma and Delta, the latter being devoted to manuscripts. Some of the cases had only four shelves, but others (M–P) as many as nine. Perhaps these ran down the centre of the room, where the roof-line gave more height. Most of the shelves up to L seem to have been full in 1674, but

---

[11] Arthur M. Hind, *Engraving in England in the Sixteenth and Seventeenth Centuries*, Part II, *The Reign of James I* (Cambridge, 1955), p. 375, pl. 234a.
[12] A facsimile of this letter was published privately by G.E. Paget of Caius in 1849.
[13] *Cambridge under Queen Anne*, pp. 162–3.
[14] It can be seen placed on a table at one end of the Old Library in a Walter Scott postcard (H231). This may reflect its position in the pre-1776 library.

thereafter only odd shelves were filled. The accounts contain a few references to library furniture, but it is not clear from these how the books were originally housed. A payment in 1611 of £4 7s for 'the new settles in our Librarye' probably refers to bookcases of the type still to be found in the Old Library at Trinity Hall, for at St John's College in 1623 the word 'sedile' is used for a bookcase.[15] Another payment of £3 4s 9d for 'a new locker in our Library' in 1619, soon after the arrival of Bishop Montagu's collection, suggests the installation of a case protected by a grille, perhaps like those still to be seen in the Bodleian Library.[16] A peculiarity of the Sidney library is the uniform titling of the early acquisitions, until the 1640s, in ink across the head of the book (Pl. 5a). Does this indicate that the books were shelved with the fore-edge downwards, an arrangement unparalleled elsewhere, or is it a relic of the storage of books in chests, like the *capsae* of the Sistine Library in the Vatican?[17] At first books were identified as College property by an ink inscription on the title-page. Several of the donations were provided with printed book-labels, the provision of which is sometimes documented in the accounts.[18] However, neither system was followed systematically, and it was not until 1701 that all the books were given a College book-plate.

Though the books were not chained, borrowing regulations were still very restrictive. Rules formulated in the early 1620s state that 'no Fellow or Master of Art (without speciall dispensation to the contrary graunted by the Master and Fellows) shall have any Booke out of the Library above 6 dayes in a Moneth, and those 6 days not together but 3 dayes in one Weeke and 3 dayes in another'.[19] Those who neglected to sign out a book in the borrowing register were to be fined 20 shillings, and those who failed to return the book at the end of three days had to pay the price of the book or 10 shillings. In 1637 these rules were tightened up. The borrowing period was reduced to three days per month, and it was firmly stated that 'noe Master of Arts or other student shall take out any booke at all'.[20] That there was a difference between precept and practice is highlighted by the case of the copy of Erpold Lindenbrog's *Scriptores rerum Germanicarum septentrionalium* (Frankfurt, 1609), borrowed by Colonel Robert Walpole, when an undergraduate of Trinity College, in 1667–8. This passed into the Walpole collection at Houghton Hall, where it remained until returned by the Marquess of Cholmondeley in 1956, following its discovery by J.H. Plumb. This absence of 289 years has earned for this book a place in the *Guinness Book of Records* as

---

[15] SSM, MR.61, p. 86; John Willis Clark, *The Care of Books* (Cambridge, 1901), pp. 168–9, figs 65, 66. I am grateful to Dr Elisabeth Leedham-Green for her advice in this matter.
[16] SSM, MR.61, p. 154.
[17] Clark, *Care of Books*, pp. 228–9, fig. 100.
[18] In 1640 5 shillings was paid for labels for the Earl of Chesterfield's donation, and 5s 6d for ones for Dr Micklethwaite's bequest (MR.61, pp. 322, 327).
[19] SSM, MR.1, p. 16a.
[20] SSM, MR.1, p. 25.

the most overdue book in the world.[21] This case is exceptional, though; apart from a few losses occasioned by wear and tear, and sales of duplicates or books perceived as no longer useful, the early library has survived largely intact.

Sidney did not receive any books from its foundress, who left scarcely enough money to found a college. One of her two executors, Sir John Harington, made the princely donation of the eight folio volumes of the *Biblia Regia*, the polyglot Bible printed by Christopher Plantin at Antwerp between 1568 and 1572, which was, and long remained, the most reliable biblical text available.[22] The poverty of the College meant that more than others it had to rely on donations rather than purchases. However, donations could be directed. Looking down the lists of books given by Sir Edward Montagu, Sir John Hart and Sir George Goring it is soon evident that these do not reflect their tastes but are shopping-lists of standard folio editions of much-needed authors. This practice continued; many of the books listed as donations in the 1630s and 1650s are specifically stated to have been purchased with money given by the donors. This procedure guarded against duplication, and ensured that the College got what it really wanted. It is, however, a pity that we do not have a choice of books actually selected by the Laudian Dr Pocklington of Peterborough, the author of *Altare Christianum* and *Sunday no sabbath*, which were ordered by Parliament to be burnt publicly in 1641.[23]

The first donations which may reflect the interests of the donors are twelve books given by Francis Aldrich, the short-lived second Master, and thirty given by Robert Rhodes, one of the first Fellows. Although the early entries in MS 91 are undated, the College accounts reveal that Mr Cliburne was paid in 1604 for various expenses including that of bringing Mr Rhodes' books from Ely.[24] Rhodes' thirty volumes include seven works by Calvin, and seven Greek texts, as well as the fine *Hortus Sanitatis*, probably printed in Strassburg by Johann Prüss c.1507.[25] Aldrich's collection is more varied theologically, ranging from Duns Scotus and Gibbons's *Concertatio Ecclesiae Catholicae in Anglia* to Tyndall, Hus and Luther. In accordance with his will of 1609, the books were selected by his brother, his copy of the *Summa* and works by Zanchius going to Humphrey Moorer, one of the Fellows.[26] Another donor of this period, Thomas Jennings, the Rector of Willingale Spain, Essex (d.1607), seems to have been more of a book collector. His bequest included the mid-thirteenth-century North French Bestiary (MS 100, part 1), and several early sixteenth-century canon law and

---

[21] *Sidney Sussex College Annual*, 1956, p. 25; *The Guinness Book of Records 1994*, ed. Peter Matthews (London, 1993), p. 164.
[22] On the *Biblia Regia* see Leon Voet, *The Plantin Press (1555–1589)*, I, A–B (Amsterdam, 1980), pp. 280–315. Ordinary paper copies sold for 70 fl.
[23] On Pocklington see *Dictionary of National Biography*, ed. S. Lee, XLV (London, 1896), pp. 450–1. His interest in ecclesiastical history is revealed in a letter of 1632 to Samuel Ward (SSM, Box 1).
[24] SSM, MR.61, p. 44.
[25] MS 91, pp. 11–13.
[26] MS 91, pp. 10–11; G.M. Edwards, *Sidney Sussex College* (London, 1899), p. 62.

devotional works, most notably a copy of Ludolph of Saxony's *Vita Christi* which had formerly belonged to a monk of Woburn Abbey.[27] Several Fellows in the first two decades of the century gave one or two books, often, it would appear, on the occasion of leaving their fellowships. John Young, the Scotsman who became Dean of Winchester, gave the *Antiquitatum Romanorum corpus* of his fellow-countryman Thomas Dempster, an Aristotle and the works of the Cambridge Calvinist William Whitaker.[28] There are also the first gifts of old Sidney men. William Willmer of Sywell, Northants., the first pensioner to matriculate at Sidney, provided some beautifully bound copies of works by the Jesuit theologians Suarez and Vasquez, gilt-stamped with his arms and a presentation inscription (Pl. 5b). Some of the volumes also have an engraved book-plate of similar design to the binding stamp.[29]

By April 1617 there were 207 donations in the library, plus an unknown, probably very small, number of purchases. At that point the number was doubled by the gift by Anne, Lady Harington and Lucy, Countess of Bedford of 245 books. Although they were recorded as the donors in MS 91, the books are referred to in the accounts as 'my Lord Harringtons', and there is little doubt that the bulk of them had belonged to the second Lord Harington, who had been educated at Sidney and died at the early age of twenty-one in 1614.[30] The accounts give some glimpses into the process of acquiring the books: 30s 4d was paid to Mr Hobson the carrier for bringing them from London; a further 44 shillings went to the Countess of Bedford's steward for his pains; and the Master spent 18s 9d on a journey to London and hiring porters. When the books got to Sidney, Mr Bosse was paid 6 shillings for writing the names in the library book. Further expenses were incurred in binding a few items which were still in loose quires.[31] Many of the volumes are distinguished by a binding incorporating the Harington fret. Even where the original binding does not survive or lacks the fret device, the list in MS 91 is sufficiently detailed to enable all but 54 items to be identified with reasonable certainty. The losses are chiefly among the mathematical and scientific works, perhaps discarded when outmoded. The collection gives a good idea of the scope of the library of a Renaissance gentleman, and supports the claim of a funeral panegyric that the young Lord Harington, a close friend of Prince Henry, was 'well read' in logic and philosophy.[32] Two items can be directly connected with his education: a gilt-edged presentation copy of *Ero-paideia, or the institution*

---

[27] MS 91, pp. 13–15, 16. On Jennings see John Venn and J.A. Venn, *Alumni Cantabrigienses*, Part I, *From the Earliest Times to 1751*, II (Cambridge, 1922), p. 471.
[28] MS 91, pp. 18, 19.
[29] STC 3368.5.
[30] MS 91, pp. 21–30; SSM, MR.61, p. 146; *Dictionary of National Biography*, XXIV, p. 389.
[31] SSM, MR.61, pp. 138, 141, 146.
[32] Richard Stock, *The Churches Lamentation for the losse of the Godly. Delivered in a Sermon, at the Funerals of... John Lord Harington...* (London, 1614), p. 68. It is possible that some of the books were acquired during his travels in the Low Countries and Italy in 1608–09, when he corresponded regularly in French and Latin with Prince Henry.

of a young noble man, published by his tutor James Cleland in 1607, and a manuscript *Mathematicall Discourse* (MS 24), dedicated to him by John Waymouth.[33] As listed in MS 91, the books are arranged according to broad subject categories, which may reflect their disposition in Lord Harington's library. There is a large quantity of history, including several interesting works on classical antiquities, such as two editions of Occo's *Numismata* and a copy of Levinus Hulsius's *Impp. Romanorum numismatum series* from the library of Sir Robert Cotton.[34] Among the 'Libri Historici' are several travel accounts, such as a set of Hakluyt. The 'Libri Mathematici' form an equally diverse group, covering astronomy, engineering and architectural theory. There is a reasonable, though not remarkable, range of classical authors. Thirteen of the scientific and classical texts formerly belonged to Sir William Bulstrode, a relative of the Haringtons. One item is to be associated with Lucy, Countess of Bedford, rather than her brother: a copy of Dionysius Gothofredus, *Auctores Latinae linguae* (Geneva, 1595) given to her by John Donne.[35] The virtual absence of theology is explained by Lady Harington's gift of that section of the library to Oakham parish church, to form a parish library (now housed in the University of Nottingham).[36]

Unfortunately Mr Bosse was not on hand to record the next large donation. When James Montagu, the first Master, died in 1618 after two years as Bishop of Winchester, he left all his books, valued *post mortem* at £200, to Sidney.[37] The account book records the expenses of carriage from the Bishop's houses in Waltham and Farnham. Palmer the Farnham carrier got £3 7s 6d and Hobson £3 5s 3d; 32 shillings was spent at Waltham on packing the books into hogsheads for carrying. Another batch of books in London cost a further £4 10s 9d to transport.[38] These charges indicate a collection of some size, perhaps four times as large as the Harington collection.[39] Unfortunately it is difficult to identify many of them positively. Only a small number have Montagu's arms as Bishop of

---

[33] Waymouth, a shadowy figure, was the author of *A Plaine and Easie Table, whereby to Reade the Whole Bible in a Yeere* (London, 1613), and *Low-Countrie Trayning: or, Certaine Demonstrations, how a Company should March* (London, 1617).

[34] Acquired by Cotton in 1603, the year of its publication. The inscription 'I HAR' in capitals on the verso of the title-page could refer to either the first or the second Baron Harington of Exton.

[35] In R.C. Bald, *John Donne: A Life* (Oxford, 1970), p. 558, the erroneous suggestion is made that Donne himself may have given the book to the College.

[36] Anne L. Herbert, 'Oakham Parish Library', *Library History*, 6, no. 1 (1982), pp. 1–11.

[37] Evelyn Philip Shirley, 'The Will, Inventories, and Funeral Expenses of James Montagu, Bishop of Winchester, Anno 1618. From the Original in the Possession of the Baroness North', *Archaeologia*, 44 (1873), 398.

[38] SSM, MR.61, pp. 150–1.

[39] Cf. Andrew Perne's library of some 900 books (David McKitterick, 'Andrew Perne and his Books', in *Andrew Perne: Quatercentenary Studies*, ed. David McKitterick (Cambridge, 1991), pp. 35–69).

Winchester gilt-stamped on the covers. A few early acquisitions bear his signature and a note of the price, but he did not continue this practice. Some can be identified from dedicatory inscriptions: the library has books presented to Montagu by Isaac Casaubon, Sir Edward Coke, John Barclay and Patrick Young, among others. One remarkable presentation copy is the *Arcana arcanissima* of Michael Maier, printed by Thomas Creede c.1614, which has a unique letter-press dedication to Montagu (Fig. 1).[40] For the most part one can only suspect a Montagu origin. He was the editor of King James's works, so it is not surprising to find a plethora of books by or about the king, or dedicated to him, such as a Czech translation of Calvin's *Institutes*, very obviously unread.[41] Montagu's acquaintance with Patrick Young, the royal librarian, may explain the presence at Sidney of two items from Henry VIII's library.[42] Another source for Montagu may have been the confiscated libraries of Catholics: at Sidney are two books which belonged to individuals implicated in the Gunpowder Plot,[43] and a collection of five volumes, with imprints between 1585 and 1596, which seem to be the working library of an English Jesuit.[44]

Another large bequest was that of Francis Combe of Hemel Hempstead, who died in 1641. He had been admitted as a pensioner at Sidney in 1600, but had then migrated to Trinity College, Oxford. Consequently he left the manor of Abbot's Langley to be held jointly by the two Colleges, and willed that his library should be split between them.[45] Although this collection, too, escaped inclusion in MS 91, the books can be identified by a printed book-label inserted when the collection came to Sidney, or by Francis Combe's signature on the title-page. A document in St Paul's archives describes him as 'always an enemy to the ministry, to injure those who stood up for prelacy. He came only three times to church in three years, and then only in hopes to be elected a parliament man'.[46] This, and

---

[40] STC 17196.5. The copy in Dr. Williams's Library, London, has a printed dedication to Lancelot Andrewes. In a copy formerly in the possession of J. Rosenthal of Munich the engraved frame surrounds a manuscript dedication to Sir Thomas Smith (J.B. Craven, *Count Michael Maier* (Kirkwall, 1910), p. 5, pl. opp. p. 5).
[41] E.P. Tyrrell and J.S.G. Simmons, 'Slavonic Books before 1700 in Cambridge Libraries', *Transactions of the Cambridge Bibliographical Society*, 3, part 5 (1963), p. 394. No other copy of this special issue of Georg Streyzius's translation with a dedication by Johannes Opsimathes to James I is known.
[42] Henry VIII, *Illustris. ac potentis. regis . . . sententia, et de eo concilio . . . et de ea bulla . . .* (London, 1537) (no. 775), and Pseudo-Dionysius, *Coelestis hierarchia* (Paris, 1515) (no. 1076). Professor James Carley is at present working on this library.
[43] *The Chastysing of Goddes Chyldern* (Westminster, 1493), belonged to Dorothy Abington, sister of Thomas Habington or Abington of Hindlip, Worcs. (cf. John Morris, *The Condition of Catholics under James I*, second edition (London, 1872), p. 283), and Rodolphus Agricola, *De inventione dialectica* (Cologne, 1557) came from the library of Everard Digby.
[44] The books are uniformly inscribed 'Jhs' at the head of the title-page. One bears the signature of Edward Leveson, perhaps a member of the Staffordshire family of that name.
[45] SSM, Box 16/1.
[46] *The Victoria History of Hertfordshire*, ed. William Page, II (London, 1908), p. 220.

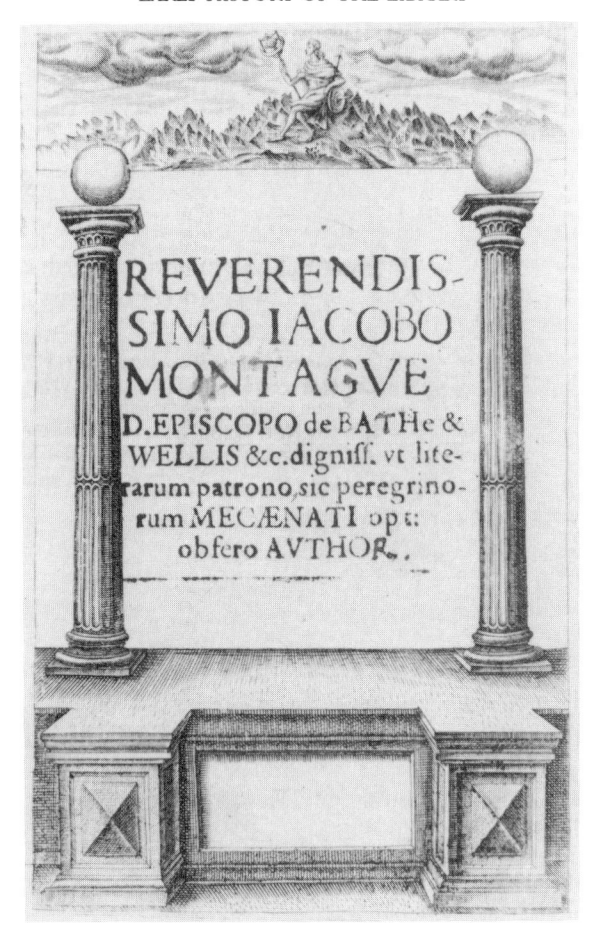

Fig. 1. Michael Maier, *Arcana arcanissima*
(London, c.1614), dedication page.

the provision for preaching in his will, suggest that he was a Puritan, but the contents of his library reveal a more complex personality, Familist rather than classical Nonconformist, and well-read in medicine, classics, logic, philosophy and theology, in which his taste was for the speculative and mystical, such as Jan van Ruusbroec and Teresa of Avila. Over eighty-six per cent of his library consisted of foreign imprints; a significant proportion are in Italian, and he even occasionally inscribed these in Italian.[47]

A much more specialised collection was bequeathed to the College in 1639 by Paul Micklethwaite, who was a Fellow of Sidney before migrating to London to

---

[47] E.g. Torquato Tasso, *Il secretario* (Venice, 1601).

become Master of the Temple.[48] Much work remains to be done on his donation of seventy-three Hebrew works, which provide a valuable insight into the material available for the pursuit of Hebrew studies at a time when there was no open Jewish presence in England. Several of the books can be associated with an earlier generation of English Hebraists.[49] Of particular note is a biblical concordance, printed in Venice, which was acquired in 1565 by the astrologer John Dee. His occult activities did not find favour with his neighbours in Mortlake, who ransacked his house in 1583, during his absence on the Continent. On his return in 1589 Dee was able to recover about three-quarters of his books, including the concordance, but some had to be sold later on to meet the cost of his experiments.[50] As well as a wide range of Italian Hebrew presses, the Micklethwaite collection includes books published in Cracow and Lublin.[51]

Sidney was founded too late to take advantage of the first wave of manuscript-collecting after the Dissolution. Such manuscripts as were acquired were incidental additions. By 1620 only three seem to have reached Sidney: the Bestiary and the *Mathematicall Discourse* already mentioned, and Dean Gunthorpe's copy of Albertus Magnus, *De Animalibus*, one of a small group of scientific texts given by Roger Montagu.[52] At least ten more were given in the 1620s and 1630s; this increase may reflect the interest of Samuel Ward, whose own collection of manuscripts, willed to the College in 1643, accounts for one fifth of the total holding.[53] The Ward manuscripts, most of which are identified by a printed book-label (Fig. 2), reveal a not unexpected interest in unusual texts, especially those which might be of use in contemporary theological debates, such as Franco of Afflighem, *De Gratia*, Thomas Bradwardine, *De causa Dei*, Matthaeus Blastaris, *De sacris synodis synopsis*, or the collection of Wycliffite sermons. But Ward's acquisition of items such as the miniature Augustinian diurnal (MS 62) or Gower's *Confessio Amantis* (MS 63) seems to have been motivated by a simple

---

[48] J. Bruce Williamson, *The History of the Temple, London* (London, 1924), pp. 384–96. I am indebted to Mr John Thornely for this reference.

[49] A Hebrew Psalter (Basel, 1516) contains the mid-sixteenth-century ownership inscription of one John Rottenwode; the Lexicon of Nathan ben Jehiel (Basel, 1599) and *Midrash Tehillim* (Venice, 1546) belonged to Hugh Broughton (1549–1612); and Fagius's *Exegesis . . . in quatuor capita Geneseos* (Isny, 1547) was presented to William Smith of King's in 1595.

[50] The concordance is no. 1560 in *John Dee's Library Catalogue*, ed. Julian Roberts and Andrew G. Watson (London, 1990).

[51] *Tefillah mekol ha-Shanah* (Cracow: Isaac ben Aaron, 1597); Joseph Albo, *Sefer ikrim* (Lublin: Kalonymos ben Mardochai, 1594). I am grateful to Harvey Hames for identifying the *Tefillah*.

[52] MS. 91, p. 11.

[53] Ward owned MSS 44, 45, 47, 54, 55, 58, 61–63, 65, 66, 70, 71, 74, 75, 90, 92–94, 101, and also possibly MSS 30 and 51 which, like 55, had previously been owned by John Pilkington.

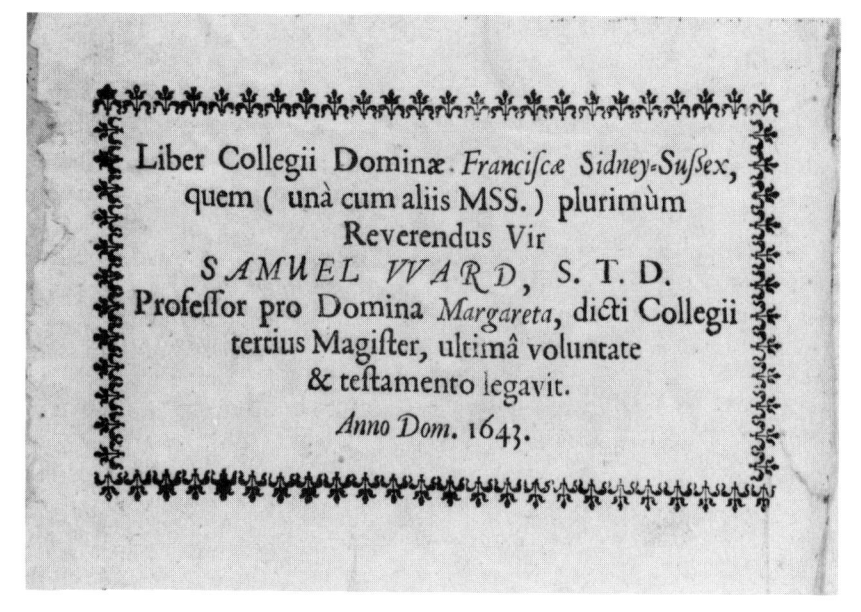

> Liber Collegii Dominæ. *Francifcæ Sidney-Suffex,*
> quem (unà cum aliis MSS.) plurimùm
> Reverendus Vir
> S*AMUEL* WA*R*D, S. T. D.
> Profeffor pro Domina *Margareta,* dicti Collegii
> tertius Magifter, ultimâ voluntate
> & teftamento legavit.
> *Anno Dom.* 1643.

Fig. 2. MS 54, printed book-label recording bequest by Samuel Ward.

interest in antiquity, which also manifested itself in his collection of Roman coins.[54]

That Fuller's 'Benjamin-Colledge' had reached 'a competent strength and stature' is reflected by the growing practice of authors and publishers, not necessarily connected with the College, making donations of books. Thomas Buck, the University Printer, gave several examples of his art, including a fine Greek New Testament of 1632. In 1668 Margaret Cavendish, Duchess of Newcastle, bestowed ten folios of her works.[55] The most fascinating gift of this kind were the six works printed on the private press of William Dugard, who had studied at Sidney under his uncle Richard Dugard before going on to be headmaster of Merchant-Taylors' School. His political sympathies were clearly expressed by his printing the *Eikon Basilike* in 1649. Early in the following year, while he was engaged in printing Salmasius's *Defensio regia,* he was arrested and sent to Newgate, and his printing effects, worth £1000, were seized. He was released after six months through Milton's intervention, and partly out of gratitude, it would appear, printed an edition of Milton's reply to Salmasius, the

---

[54] In his will (SSM, MR.103) Ward bequeathed to the College 'certaine old Coynes of silver som .80. of the old Emperours of Rome, allso one of gould of Constans the Emperour second sonne of Constantine the great'. There is now no trace of these.
[55] MS 91, p. 103; SSM, MR.61, p. 680.

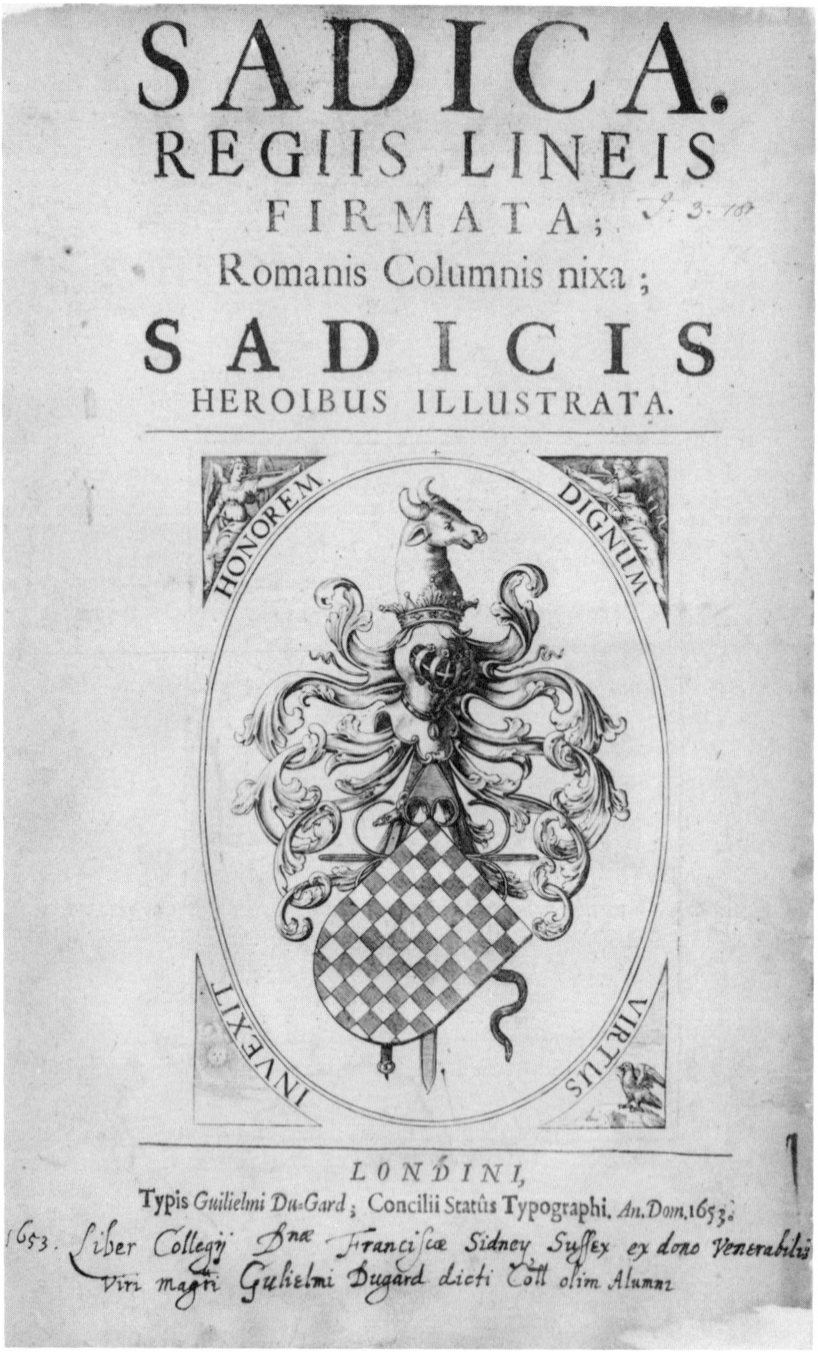

Fig. 3. Francisco de Santo Agostinho Macedo, *Sadica* (London, 1653), title-page.

Pro populo Anglicano. A copy of this was included in the gift, but was burnt 'by the King's proclamation' on the Restoration.[56] Its loss is to be regretted since it would have enabled the real Dugard edition to be distinguished from various pirate editions, something which Madan, in his article on the subject, was unable to do.[57] Fortunately there was no reason to burn one of two known copies of a history of the Portuguese family of Sa by Francisco de Santo Agostinho Macedo, chaplain to the Portuguese ambassador, which was printed by Dugard in 1653 (Fig. 3).[58]

Bush and Rasmussen, in their study of the early history of Emmanuel College library, note that it was fifty-three years before Emmanuel acquired any of the works of the philosopher and logician Petrus Ramus, which were standard texts in the early seventeenth-century Cambridge curriculum.[59] This is a powerful reminder that the individual collections of students and Fellows, as well as the holdings of the University Library, have to be considered in any analysis of the sources of information available to Sidney men in the seventeenth century. Several of the volumes cited by George Palfrey in his note-book, compiled while he was Blundell Scholar in the 1620s, do not appear to have been in the College library.[60] However, Sidney's dependence on donations, which included the working libraries of several members of the College, means that the collection provides a reliable guide to the academic concerns of various generations: the 1630s are full of ecclesiological speculations; in the 1640s very little is acquired, because of the troubles of the Great Rebellion, apart from copious literature on the Covenant and similar ephemera; in the 1650s one can detect a resurgence in biblical studies, with a new edition of the polyglot Bible and new translations. The third quarter of the century also sees a flowering of historical and antiquarian studies, often with a contemporary political message. Comparing the library left to Sidney in 1707 by Thomas Goodlad, who had entered the College as a sizar in 1661 and became a Fellow in 1666,[61] with the earlier donations of Montagu, Harington and Combe, we find not only a marked increase in the number of books printed

---

[56] MS. 91, p. 111.
[57] F.F. Madan, 'Milton, Salmasius, and Dugard', *The Library*, fourth series, 4, no. 2 (1923), pp. 119–45.
[58] Donald Wing, *Short-title Catalogue of Books printed in England . . . 1641–1700*, second edition, 3 vols (New York, 1972–88), M121B. The other copy is in the Folger Library, Washington, D.C.
[59] Sargent Bush, Jr. and Carl J. Rasmussen, *The Library of Emmanuel College, Cambridge, 1584–1637* (Cambridge, 1986), pp. 27–8.
[60] Peter Salt, in unpublished notes on the notebook, now in the possession of Sheriff Smith of Kilmarnock, identifies extracts from Franz Titelmann, *Compendium physice*; Franciscus Toletus, *Commentaria in tres libros Aristotelis de anima*; and Jacopo Zabarella, *In Aristotelis libros physicorum commentaria*.
[61] *Alumni Cantabrigienses*, Part I, II, p. 235. Goodlad's library contains several books previously belonging to Edmund Matthews (1616?–1692), another Sidney Fellow.

in England rather than abroad, but also a definite shift even in academic circles in the seventeenth century towards the use of the vernacular. It is in the library that we can most easily understand the mentality of Sidney men in the early years of the College.

Sidney's 'Errand into the Wilderness':*
The American Careers of Sidney Men in the Pre-Commonwealth Era

KARL S. GUTHKE

I

Eighteenth- and nineteenth-century demographic events such as the 'clearances' in Scotland, the potato famine in Ireland and the pogroms in Eastern Europe tend to overshadow the fact that the educated classes, too, left their mark on the profile of the peopling of North America, long before the influx of the 1848ers. Indeed, the very first generation of settlers, in both foci of immigration, Virginia and New England, is remarkable among colonial populations for its considerable component of university men. Whether 'scholars' or 'gentlemen' or both, they were determined to leave an intellectual legacy. As early as 1619, ten thousand acres were set aside for a college in Henrico, Virginia, designed to teach the Indians 'true religion and civil course of life';[1] and the college in the 'other' Cambridge bears the name of the Cantabrigian who bequeathed his more than 300 books to it in the 1630s.[2] 'These university-trained emigrants were the people who founded the intellectual traditions and scholastic standards [. . .]. They created that public opinion which insisted on sound schooling, at whatever cost; and through their own characters and lives they inculcated, among a pioneer people, a respect for learning.'[3] The earliest settlers of Virginia, from 1607 on, were cultured if nothing else, while the 'Great Migration' of some 13,000 by-and-large reasonably prosperous Puritans to New England during the 1630s included 118 university men, an estimated 85 per cent of them clergy. About three quarters of them were Cambridge graduates, and Sidney Sussex College,

---

[1] Richard L. Morton, *Colonial Virginia*, I (Chapel Hill, N.C., 1960), p. 60.
[2] For the broader context, see Frank Thistlethwaite, 'Cambridge: The Nursery of New England', *Cam*, Spring 1992, pp. 8–12.
[3] Samuel Eliot Morison, *The Founding of Harvard College* (Cambridge, Mass., 1935), p. 41.

* *A Brief Recognition of New England's Errand Into the Wilderness* was the title of the election sermon preached on 11 May 1670 by the Rev. Samuel Danforth (Cambridge, Mass., 1671): it was given wide currency by Perry Miller's book *Errand into the Wilderness* (Cambridge, Mass., 1956). I am grateful to Nicholas Rogers for helping me on my errand into the College's past.

with no fewer than four graduates coming to America in the 1630s, contributed its fair share, comparable to, say, Pembroke, Clare and King's, though not to Emmanuel, which sent no fewer than thirty-five alumni to New England by 1645, virtually all of them during the 1630s. (The total of university men emigrating to New England before 1630 and after 1640 was no more than ten.)[4]

Typically, all four Sidney men were clergymen. Yet while three of them, George Burdett, George Moxon and John Wheelwright, left Old England for the New to escape various forms of alienation and oppression of Puritans common in the pre-Commonwealth era, the fourth, Thomas Harrison, came to Virginia as a High Church man, but moved from Anglican Virginia to non-conformist Boston as a newly re-born Puritan become *persona non grata* in the colony of Cavaliers. But he was by no means the only one of the four reverends who ran afoul of religious orthodoxy. In fact, each of the other three had his difficulties with the Puritan orthodoxies which emerged rapidly in the colony designed to be the Almighty's kingdom on transatlantic Earth. Oddly enough – or perhaps not – both Virginia and New England, each in her denominationally separate way, created the same climate of religious intolerance, oppression and harassment that many of the university men had found unbearable at home, when Archbishop Laud reigned supreme, imposing Arminian 'popery' on recalcitrant Calvinists.[5] No wonder all four Sidney graduates were among those – nearly half of the intellectuals, ministers and university men who had embarked on the 'errand into the wilderness' of New England out of a sense of mission – who returned to England from 1640 on, until 1660 when the tide turned with respect to opportunities for both political action and clerical employment.[6] While around

---

[4] Virginia DeJohn Anderson, *New England's Generation: The Great Migration and the Formation of Society and Culture in the Seventeenth Century* (Cambridge, 1991), p. 15; Samuel Eliot Morison, pp. 359, 360, 362; Harry S. Stout, 'University Men in New England 1620–1660: A Demographic Analysis', *Journal of Interdisciplinary History*, 4 (1974), 377, 378. David Cressy, *Coming Over: Migration and Communication between England and New England in the Seventeenth Century* (Cambridge, 1987), speaks of seventy-six ministers emigrating in the period in question (p. 87). Also based on seventy-six clergymen, mostly Cambridge graduates, is Richard Waterhouse's 'Reluctant Emigrants: The English Background of the First Generation of the New England Puritan Clergy', *Historical Magazine of the Protestant Episcopal Church*, 44 (1975), 473–488.

[5] On the religious motives for emigration see T.H. Breen and Stephen Foster, 'Moving to the New World: The Character of Early Massachusetts Immigration', *William and Mary Quarterly*, 30 (1973), 189–222; Perry Miller, 'Religion and Society in the Early Literature of Virginia', in P.M., *Errand Into the Wilderness* (Cambridge, Mass., 1956); David Cressy, ch. 3; Virginia DeJohn Anderson, ch. 1. On Arminianism and the general political and religious background, see Conrad Russell, *The Crisis of Parliaments* (Oxford, 1971), esp. pp. 210–217.

[6] William L. Sachse, 'The Migration of New Englanders to England, 1640–1660', *American Historical Review*, 53 (1948), 251–278; Harry S. Stout, 'The Morphology of Remigration: New England University Men and Their Return to England, 1640–1660', *Journal of American Studies*, 10 (1976), 151–172; Stout (see n. 4), 382, 394–397.

1630, according to Captain Roger Clap, 'How shall we go to Heaven' was a more popular topic of discourse than 'How shall we go to England',[7] the reverse seems to have been true a decade later. By that time, Heaven had all but been established in the Boston area, but Old England was widely considered 'the more tolerant country' as one remigrant put it.[8]

In the metaphoric language of the Statutes of Sidney Sussex College, the four men I shall try to take a closer look at were no doubt the bees that swarmed the farthest from their hive in what was then still a mere extension of Bridge Street 'ita ut tandem ex Collegio, quasi alveari evolantes, novas in quibus se exonerent sedes appetant.'[9] Was it a worthwhile trip? And what manner of bees were they? Not the drones ('fuci'), surely, which the Statutes providentially included in their extended simile, but a very mixed lot, nonetheless. That is the short answer. The slightly longer one offers some curious glimpses of American frontier life, Cambridge-style.

II

Thomas Harrison arrived in North America in the very year, 1640, when back-migration of Puritans began in a statistically significant way – a symbolic coincidence perhaps, since he came as a Church of England divine; Venn, *Calamy Revised*, *Alumni Dublinenses*, Urwick's *Early History of Trinity College Dublin*, and other authorities all state or imply that he came as chaplain to Virginia's governor, the scholar and playwright Sir William Berkeley. But this is hardly possible as Berkeley did not set foot on the colonial shore until 1642, while the inhabitants of Virginia's Lower Norfolk County chose Thomas Harrison as their minister 'at a Court Held 25th May 1640', offering him an annual salary of one hundred pounds.[10] Whether he did eventually become Berkeley's chaplain, as rumour has it, is highly doubtful.[11] What is recorded is only that he was the minister of Elizabeth River Parish and later (concurrently?) of nearby Nansemond Parish from 1640 until 1648.[12] Who was he? The Sidney Sussex College Records give us a relatively full picture of his background:

---

[7] Cited from Sachse, p. 252.
[8] Sachse, p. 253.
[9] G.M. Edwards, *Sidney Sussex College* (London, 1899), p. 25; paraphrased in C.W. Scott-Giles, *Sidney Sussex College* (Cambridge, 1975), p. 25.
[10] Philip Alexander Bruce, *Institutional History of Virginia in the Seventeenth Century*, 1 (New York and London, 1910), pp. 132, 149; *Virginia Magazine of History and Biography*, 1 (1893–1894), 327. For this point, and generally, see J. and J.A. Venn, *Alumni Cantabrigienses*, 4 vols (Cambridge, 1922–27).
[11] See Francis Burton Harrison, 'The Reverend Thomas Harrison, Berkeley's "Chaplain"', *Virginia Magazine of History and Biography*, 53 (1945), 306, n. 4.
[12] Harrison, pp. 306–307; Bruce, p. 256, n. 2; Edward D. Neill, *Virginia Carolorum [. . .]. Based upon Manuscripts and Documents of the Period* (Albany, N.Y., 1886), p. 195: 'While Daniel Gookin removed from Nansemond, after the non-conformist ministers were

[1634] Thomas Harrison Eboracensis filius Roberti Harrison Mercatoris natus Kingstoniae super Hull, et ibidem literis grammaticis institutus in Schola communi sub M[agist]ro Jacobo Burney per quinquennium, dein ibidem sub M[agist]ro Antonio Stephenson per biennium adolescens annorum 16 admissus est pensionarius ad convictum Scholarium discipulorum Apr: 12. Tut. Ri. Dugard SS. Theol. Bacc. solvitq[ue] pro ingressu.[13]

According to Venn, he received his B.A. in 1638. What he did during the next two years is not known. Nor are we well informed about his doings during the early years in Virginia, other than that the Lower Norfolk County Records show that in 1645 he received a fee of one thousand pounds of tobacco, then worth five pounds sterling, for conducting the burial service over the graves of Mr. and Mrs. Sewell of Lower Norfolk and delivering a sermon in their memory.[14] By this time, however, he had done Sidney's intellectual heritage proud in a more spiritual way. In April 1645 the County Court registered a complaint against him for non-conformity. The church wardens of his parish

> have exhibited there presentment against Mr. Thomas Harrison Clark (Parson of the Said parish) for not reading the booke of Common Prayer and for not administring the Sacrament of Baptisme according to the Cannons and order prescribed and for not Catechising on Sunnedayes in the afternoone according to Act of Assembly upon wch prsentmt the Court doth order that the Said Mr. Thomas Harrison shall have notice thereof and bee Summoned by the sherriffe to make his psonall appearaunce at James Citty before the Right worrl the Governor & Counsell on the first daye of the next Quarter Court and then and there to answere to the Said prsentment.[15]

Harrison's conversion to Puritanism had a distinctly New World flavour. For it seems to have taken place under the impression of the 1644 massacre of white settlers by Indians led by Chief Opechancanough, which in Puritan circles was widely held to be God's retribution for the persecution of Puritans in Virginia.[16] By 1647, when the Virginia Assembly under Berkeley had passed an act declaring that ministers refusing to read the Book of Common Prayer were no longer entitled to receive their parishioners' tithes,[17] Harrison's position was officially

silenced, quite a congregation in that region maintained services without the Book of Common Prayer. Thomas Harrison, a minister who had been a friend of Governor Berkeley and approved of the act which had been passed requiring services to be held according to the canons of the church of England, after the Indian massacre repented of the course he had pursued, and went and preached to the Nansemond people, and avowed his sympathy with Puritanism.'

[13] MR. 30, p. 231.
[14] Bruce, p. 160.
[15] *The Lower Norfolk County Virginia Antiquary*, ed. Edward W. James, II (Baltimore, 1897), p. 12.
[16] Bruce, p. 255; Harrison, 306–307.
[17] Bruce, p. 256, n. 1; Neill, pp. 198–199. See also *The Statutes at Large; Being a Collection*

heretic. He made no bones about this himself in three letters written 1646–1648 to Massachusetts Governor John Winthrop. The initial contact between the two men is no doubt connected with the presence of three Puritan pastors from Massachusetts in Virginia, sent there by Winthrop in 1642 at the request of local dissenters, but obliged to return the following year.[18] Writing on 2 November 1646, Harrison thanks Winthrop profusely for an unspecified 'signall favour' which must indicate at least spiritual support; he also says that Winthrop has encouraged him to 'giue you an account of our matters', and assures him of his willingness to 'seke and take directions (and if you please commands) from you'.[19] On 14 January 1648 he proudly announces, amid a hodgepodge of political news from Old England, '74 haue ioyned here in Fellowship, 19 stand propounded, and many more of great hopes and expectations'.[20] At home, Charles' kingdom still, the Levellers are cause for concern, he tells the Governor of his spiritual home-in-exile province on 10 April 1648; all the more reason to rejoice that the true Kingdom lies to the West: 'Sir whether it be true or false, the Saints in these goings downe of the Sun had never more light to see why their Father hath thus farre removed them, nor ever more strong engagements to be thainkfull for it.'[21]

With these sentiments, Harrison's days in Virginia were numbered. He was banished from the colony in the summer of 1648. By October, he 'is cam to boston'.[22] As Adam Winthrop writes to his brother John, Jr at the Pequod plantation on 1 November 1648: 'Mr. Harrison the Paster of the church at verienya being banished from thence is arrived heer to consult about some place to settle him selfe and his church some thinke that youer plantation will be the fittst place for him, but I suppose you haue heard more amply before this.'[23]

Opposition against Harrison's banishment for not conforming to the Book of Common Prayer soon arose not only among Harrison's parishioners and in the Virginia Council of State but also in Cromwell's Whitehall.[24] To the latter's protest there was a staunchly loyalist reply in March, 1651: "'Tis true, indeed, Two Factious clergy men chose rather to leave the country than to take the oaths of

---

of All the Laws of Virginia . . ., ed. William Waller Hening, I (New York, 1823), pp. 277, 341.

[18] Harrison, 306; Morton, p. 151. Morton states also that one of them, William Thompson, was instrumental in converting Harrison, who had previously 'aided in expelling the Puritan ministers' (p. 152).

[19] *Winthrop Papers*, V (The Mass. Hist. Soc., 1947), 116–117.

[20] *Winthrop Papers*, V, 198.

[21] *Winthrop Papers*, V, 213.

[22] *Winthrop Papers*, V, 273. Morton reports that when Harrison appeared before the Quarter Court, the Governor and Councillors allowed him to remain three years longer in Virginia (p. 152).

[23] *Winthrop Papers*, V, 277.

[24] See the documents printed in the *Virginia Magazine of History and Biography*, 17 (1909), 19–20, 286.

Allegeance and Supremacy, and we acknowledge that we gladly parted with them'.[25]

The case was still not settled in July, 1652.[26] But by that time, Harrison could probably not have cared less. In 1651 he had assumed the ministry at Dunstan-in-the-East in London, 'a large and important parish. Oliver Cromwell was occasionally before him as he preached.'[27] Eventually, when Henry Cromwell became Commander-in-Chief of the Irish army, Harrison became his Chaplain, and his career continued with distinction until his death in Dublin in 1682.[28]

Personally, Harrison seems to have been the most pleasant of the four Sidneyans in America. According to Calamy,

> he was extreamly popular, and this stirr'd up much Envy. He was a most agreeable Preacher, and had a peculiar way of insinuating himself into the Affections of his Hearers; and yet us'd to write all that he deliver'd: and afterwards took a great deal of Pains to impress what he had committed to Writing upon his Mind, that he might in the Pulpit deliver it *Memoriter*. He had also an extraordinary Gift in Prayer; being noted for such a marvellous fluency, and peculiar Flights of Spiritual Rhetorick, suiting any particular Occasions and Circumstances, as were to the Admiration of all that knew him. He was a compleat Gentleman, much Courted for his Conversation; free with the meanest, and yet fit Company for the greatest Persons. My Lord Thomund (who had no great Respect for Ecclesiasticks of any sort) declar'd his singular value of the Doctor, and would often discover an high Esteem of his abilities. He often us'd to say, that he had rather hear Dr. Harrison say Grace over an Egg, than hear the Bishops Pray and Preach.[29]

III

It is doubtful whether George Burdett, on the other hand, could have said grace over an egg without risking scandal – as he did with everything he did, or didn't. No reference to him, whether in documents of the time or in assessments by colonial historians, fails to mention his remarkable consistency in objectionable behaviour. Perhaps this is why there is no trace of him in the Sidney Sussex College records. A discrete form of academic disowning? Still, less purist sources, Venn among them (I, 256), indulge their passion for completeness by including the man who, coming to Cambridge from Trinity College, Dublin, was admitted to

---

[25] *Virginia Magazine of History and Biography*, 5 (1898), 230.
[26] *Virg. Mag.*, 17, 286.
[27] Harrison, p. 308.
[28] For the rest of his career, see Harrison, pp. 308–311.
[29] Edmund Calamy, *An Account of the Ministers, Lecturers, Masters and Fellows of Colleges and Schoolmasters, who were Ejected or Silenced after the Restoration of 1660*, 2nd ed., II (London, 1713), p. 122.

Sidney in 1623–24 where, on an unknown date, he must have acquired the M.A. that is attributed to the troublemaker extraordinaire in reference works such as Frederick Lewis Weis, *The Colonial Clergy and the Colonial Churches of New England* (Lancaster, Mass., 1936, p. 46) and Anne Laurence, *Parliamentary Army Chaplains, 1642–1651* (Woodbridge, 1990, p. 105). Venn, to be sure, stands on academic nicety and volunteers no more than a grudging 'called M.A.', as though giving Burdett more than he deserved.

Venn's curt 'was constantly in trouble' understates the case, however, as it refers only to Burdett's years in America. As a matter of record, Burdett was well on his way to his later image while still in England. Admittedly, he was batting on a sticky wicket. For from 1632 to 1635 he was a Puritan 'Lecturer' (thus the formal designation of a 'town preacher') in Great Yarmouth[30] where, as in much of East Anglia even before the Arminian Bishop Matthew Wren of Norwich was installed in 1636 as Archbishop Laud's watch-dog, non-conformists with strong feelings about predestination versus the beneficial power of the sacraments had a particularly difficult stand, with many Puritan ministers embarking for New England from that very port.[31] Burdett's early brush with ecclesiastical authority is amply documented in the Acts of the Court of High Commission (which also reveal that in the six or so years before coming to Great Yarmouth, 1626–1632, he had been preaching in no fewer than three parishes, Brightwell, Saffron Walden, and Havering[32] – perhaps indicative of a rolling stone gathering no moss, but no sympathy either). In any case, in Great Yarmouth, the records in the Calendar of State Papers indicate, trouble flared up between the Lecturer and his Curate, Matthew Brookes, almost immediately after Burdett arrived. The charges of spiritual deviancy range from 'blasphemy' to 'raising new doctrines', from 'not bowing at the name of Jesus' to unorthodox views on redemption and Communion, from which he wished to exclude whoremongers and drunkards. (He was himself accused of being at least one of these later.) The Court of High Commission suspended him in February 1635. By July that year 'his poor wife' petitioned for an annuity for the support of herself and their children, her husband 'being gone for New England'.[33]

Burdett had sailed to Salem, Massachusetts, from where in December that year he wrote to Laud complaining about the circumstances leading to his 'voluntary

---

[30] Paul S. Seaver, *The Puritan Lectureships: The Politics of Religious Dissent, 1560–1662* (Stanford, Cal., 1970); on Burdett, p. 40.
[31] See R.W. Ketton-Cremer, *Norfolk in the Civil War* (London, 1969), ch. 4; Norman C.P. Tyack, 'The Humbler Puritans of East Anglia and the New England Movement: Evidence from the Court Records of the 1630s', *The New England Historical and Genealogical Register*, 138 (1984), 79–106; references to Burdett on pp. 80 and 90.
[32] See Henry A. Parker's gathering, from the Calendars of State Papers, of all entries in the Acts of the Court of High Commission concerning Burdett in *Publications of the Colonial Society of Massachusetts*, 8 (1906), 359–373; p. 367 on Burdett's pre-Yarmouth positions.
[33] Ibid., p. 371; on Burdett's unorthodox views and suspension, see ibid., pp. 360–369.

exile'.[34] This is interesting in connection with a later letter (1638) to the Archbishop of Canterbury which has given rise not only to the accusation that he was Laud's emissary, spying on the unorthodoxies of New England, but also that he had only 'pretended' to quarrel with the ecclesiastical authorities at home in order to be all the safer in his contemplated subversive role overseas.[35] While the Court records leave no doubt about his protracted conflict with his ecclesiastical superiors in Laudian England, there is no denying that the man who was 'held in high esteem' in Puritan Salem, where he was admitted as a freeman of the colony and given a piece of land 'upon the rock beyond Mr. Endecott's fence',[36] did ingratiate himself to the arch enemy of all Puritans a little later. This was after he had moved, again as a preacher, in 1637, to the settlement called Pascataqua[ck], now Dover, New Hampshire. From this safe haven he denounced Massachusetts in 1638 in at least three letters to Archbishop Laud for unorthodox thinking and seditious plotting.[37] Somehow John Winthrop, the Governor of Massachusetts (already nettled by 'a scornful answer' he had received earlier that year from Burdett in reply to his remonstrances about Pascataquack harbouring residents 'we had cast out'),[38] got wind of the matter, and a serious matter it was, 'discovering what they [Burdett and an associate] knew of our combination to resist any authority, that should come out of England against us'.[39] As Winthrop explained the case himself,

> one of Pascataquack, having opportunity to go into Mr. Burdet his study, and finding there the copy of his letter to the archbishops, sent it to the governour, which was to this effect: That he did delay to go into England, because he would fully inform himself of the state of the people here in regard

[34] Ibid., p. 371.
[35] See A.H. Quint's *Historical Memoranda* as quoted in the *Publ. of the Col. Soc. of Mass.*, VIII, 358 ('pretended quarrel'); Jeremy Belknap, *The History of New-Hampshire* (Boston, 1792), I, 33–34 ('either really or pretendedly taking offence').
[36] Sidney Perley, *The History of Salem, Massachusetts* (Salem, 1924), p. 296, quoting and paraphrasing town records. William Hubbard notes in *A General History of New England* (Boston, 1848): he came 'to Salem, where he was received a member of their church, and was employed to preach amongst them for a year or more, being an able scholar, and of plausible parts and carriage. But finding the discipline of the church as much too strict for his loose conscience, as the other was, in pretence, too large, he left his brethren at Salem, out of love to his friends at Pascataqua, where he continued for some time in good esteem (as least in appearance) with Mr. Wiggans, that had the power of a Governour thereabouts, until he declared himself of what sort he was' (p. 353). There is a similar account in Belknap, I, 34.
[37] See excerpts in William D. Williamson, *The History of the State of Maine* (Hallowell, 1832), I, 270; John Gorham Palfrey, *History of New England* (Boston, 1859), I, 518; Thomas Hutchinson, *The History of the Colony and Province of Massachusetts-Bay*, ed. L.S. Mayo (Cambridge, Mass., 1936), I, 77.
[38] John Winthrop, *The History of New England from 1630 to 1649*, ed. James Savage, I (Boston, 1825), p. 276; cp. p. 291.
[39] Ibid., I, 281.

of allegiance; and that it was not discipline that was now so much aimed at, as sovereignty; and that it was accounted [perjury] and treason in our general courts to speak of appeals to the king.

The first ships, which came this year, brought him letters from the archbishops and the lords commissioners for plantations, wherein they gave him thanks for his care of his majesty's service, &c. and that they would take a time to redress such disorders as he had informed them of, &c. but, by reason of the much business now lay upon them, they could not, at present, accomplish his desire. These letters lay above fourteen days in the bay, and some moved the governour to open them; but himself and others of the council thought it not safe to meddle with them, nor would take any notice of them; and it fell out well, by God's good providence; for the letters (by some means) were opened, (yet without any of their privity or consent,) and Mr. Burdett threatened to complain of it to the lords; and afterwards we had knowledge of the contents of them by some of his own friends.[40]

But Burdett seems to have been a man of such irrepressible propensity for making enemies that even without the Laud/Winthrop connection he managed to make himself unpopular in Dover almost from the start. 'He aspired to be a sort of Pope', one local historian says.[41] If not pope, then at least spiritual and administrative leader, preacher and 'governor'. Historians disagree on whether Burdett's personal failings contributed to his leaving Dover after no more than two years (see n. 41 and n. 37). In any case, by 1639 he had once again changed places and provinces: he now served as minister[42] in Agamenticus, Maine (presently York), and here the scandal which appears to have been brewing just below the surface of earlier documents broke out with full fury.

'It would seem that he no longer preached', in the judgment of the distinguished Massachusetts historian Charles Francis Adams, based on a variety of early accounts, 'as, selecting for his companions "the wretchedest people of the country", he passed his leisure time "in drinkinge, dauncinge [and] singinge scurrulous songes." He had, in fact, "let loose the reigns of liberty to his lusts, [so] that he grew very notorious for his pride and adultery". At Agamenticus, also, Deputy-Governor Gorges found the Lords Proprietors' buildings, – which had cost a large sum of money, and were intended to serve as a sort of government house, – not only dilapidated but thoroughly stripped, "nothing of his household-stuff remaining but an old pot, a pair of tongs, and a couple of cob-irons".'[43]

The *Province and Court Records of Maine* do indeed paint a picture of the final

---

[40] Ibid., I, 298. See also Belknap, I, 34–35.
[41] George Wadleigh, *Notable Events in the History of Dover, New Hampshire, from the First Settlement in 1623 to 1865* (Dover, N.H., 1913), p. 14; cp. p. 15. See also John Scales, *Historical Memoranda Concerning Persons and Places in Old Dover, N.H.* (Dover, N.H., 1900), pp. 17–18, 25–26.
[42] *Province and Court Records of Maine*, I (Portland, Me., 1928), p. 74.
[43] *Three Episodes of Massachusetts History* (Boston and New York, 1892), I, 310–311. The quotation at the end is from Hubbard, p. 361.

stage of Burdett's errand into the wilderness which is not pretty, but all the more colourful. Whilst his offences in Dover, according to Governor Winthrop, included, at least by implication, doctrinal deviations, the court in Saco, Maine, in 1640 dealt with more this-worldly issues. Burdett brought at least three suits of slander against some of his neighbours who alleged sexual escapades with one George Puddington's wife 'and that his bed was usually tumbled' (I, 71). In the event, he was 'indicted by the whole bench for a man of ill name and fame, infamous for incontinency, a publisher and broacher of divers dangerous speeches the better to seduce that weake sex of women to his incontinent practises' and fined a total of forty-five pounds for 'entertaining' Mrs. Puddington, breaking the peace and 'deflowring Ruth the wife of John Gouch' (I, 74–75). By 9 September 1640 he is already the 'late minister of Agamenticus' (I, 77), and the last we hear about him in the records is: 'Richard Colt sworne and examined saith that he heard John Baker say he heard John Gouch say that he was minded to shoote Mr. Burdett, but that his wife perswaded him to the contrary, and further that he heard the said Baker say that he thought the said John Gouch carryed a pistoll in his pockett to shoote Mr. Burdett' (I, 80).

Winthrop thought he had the last word: 'Upon this Mr. Burdett went into England, but when he came there he found the state so changed, as his hopes were frustrated, and he, after taking part with the cavaliers, was committed to prison.'[44] But there was life after prison. Under Charles II, Burdett became Chancellor and Dean of the diocese of Leighlin, Ireland.

IV

From the most obnoxious to the least troublesome – George Moxon, whose entry in Sidney's Admissions Register (MR. 30) reads:

> Georgius Moxon Eboracensis filius Jacobi Moxon agricolae, natus in paroecia de Wakefield, educatus ibidem in publico literaru[m] ludo sub praeceptore Mro. Izack per annu[m] adolescens annu[m] aetatis agens decimu[m] octauu[m]: admissus est in Collegium pauper scholaris Junij 6. 1620. Tutore & fideiussore Mro. Bell. (P. 159)

According to Venn (I:3,225), he received his B.A. in 1624, was ordained in 1626 and appointed to the perpetual curacy of St Helen's, Chester. Perpetual was a respectable dozen years; not until 1637 was he cited for non-conformity over disuse of the ceremonies, and he lost no time embarking from Bristol in disguise. He turned up in Dorchester, near Boston, the same year. Here Moxon was admitted as a freeman on 7 September.[45] Very soon thereafter, William Pynchon,

---

[44] *History of New England*, II, 10.
[45] *Calamy Revised*. There is a brief account of Moxon's career in James Moxon, *The Moxons*

the founder of the trading post in Springfield, then called Agawam, must have persuaded Moxon to join his year-old Puritan settlement and spread the gospel in the Wild West of Massachusetts. He arrived early in 1638 'at the season of general thanksgiving through New England at the overthrow of the Pequots'. By 'the spring of 1638 it had been voted that the expenses of fencing his home-lot on the main street and of building his house should fall upon those who might join the plantation thereafter'.[46] From then on, until Moxon's return to England in 1652, one hears nothing but his praises sung. His 'sermons were of love', if on the curiously pragmatic ground that 'we are in a new country, and here we must be happy, for if we are not happy ourselves we cannot make others happy'.[47] 'Others' do not seem to have included the Indians, though, for the Rev. Moxon is on record as having opined that 'an Indian promise is noe more than to have a pigg by the taile'.[48] With this exception, his charity was boundless, for in his sermons he would cover 'about all that could be said upon his subject, dividing and subdividing his topic with reckless prodigality of time' – with the then predictable result that, as Pynchon wrote to Governor Winthrop in 1644, 'the Lord has greately blessed mr. Moxons ministry'.[49] And to this day the fat little man remains fixed in local memory as he was described in a poetical portrait written shortly after his return to England:

> As thou with strong and able parts are made,
> The person stout, with toyle and labor shall,
> With help of Christ, through difficulties wade.[50]

Difficulties he did have in Western Massachusetts. In part they were of this world, such as the suit for unspecified slander brought by Moxon against one John Woodcock in December, 1639, in which he demanded £9 19s in damages and, with three of his witnesses sitting on the jury, due to the scarcity of upright citizens in what was then 'the interior', got no more than £6 13s 4d, even though Woodcock declared that he was ready to repeat the offence.[51] Spiritual malaise erupted when both of Moxon's daughters started having 'fits', which suggested traffic with the devil. For while tiny, the outpost was not small enough not to have a male witch in residence, Hugh Parsons, he of the red coat, who was tried

---

of Yorkshire (Ludlow, Shrops., 1987), pp. 20–21, 91–93. My own account is based on the sources indicated.
[46] Mason A. Green, *Springfield, 1636–1886* (Springfield, 1888), pp. 17, 43.
[47] Harry Andrew Wright, *The Story of Western Massachusetts* (New York, 1949), I, 134.
[48] Green, p. 26.
[49] Green, pp. 76–77; *Winthrop Papers*, IV (The Mass. Hist. Soc., 1944), 443.
[50] *First Church of Christ 1637–1937*, published by The Three Hundredth Anniversary Committee, Springfield, Massachusetts, 1937, section entitled 'The Church and its Ministers'. There is a commemorative article on Moxon in the *Springfield Union* of 11 May 1987 where he is made out to have been 'as popular with English monarchs as a Marxist might be with Ronald Reagan' (p. 13). This is meant to be praise.
[51] Green, p. 53.

for witchcraft in Boston in 1651 along with his wife, Mary. Still, by this time Moxon was well enough ensconced spiritually to weather the storm. A forty-foot long meeting house had been built for his congregation in 1645, and the following year 'it was agreed with John Matthews to beat the drum for the meetings at 10 of the clock on lecture days and at 9 of the clock on the Lord's days, in the forenoon only, from Mr. Moxon's to Rowland Stebins – from near Vernon Street to Union Street, and for which "he is to have 6 pence in wampum, of every family, or a pick of Indian corn, if they have not wampum" '.[52]

Real – and that meant doctrinal in Massachusetts at the time – 'difficulty' did however loom large at about the time when the Parsons were tried for witchcraft in Boston. Moxon's sponsor and mentor, the local squire William Pynchon, no mean theologian himself, had published a book in 1650 entitled *The Meritorious Price of Our Redemption, Justification,* etc. The General Court of Massachusetts had the book burned as heretical and directed the author to appear at its next meeting, 14 October 1651, to retract his errors. Pynchon and his wife left the colony instead, sometime in 1652. 'With them went the Reverend George Moxon [whose Puritan orthodoxy had been officially suspect to Boston divines as early as 1649][53] who, as Pynchon's sympathizer and spiritual adviser, must have known that his turn to be questioned, censured, and ejected would come next.'[54]

Moxon's afterlife in England was auspicious at first: he shared the Rectory of Astbury, Cheshire, with one George Machin and was made Assistant-Commissioner to the 'Triers', the examining board for prospective ministers appointed by Cromwell to make sure that candidates did not encourage dancing or play-acting, or speak irreverently of Puritans.[55] His luck did not outlast the Commonwealth by long, however. When the Act of Uniformity was passed in 1662, Moxon was removed from his post. The once popular minister was now reduced to preaching in barns and farmhouses. But there must have been consolation in the fact that he lived to see James II's declaration of liberty of conscience, though he did not live to inaugurate the meeting house built for his congregation at Congleton, in the parish of Astbury.

V

Sidney's graduate in America who looms largest in the early history of New England was the one of the four who returned to England only briefly, for a few years during the Commonwealth and early Restoration, and then all the more firmly transplanted himself to the New World, dying on the edge of the wilderness

---

[52] Henry M. Burt, *The First Century of the History of Springfield: The Official Records from 1636 to 1736,* I (Springfield, Mass., 1898), pp. 144–145.
[53] See the document reprinted in Green, p. 111.
[54] Samuel Eliot Morison, *Builders of the Bay Colony* (Boston, 1964), p. 374.
[55] J.E. Gordon Cartlidge, *Newbold-Astbury and Its History* (Congleton, 1915), p. 90.

and leaving a family tree of descendants which flourishes to this day.[56] This was John Wheelwright, the son of a Lincolnshire yeoman, born two years before the founding of the College to which he was admitted on 28 April 1611 as a 'Pensionar[ius]',[57] earning his B.A. in 1614–15 and his M.A. in 1618, according to Venn. Ordained the following year, his career was true to form: suspended from his position as vicar at Bilsby, Lincs., in 1632, for alleged simony – which may have been his bishop's way of getting rid of a nonconformist such as Wheelwright is assumed to have been (by Venn and others) – he left Old England for Massachusetts in 1636 after a brief spell as preacher at Belleau, Lincs.[58] Whatever may ultimately have triggered his emigration, it was probably not the re-issue of the *Book of Sports* in 1633, which encouraged sports on the sabbath and drove many Puritans to distraction, or to Massachusetts.[59] For one of the most enduring Sidney anecdotes has it, as Cotton Mather reported to George Vaughan, 'that [...] waiting on Cromwell, with whom he had been contemporary at the University, Cromwell declared to the gentlemen about him "that he could remember the time when he had been more afraid of meeting Wheelwright at *football*, than of meeting any army since in the field; for he was infallibly sure of being *tript up* by him" '.[60]

In Boston, where he arrived on 26 May 1636, Wheelwright was tripped up himself soon enough in the field of Puritan doctrinal tackling which was just then hastening the climax of the game. While readily accepted into the Boston church and given the newly formed parish in the then somewhat outlying southern suburb of Mount Wollaston (now semi-metropolitan Braintree), this none too soft-spoken gentleman of the cloth was hardly off the boat before he got himself embroiled in the Antinomian controversy and, considering himself as Puritan as the next victim of English conformism, ran afoul of the Puritan orthodoxy which had in the meantime developed its own formula of indictable nonconformism on its virgin soil, which included Antinomianism. Leaving no hair unsplit, the Antinomians, most prominently Wheelwright's voluble sister-in-law Ann Hutchinson, took the position that the real evidence of being 'elected' by the Lord was not wealth and model civic and moral behaviour, including good works, but the regenerate Christian's spiritual certainty – something like a personal revelation of grace – which allowed the true believer to neglect sine-qua-non features of Puritan life such as church-attendance and Indian massacres.[61] Wheelwright came

---

[56] See the afterword in John Heard, Jr., *John Wheelwright, 1592–1679* (Boston, 1930). See also note 58 below. Wheelwright's year of birth is a matter of disagreement.
[57] MR. 30, p. 144.
[58] See Edmund M. Wheelwright, 'A Frontier Family', *Publ. of the Col. Soc. of Mass.*, 1 (1895), 271–272; Belleau: acc. to Venn; see also Charles H. Bell, *Memoir of John Wheelwright* (Cambridge, Mass., 1876).
[59] See Waterhouse, p. 483.
[60] Jeremy Belknap, *The History of New-Hampshire*, III, 339.
[61] There is a vast body of literature on this subject. I mention only Emery Battis, *Saints and*

under official scrutiny in January 1637, after he preached a fast-day sermon in Boston in which he belligerently charged the ruling authorities with supporting a covenant of works rather than inner certainty of election. The General Court found him guilty of sedition and contempt of authority (right after settling a dispute about damage done by imported goats to neighbours' crops) and later in the year disfranchised and 'banished' him from the Bay Colony. He was given '14 dayes to settle his affaires', whilst all those merely suspected of the Antinomian heresy were ordered to hand over 'all such guns, pistols, swords, powder, shot, & match as they shalbee owners of' and one Rolfe Mousall, charged with having spoken 'in approbation of Mr. Wheelwright, was dismissed from being a member of the Courte'.[62]

In November 1637 Wheelwright left for New Hampshire with a group of followers and became one of the founders of what is now Exeter. One of the attractions of the remote place must have been that since 1635 that colony 'had been without any central government'.[63] By the same token, when in 1643 Exeter came under the jurisdiction of Massachusetts, Wheelwright moved again, this time to Wells, Maine, perhaps the most outlying part of the New England wilderness. His voice, however, was heard here as he took his principal parishioners with him. Indeed, they became a sort of local aristocracy,[64] if a tree-felling and log-cabin-building one. Whether it was the terminal boredom of this pioneer place or a surprise insight into his doctrinal error, we shall never know: in any case, in 1643, in two letters to Governor Winthrop, Wheelwright announced a change of heart about his Antinomianism, humbly requesting him to 'pardon my boldness'.[65] As a result, he had 'his banishmte taken offe, & is reced in agayne as a membr of this colony', the General Court of Massachusetts decreed the following year.[66]

If Wheelwright's remorse was calculation rather than middle-age mellowing, it did not bear fruit immediately. It was not until 1647 that he was called to serve the Bay Colony again, at Hampton on the North Shore, and then only as an assistant to the pastor, as a mere 'help in the worke of the Lord with [. . .] Mr

---

Sectaries: Ann Hutchinson and the Antinomian Controversy in the Massachusetts Bay Colony (Chapel Hill, N.C., 1962) and Ronald D. Cohen, 'Church and State in Seventeenth-Century Massachusetts: Another Look at the Antinomian Controversy', *Journal of Church and State*, 12 (1970), 475–494.

[62] *Records of the Governor and Company of the Massachusetts Bay in New England*, ed. Nathaniel B. Shurtleff, I (Boston, 1853), pp. 189, 207, 211, 236. For a contemporary account see John Winthrop's *The History of New England from 1630 to 1649* (see n. 38 above), I, 215–246. See also Heard, ch. 5.

[63] Charles E. Clark, *The Eastern Frontier: The Settlement of Northern New England, 1610–1763* (Hanover, N.H., 1983), p. 39.

[64] See Charles H. Bell, *History of the Town of Exeter* (Exeter, 1888), chapters 1 and 2; Edward E. Bourne, *The History of Wells and Kennebunk* (Portland, Maine, 1875), chapters 1–5.

[65] Winthrop, *The History of New England*, II (1826), pp. 162–164.

[66] *Records of Mass. Bay*, III (Boston, 1854), p. 6.

Dalton our prsent & faithfull Teacher', as the contract specifies, which also assured him of a house-lot, a farm, and £40 per annum.[67] In 1656 or 1657 Wheelwright left for England for what turned out to be no more than an extended interlude during which he met with his erstwhile college antagonist on the football field, 'with whom', he wrote to his Hampton parishioners on 20 April 1658, 'I had discourse in private about the space of an hour', arguably not limited to prowess in sports, as 'all his [Cromwell's] speeches seemed to me very orthodox and gracious'.[68]

So were Wheelwright's by this time. His own church gave him a clean bill of doctrinal health. When in 1654 the pillars of Hampton saw fit to protest to the General Court that Wheelwright was being accused unfairly of heretical beliefs in Boston, they stated that he 'hath for these many years approved himself a sound, orthodox, and profitable minister of the gospel', and the General Court heartily agreed.[69]

After the Restoration the attraction of New England became irresistible once again. In 1662 we find Wheelwright tending a Puritan flock in Salisbury, in Northern Massachusetts. Though he was at least close to retirement age by now, some of his belligerence was still virulent, or perhaps it re-emerged in the form of the last-chance radicalism of the elderly. His relationship with the Magistrate of Salisbury, whom he excommunicated early on and then had to take back into the fold, was an armed truce at best. 'Another argument between Pike [the Magistrate] and Wheelwright began on a Sunday evening when Pike was on his way to Boston. It was winter and he knew it would be a long trip. Pike was a Deputy of the General Court and had to be in Boston on Monday morning. Therefore, he decided to get an early start. As soon as the sun went down he started on his journey. After crossing the river though, the sun came back out. Reverend Wheelwright had Pike arrested for working on a Sunday, which was against the law. He accused Pike of knowing it was just a cloud passing over. Pike was fined ten shillings.'[70]

Such was life on the religious frontier. And Wheelwright made the most of it, plodding on in the service of the Lord until he was gathered to his spiritual fathers in 1679, in his mid-eighties then, but apparently still vigorously unretired, and the Salisbury Sabbath inviolate, changeable weather notwithstanding.

---

[67] Joseph Dow, *History of the Town of Hampton, New Hampshire* (Salem, Mass. 1893), p. 352.
[68] Ibid., p. 363.
[69] Dow, p. 281; *Records of Mass. Bay*, III, 344.
[70] Carolyn Sargent, *Salisbury History* (Newburyport, Mass., 1991), pp. 3–4.

VI

It was rather a mixed lot of pioneering bees, then, that swarmed to the then end of the world from the then far end of Bridge Street. What they said or did, or didn't say or didn't do, raised eye-brows then and adds colour in retrospect. But, of course, such human shortcomings and foibles were the very foundation on which the Puritan theocracy of New England was built. Nobody this side of saintliness, not even a Cambridge-trained cleric, was excepted from that civic, moral and doctrinal policing which such weaknesses and imperfections made so irresistibly desirable and which, in those early years, was the signal feature that distinguished New England from other British colonies. Still, though *nil humani* was missing in the four Sidney graduates, one thing not one of them was accused of was lax scholarship. Their *alma mater* need not disown them.

The Posthumous History of Oliver Cromwell's Head

CHRISTOPHER PARISH

The last lines of a fourth leader in *The Times* of 13 October 1960 read as follows: 'the most fervent royalist must surely feel ashamed for the indignities that were then inflicted on the dead, and be glad to think that at last this pitiful head lies easy that never wore a crown'. The reference relates to a committal service which took place at 12.30 p.m. on 25 March 1960 in the precincts of Sidney Sussex College Chapel, Cambridge when an embalmed human head, transfixed by a metal spike on a wooden pole, was buried in the presence of the Master (Dr David Thomson), the College Chaplain (the Rev. J. Murray Irvine), Mr J.W.A. Thornely, Professor D.E.D. Beales, Professor T.M. Charlton and Dr H.N.S. Wilkinson (the donor of the head) and his sister, Miss Wilkinson. There is strong evidence for believing that it was the head of the most famous son of Sidney, Oliver Cromwell, Lord Protector of the Commonwealth (who entered Sidney as a Fellow Commoner on 23 April 1616).[1] Cromwell still has passionate admirers who think of him as 'the finest type of middle class Englishman' or 'the greatest Englishman of all time' as well as fervent enemies who consider him 'a hypocritical tyrant'. This is not the place to debate his position in history, but it is an opportunity to record some facts about the story of the mortal remains of Cromwell between the time of his death on 3 September 1658 and 25 March 1960.

The Gazette (No. 432 (801)) of 2–9 September 1658 records that

> His most serene and renowned Highness, Oliver Lord Protector, being after a sickness of about fourteen days (which appeared an ague in the beginning) reduced to a very low condition of body, began early this morning to draw near the gates of death, and it pleased God about three o'clock afternoon to put a period to his life.

The post mortem examination by Dr George Bates (physician to Charles I, Cromwell and Charles II) on the day of Cromwell's death is fully described in

---

[1] Except where otherwise stated, the evidence cited in this article comes from the remarkable study by Karl Pearson and G.M. Morant, *The Portraiture of Oliver Cromwell with Special Reference to the Wilkinson Head* (Biometrika, Cambridge, 1935). See Plate 6.

Bates's *Elenchi Motuum Nuperorum in Anglia* (London, 1663), p. 217. The translation by A. Lovell in 1685 is as follows:

> His body being opened; in the Animal parts, the vessels of the Brain seemed to be overcharged; in the Vitals, the Lungs a little inflamed; but in the Natural the source of the distemper appeared, the Spleen though sound to the Eye, being filled with matter like to the Lees of Oyl. Nor was that incongruous to the Disease that for a long time he had been subject unto, seeing that for at least thirty years he had at times heavily complained of Hypochondriacal indispositions . . .

George Bates, a chameleon-like character who changed his disposition to suit the times, was born in Maids Moreton, Bucks, and educated from the age of fourteen at New College, Oxford. It was rumoured by his friends that he brought about the premature death of Cromwell by poison and that this led to his reappointment at the Restoration and his election as a Fellow of the Royal Society!

Mercurius Politicus of 4 October 1658 states that Cromwell's body was embalmed on 4 September. In order to examine the brain, Bates must have sawn off the top of the skull, a technique described in 1615 by Philbert Guibert, a physician in Paris. Thus Cromwell's head at his burial must have had a covering of embalmed skin and a reattached cranial cap. The account of Cromwell's autopsy parallels that of James I in 1625 in that the cranial cap was removed in both cases, the bowels were put in a leaden vessel and buried and the bodies of both were embalmed. Cromwell's state funeral followed the pattern of that of James I in every respect.

Two and a half weeks after his death, his body was taken from Whitehall to Somerset House on 20 September 1658 on a hearse drawn by six horses. A formal lying in state ensued, followed by a standing in state representing purgatory followed by heaven; some thought this to be a popish practice. Burial eventually took place in the Henry VII Chapel of Westminster Abbey on the morning of 27 October 1658, eight weeks after Cromwell's death. Edward Burroughes, a Quaker, protested in a pamphlet against the later state funeral without a body. On 23 November 1658, at a cost of £60,000, the state funeral took place with some 9,000 in the procession, the wax effigy from the lying in state being placed in the chancel in the Abbey. There were no candles, no prayers and no sermons or orations. Only the trumpets were sounded.

On 25 May 1659 Richard Cromwell abdicated and exactly a year later Charles II landed in England. The task of revenge began. Hugh Peters (Cromwell's Chaplain), Col. Harrison and John Cook were hung, drawn and quartered. Peters was forced to watch Cook's execution and Harrison was dragged on a hurdle to the gallows.[2]

On 6 December 1660 the House of Commons ordered the exhumation and

---

[2] Sir George Wharton, *Gesta*.

hanging 'in their coffins' of Cromwell, Bradshaw, Ireton and Pride. On the same day they passed a Bill against profane cursing and swearing!

On Saturday 26 January 1661, John Lewis, a mason, was paid fifteen shillings by the Worshipful Sergeant Norfolke of the Herald's office for the exhumations of Cromwell and Ireton, whose bodies were taken to the Red Lion at Holborn. Bradshaw was exhumed on Tuesday 29 January 1661. On Wednesday 30 January 1661, the anniversary of the execution of Charles I twelve years earlier, all three bodies were taken on sledges to Tyburn and there hung up (but not in their coffins). Sainthill, a Spanish merchant, described the gruesome scene:

> Oliver Cromwell in a green cerecloth [Bates had wrapped it in four layers of cerecloth] very fresh embalmed. Bradshaw in his winding sheet, the fingers of his right hand and nose perished. Of his toes, I had five or six in my hand which the 'prenties had cut off. Ireton like a dried rat, corrupt about the fundament.

At sunset, the bodies were taken down and the heads cut off. It was not surprising that it took eight blows to sever Cromwell's head, since it was covered by embalmed skin and eight levels of cerecloth. Nor is it surprising to find damage to the nose and front teeth after eight blows in the prone position. The following day, 31 January 1661, all three heads were set up on poles on the top of the south end of Westminster Hall immediately above the single-story State Treasury, which was guarded by troops. Ten years later, Dr Charles Patin of Paris recorded the heads still *in situ*. Twenty-four years on, in 1684, *The London Gazette* stated that Sir Thomas Armstrong's head was put up between Cromwell's and Bradshaw's.

From 1684 to 1710 the evidence is anecdotal. In November 1688 there was a great storm. Dutch William was landing in England. James II was trembling, and probably so was Private Barnes of Lord Arlington's regiment, who, being on duty at the Treasury, was surprised when Cromwell's head with the broken pole and transfixion spike dropped at his feet. Taking it home he hid it in a chimney, fearful of disclosure after hearing of the Earl Marshal's threat of severe punishment for the possessor of the head. On his deathbed in 1702 he told his daughter about the head. Whether she sold it to Claudius Du Puy, a French-Swiss calico printer, we do not know, but in a diary written by Count von Uffenbach we have a description of Cromwell's *head* (not a skull) in the second room of a museum of curiosa kept by Du Puy. Von Uffenbach visited several Cambridge libraries, including that at Sidney, and his records of their contents are supremely accurate. We can, therefore, accept his evidence of the head on his visit in 1710. Du Puy, a bachelor, died intestate on 11 August 1758 leaving his four-room collection of humming birds, marine animals, waxworks, musical instruments, strange footwear, etc. Uffenbach's description clearly states that a wooden shaft was piercing the head.

Again there is a gap in the story, until 1775 at the latest. Dr Elliston, Master of Sidney (1760–1807), dined with William Samuel Powell, Master of St John's (1765–1775). Powell in his diary records that Elliston told him that he had been offered the head of Oliver Cromwell – this must have happened before the death of Powell in 1775. The offer was made by a comedian named Russell. Why? Elliston was the son of a farmer in Orford, Suffolk. His brother, Robert, was a Bloomsbury watchmaker. Robert's son, Robert William, was educated by his uncle, the Master of Sidney. Robert William ran away and became an actor at Bath under the management of Samuel Thomas Russell at the Surrey Theatre. Samuel Thomas's father was an impecunious comedian. Robert William Elliston probably advised Russell's father to approach his uncle at Sidney. He did so and was refused. In 1775 Southgate, the numismatist and librarian of the British Museum, said the head was like Cromwell's when he was shown it. John Kirk the medallist said it was like the Cooper portrait (now in the Hall at Sidney). Russell, the comedian, borrowed money from Cox, a London jeweller in 1780. Cox reclaimed his loan in 1787 and took the head in part exchange for the sum of £118. (The deed of exchange is in the Sidney Muniment Room.) A newspaper account says that Sir Joshua Reynolds borrowed the head and showed it to George III. (Reynolds's wife was a descendant of the Cromwells.) Cox eventually sold the head to three brothers, named Hughes, for £230. They exhibited it in Mead Court, Old Bond Street, in 1799, charging two shillings and sixpence for admission. The exhibition was a failure and all the papers connected with the head went to John Cranch (1751–1821), an antiquary from Devon, who had drawn up a brochure for the exhibition and painted an oil portrait of the head. Both are now in the possession of the College. The painting and the copperplate sketch of the head on the brochure are accurate portrayals of the head which was buried in 1960. About 1814, Josiah Henry Wilkinson purchased the head and in an account written in 1827 he relates the tradition of the head falling at the feet of the sentinel on the parapet outside Westminster Hall, its concealment in the chimney, the hue and cry and the deathbed disclosure. J. H. Wilkinson showed the head to Maria Edgeworth in 1822. In her letter of 9 March 1822 she says:

> ... but to go back to our breakfast ... we saw – What do you think? Oliver Cromwell's head – not his picture – nothing of stone or marble or plaister of Paris, but his real head ... This head as he well observed is the only head on record which has after death been subject to the extremes of horror and infamy ...

In 1857, Dr Stanley, Dean of Westminster, examined and described the head. Dr Rolleston, Professor of Anatomy at Oxford, asked to see the head and stated that the skull (not head) in the Ashmolean Museum was not authentic. In 1898 Canon Wilkinson received a letter from Mrs Bond, a poor widow in America, offering the Cranch portrait, the Russell-Cox deed and other papers including the brochure, for £10. The offer was accepted and they returned across the Atlantic which they had crossed when Cranch in his old age had gone to live with his granddaughter in the U.S.A. The Royal Archaeological Institute exhibited the head in 1911.

This brings us to the donation of the head by Dr H.N.S. Wilkinson to Sidney Sussex College in 1960. Much of the story so far is to be found in a very scholarly work by Karl Pearson, F.R.S. and G.M. Morant, D.Sc. entitled *The Portraiture of Oliver Cromwell with Special Reference to the Wilkinson Head*, published by Biometrika in 1935 and printed by Cambridge University Press. They compared the facial measurements on the Wilkinson Head with those on the death and life masks and on the busts of Cromwell. They took nineteen measurements of the Chequers Life Mask, the Ashmolean Death Mask, the distorted Ashmolean Mask, the British Museum Wax Mask, the modified Museum Mask, the Florence Bust, the Ashmolean Bust and the King's College Bust. Taking the mean of all these measurements and comparing them with the Wilkinson Head figures, they stated that 'the accordance between the mean of the masks and bust and the Wilkinson Head is astonishing'. 'We can find no external characters, nor any measurements which we have found it possible to take, which contradict the hypothesis that the Head is that of Cromwell.' The gaps in the history hinder conclusive proof that it is Cromwell's. But Pearson and Morant conclude:

> We started this inquiry in an agnostic frame of mind, tinged only with scepticism as to whether the positive statements made in the past with regard to it were not based solely on impressions unjustified by any attempt at a scientific investigation. We finish our inquiry with the conclusion that the Wilkinson Head is the genuine head of Oliver Cromwell, Protector of the Commonwealth.

The question arises about the possibility of the head being a forgery. Could Cox have forged it and therefore the Russell-Cox deed? The British Museum Manuscripts Department attested the deed as genuine. If the head is a forgery, why did those responsible damage the lips, the nose, the teeth and the ear? An undamaged head would have been more acceptable as Cromwell's. The worm holes through the embalmed skin and jaw tissue would be almost impossible to fabricate. If it was not Cromwell's, whose head was it? A man of his age who was subject to a post-mortem examination, an embalmment, a decapitation and an exhibition on a spike. If someone other than Cromwell fitted the detailed analysis undertaken by Pearson and Morant, surely historical evidence could be produced to identify him. None is forthcoming. All the evidence of the way that the head was treated after death points to its being that of a personage of the very highest degree. It is difficult to think of any other contender than Oliver Cromwell.

All this leaves the problem of the disposal of his body after Tyburn. Was it simply deposited in a pit below the gallows? In *Short Meditations on . . . the Life and Death of Oliver Cromwell* (1661) it is said that he 'hath no other Tombe but a Turf under Tyburn'. However, in the eighteenth century, reports circulated that, at his own request, Cromwell's body had been either cast into the Thames in a leaden coffin or buried in Naseby field. The last lineal male descendant of Cromwell, another Oliver Cromwell, who died in 1821 and who was Clerk of the Governors of St Thomas's Hospital, London and a solicitor, stated that an aged servant who once served Richard Cromwell had told his mother that the body was carried via Cheshunt to Huntingdon and then much further. A distant relative, Dr Cromwell Mortimer, in 1809 related that it was buried twenty feet deep in a field in a paternal estate in Huntingdonshire.

Cromwell's daughter, Mary, married Lord Fauconberg, a descendant of Anthony de Bellasis, who was Henry VII's Chaplain and whose offspring became Barons, Viscounts and Earls of Fauconberg. At the Dissolution of the Augustinian Priory of the Black Friars in 1538, Anthony acquired their property at Newburgh, near Coxwold in Yorkshire. The Fauconbergs also owned property in Chiswick, Mary being buried in St Nicholas's Church and, as they were in royal favour at the Restoration (Lord Fauconberg became Lord Lieutenant of the North Riding and Ambassador to Venice), it has been suggested that Mary was allowed to take the body of Cromwell to Chiswick before taking it to Newburgh Priory for burial. There is, in fact, a walled-up stone vault in the Priory which is said to contain the headless body of Oliver Cromwell. The Wombwell family who now live there have refused all requests for further investigation of the body. It would be of interest to compare it with the head; but perhaps the Wombwells are right to let it 'lie easy', as does the head in Sidney Sussex College Chapel.

Joshua Basset, Popery and Revolution

MARK GOLDIE

That the two universities were the 'seminaries of the Church of England' was an obvious truth in seventeenth-century England. That Sidney Sussex College had a special mission to protect the Protestant religion was enshrined in its statutes. King James II's imposition of a Roman Catholic Master was bound to be a catastrophe. It brought the enemy within the gates and planted the Roman viper in the bosom of the Reformed religion. The advent of Joshua Basset not only afflicted Sidney Sussex but also led the whole university into conflict with the Crown. The collision resulted in the sacking of the Vice-Chancellor and provoked to unaccustomed militancy a Fellow of Trinity College, Isaac Newton. When militancy of a more unstoppable kind – the invading army of Prince William of Orange – destroyed the regime of England's last Catholic monarch, the attempt to propagate Catholicism in Cambridge collapsed. King James fled, and so did the Master of Sidney. The Catholic Counter-Reformation and the Protestant 'Glorious Revolution' had caught the College in their slipstreams.

The old Master, Richard Minshull, died on 31 December 1686, after forty-three years in office. Elected at the height of the Civil War, he survived the Cromwellian regime, the restoration of Crown and Church in 1660, and the accession of James II in 1685, 'during which period he saw many revolutions ... through all which confusion he so poised matters that he kept himself steady in the government of this House'.[1] But it was an inauspicious moment at which to die. Two weeks earlier King James had installed John Massey, a Roman Catholic convert, as Dean of Christ Church in Oxford.[2] The King had by now lost patience with his erstwhile allies, the Anglican High Churchmen and Tory politicians, who refused to accommodate his aspirations for the Catholic community. In June the judges had declared legal the King's power to dispense with the laws that excluded Catholics from public office. In July the Ecclesiastical Commission had been established: it suspended the Bishop of London for failing to suppress anti-Catholic preaching. In the autumn several Catholics were appointed to the Privy Council. And in December James resolved to sack two of his chief ministers, his

---

[1] British Library [hereafter BL], Add. MS 5821, f. 118: the antiquarian William Cole, writing in 1748.
[2] The number of colleges given Catholic heads during James II's reign was four, the other two being Magdalen and University in Oxford.

Protestant brothers-in-law, the Earls of Rochester and Clarendon. Those who took for granted their hegemony in English public life were now on the defensive.

With remarkable alacrity, on 3 January 1687, the King wrote to the Fellows of Sidney recommending that they elect Joshua Basset. Born in about 1641, Basset was the son of a merchant and alderman of King's Lynn, and was admitted a sizar of Gonville and Caius College in 1657. He became a Fellow there in 1665, and was dutifully active as chaplain, steward, and dean, and as university preacher and praelector rhetoricus.[3] He converted to Catholicism in 1686 and publicised his reasons in a book called *Reason and Authority*, published by the King's Catholic printing house. Like other converts, he arrived at his conviction by way of radical doubt. The Protestant doctrine of *sola scriptura* – that Christian truth is discernible from Scripture alone – left him at a loss to find even such fundamental doctrines as the Trinity and the divinity of Christ. Only through the authority of Catholic teaching could the true meaning of Scripture be secured. Without that, Christianity collapsed into a 'confused Babel of religion', for it was evident 'how grievously our poor nation was . . . torn and divided with such sects and schism'.[4]

Basset's conversion quickly made itself felt in Cambridge. On 5 November 1686, Edward Spence, Fellow of Jesus College, satirically attacked Catholicism in a sermon. He did what Anglican clergy were accustomed to do on the day set aside to celebrate England's providential deliverance from the Gunpowder Plot. But, equally, he knew the fate of the Bishop of London, and of a London preacher recently suspended for anti-popish preaching. Basset, by threatening royal retribution, secured from Spence a public recantation in the Senate House, 'the disgrace of which struck so much upon his spirits, that it turned his head, and he continues distracted to this day'.[5] Basset's vigilance secured the King's nomination to a mastership.

The King's first letter to Sidney Sussex produced from the Fellows the response that they would accept Basset if he took the customary oaths. On 12 January there came another, requiring them to elect Basset without administering the oaths of Allegiance and Supremacy, which contained clauses obnoxious to Catholics. Lord Dartmouth, one of the King's naval cronies, begged his majesty to desist, but was told that 'Basset had done him eminent service, and that he

---

[3] See *Dictionary of National Biography*; J. Gillow, *Biographical Dictionary of the English Catholics* (London, 1885), I, 153–4; J. Venn, ed., *Biographical History of Gonville and Caius College* (Cambridge, 1897), I, 400. Biographical information about Basset is exiguous. Even Charles Dodd, whose *Church History* (1742) faithfully memorialized the lives of prominent Catholics, failed to include Basset.

[4] *Reason and Authority: Or the Motives of a Late Protestant's Reconciliation to the Catholic Church* (1687), pp. 8–9. In his reply, Thomas Bainbridge ridiculed Basset's self-enslavement to infallible authority after having so 'narrowly escaped being an atheist': *An Answer to a Book, entituled, Reason and Authority* (1687), p. 1. There is a brief comment in L. Bredvold, *Contexts of Dryden's Thought* (Ann Arbor, 1956), pp. 96–7.

[5] BL, MS Lansdowne 988, f. 190: Joseph Craven, writing in 1725.

should have it'.[6] The Fellows continued to procrastinate: they neither elected Basset, nor defied the King by electing a Protestant instead. By 19 February they still had not acted. Isaac Newton, pugnacious from this first moment of Cambridge's confrontation with the Crown, found their indecisiveness puzzling and irresponsible. 'I wonder that the good men of Sidney do not elect their Master. An honest courage in these matters will secure all, having law on our sides'.[7] The fact was that the senior Fellow, the College's President, was at loggerheads with his juniors. Edmund Matthews, now seventy and twice the age of most of his colleagues, was inclined to acquiesce and elect Basset. He was no crypto-Papist: he had merely been slow to convene the Fellows and now was overawed by the royal command. His generation, adults during the Civil War and Cromwellian 'usurpation', had become inured to, and scarred by, the revolutions of that violent century. Against Matthews stood the third most senior Fellow, James Johnson, tutor and steward, twenty-five years younger, a man 'of a rough and somewhat boisterous behaviour'. He later got his reward by being elected Master when the King and Basset fled.[8]

Unfortunately, it was difficult to deny that the King had a right to instruct colleges to fill fellowships and headships by mandate, and to override statutes in doing so. In earlier years, the Crown had issued scores of such mandates, and colleges and individuals had themselves sought mandates in order to bypass inconvenient statutes, or to secure preferment. The King's propagandist, Nathaniel Johnston, ransacked the public records and offered 'many ... modern instances of the entire obedience paid to the King's mandates by Masters and Fellows of colleges'. A modern historian has produced a similar catalogue, judging that 'it is, I think, difficult to accuse James II of a monstrous illegality'.[9] Sidney Sussex had received more mandates than most colleges. About a dozen of the men – one third of the total – who entered fellowships during the Restoration period (1660–88) were elected 'ex Mandato Regis', though it is true that objections had been raised to two mandates, in 1663 and 1673.[10] James Johnson himself became a Fellow by mandate. It was not the King's use of the royal prerogative that vexed the universities, but its use on behalf of Catholics. And once the Protestant bit

---

[6] Sidney Sussex College Muniments, MR 108/1/4: Joseph Craven to John Lent, 18 January 1725. This, and MR 108/1/2, are key sources: the latter is cited here from the copy in BL, MS Lansdowne 988, ff. 189–91. I am most grateful to Nicholas Rogers for help with the muniments and for several items of information.

[7] *The Correspondence of Isaac Newton*, ed. H.W. Turnbull (Cambridge, 1961), II, 468.

[8] Dr Williams's Library, London: Roger Morrice, Entring Book, Q, 127; BL, Add. MS 5821, f. 120.

[9] Nathaniel Johnston, *The King's Visitatorial Power Asserted* (1688), pp. 273ff, 352; E.F. Churchill, 'The Dispensing Power of the Crown in Ecclesiastical Affairs', *Law Quarterly Review*, 38 (1922), 315.

[10] These figures are drawn from the list of Fellows in Cambridge University Library [hereafter CUL], MS Baker, Mm.2.25. Cf. G.M. Edwards, *Sidney Sussex College* (London, 1899), pp. 137–9.

was between the dons' teeth, the rhetoric of constitutionalist principle soon followed. Joseph Craven, Fellow since 1676 and future Master, wrote that Basset was a 'forward tool for arbitrary power and popery', and that the King had, 'against the College statutes and the laws of the land, by a high stretch of his dispensing power . . . forced him upon us.'[11]

The Fellows continued to demur. It is probable that they challenged the evidence for Basset's dispensation, for on 25 February the Crown prepared a warrant under the Great Seal formally dispensing him, together with four other Cambridge converts, from the usual oaths.[12] The Fellows 'made what application they could at Court by petition and [the] interest of friends, but found nothing could prevail'.[13] Finally they acquiesced and admitted Basset, though it is doubtful that they actually *elected* him.[14] The Election of Officers book in the College archive lists the election of Basset's predecessor and successors but not his, and against his successor is recorded 'Magister Collegii Quintus electus fuit et admissus' – fifth and not sixth Master.[15] In 1748 the antiquarian William Cole remarked that Basset 'is left out in the catalogue of Masters on the MS Table, on account, I suppose, of his not being elected by the society'.[16]

On 7 March 1687 Basset installed himself in the College by *force majeure*, under the protection of the King's assize judges. The assize circuit provided the most visible display of royal authority in the provinces, the judges arriving in formal procession, and delivering an address outlining royal policy. Anthony Wood, the Oxford gossip, got an account of Basset's arrival from Edward Sclater, the vicar of Putney in Surrey, another recent convert to Rome.

> The same day that the judges went into Cambridge, Joshua Basset, who had a mandamus for the headship of Sidney College in Cambridge went with his attendants from his house (Pembroke Hall)[17] to the said College and a week or a fortnight after he was settled <had mass said publicly in the College chapel to him and his and turned out the Fellows>.[18]

Sclater's enthusiasm led to exaggeration in the telling, and Wood later scored out the final, bracketed passage as 'false'. Basset did threaten to take over the chapel,

---

[11] BL, MS Lansdowne 988, ff. 189–90.
[12] The others were Clement Boult, Fellow of Caius; William Thompson, scholar of Caius; Clement Scott, Fellow of Corpus Christi and junior proctor; and John Basset, Fellow of Pembroke. *Calendar of State Papers, Domestic* [hereafter *CSPD*], 1686–7, p. 375.
[13] BL, MS Lansdowne 988, f. 189.
[14] When Leopold Finch was installed by royal mandate as Warden of All Souls, Oxford, in 1687, the Fellows admitted him but refused to elect him: he has gone down in college folklore as the 'unelected Warden'.
[15] Muniments, MR 41, p. 69.
[16] BL, Add. MS 5821, f. 120.
[17] This is plausible, since Basset, though a Fellow of Caius, probably lodged with John Basset, Catholic Fellow of Pembroke, who was perhaps his brother.
[18] *The Life and Times of Anthony Wood*, ed. A. Clark (Oxford, 1891–1900), III, 214–15.

Plate 1 Portrait of Ralph Simons, artist and date unknown

COLL. DOMINÆ FRANCISCÆ SIDNEY SUSSEX

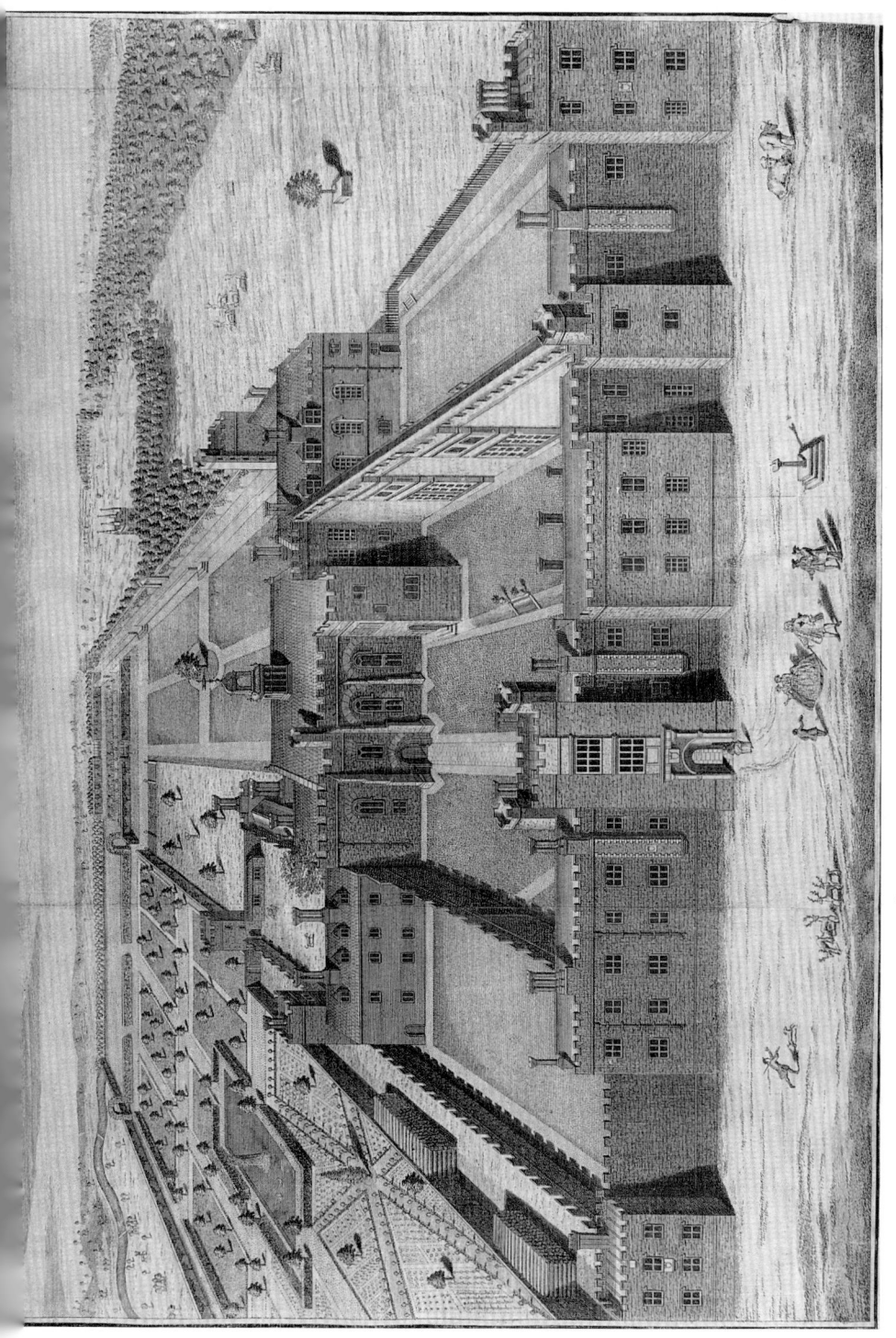

Plate 3 View of Penshurst Place, engraved by George Vertue, 1747

Plate 4 Wooden box containing incrusted skull, presented by Captain William Stevens in 1627

Plate 5a A selection of volumes by Suarez from the College Library, showing titling across the head of the book

Plate 5b Gabriel Vasquez, *Paraphrasis et compendiaria explicatio ad nonnullas Pauli epistolas* (Ingolstadt, 1613), binding with Willmer arms

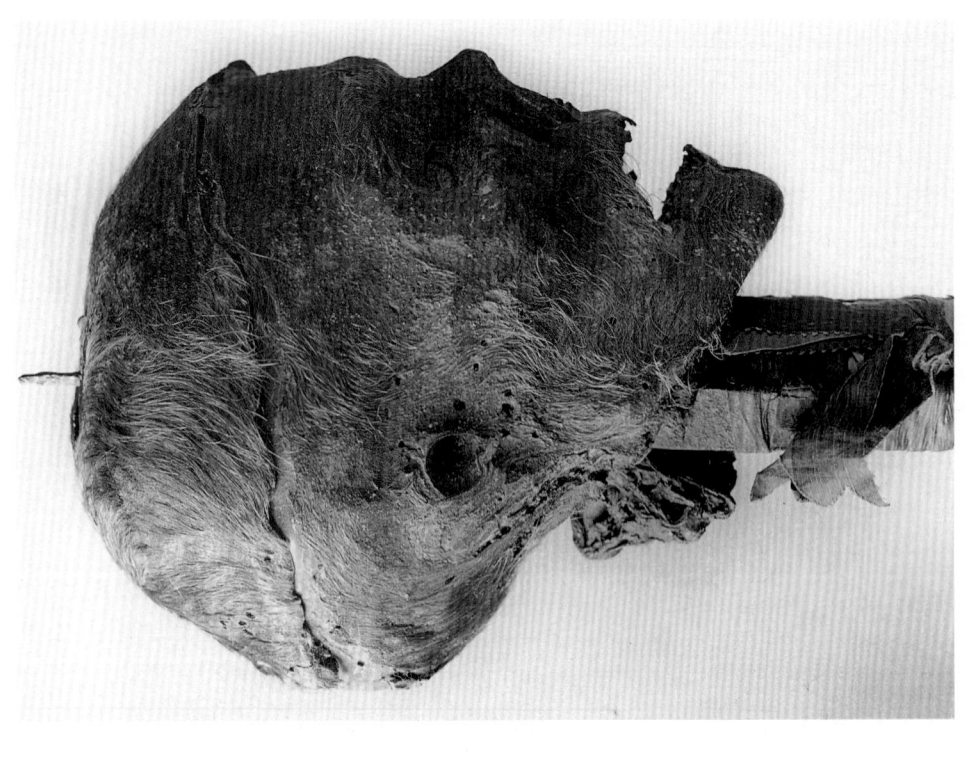

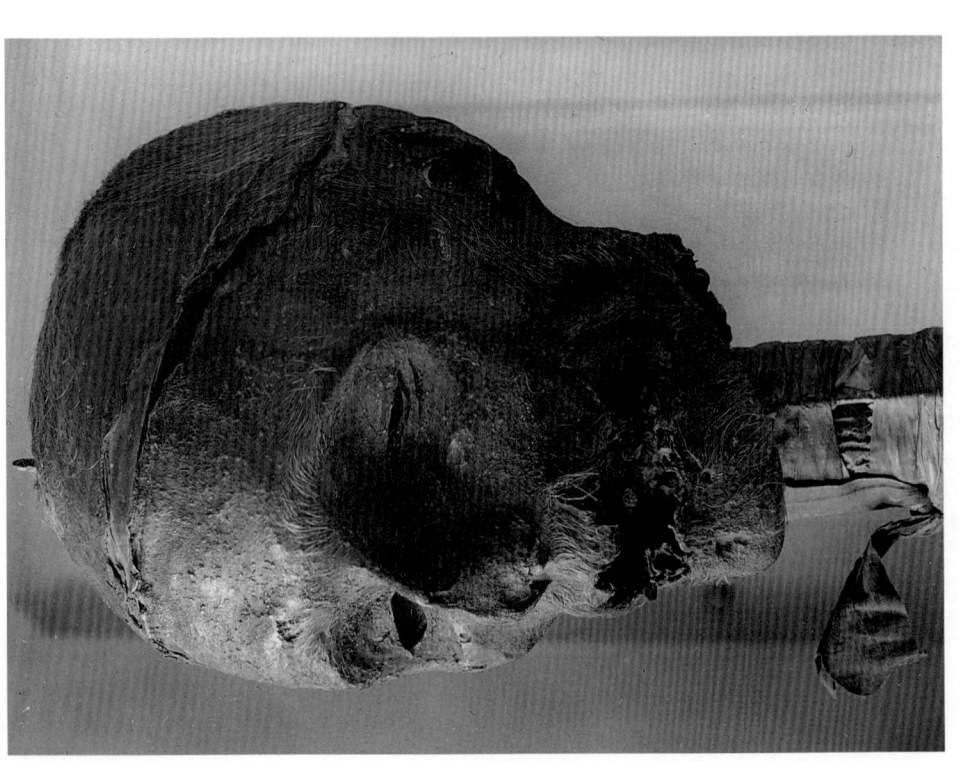

Plate 6 Two views of Cromwell's head, showing metal spike on wooden shaft, wart site over right eye, trial axe cuts on back of neck, and worm holes in upper mandible

Plate 7 Canon Horace Wilkinson holding Cromwell's head, Woodbridge, c.1949

Plate 8a The west front of the College immediately prior to Wyatville's remodelling

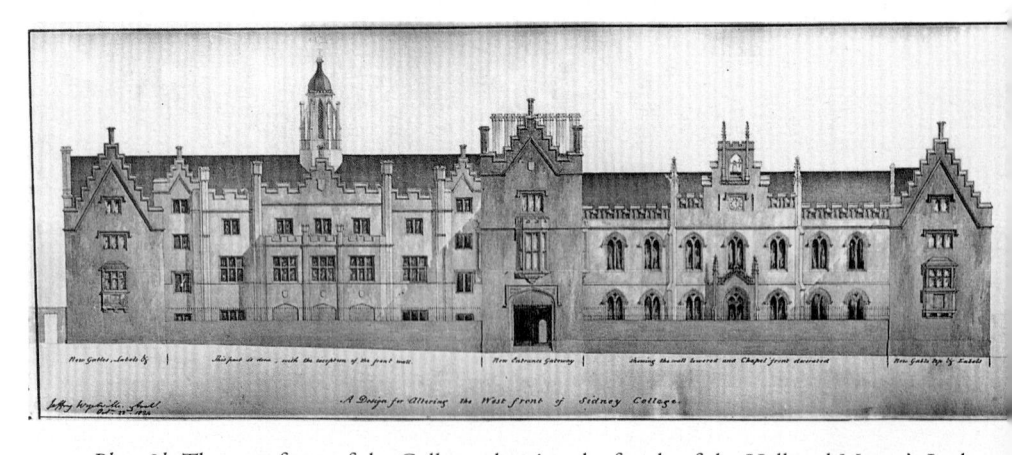

Plate 8b The west front of the College, showing the façade of the Hall and Master's Lodge as built to Wyatville's designs, 1822–4, and the proposals for the second phase, 22 October 182

Plate 9 William Chafy, artist unknown

Plate 10 The 1820s houses on the north side of Sussex Street in 1936

Plate 11a The New Cleethorpes area from the air: Blundell Park Football Ground is to the centre top, Grimsby Road runs from left to right across the top half of the photograph. Sidney Park is at the bottom centre. The edge of the area developed by the College can be seen to the top right. The main features shown on the photograph, which looks north-east, can be located on Map 2, p. 186.

Plate 11b Fellows on their annual visit to Cleethorpes, c.1959: visit to British Titanium Products Ltd, Grimsby: *(left to right)* Dr Agar, Mr Angus, host, Dr Clemmow, Professor Robinson, Mr John Mountain (College agent), Mr Dibden, Dr Beales, Mr Thornely, Mr Roy, two hosts.

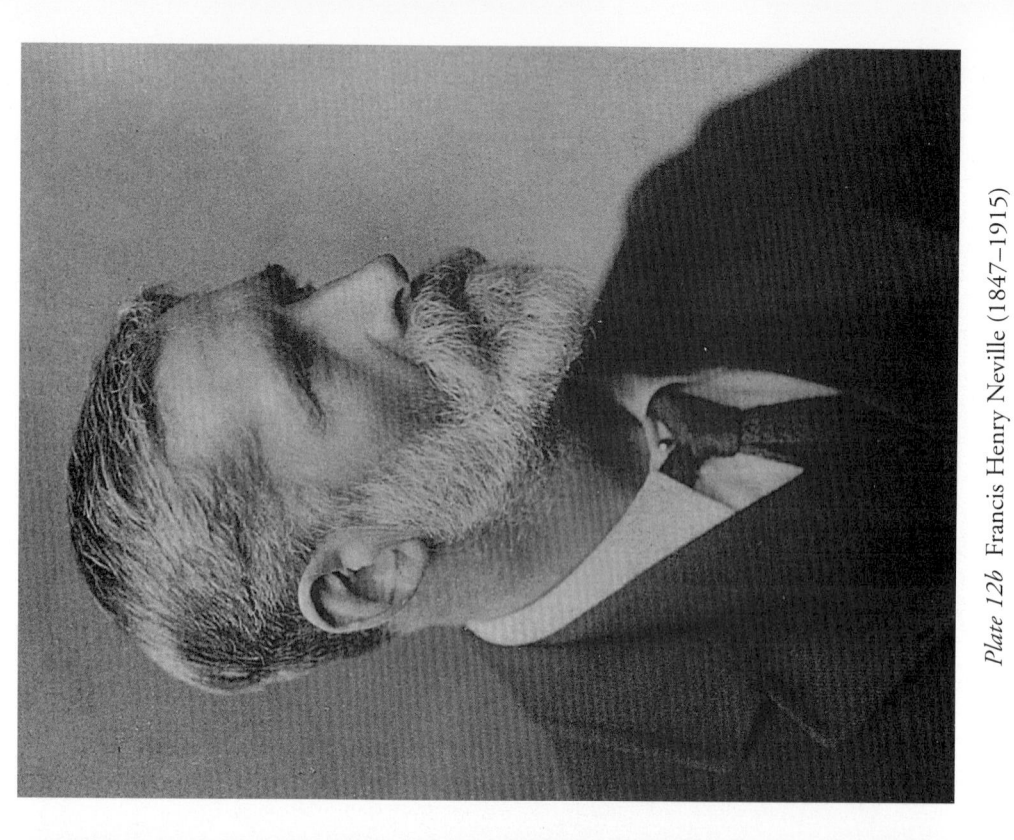

Plate 12a Charles Thomas Heycock (1858–1931)

Plate 12b Francis Henry Neville (1847–1915)

Plate 13a View of the main laboratory, in building (a), looking north. This photograph, and Plate 13b, were taken towards the end of the laboratory's life, c.1908.

Plate 13b View of buildings (a), (b) and (c), looking south-west. The North range of Hall Court is visible in the background. Building (a) has a chimney over the fume cupboard shown in Plate 13a, and skylights. A glazed addition to building (a) is visible at far left.

Plate 14 George Ralph Mines (1886–1914)

Plate 15a J.L. Pearson's plans for a new Chapel: exterior from Jesus Lane

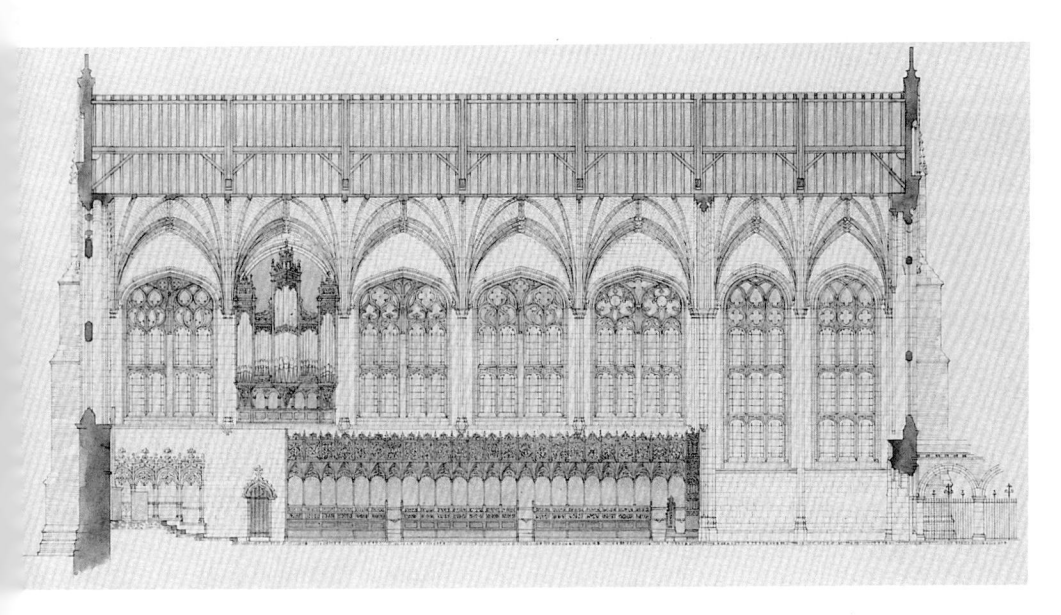

Plate 15b J.L. Pearson's plans for a new Chapel: interior section, showing stalls

Plate 16a The old College Chapel

Plate 16b The rebuilt Chapel

or to require that it be shared between the two religions, and on 5 November he locked the chapel door to prevent the annual Gunpowder Day service. But, more prudently, he fitted up a private Catholic chapel in the Master's Lodge. The altarpiece, described as having 'the IHS in a glory and cherubims about it', was hung in later years over a door in the College audit room. William Cole remarked that he had 'met with several people in Cambridge who remember to have been present' at mass in the Lodge.[19]

For the next twenty-one months Catholic Master and Protestant Fellows were at loggerheads. Craven recollected:

> As to his government we found him a passionate, proud and insolent man, whenever he was opposed, which made us very cautious in conversing with him, who saw he waited for and catched at all occasions to do us mischief in what concerned our religion. I don't deny, that he had learning and other abilities to have done us good, but his interest lay the contrary way.[20]

Basset bragged that he was exempt from the statutory residence requirement, so that he had 'free liberty to come to London and Westminster and wait on the King, Queen Consort and Queen Dowager'.[21]

Earlier histories of the College give no hint that the Fellows persisted in their resistance to Basset and that they were summoned to London to face the wrath of the Ecclesiastical Commission. The evidence is in the diary of the Presbyterian political agent, Roger Morrice. He reported that, during April 1687, the Fellows were planning to depose Basset, not now on the ground that he had refused the oaths, but because he was in breach of the College's own special statutory provisions. The Master, he explained, was required 'every month [to] collate in the College upon some point in defence of the Reformation against Popery and that he shall in the public schools[22] once a month or two defend some point of the like kind'. Since Basset had 'neglected, forborne and refused' this requirement, the Fellows intended to assemble and expel him. 'But it seems he had notice (by some false brother among them) of their purposes', and took horse to London to denounce them. As a result, their 'purpose is disappointed' and the Fellows are summoned to appear before the King's Commission. The upshot, as we shall see later, was the peremptory rewriting of the College's statutes.[23]

The resolve of the Sidney men was stiffened by news from Oxford. On 5 April the King sent a mandate to instal Anthony Farmer as President of Magdalen College, the richest foundation there. Farmer was a Catholic convert, a former student of Trinity in Cambridge, and, according to his enemies, a drunken

---

[19] BL, MS Lansdowne 988, f. 190; Add. MS 5821, f. 119.
[20] BL, MS Lansdowne 988, f. 190. Basset's learning is visible in his *Reason and Authority*, where his citations included Aristotle, Epicurus, Lucretius, Augustine, Averroes, Luther, Calvin, Beza, Melanchthon and Grotius.
[21] Muniments, MR 108/1/4.
[22] 'Public schools' here means the lecture halls of the university at large.
[23] Morrice, Entring Book, Q, 127.

debauchee. On 15 April, Magdalen, bolder than Sidney, defied the King and elected one of their own number, a Protestant. News was exchanged in correspondence between Arthur Charlett, President of University College, and John Laughton of Trinity in Cambridge – they believed their letters were opened by the government in London. On 25 April Laughton told Charlett how Magdalen's stand was galvanizing Sidney:

> I have communicated what you relate concerning the brave resolution of Magdalen to my friends of Sidney College here, and perhaps you'll hear very shortly good effects of it, for they are already seriously intending to take such a course as probably may retrieve the unhappy miscarriage of their weak and timorous President [Matthews] who is now removed into the country very much discontented and disturbed in mind for the irreparable scandal and mischief that his wretched frailty hath brought upon us all.

Nor was this the only link between the two crises at Cambridge and Oxford. The dons set about digging dirt on Farmer's Cambridge past in order to destroy his reputation. Among the charges was that Farmer had committed rape – and that Basset was suppressing the evidence through his influence over the girl and her mother. Farmer's and Basset's reputations were irretrievably blackened.[24]

From the evidence now available, it is clear that, Edmund Matthews apart, the Fellows of Sidney were ready enough to take a stand against their intruded Master. Accordingly, we need to modify the impression of supineness given by two recent historians, who remark that Sidney 'dutifully elected' Basset and that 'the college offered no serious resistance'.[25]

The readiness of Sidney Sussex to resist the King was part of a national wave of Anglican civil disobedience against James's Catholicizing policies, which was to culminate in the trial of the Seven Bishops for sedition in the summer of 1688. The Fellows were steeped in the instinctive royalism of the Restoration era, yet also in its no less passionate Anglicanism. The Church of England, risen from the ashes of the Puritan Revolution, was increasingly self-confident, and took its uncompromising stand for 'true religion' half way between Rome and Geneva. The Anglican Church's canonization of Charles I as the martyr-king, and the shared experience of the defeat and restoration of monarchy and episcopacy, created an alliance of crown and altar which left churchmen starkly uncomprehending when confronted by a Stuart king who was disloyal to Anglicanism. The pain of the events of 1687–88 was the sharper given the intense and risky loyalty of churchmen towards James during the political crises of 1679–85, from which they emerged with the newly coined label of 'Tory'. They had defended the

---

[24] Bodleian Library, MS Ballard 23, ff. 3, 11. I am grateful to Robert Iliffe for drawing these letters to my attention.
[25] J. Gascoigne, *Cambridge in the Age of Enlightenment* (Cambridge, 1989), p. 38; J. Twigg, *The University of Cambridge and the English Revolution, 1625–1688* (Woodbridge, Suffolk, 1990), p. 279.

Catholic heir's right to succeed to the throne, against the onslaught of the Whigs, who sought to exclude James from the succession. The Whigs' apparent revival of the violent radicalism of the Puritan Revolution seemed a worse threat than Catholicism, for James showed reassuring signs of confining his religion to his private devotions. The reality of James's ambitions, once upon the throne, came as a brutal blow. What the Whigs failed to achieve by parliamentary means in 1679–81 they achieved by William of Orange's invasion in 1688 – this time with the connivance of bewildered Tories, their consciences rent asunder by the competing claims of Protestant and Stuart loyalism.

The Fellows of Sidney were typical of a Cambridge college at this time. At the turn of 1687 there were twelve of them.[26] Most were around thirty years old and expected to proceed to a parish living before long. Three went off to parishes during 1687, taking flight from the Popish Master. As scholars they were undistinguished. None published a book or even a sermon; none rates an entry in the *Dictionary of National Biography* – not even the future Masters and Vice-Chancellors, Johnson and Craven. Practically the same can be said of the Fellows during the Restoration period as a whole. Only David Jenner – one among thirty-four Fellows elected between 1660 and 1688 – broke into print.[27] Of course, the chief duty of a Fellow was to teach and catechise students. Even so, other colleges responded more fulsomely to the imperative of the age, the publishing of learned polemics against Protestant Nonconformity and Roman Catholicism – against Geneva and Rome.[28]

Yet we can be confident that the mind-set of the Fellows was characteristic of the Tory-Anglicanism of the 1680s. David Jenner spoke for them all. Awarded the degree of Master of Arts by royal mandate in 1662 and of Bachelor of Divinity in 1668, he was a Fellow from 1662 until 1676, then prebendary of Salisbury Cathedral, and one of Charles II's chaplains. He was the type of churchman who in due course might expect a bishopric for his ideological services. He published two books: *Beaufrons: Or, a New Discovery of Treason, under the Fair Face and Mask of Religion, and Liberty of Conscience* (1683), a savage attack on religious toleration, and on Protestant Nonconformity as a source of fanaticism and rebellion; and *The Prerogative of Primogeniture* (1685), which vindicated James II's inviolable right to inherit the throne, regardless of his religion. Other Fellows spoke for themselves, albeit with mechanical brevity in verse eulogies. Thus

---

[26] So far as can be ascertained. There are inconsistent tallies of elections to Fellowships in CUL, MS Mm.2.25 (Baker X), and BL, Add. MS 5821, ff. 137–38; and lists of Fellows in the College Muniments: MR 32 and 42. Biographical information derives from J. and J.A. Venn, *Alumni Cantabrigienses, Part I*, 4 vols (Cambridge, 1922–27).

[27] Jenner is the only Restoration Fellow in the *DNB*; the next to rate an entry is Thomas Woolston, elected in 1690.

[28] They did, however, buy and read such material, as is evident from the approximately 260 books left to the College library by Thomas Goodlad, Fellow from 1666.

Thomas Walker, a twenty-five year old Fellow, writing on the accession of James II:

> Hail! Mighty James! kind heavn's peculiar care,
> Whom roaring guns, and dangerous waves did spare;
> Waves less tumultuous, than the rabble were.
> Begin, sweet muse, his deathless fame rehearse . . .

Walker went on to rehearse royal successes – including that 'By force the Whigs [were] repressed' – and then exclaimed:

> Cease, faction, cease, and smooth thy angry brow;
> No more the blasted seeds of treason sow:
> Let no disloyal murmurs stain
> The long, and ever-peaceful reign
> Of James, the Martyr's son.

The celebration concludes:

> Methinks I see his guardian angel stand, . . .
> Ready to twine about his radiant brow
> More verdant laurels, than on earth do grow,
> And with loud acclamations sing
> Praise to the heavenly, for the earthly king.[29]

In 1683 the university had dutifully obeyed a royal mandate to depose its Chancellor, Charles II's Protestant but illegitimate and rebellious son, the Duke of Monmouth. The dons solemnly burnt Kneller's portrait of Monmouth. In short, the accession of England's last Catholic monarch was acclaimed with unalloyed enthusiasm and with scarcely a hint that the Protestant cause was in danger.

Basset was nominated Master at precisely the moment when scales were rapidly falling from Anglican Tory eyes. The wider, indeed international, context in which the appointment at Sidney was seen is well captured in a diary written in Dublin:

> Feb. 6. Tyrconnel lands at Dunleary, and was brought to town by a great train of his party, but few or none of the Protestant gentry . . . The King made one Basset rector of Sidney College in Cambridge, a Roman Catholic. In France dragoons were sent to Languedoc. In England Berwick made Master of the Horse and colonel of horse. The Lord Maitland, a Roman Catholic, made Secretary of State in Scotland. . . . In Ireland, Peters, a Roman Catholic, made Archbishop of Cashel.[30]

---

[29] *Moestissimae ac Laetissimae Academiae Cantabrigiensis* (Cambridge, 1685), sig. Aa4v–Bb3r. For Basset's effusion see sig. E1r, which indicates an early Catholic bias.

[30] Historical Manuscripts Commission, *Ormonde*, VIII, 348.

Tyrconnel was about to transfer power to Catholics in Ireland for the first time since Cromwell's conquest. In France, Louis XIV had ended toleration for Protestant Huguenots, and troops were being used to drive them out or forcibly convert them – Sidney Sussex contributed £40 to the national collection for Huguenot refugees.[31] Berwick was James II's illegitimate son, and was added to the growing Catholic officer corps in the army. In sum, the fate of the Reformed religion seemed increasingly precarious.

Protestants now rapidly began to take a catastrophist view of James's ambitions. A century of apocalyptic anxiety, fed by John Foxe's *Book of Martyrs*, ingrained a visceral hatred of Catholicism. James II would soon join 'Bloody Mary', the Spanish Armada, the Gunpowder Plot, and the Irish Massacre of 1641, in the litany of the Popish onslaught upon England. In so far as English national identity has had a founding mythology, it is rooted in Protestant patriotism. In Victorian times, it achieved its most influential narrative celebration in Lord Macaulay's *History of England* (1848). It was natural for G.M. Edwards, writing the history of Sidney Sussex in 1899, to refer his readers to Macaulay for evidence of James II's 'tyrannical dealings'.[32]

By and large, James II has had a better press in recent decades. Inflexible, unimaginative, and choleric he certainly was. That he was determined to coerce his subjects into the Catholic Church is doubtful. He knew his limitations: until the summer of 1688 he expected to be succeeded by his Anglican daughter Mary; there were never more than eleven per cent of Catholics among the army officer corps; and he knew that only two per cent of the population was Catholic. Yet he was also in a hurry: he inherited the throne at fifty-two, and might not have long to establish a Catholic foothold. At headlong pelt he inaugurated a missionary campaign: chapels and schools were opened, thousands of books printed, and courtiers subjected to theological disputations. Catholic higher education was non-existent and a start had to be made: to him, the universities' charade of outraged conscience served merely to protect Anglican exclusiveness – the 'liberties' of the colleges masked the privileges of religious monopoly. Whatever James's ultimate allegiance to a Counter-Reformation vision of the English Church restored to Rome, for the duration he was, paradoxically, committed to principles which modern liberals and secularists hold dear: a university open to a plural society, unencumbered by the strictures of the Anglican Establishment. 'The King had imagined it would be a means to familiarise those of different religions, and make them live together in greater peace and unity together, pursuant to the intent of liberty of conscience . . . [if] some few Catholics, were incorporated into the universities.'[33] That is why James made two moves: to license any Master or Fellow who converted to Rome, and to see if he could secure at least one college for Catholic higher education.

---

[31] In June 1687 and January 1689: Muniments, MR 32, pp. 463, 485.
[32] Edwards, *Sidney Sussex*, p. 150.
[33] *The Life of James the Second*, ed. J.S. Clarke (London, 1816), II, 125.

The King's – and Joshua Basset's – missionary effort in Cambridge did not stop with Sidney Sussex. Basset soon brought the whole university into collision with the Crown. A Benedictine monk called Alban Francis arrived as missioner. On Ash Wednesday, 9 February 1687, the Vice-Chancellor received a mandate from the King to award Francis the degree of Master of Arts. According to one diarist, 'it was presumed the design was to capacitate Francis to be head of a house'.[34] Basset and Francis were close associates. Francis brought to Cambridge the King's mandate to install Basset at Sidney, and Francis was described as Basset's 'chaplain' – probably his confessor. Basset had Francis admitted a Fellow Commoner at Sidney and he dined regularly; he was anxious to have him made a full Fellow.[35] When a Suffolk rector converted to Rome it was to Basset and Francis that he came for advice about how to conduct himself.[36] Previous histories of the College have said nothing of the Alban Francis affair, but the Master of Sidney was at the heart of the business.[37]

The Vice-Chancellor, Dr John Peachell, was Master of Magdalene, a genial companion of Samuel Pepys, but weak and vacillating. He struggled to find the courage to lead the university against the King and had not the confidence to do so effectively. The King's mandate was read to a Congregation of the Senate on 21 February. The Senate resolved, with only a handful of dissentients among 150 to 200 present, to refuse Francis his degree unless he took the oaths. A Grace, or resolution, was drawn up, but it was quickly apparent that it was impossible to proceed in this customary way. The Senate's business was filtered through the Caput, a body of six senior dons, each of whom had a veto. The Master of Sidney was a member, and plainly Basset would exercise his veto. In order to evade him, the Senate resorted to acting by way of a petition instead of by Grace. But since it was feared that such a petition might look 'tumultuory' – mass petitioning got a black name during the Civil War – two representatives were deputed to voice the collective view that the King be begged to withdraw the mandate. Peachell meanwhile persuaded the Chancellor, the Duke of Albermarle, to intercede with

---

[34] *The Autobiography of Sir John Bramston*, ed. Lord Braybrooke (London, 1845), p. 276.
[35] Muniments, MR 108/1/4; *The Diary of Samuel Newton, Alderman of Cambridge, 1662–1717*, ed. J.E. Foster (Cambridge, 1890), p. 90; Wood, *Life and Times*, III, 221. Francis delivered the mandate in the company of two Fellows of Caius, Clement Boult and James Holman.
[36] Bodleian Library, MS Tanner 29, f. 108.
[37] For what follows the chief source is *The Cambridge Case* (1689). This is reprinted in T.B. Howell's *State Trials* (London, 1811), and is the source of later accounts, such as Lord Macaulay's, and C.H. Cooper, *Annals of Cambridge* (Cambridge, 1845), III, 615–32. The fullest modern account is P.C. Vellacott, 'The Struggle of James the Second with the University of Cambridge', in *In Memoriam: Adolphus William Ward* (Cambridge, 1924). See also Twigg, *Cambridge and the English Revolution*, pp. 281–4. There is fresh material in the Isaac Newton (Keynes) papers at King's College, and in Morrice's Entring Book, Q, 104–5, 111–12, 122, 129–31, 147.

the King, but James brushed him aside. In a state of high anxiety Peachell unburdened himself to Pepys:

> I could not tell what to do – decline his Majesty's letter, or his laws: I could but pray to God to direct, sanctify, and govern me . . . 'tis extraordinary distress and affliction to me, after so much endeavour and affection to his royal person, crown, and succession, I should at last by the providence of God, in this my station, be thus exposed to his displeasure.

It was 'fear of the last judgement' that led him to defy his king. The doe that Pepys sent for the audit feast was small consolation.[38]

Poor Peachell needed constant coaxing from his colleagues throughout the ensuing ordeal. More forthright politicians and churchmen, with an eye to the national scene, were eager to use the Cambridge case for a showdown with the King, and were anxious that the dons should not cave in. The university took counsel from two senior lawyers, who were later to act at the Seven Bishops' trial: Heneage Finch, former Solicitor General, and Sir Francis Pemberton, former Lord Chief Justice, both now out of office. They were categorical on the illegality of the King's demand, and on the pivotal role of the universities as 'seminaries of learning and religion [and] a mighty influence on the religion here established'.[39] The bishops were also ready for a fight. On 25 February Bishop Francis Turner of Ely – widely tipped as the next Archbishop of Canterbury – wrote to Humphrey Gower, Master of St John's:

> You have had a most glorious part in this great transaction. The scene opens to all eyes, and the mouths of all good men are full of the praises due to the whole university for making the first stand, and that in a brave body. I trust your example will do wonders, and work like efforts at Oxford, where they are to be tried (I hear) immediately. I do almost promise myself, your courage and consistency will reassure the old man of Sidney. For myself, I expect to stand or fall with you . . . The good Archbishop is mightily revived by this account . . . God Almighty fit and prepare us for whatever He pleases to send . . .[40]

Turner's remark about 'the old man of Sidney' must refer to Matthews. Evidently, the university's stand in the case of Alban Francis provided a stiffening of the resolve of the Fellows of Sidney in overruling their aged President.

Immediately after the Congregation of Senate, Alban Francis rode to London. Close behind came the two representatives of the university. Peachell soon received a second letter from the King, demanding compliance. The Senate again demurred. The King pronounced that he 'was offended at the proceedings of the

---

[38] *The Diary and Correspondence of Samuel Pepys*, ed. J. Smith and Lord Braybrooke (London, 1854), IV, 236–7.
[39] BL, Add. MS 32,095, f. 238.
[40] CUL, MS Mm.2.23, p. 307 (Baker VI, p. 359).

university', and on 9 April the Vice-Chancellor was summoned to appear before the Ecclesiastical Commission. The Commission's chairman was Lord Chancellor Jeffreys, notorious for his harsh treatment of the Monmouth rebels in the 'Bloody Assize'. He was unswervingly devoted to the King, and given to splenetic hectoring in court. He reduced Peachell to stammering befuddlement. The Vice-Chancellor had with him eight delegates of the Senate, among them Isaac Newton. Several attempted to speak up, but were cut short, Jeffreys slapping one down with the sneer that he was not yet Vice-Chancellor.

Newton said nothing, and one historian judged that his mind was on other things, for he was in the throes of printing the *Principia Mathematica*.[41] On the contrary: now that the writing of the *Principia* was complete, and Edmund Halley was seeing to the publishing, Newton had turned with furious energy to the defence of the university. On 19 February, when he complained about Sidney Sussex's irresolution, his correspondence took an abrupt turn from geometry to popery.[42] When the delegates were about to go to London it was suggested that Alban Francis be given his degree with a caveat that no precedent should thereby be created. Newton got up, paced about, and then said 'this is giving up the question': 'if one priest be [made] a Master [of Arts] you may have a hundred'.[43] Among Newton's papers in King's College are several documents bearing on the case, including drafts of the university's defence submitted to the Commission. Newton may have had a hand in writing *The Cambridge Case*, published immediately after the Revolution, which provides our main source for the affair.[44] The Alban Francis case fuelled Newton's lifelong antipathy to popery and his preoccupation with religious history and prophecy.[45] That millenarianism and modern physics could subsist together in the same mind has offered a classic conundrum to historians of science.

The university's defence was fourfold: that statutes required graduands to take the oaths of Allegiance and Supremacy; that university officers were bound to require those oaths; that the granting of a degree was not an ecclesiastical matter, so that the Commission had no cognizance; and that the Commission was outlawed by the Act of 1641 which abolished the Court of High Commission.

---

[41] Vellacott, 'Struggle', p. 98.
[42] Newton, *Correspondence*, II, 467. For Newton's role in this affair see R.S. Westfall, *Never at Rest: A Biography of Isaac Newton* (Cambridge, 1980), pp. 473–9. The fullest investigation has been undertaken by Dr Robert Iliffe in his forthcoming paper, 'Dispensing Justice: The Political Life of Isaac Newton, 1687–91'. I am most grateful to him for his help and for transcripts from the Keynes papers.
[43] L.T. More, *Isaac Newton* (New York, 1934), p. 342.
[44] Westfall, *Never At Rest*, p. 475. Keynes MS 113 is a manuscript of the *Case* in Humphrey Newton's hand. There are several other manuscript copies elsewhere.
[45] See F. Manuel, *Isaac Newton, Historian* (Cambridge, 1963). It has even been argued that the *Principia* includes a veiled critique of James II: G. Grinnell, 'Newton's *Principia* as Whig Propaganda', in *City and Society in the Eighteenth Century*, ed. P. Fritz and D. Williams (Toronto, 1973).

In private memoranda Newton was even more forthright. To sacrifice the oaths would 'diminish the security of the nation against their being enslaved to the authority of the bishop of Rome'. The danger was manifest, as the case of Sidney Sussex showed:

> Men of the Roman faith have been put into masterships of colleges. The entrance into fellowships is as open. And if foreigners be incorporated 'twill be as open to them as others. A mixture of Papists and Protestants in the same university can neither subsist happily nor long together.[46]

The university's defence was met by a harangue from Jeffreys, which dwelt on two themes. He reminded the Cambridge delegates of the regular practice of accepting royal mandates. (That a degree had earlier been awarded to the Moroccan ambassador's secretary, a Muslim, led to national amusement – 'This piece of raillery was everywhere set up, that a Papist was reckoned worse than a Mahometan'.[47]) Jeffrey's second complaint was that the Senate had proceeded by petition rather than Grace. It is possible that Basset had privately expressed his anger to Jeffreys about this device. Jeffreys demanded to know how the Vice-Chancellor knew the Senate's mind without a Grace. Peachell replied: because opinions were brought to him by Mr Newton and his colleagues. 'This new way of giving opinions' was tumultuous, retorted Jeffreys. 'There was no other way', stammered John Billers, the University Orator, before being cut off. There was no tactful way of explaining to the Lord Chancellor that they were driven to tumultuory petitioning by the obstruction of the Popish Master of Sidney.

It was said that Jeffreys treated the dons 'just as he used to treat the fanatics' – the Nonconformist rebels he had sent to the gallows in the West Country.[48] Peachell's inability to stand up to Jeffreys shamed the university. 'It was no small reflection on that great body, that their chief magistrate was so little able to assert their privileges, or to justify their proceedings. He was treated with great contempt by Jeffreys.'[49] Jeffreys pronounced that Cambridge University had been 'pernicious and obstinate' and 'guilty of an act of great disobedience to the King's commands'. Peachell was sacked from the Vice-Chancellorship and suspended from his mastership. But with the eight delegates Jeffreys, under a counsel of restraint from the King, was gentler, adjuring them, in the words of Scripture, to 'go your way and sin no more, lest a worst thing come unto you'. Even the King could grasp that the Commission was antagonizing the entire diaspora of Cambridge alumni in public life, and that if Newton and his colleagues were punished 'they would be received by the whole university as martyrs'.[50]

For all Jeffreys' bluster, and Peachell's humiliation, the King decided not to

---

[46] King's College, MS Keynes 116, f. 2; and see MS 118.
[47] Gilbert Burnet, *History of his Own Time* (1720), I, 698.
[48] Morrice, Entring Book, Q, 122.
[49] Burnet, *History*, I, 698.
[50] Morrice, Entring Book, Q, 130.

continue to press for Alban Francis's degree. The university had, in Gilbert Burnet's words, resisted 'with a firmness that the Court had not expected'. The new Vice-Chancellor, Dr John Balderston, Master of Emmanuel, made clear he was ready to repeat Peachell's stand, promising, in a defiant inaugural speech, that 'during his magistracy, neither religion, nor the rights of the [university] body, should suffer'.[51] The Presbyterian Roger Morrice was amazed at the university's boldness. It was 'of very great consideration, for England wants nothing but a back[-bone], and if they should but now make a stand, the common genius and strength of the kingdom would fall in with them, and a stop would certainly be put to all proceedings of this kind'.[52] The affair of the Master of Sidney's confessor had demonstrated the willingness of the Protestant nation to face down its Catholic monarch.

In the coming months, it was an Oxford college which bore the brunt. The Ecclesiastical Commission had embarked on a more determined crusade against Magdalen College. In due course, all its Fellows, bar one convert, were expelled and the College turned over to Catholics. In Oxford the Commission was able to break a single college without the mistake of a head-on collision with the university at large. In Cambridge, the King's retreat left Joshua Basset high and dry at Sidney. Peachell's timorous resolution and Newton's ferocious memoranda had ensured that Sidney did not go the way of Magdalen, nor its Fellows acquire the laurels of Protestant martyrdom. Accordingly, the Magdalen affair and not the Sidney affair has had the lion's share of historical attention.[53]

The Ecclesiastical Commission had not quite finished with Cambridge. We earlier saw that the Fellows of Sidney planned to depose Basset for breach of the anti-popish statutes. On 21 April 1687 the Commission demanded to see the college's statutes. Its authority to 'correct, amend, and alter' university and college statutes was clearly stated in its commission.[54] The statutes were delivered up on 5 May and passed to lawyers for revision, and new statutes were issued on 13 June.[55] John Laughton told Charlett of his fears that Sidney was but the first and that 'all other colleges in both universities will be dealt with one after another, as the goose (in the emblem) was plucked of all her feathers'.[56] Bishop Thomas Sprat, a member of the Commission, in pitiful self-exculpation after the Revolution, protested his innocence: 'I absolutely resisted all the alterations in the statutes of

---

[51] Burnet, *History*, I, 698.
[52] Morrice, Entring Book, Q, 131.
[53] Two books are devoted to it: J.R. Bloxam, ed., *Magdalen College and King James II, 1686–1688* (Oxford, 1886); L. Brockliss, G. Harriss, and A. Macintyre, *Magdalen College and the Crown* (Oxford, 1988).
[54] *The History of King James's Ecclesiastical Commission* (1711), pp. 6–7.
[55] BL, Add. MS 5847, ff. 111–12; Bodleian Library, MS Rawlinson D365, ff. 16, 19, 20. The King's confirmatory letter is dated 2 July.
[56] BL, MS Ballard 23, f. 7.

Sidney College, and all other changes and abrogations . . . for the advantage of Popish priests and students'.[57]

Yet, oddly enough, not all contemporary Protestant comment was hostile to the revision of the college statutes. On 3 June John Freke wrote to the philosopher John Locke:

> We have no news but what the Ecclesiastical Commissioners make us . . . The university of Cambridge is to bring their statutes to them to receive such corrections and alterations as their lordships shall think fit and they say also that Caius College [sic] statutes are likewise to run the same fate and I believe few colleges in either university have such correct statutes as to need no amendment if well looked into and strictly examined.

Freke seems surprisingly oblivious of the Catholicizing intent of the statutory revisions. He was an anticlerical Whig, and a kinsman of William Penn, the King's devoted Quaker supporter. Like many of his kind, he believed the universities were stocked with self-serving clerical reactionaries, whose doctrines of the Divine Right of Kings and of bishops had sponsored a terrible repression of Whigs and Nonconformists. In 1683 Locke himself had been expelled from Christ Church, Oxford, as a seditious Whig, and Freke was contemplating using influence at Court to get Locke restored.[58] Whigs were keenly aware that Anglican-Tory authorities had been as ready as the King now was to order summary expulsions of the religiously and politically incorrect. In Cambridge the master of the workhouse had been sacked for being a Protestant Nonconformist.[59] Among the Whigs there was also a strain of Puritan Baconianism which deplored the theological scholasticism of the universities. In 1683 Whig conspirators (whom Freke knew) planned, after their insurrection, to turn some colleges over to 'mechanical arts and agriculture', as being more useful than the production of 'supernumerary clergy'. They might have been surprised to learn that in 1684 the Fellows of Sidney purchased Joseph Moxon's *Mechanick Exercises*.[60]

No member of the Ecclesiastical Commission was, in fact, a Catholic, and the Commission's most recent historian, John Kenyon, has shown that, far from being merely a juggernaut for the King's Catholic missionary work, it engaged in a good deal of routine work of adjudication, discipline and reform, in such areas as simony, clandestine marriages, divorce, and corruptly governed schools and charities. However, Kenyon remarks that the Commission 'never used its sweeping powers to review and alter statutes of universities and colleges'.[61] At Sidney

---

[57] Thomas Sprat, *A Letter from the Bishop of Rochester* (1688), p. 13.
[58] *The Correspondence of John Locke*, ed. E.S. De Beer (Oxford, 1976–89), III, 210, 201.
[59] *CSPD*, 1687–89, p. 216.
[60] R.L. Greaves, *Secrets of the Kingdom: British Radicals from the Popish Plot to the Revolution of 1688–1689* (Stanford, 1992), p. 148; Muniments, MR 32, p. 450.
[61] J.P. Kenyon, 'The Commission for Ecclesiastical Causes: A Reconsideration', *Historical Journal*, 34 (1991), 735.

it certainly did. It was no doubt with those revisions in mind that, in April 1689, Isaac Newton – by this time MP for the university – drafted a Bill empowering the Crown to revise statutes 'and strike out whatever favours Popery, and instead thereof to insert other precepts agreeable to the Reformed religion'.[62]

Sidney Sussex's statutory revisions had been drawn up by Basset himself. In the College archive is a copy of the original statutes corrected by him.[63] The Commission meticulously deleted all the clauses relating to 'popery, heresies and superstitions'. The Master was also given power to admit students on his own authority. Apparently only six students were admitted in Basset's time, two of whom migrated from Caius where they had probably been his pupils. One of these, William Thompson, was certainly a Catholic, and in November 1687 he was intruded into a Fellowship, without consultation with the Fellows.[64]

James II's regime did not long survive. When William of Orange published his Declaration of the reasons for his 'expedition' to England in the winter of 1688 he denounced the maltreatment of the universities. And the Bill of Rights of 1689 condemned the Ecclesiastical Commission as 'illegal and pernicious'. The process of restoring the colleges to Protestancy began as William's revolution got under way. In the autumn of 1688 James, having grasped the reality of the impending invasion, rapidly went into abject retreat in a desperate bid to recover domestic support. In October the bishops delivered a long list of demands, including the calling of a free parliament, and the sacking of Popish heads of colleges. On 24 October Peachell was restored as Master of Magdalene.[65] On 5 November William of Orange's army landed at Torbay. On the 14th the Bishop of Durham, who had sat in the Ecclesiastical Commission, and was now, like Bishop Sprat, frantically back-tracking, asked the King

> that the Fellows of Sidney College in Cambridge, for whom I have so often moved your Majesty, may have leave to elect a new Master, in the place of Mr Basset (he being ... unqualified ...) [and] to proceed on all other affairs relating to that society, according to their original statutes and constitution.[66]

In the following days the King, by failing to fight the Battle of Salisbury Plain, threw away his crown. The wheels of royal retreat continued to turn, and on 1 December he rescinded Sidney Sussex's new statutes and the Fellows were authorised to elect a Master.[67] Basset was thereby deposed. On 9 December the

---

[62] Newton, *Correspondence*, III, 20–21.
[63] Muniments, Box 19, no. 2.
[64] *CSPD*, 1687–89, p. 95; Muniments, MR 108/1/4.
[65] *CSPD*, 1686–87, p. 443; 1687–89, p. 329. Dartmouth's notes on Burnet's *History* record of Peachell that 'After the Revolution he starved himself to death, in consequence of having been rebuked by Archbishop Sancroft for drunkenness and other loose habits'.
[66] Quoted in C.E. Whiting, *Nathaniel Lord Crewe, Bishop of Durham (1674–1721)* (London, 1940), p. 184.
[67] BL, Add. MS 5847, f. 112; *CSPD*, 1687–89, p. 369.

Fellows elected James Johnson as the sixth Master. On 11 December the King fled London in fear for his life.

Anti-popish riots swept the country and Catholic chapels were destroyed. On 13 December Alderman Newton recorded events in Cambridge:

> This night and several nights before there were up in arms a great many in this town, some nights 2 or 300 (many scholars among them) of the rabble called the mobile [mob], who at first under a pretence to seek for papists and such who had favoured them and to ransack their houses for arms, at last came to be very insulting and wherever they pleased, to enter men's houses and do them much mischief.[68]

One Catholic was made to dance naked in a ditch until he agreed to change his religion.[69] At Sidney, Basset's chapel was attacked and vestments and other accoutrements of worship were destroyed. The College spent eleven shillings for 'mending the chamber broken by the rabble'.[70] Basset fled to his native King's Lynn but quickly moved on to escape 'the then enraged mob'. He left the College so precipitately that he abandoned his belongings. When he attempted to recover them, Johnson brusquely told him that unless he desisted he would be informed against as a Popish priest.[71]

Basset settled in London, and died there in 1720, 'in no very affluent circumstances'.[72] We know next to nothing about the last thirty years of his life. He was a friend of Bishop Bonaventure Gifford, appointed Vicar Apostolic under James II, and of John Gother, James's chief Catholic propagandist, whose prayer books were used by English Catholics until Victorian times. We learn this from Edward Stephens, who, in 1705, pronounced that Quakers, Deists and Catholic missioners were England's greatest enemies.[73] Basset published his chief work of Catholic apologetic, *An Essay towards a Proposal for Catholic Communion*, in 1704: it was reissued in 1781, 1801 and 1879.[74] Like all Catholic books, it was the subject of government attention. The printer was arrested, and was so angry at

---

[68] *Diary of Alderman Newton*, p. 96.
[69] BL, MS Lansdowne 988, f. 189.
[70] W.L. Sachse, 'The Mob in the Revolution of 1688', *Journal of British Studies*, 3 (1964), p. 28; Muniments, MR 32, p. 486.
[71] BL, Add. MS 5821, f. 120. An inventory of the Master's Lodge, dated 12 December 1688, is in Muniments, MR 31D, pp. 13–15. Basset's inventory of his personal goods, including curtains for the 'chapel-chamber', is in MR 105/1. It also includes trees: it seems he improved the College gardens.
[72] BL, Add. MS 5821, f. 120.
[73] Edward Stephens, *An Essay* (1705), pp. iii, 5. See also his *Achan* (1704).
[74] Basset's third published work was a critique of the ecclesiology of the Anglican High Churchmen Henry Dodwell: *Ecclesiae theoria nova Dodwelliana exposita* (1713). Basset presented a copy to Sidney.

being the sole victim that he entrapped Basset in order to have him seized too. But Basset 'gave him a great blow with his cane', escaped, and disappeared.[75]

In 1725 Michel Le Quien, professor of theology in Paris, charged that Basset had suffered persecution at the hands of Protestants, and had been forced into hiding in the countryside, there to scratch a living teaching peasants to read.[76] When the Bishops of Lincoln and Norwich – and through them Archbishop William Wake of Canterbury – drew this charge to the attention of the then Master, Joseph Craven, they got a lengthy response. 'I never heard of any persecution he suffered from Protestants, or that he ever had any hard dealings from them.' As far as he knew, Basset had not been jailed. As for his ejection from Sidney, that 'was not done by Protestants, but by his good Roman Catholic King'. No 'menace' was used to evict him; indeed he 'willingly submitted' and sent a letter to the College 'soon after our election was over, [in which] he wishes the person joy who was chosen'. The College, Craven continued, magnanimously did not seek to have Basset excepted from the new regime's Act of Indemnity, though lesser enemies of religion and the constitution had been excepted. 'And thus . . . the Papists would fain make something of nothing'.[77]

We need lastly to turn to a singular irony. Like many articulate English Catholics in the late seventeenth century, Joshua Basset was, in fact, scarcely orthodox in his Catholicism. Craven wrote that he was

> such a mongrel papist, and had so many nostrums in his religion, that no part of the Roman Church could own him, . . . so that had he lived in a country, where the Inquisition reigns and had declared his opinions he would have been taken up for a heretic. Besides, his utmost contempt of the ordinary missionaries that came into England is well known to those, who had intimate conversation with him.[78]

Edward Stephens, an Anglican minister who had 'much conversation with him', agreed that, though a Catholic, Basset was 'indeed a very moderate one, as any I know, but yet so fixed'.[79] Another Anglican remarked that Basset's aim was 'to disguise Popery, as far as possibly he can in a Protestant dress, by palliating some parts of it, denying others, pleading for others that they are not obligatory'. It was such heretical stuff that he would not 'dare to write at this rate in Italy, or Spain'.[80]

---

[75] Pierre de Courayer, *A Defence of the Dissertation on the Validity of the English Ordinations* (1728), II, 387–8.
[76] Michel Le Quien, *Nullite des ordinations anglicanes* (Paris, 1725), pp. xxx–xxxii.
[77] Muniments, MR 108/1/2 (and see items 1, 3, 4); BL, MS Lansdowne 988, ff. 189–90. Craven's letter was published in Courayer's *Defence of the Dissertation*, II, 385–8. Courayer was a renegade Catholic priest who had fled France.
[78] BL, MS Lansdowne 988, f. 190.
[79] Basset, *Essay*, p. ix.
[80] Nathaniel Spinckes, *An Essay Towards a Proposal for Catholick Communion . . . Answered* (1705), sig. A3r, p. 304.

The character of Basset's Catholicism is best expressed in his *Essay* of 1704. He wrote that 'I have in every point enquired what is the most moderate sense in which the doctrine of the Roman Church is delivered'. The essence of Catholicism, he insisted, was not to be deduced from the outlandish opinions of some of its theologians, nor from the moral corruptions of some of its devotees. On this principle, he set out to draw the sting of every Protestant caricature of Roman doctrine. For example, he declared that the idea of papal infallibility was only a school of thought, which he himself did not share, preferring the conciliarist doctrine exemplified in the Gallican tradition. His litany of the liberties of the French Church was intended to imply that a re-Catholicized Anglican Church would scarcely have to do more than nod in the direction of the pope as a universal spiritual patriarch. Basset was convinced that Anglican priestly orders were valid, so that reunion with Rome would not require the humiliating act of re-ordination. In all this, his hero was J.B. Bossuet, the great French theologian and defender of Gallican independence, who had explored doctrinal accommodation with the German Protestant philosopher Leibniz.[81]

Basset left two distant shadows in Victorian times, the one concerning the state's right to interfere in the universities, the other concerning the relations between Catholics and Anglicans. In 1839 George Corrie, Professor of Divinity, future Master of Jesus College, and a leader of Conservative opinion in Cambridge, published *Brief Historical Notices of the Interference of the Crown with the Affairs of the English Universities*. Prompted by outrage against the commission which a Liberal, secular, and Erastian government imposed upon the universities, he recalled James II's tyrannous interferences, especially at Sidney, and came to the optimistic conclusion that under the Bill of Rights the universities were perpetually exempt from inspection by Royal Commissioners.[82]

Basset's theological shadow, almost his reincarnation, was Henry Oxenham, an Anglican minister who converted to Catholicism in 1857, but who could never abandon belief in the validity of his Anglican orders and declined to become a Catholic priest. He taught at Cardinal Newman's Oratory in Birmingham and published extensively for the cause of Anglican-Catholic relations. Like Lord Acton, England's most prominent Catholic lay intellectual, Oxenham was a disciple of the great theologian Dr Döllinger, under whom he studied at Tübingen. Oxenham was deeply hostile to ultramontanism, and rejected the declaration of papal infallibility in 1870, for a time adhering to Döllinger's breakaway Old Catholic Church. He admired 'the great name of Bossuet', and condemned the French Revolution for destroying the Gallican tradition, whereby 'the last

---

[81] Basset, *Essay*, in *An Eirenicon of the Eighteenth Century*, ed. H.N. Oxenham (London, 1879), pp. 101, 119ff, 288ff, and passim. Stephens said that the *Essay* 'is but an improvement' of Bossuet, and of Gother's *Papist Misrepresented* (1687), the most influential Catholic work published under James.

[82] George Corrie, *Brief Historical Notices* (1839), p. 100.

corporate protest against the modern pretensions of the Papacy was extinguished'.[83] In 1879 he republished Basset's *Essay* under the title *An Eirenicon of the Eighteenth Century*. In his introduction he praised the ecumenical tradition, reverencing Erasmus, Cassander, Grotius, Bossuet, Leibniz, and Döllinger. His footnotes used Newman as a commentary on Basset. He recited the history of attempts to reconcile Catholicism and Protestantism, and deplored the 'ruthless and uncompromising partisanship' of the Jesuits. Like Basset, Oxenham was a 'mongrel Papist', eclectic in his theology, a convert who did not become more Roman than Rome. Two centuries earlier, Basset had hoped for a rapprochement with the Church of England, not its humiliation or destruction. But no Protestant could see it like that.

It is striking how recently the Cold War of the Reformation has thawed in Cambridge. Catholics were not permitted to become Fellows of colleges until 1871: Sidney's first Catholic Fellow was F.H. Neville, in 1904.[84] Baron Anatole von Hügel, in 1883, was the first Catholic since the Reformation to hold a university post; Lord Acton, in 1895, the first professor; Nicholas Lash, in 1978, the first Catholic divinity professor; and Sir John Lyons, in 1984, at Trinity Hall, the first Catholic Master.[85] Sidney Sussex has not had another Popish Master since Joshua Basset.

---

[83] Henry Oxenham, *Short Studies in Ecclesiastical History and Biography* (London, 1884), pp. 71–2.
[84] W.G. Gorman, *Converts to Rome* (London, 1910), p. 200.
[85] I am grateful to Christopher Brooke and Timothy Smiley for this information.

Dictionary Johnson amidst the Dons of Sidney: A Chapter in Eighteenth-Century Cambridge History

JAMES BASKER

The great Samuel Johnson, certainly the Other Place's most famous dropout, is rarely associated with Cambridge. Yet during a tumultuous three-day visit in 1765, Johnson embraced Cambridge – and Sidney Sussex College – with an ardour that almost changed the course of his life and with it the history of the University. Slighted by his biographers and almost lost from memory, Johnson's Cambridge visit is little known or remarked upon. Boswell, having little information, gives it scarcely a mention, and once his celebrated *Life of Johnson* (1791) had appeared the additional details that emerged in the nineteenth century were lost in the shadows. Apart from Sidney's own historian C.W. Scott-Giles, who mentions it briefly,[1] few have remembered that Johnson's Cambridge visit centred on Sidney and that the whole occasion was chiefly the responsibility of a young Sidney Fellow named John Lettice. The frenetic and intensely social weekend Johnson spent in Cambridge not only adds a colourful episode to the history of the College; it also opens a window on the intellectual and literary life of the University during a period too often regarded as dull and dormant.

In 1765 John Lettice was an energetic and promising twenty-seven-year-old with literary aspirations. Having matriculated at Sidney in 1756, taken his BA (1761) and continued MA (1764), he had been elected to a College Fellowship which he would continue to hold until 1785.[2] His poem *The Conversion of Paul* had just won the Seatonian Prize for 1764, placing Lettice in rather select company: in the 1750s the brilliant but intermittently mad poet Christopher Smart, also a friend of Johnson's, had won the Seatonian Prize for five of its first

---

[1] C.W. Scott-Giles, *Sidney Sussex College: A Short History* (Cambridge, 1975), p. 87. See also H.P. Stokes, 'Dr Samuel Johnson's Visit to Cambridge in 1765', *The Cambridge Review*, 44 (1922–23), 229, 300–01, and 314–15.

[2] For details on John Lettice (1737–1832), see his entry in the *DNB* and in J.A. Venn, *Alumni Cantabrigienses, Part II*, 6 vols (Cambridge, 1940–54). Hereafter, all biographical information about Cambridge men is derived from Venn unless otherwise indicated.

six years after it was established in 1750.[3] As Lettice would disclose more than fifty years later, in the early 1760s he had also published an anonymous pamphlet called *A Council in the Moon*, in which he had made the daring proposal that college Fellows be allowed to marry.[4] (It would not be until the nineteenth century that Fellows were allowed to marry, but of course Lettice was far from the first young don to chafe under the restriction.)

It was a sign of his talent and enterprise that, by 1764, Lettice had somehow become acquainted with Samuel Johnson – 'well acquainted', Lettice's close friend Baptist Noel Turner remembered when he wrote about the episode, in collaboration with Lettice, for a London magazine in 1818–19.[5] Lettice had probably met Johnson through one of three people he already knew in Johnson's circle: James Grainger (1729–1766), a minor poet who had successfully cultivated Johnson's acquaintance since the mid-1750s and with whom Lettice had joined in the late 1750s or very early 1760s to work on a translation of Ovid's *Epistles* (the project was later abandoned); Thomas Percy (1729–1811), later Bishop of Dromore, a poet and antiquarian who had been introduced to Johnson by Grainger as early as 1756 and who, while remaining a lifelong member of the Johnson circle, also developed such a close friendship with Lettice that it would be remembered in Lettice's obituary in 1832; or Robert Levet (1705–1782), the poor physician who was one of Johnson's housemates and most beloved friends, whom Lettice had come to know by the 1760s and by whom he had been alerted to watch closely Johnson's tea-drinking habits (they proved remarkable).[6] Through whatever channels, Lettice had met Johnson in London and had come to know him sufficiently well that, when Johnson arrived in Cambridge, it was Lettice whose company he first sought out, it was Lettice who hosted the first social event in Johnson's honour, and it was Lettice who emerged as the only person known to have spent all three evenings of Johnson's visit (16–19 February 1765) in the great man's company.

Not surprisingly, it was also Lettice who put his friend Turner in touch with Johnson sometime before 1765. Turner, two years Lettice's junior, had been at

---

[3] Graham Chainey, *A Literary History of Cambridge* (Cambridge: The Pevensey Press, 1985), p. 81.
[4] Manuscript letter, Lettice to James Plumtre, 26 November 1819, preserved in the University Library, *Add.5866*.
[5] Baptist Noel Turner, letter of 17 October 1818, printed in *The New Monthly Magazine*, quoted here from John Nichols, *Illustrations of the Literary History of the Eighteenth Century*, VI, 147. Most of the detail about Johnson's visit to Cambridge did not emerge until Turner published this account in 1818–19, more than fifty years after the event; he composed it in collaboration, he says, with his 'dear and very old friend' John Lettice. (Lettice was eighty-one, Turner eighty.) Turner's account, including direct quotations from Lettice, is reprinted in full in Nichols (VI, 141–71) and is cited hereafter as *Turner*.
[6] *Boswell's Life of Johnson*, ed. George Birkbeck Hill and L.F. Powell (Oxford: Clarendon Press, 1934–58), I, 48 and 243–4, and II, 455; Nichols, *Literary Illustrations*, VII, 233; *Gentleman's Magazine*, 102 (Nov. 1832), ii, 477–80; *Turner*, p. 153.

Oakham School with Lettice and had followed him to Cambridge, taking his BA at Emmanuel in 1762 and staying on for his MA and a Fellowship at Emmanuel until 1769.[7] While Turner was still a student at Emmanuel he and Lettice projected a joint plan for a new translation of Plutarch's *Lives*. Lettice had suggested they seek Johnson's opinion of the project before proceeding and so, at Lettice's urging, Turner called on the 'literary Colossus' during one of his jaunts to London.

The result was a memorable meeting for Turner that also seems to have stirred Johnson's curiosity about Cambridge. Turner recalls that first encounter with Johnson this way: 'at the top of a few steps the door opened into a dark and dingy looking old wainscotted anti-room, through which, a little before noon, came rolling, as if just roused from his cabin, the truly uncouth figure of our literary Colossus, in a strange black wig, too little for him by half . . . He seemed pleased to see a young Cantab in his rooms, and on my acquainting him with the business on which I had taken the liberty of consulting him, he rather encouraged our undertaking than otherwise.' Despite this encouragement, which must have lifted spirits when reported back to Lettice in Cambridge, Lettice and Turner would later drop the Plutarch plan as too demanding. Eventually, Turner recalls, the conversation turned from the young authors' projects to larger subjects: 'After this, the great man questioned me about Cambridge, and whatever regarded literature, and attended to my answers with great complacency.'[8]

Curiosity about Cambridge soon turned into action. Plied with invitations from his young friends Lettice and Turner, interested as always in seeing new places (especially centres of learning), and eager to meet such figures as the Shakespearean scholar Richard Farmer (whose scholarship he admired), Johnson found himself riding into Cambridge one Saturday in mid-February 1765 in a phaeton driven by his young friend Topham Beauclerk. Beauclerk, a twenty-five-year-old aristocrat who had come down from Trinity College, Oxford to pursue a literary life in London, had been friends with Johnson since the late 1750s. Beauclerk was typical of the many bright young people, male and female, whose company Johnson treasured and on whose energies he thrived all his life. It was easy for Beauclerk to think of going to Cambridge, for he had a friend at Trinity (the young Fellow George Leycester) and he had his own carriage; in offering transportation and company on the journey, he provided Johnson with the final inducements to accept Lettice's and Turner's invitation to come to Cambridge. Beauclerk and Johnson arrived on Saturday evening, driving directly to the Rose Inn in the marketplace.[9]

---

[7] Turner (1740–1826) left Emmanuel in 1769 to get married and assume the Headmastership of his and Lettice's alma mater, Oakham School (1769–1778); he pursued a career as a cleric and author of minor writings on literature and religion. See Nichols, *Literary Illustrations*, VI, 141–71 passim.

[8] *Turner*, p. 148.

[9] The Rose Inn was for many years located on the north side of the marketplace, but is now

Thus the weekend began. Never one to yield to the fatigues of travel, Johnson immediately sent a message to John Lettice at Sidney to join him for dinner. It would no doubt have been thrilling in any circumstances for a young College Fellow to receive such an invitation. What became a particular point of pride for Lettice was that he 'had the honour' [in Turner's words] 'to be the only gownsman sent for by the great man to spend the first evening with him'.[10] Whether Beauclerk joined them or Johnson and Lettice dined on their own, where they took their meal, what they ate and drank and talked about, how late they stayed out: all the details, sadly, have disappeared from memory.

The following morning was Sunday, but despite the presence of St Mary's just yards away, Johnson did not go to church. This Turner chose to interpret as a deliberate decision on Johnson's part, a tribute to his piety and consideration. Had the famous Johnson turned up at church, Turner reasoned, he would have attracted 'the general gaze during the whole service' and thus 'turned . . . a Christian church into an idol temple'. Turner may not have known, or not wanted to think, that Johnson frequently slept late and missed church wherever he was. If his dinner with Lettice had turned into a late night – a strong possibility, given the sessions that were to unfold over the next two evenings – then Johnson may have had other reasons for not stirring from his bed on Sunday morning.

Indeed, for many years the tradition prevailed that Johnson did not resurface at all until Monday. Dr John Sharp of Trinity, in an irreverent and self-serving account published in the *Gentleman's Magazine* in 1785, reports that 'Caliban, you may be sure, was not roused from his lair before next day noon, and his breakfast probably kept him till night. I saw nothing of him, nor was he heard of by any one, till Monday afternoon, when I was sent for.'[11] In fact Sharp, a Fellow of Trinity since 1746, does seem to have hosted Johnson and his youthful company at tea on Monday and to have observed a raucous dinner party in Johnson's honour at Trinity later the same evening. But Sharp contrives (not for the first time in the history of Cambridge dinner parties) to make himself seem the focus of Johnson's Cambridge visit, rather than the peripheral and rather accidental observer he was, and in his very patchy account can offer nothing about Johnson's whereabouts at any other time over the weekend.

What Johnson actually did on Sunday, as revealed by Turner and Lettice fifty years after the event, was go round to Sidney for a party in his honour thrown by John Lettice. In his rooms at Sidney Lettice hosted a little 'Sunday party', to which he had invited a handful of guests. In addition to Johnson, they included: Lettice's close friend and future reporter of the weekend's events B.N. Turner from Emmanuel; Johnson's travelling companion Topham Beauclerk; Beauclerk's

---

remembered only in the name of 'Rose Crescent' which runs through what were the inn's stable yards.
[10] *Turner*, p. 152.
[11] Sharp's letter, dated 1 March 1765, published in the *Gentleman's Magazine* in 1785 and reprinted by Birkbeck Hill and Powell in *Boswell's Life of Johnson*, I, Appendix C, 517–18.

Cambridge friend, a Trinity Fellow named George Leycester; and the Regius Professor of Greek, also a Fellow at Trinity, Dr Michael Lort.[12] Of this little party, which Turner in his recollections terms the 'Sidney Symposium', Lettice himself gives a very brief account:

> Our distinguished visitor shone gloriously in his style of dissertation on a great variety of subjects. I recollect his condescending to as earnest a care of the animal as of the intellectual man, and after doing all the justice to my College bill of fare, and without neglecting the glass after dinner, he drank sixteen dishes of tea. I was idly curious enough to count them, from what I had remarked, and heard Levett [Johnson's friend Dr Robert Levet] mention of his extraordinary devotion to the tea-pot.[13]

Whatever was served in 'the glass after dinner', it must have been quite invigorating, because Turner goes on to reveal that the party lasted past sunrise: 'we kept it up till day-light', he writes, and 'the great man [Johnson] was in high glee'. Sometime after dawn Turner staggered home to Emmanuel, filled with anxiety, a friend later reminded him, about being seen in the streets 'at so improper an hour'. Upon arriving at his college he was relieved to find the gate unlocked, but then abashed to stumble upon some workmen who were 'astonished at seeing . . . a grave fellow of the College in his gown . . . retiring to sleep just as they rose to work'.[14]

Johnson probably fared better. He was known for his late-night stamina and on more than one occasion had stayed out all night on London frolics with men half his age. Of the 'great variety of subjects' on which Johnson 'shone gloriously' through the night at the Sidney Symposium, neither Lettice nor Turner gives specific details, but they were undoubtedly the same topics as those on which he is known to have expounded at other points in his Cambridge weekend: recent books, politics, and literature, especially (it is interesting to note) the writings of Cambridge authors. Thus, when a question arose about one of Milton's sonnets, for example, Johnson stunned his auditors and revealed much about his esteem for Milton by reciting, one witness recalls, 'the whole sonnet instantly *memoriter* . . . after which he learnedly harangued on sonnet-writing and its different numbers'.[15] Coming from the critic who fifteen years later, in his 'Life of Milton', would systematically denounce Milton's finest lyric poem *Lycidas* ('the diction is harsh, the rhymes uncertain, and the numbers unpleasing') and say of Milton's sonnets that of even the best of them 'it can only be said, that they are not bad', Johnson's impromptu recital is astonishing. Perhaps it was also on this evening he first expressed his view that the English language itself was no good for sonnets:

---

[12] *Turner*, pp. 152 and 165.
[13] *Turner*, pp. 152–3.
[14] *Turner*, p. 165.
[15] Sharp, p. 229.

'the fabric of a sonnet, however adapted to the Italian language, has never succeeded in ours'.

Critical pronouncements poured forth, presumably along with the drink. At another point someone mentioned Christopher 'Kit' Smart and his recent escape from a 'house of confinement', whereupon Johnson – who always took great pity on Smart and frequently extended him charity – had the following exchange with Beauclerk:

> *Beauclerk*: '[Smart] was a fool for that, for within two days they meant to have released him.'
> *Johnson*: 'Whenever poor Kit could make his escape, Sir, it would always have been within two days of his liberation.'

Johnson then, according to Turner's account of the conversation, 'proceeded to speak highly of the parts and scholarship of poor Kit; and to our great surprise, recited a number of lines out of one of Smart's Latin Triposes; and added, "Kit Smart was mad, Sir." '

> *Beauclerk*: 'What do you mean by mad, Doctor?'
> *Johnson*: 'Why, Sir, he could not walk the streets without the boys running after him.'

Shortly after this, when Johnson left the room for a moment, Beauclerk added, probably with a mixture of puckishness and compassion: 'What he says of Smart is true of himself.' Fifty years later Turner would remember that he had observed the same thing about Johnson as he walked through the streets of Cambridge that weekend in 1765.

When the topic of Johnson's least favourite Cambridge author, Laurence Sterne, arose, he offered the young academics a first-hand anecdote fresh from the London literary scene. Said Johnson:

> In a company where I lately was, Tristram Shandy [i.e., Sterne] introduced himself; and Tristram Shandy had scarcely sat down, when he informed us that he had been writing a Dedication to Lord Spencer; and *sponte sua* he pulled it out of his pocket; and *sponte sua* for nobody desired him, he began to read it; and before he had read half a dozen lines, *sponte mea*, Sir, I told him it was not English, Sir.[16]

However much his audience may have enjoyed such slams by London's 'Literary Dictator', he was to prove spectacularly wrong about Sterne. 'Nothing odd will do long', Boswell records him saying years later, '*Tristram Shandy* did not last.'[17]

The subject of politics roused Johnson even more, especially when it came time for proposing toasts: 'On being asked for a toast, his answer was, "If you wish for

---

[16] *Turner*, p. 156.
[17] *Boswell's Life of Johnson*, II, 449.

a gentleman, I shall always give you Mr Hollis; if for a lady, Mrs Macaulay, Sir." '
To the arch-Tory Johnson, the Whiggish politics of Thomas Hollis (a wealthy liberal and American sympathizer) and Catharine Macaulay (the radical Whig historian) were self-evidently ridiculous and always fair game. On his last night in Cambridge, at about midnight, Johnson reportedly 'began to be very great; stripped poor Mrs Macaulay to the very skin, then gave her for his toast, and drank her in two bumpers'.[18] But it was Hollis who unwittingly had the last laugh: the year after Johnson's visit he presented Sidney with the portrait of Oliver Cromwell – whose memory Johnson detested – that has hung in the College Hall ever since.[19]

The late-night revels grew livelier as the drink went round, but clearly Johnson could hold his own at all hours. After considerable 'sportiveness and play of wit, at the lady's [Macaulay's] expense', Johnson is reported to have been challenged by Beauclerk:

Beauclerk: 'Come, come, Doctor, take care what you say, and don't be too saucy about Mrs. Macaulay; for, if you do, I shall find means of setting her upon you as soon as we return, and she will comb your wig for you pretty handsomely.'
Johnson: 'Well, Sir, and pray by what means do you propose to achieve this notable exploit of yours, Mr. Beauclerk?'
Beauclerk: 'Oh! I'll soon tell you that, Doctor. You can't deny that it's now a full fortnight since Mrs. M. made you a present of her history [*History of England*, 1763–]; and to my certain knowledge it still remains in your study without one of the leaves being cut open; which is such a contempt of the lady's genius and abilities, that, should I acquaint her with it, as perhaps I shall, I wouldn't be in your place, Doctor, for a good deal, I assure you.'
Johnson ['sub-laughing all the while']: 'Why, in the first place, Sir, I am so far from denying your allegations, that I freely confess, before this company, that they are perfectly true and correct. The work of Mrs. Macaulay is indeed in the situation you have described. But in the second place, Sir, I may safely, I believe, defy all your oratorical powers so far as to work upon that lady's vanity as to induce her to believe it possible, that I could have suffered her writings to lie by me so long, without once gratifying myself by a perusal of them.'

Having speared Macaulay, Johnson aimed his final barb at Beauclerk with mock defiance: 'Pray try, Mr. Beauclerk, I beg you will try, Sir, . . . and then we shall see whether you will soonest bring the lady about my ears, or about your own, Sir.'[20] Through it all, however boisterous or combative the conversation got – and the young dons admitted that they 'sometimes purposely contradicted [Johnson]

---

[18] Sharp, p. 229.
[19] Scott-Giles, pp. 128–9.
[20] *Turner*, p. 158.

to elicit the sparks of his genius by collision' – the mood always remained (in Turner's phrase) one of 'convivial hilarity'.[21] Johnson loved it.

However little he slept, Johnson seems to have stayed at Sidney on Sunday night. Turner remembers coming back to Sidney on Monday morning to pick Johnson up and take him off to Emmanuel to introduce him to Richard Farmer. Because Johnson had not yet seen much of Cambridge, Turner took him on a circuitous route (according to his own recollection) via Trinity (which Johnson 'admired in course'), Trinity Hall ('I like that College', said Johnson), then Clare, King's, St Catharine's, Queens', Pembroke, and Peterhouse, before arriving at Emmanuel.

Meanwhile Lettice, after two nights of Johnsonian revels, must have been relieved to be left on his own for a while, and perhaps to get some rest. He would have been especially glad for the rest when it developed later on Monday that the whole 'Sidney Symposium' – Johnson, Lettice, Turner, Beauclerk, Lort, and Leycester, reinforced with the addition of Richard Farmer – were to reassemble in Leycester's rooms at Trinity and embark on what was for Lettice a third consecutive night of 'convivial hilarity' with Johnson. Boswell himself could hardly have asked for more – would that Lettice had also shared Boswell's obsession to scribble down every detail.

At Emmanuel, Turner presented Johnson to Farmer and their meeting went extremely well. Each had a favourable preconception of the other. Johnson admired Farmer's scholarly work on Shakespeare and was interested in consulting him about his edition of *The Works of Shakespeare*, which was just then in final preparation for publication a few months later, in October 1765. On his part, Farmer so admired Johnson's accomplishments that he had written to the Government on Johnson's behalf when he was being considered for a pension in 1762.[22] Their talk was predictably bookish, ranging from Shakespeare and some obscure medieval texts to contemporary writers such as William Shenstone and Richard Hurd. Overall, according to Turner who witnessed it, 'the long-wished-for interview . . . was uncommonly joyous on both sides'.[23] Farmer recorded his own description of this meeting just a few days after it occurred, in a personal letter to Thomas Percy. His impressions of Johnson were indeed powerful, but not without ambivalence:

> I have had the unexpected pleasure of Mr. JOHNSON'S Company at *Cambridge* – a Character the most extraordinary, that it has ever been my fortune to meet with. – I admire him, & I pity him: you will not ask me a reason for the former – his Compass of knowledge, & his manner of expressing that knowledge are really admirable. [B]ut he has *pitiable* infirmities both in body & mind. I can excuse his *Dogmatisms* & *Prejudices*; but he

---

[21] *Turner*, pp. 155 and 157.
[22] Howard Erskine-Hill, 'The Political Character of Samuel Johnson', *Samuel Johnson: New Critical Essays*, ed. Isobel Grundy (London: Vision Press, 1984), pp. 121–2.
[23] *Turner*, p. 154.

throws about rather too much of what some *Frenchman* calls the *Essence of BUT*: in plain *English*, he seems to have something to *except* in every man's Character. *Hurd* for instance comes off badly, & *Shenstone* still worse: he pitys *You* for your opinion of the latter.[24]

Farmer did note, however, that Johnson was greatly enjoying his time in Cambridge and seemed eager to spend more time among his friends there: 'He was in good spirits, & seem'd pleas'd with us: the latter he confirm'd, by promising another visit towards Summer.' Then, perhaps sensing that he had earlier sounded a bit churlish about someone who at one of the college parties had lavished praise on him in front of his Cambridge colleagues ('Gi'me your hand, gi'me your hand, you are the man after my own heart,' Johnson is reported to have said to Farmer, evidently at some late hour in the proceedings),[25] Farmer enjoins Percy to secrecy: 'What I say of *Johnson* is in confidence – [even] if my Character was sufficient for it, I would not hurt his.'

That night Farmer joined the 'Sidney Symposium' when it reconvened, its venue now shifted to Trinity, where Lettice's group of Johnsonians were beginning to resemble an eighteenth-century version not so much of 'The Apostles' as of Ken Kesey's 'Merry Pranksters'. Initially the party gathered in Leycester's rooms in Nevile's Court at Trinity, but over the course of the evening it grew or migrated or somehow became so evident that John Sharp and other unnamed Trinity members got swept up in it. About this party on Monday evening, all the surviving accounts are in general agreement: many toasts were drunk, Johnson again held forth and 'waxed great' on various topics, and once again the party roared on well past midnight. The evening seems to have taken its toll on Richard Farmer who, though more than twenty-five years younger than Johnson, lacked his late-night stamina. He struggled to recover for days afterwards, as he also reveals in his letter to Percy about the Johnson visit, when he coaches Percy about how to arrange his own meeting with Johnson. In a deft stroke of understatement, Farmer cautions Percy to be sure that any such meeting with Johnson occur out of term, 'for his hours are not very Academical & I have been obliged to work double tides ever since'.[26]

There is no information about where Johnson slept on Monday night or whether poor Lettice had to get him back to a guestroom in Sidney. But everyone confirms, perhaps with relief, that Johnson returned to London on Tuesday morning. No one dreamed that this would be the last time Johnson ever visited Cambridge. Quite the opposite: Farmer expected him to come back in the spring or early summer; Sharp says 'He tells me he will come hither again quickly, and is promised "an habitation in Emanuel College" '; and Lettice, who proved both

---

[24] Farmer to Thomas Percy, 25 Feb. 1765, reprinted in *Boswell's Life of Johnson*, I, Appendix G, 555.
[25] *Turner*, p. 157.
[26] Farmer to Percy, *Boswell's Life of Johnson*, I, 555.

hospitable and durable in 1765, represented a standing invitation to Johnson over the rest of his life, continuing as a Fellow at Sidney until the year after Johnson's death in 1784.

Given that for many years there was talk of Johnson accepting an academic post at Cambridge (usually at Emmanuel, where Farmer became Master in 1775), one wonders whether such a prospect ever glimmered in the minds of the Sidney Fellowship. During his stay in Sidney, did Johnson meet any of the other dons who might have joined with John Lettice in making such a nomination? Did he meet even fleetingly, for example, the Master, William Elliston? A Fellow since 1758 and Master 1760–1807, Elliston is revealed by the College records to have been sufficiently interested in Johnson's writings to have signed out and carried home various books of his over the years, among them Johnson's *Dictionary*, his *Rambler* essays, and a volume containing *Rasselas, Irene*, and his major poems.[27]

Or did he meet Thomas Martyn, Fellow of Sidney 1758–73 and Professor of Botany 1762–1825, with whom Lettice collaborated on various scholarly projects including *The Antiquities of Herculaneum* (1773), a massive undertaking about which Johnson was consulted and over which he commiserated with Lettice and Martyn ('They don't know what they have undertaken; the engravers will drive them mad')?[28] Perhaps in connection with these projects, Martyn regularly consulted Johnson's *Dictionary*: College records show him checking out the two folio volumes during the late 1760s, on one occasion keeping them for more than four months (August 6 to December 30, 1769). Moreover, as he eventually married the Master's sister Martha Elliston, in a Fellowship Election Martyn might have wielded influence in more ways than one.

Would Thomas Twining have taken a part, albeit as a former fellow? A brilliant classical scholar, he had entered Sidney in 1755 and held a Fellowship 1760–64, moving out just months before Johnson's visit, in order to get married. In other contexts Twining showed a deep and abiding interest in the life and works of Samuel Johnson: his private correspondence is full of references to Johnson and his work, it was to Twining that Dr Charles Burney would write in December 1784 to lament the paltry ceremonies he felt had so disgraced Johnson's burial a few days earlier, and in 1797 Twining paid homage to Johnson's memory by making a pilgrimage to an old willowtree in Lichfield said to be connected with Johnson.[29]

Surely Richard Hey would also have supported a Johnson nomination after he came to Sidney as a Fellow in 1768, though he had been only a twenty-year-old

---

[27] Elliston's borrowings, along with those of the other Sidney Fellows, are listed in the original borrowing books now preserved in the College Muniment Room. My thanks are due to Mr Nicholas Rogers for his generous help and advice in deciphering these records. Unless otherwise indicated, all further references to Sidney Fellows' reading habits are derived from them.

[28] *Turner*, p. 149; Scott-Giles, pp. 84–5.

[29] Scott-Giles, p. 83; *Boswell's Life of Johnson*, IV, 372, n. 1 and 420, n. 1.

undergraduate at Magdalene when Johnson made his descent on Cambridge in 1765. He too was a friend of John Lettice's (he donated copies of Lettice's books to the College Library) and from the moment he arrived in the College in 1768 he became one of the most frequent borrowers of Johnson's *Dictionary*, regularly lugging the two massive folio volumes off to his rooms to consult them as he worked. Still another Sidney Fellow of the late 1760s might also have been predisposed in Johnson's favour: Christopher Hunter, a prize-winning scholar who matriculated in 1763 and stayed on as a Fellow until the mid-1780s, had been an undergraduate in Sidney when Johnson visited in 1765. How could the buzz of the great man's presence not have reached him and the other undergraduates, and what impression did it make on them? As a Fellow, Hunter too is shown by the borrowing records to have used Johnson's works regularly in the College library over the course of the 1770s and '80s.

It is irresistible to extend the fantasy and speculate for a moment on what might have happened if Johnson *had* been elected and come to Sidney as a Fellow sometime after 1765. Obviously he would have felt welcomed by all these friends and admirers among the Fellows, and no doubt he would have overawed (and amused) the students. Some events would have been foreseeable. A passionate monarchist, Johnson would have been there in time to back Master Elliston's decision (c.1772) to reject the offer of Cromwell's head, though his unease at seeing Cromwell's portrait in the Hall every day can only be imagined.[30] Others are open questions. Would Johnson have joined in scholarly or literary projects with Lettice or Martyn or Twining or any of the other Fellows? When compiling his *Lives of the Poets* in the late 1770s would he have included what one source has called 'the only poet ever to emerge from Sidney Sussex College', the brilliant but self-destructive William Pattison (1706–1727)?[31] From a Cambridge base, might he have tempered, deepened, or otherwise reconsidered his treatment in the *Lives* of other Cambridge poets such as Milton, Dryden, and Gray? In the 1780s wouldn't Johnson surely have supported the anti-slavery ideas of Henry William Coulthurst, who came to Sidney as a Fellow in 1781 and who would become the Cambridge University correspondent for the Abolition Society when it formed in the late 1780s? Perhaps Johnson, who loathed slavery and had taken an active role in opposing it as early as the 1770s, might have joined with Coulthurst to accelerate the emergence of Cambridge as a centre of the anti-slavery movement from about 1784–5.[32]

The possibilities are endless. Would Johnson have lectured? Delivered sermons? Written more? Inspired a school of followers? Perhaps the one thing we can say

---

[30] Scott-Giles, pp. 128–9 and 132–3.
[31] For an account of William Pattison and excerpts from his poetry, see Chainey, *Literary History of Cambridge*, p. 69.
[32] See, for example, Johnson's legal brief against slavery addressed to a Scottish Court in 1777 on behalf of an African slave seeking his freedom, in *Boswell's Life of Johnson*, III, 202–203.

with certainty, given the record of his stay in Cambridge and his love of drink, talk, and company, is that he would have taken Combination Room nights to new heights. But perhaps in that context he might well have sparked something more, might have gathered around him a group of lively and creative minds analogous to his beloved 'Club' in London, with its Burke, its Reynolds, its Boswell and its Goldsmith. If so, then Johnson might have made the 'Sidney Symposium', an impromptu group named in jest, into a lasting reality.

Though Johnson was to live for another twenty years, he never returned to Cambridge. But Cambridge lived on in his memory and in his affections. In a conversation between George III and Johnson in 1767, the King asked him 'whether there were better libraries at Oxford or Cambridge'. Johnson answered that 'he believed the Bodleian was larger than any they had at Cambridge', but then added, in a gesture of respect for the scholars at Cambridge and perhaps a dig at his alma mater on the Thames, 'I hope, whether we have more books or not than they have at Cambridge, we shall make as good use of them as they do'.[33] A decade later, in a letter to Farmer (now Master of Emmanuel) asking about some archives in the University Library that might be useful in preparing his *Lives of the Poets*, Johnson welcomes the prospect of a return visit to Cambridge: 'If you think my inspection [of the archives] necessary, I will come down, for who that has once experienced the civilities of Cambridge would not snatch the opportunity of another visit?'[34] Conversely, there are signs that Johnson lived on in other ways in Cambridge, and in Sidney specifically. His influence continued in the lives of the young Cantabrigians he met, perhaps most evidently in that of John Lettice. Lettice remained a Fellow of Sidney until 1785, spent 1768–72 as chaplain to the British Embassy in Copenhagen, in 1785 accepted the living at Peasmarsh he would hold into his nineties, and from 1799 added the job of tutor to the Beckford family to his duties. His correspondence shows him as late as the 1820s maintaining his connections with Sidney, hiring Sidney BAs as his curates and trying to keep up on College gossip. Through it all, he never abandoned his aspirations to a literary career. Everywhere in his innumerable writings the force of Johnson's example can be seen: his efforts at biography (a translation of Holberg's *Parallel Lives of Famous Women* [c.1770] and his series of Scottish *Lives* in the 1790s), his travelogue *Letters on a Tour through Scotland* (1794), his critical essays on Gay's *Fables* in 1815–16, his volume of writings in prose and verse *Miscellaneous Pieces* (c.1820). Literary fame and, in the end, even Cambridge prizes eluded him: in 1822 at the age of eighty-five he submitted a 500-line poem in blank verse on 'Antioctus Epiphanes' [sic] for the Seatonian Prize, only to be rejected (to his chagrin) because the competition was not open to anyone 'beyond 40 years of age'.[35] Still, when he died in 1832, a month short of his ninety-fifth

---

[33] *Boswell's Life of Johnson*, II, 35.
[34] Johnson to Richard Farmer, 22 July 1777, *The Letters of Samuel Johnson*, ed. Bruce Redford (Princeton: Princeton University Press, 1992), III, 43.
[35] Lettice to Plumptre, 29 November 1822, unpublished letters of Lettice in the University

birthday, he was described in a long obituary in the *Gentleman's Magazine* as 'almost the only survivor of the literary coterie of Drs. Johnson and Goldsmith'.

More subtly but perhaps more pervasively, Johnson also lived on in the collective mind of the College – a story told largely by the College Library borrowing records. From the 1760s until about 1820, the available records show that Johnson was one of the authors most widely read (or consulted) by the College Fellows, regardless of their fields. At least twenty-four different Fellows signed out books by Johnson during that period (how many more read them on site or owned their own copies?). They borrowed only his two-volume folio *Dictionary* until 1787, when the College acquired a copy of the first collected edition of his *Works* (11 volumes), edited by John Hawkins, which had just been published that year. (The College was evidently short of money because Johnson's *Works* seem to be the only new books acquired in 1787 and, rather than purchasing them outright, the librarian arranged to trade some 'Old Folio Common Prayer Books' to get them as part of a swap with the Cambridge bookseller Deighton.) The fact that the *Dictionary* was allowed to circulate, even just among the Fellows, is most striking: not only would it seem to deprive others of access to a standard reference work, sometimes for weeks or even months at a time, but the massive size and weight of the two folio volumes fosters images of frail dons staggering around the College under their lexicographical burden. To their credit, at least Sidney's Fellows were using it seriously: the records at All Souls in Oxford show that Johnson's *Dictionary* sat in their common room without circulating from 1755 until the mid-nineteenth century because it perched next to the wager book and was used purely to settle bets among the fellows.

Along with Johnsoniana, the records also yield haphazard glimpses of eighteenth-century College life. All of Johnson's works were checked out several times, for example, but, in an inversion of the usual patterns in community and commercial lending libraries of the time, the most frequently circulated volumes were not the *Rambler* or *Idler* but the *Lives of the Poets* (by a ratio of 2:1). Some Fellows borrowed single volumes of Johnson and others seven volumes at a time; some returned them next day and some kept them months at a time; and some continued to borrow books years after leaving their fellowships (Lettice once borrowed three volumes of Johnson eight years after he had moved on to his living at Peasmarsh). At least one kindly Fellow, William Cruttenden, checked out volumes of Johnson on behalf of a final-year undergraduate, Samuel Phillipps. But the most compelling story of a Johnson reader at Sidney has to be that of Samuel Chilcott, a young unmarried Fellow who entered the library and signed for four volumes of Johnson's *Works* on 25 December 1801. One needn't be a

---

Library, *Add 5866*. Lettice's correspondence reveals many previously unknown publications of his spanning more than sixty years, from the 1760s to the 1820s.

Dickensian sentimentalist to find pathos in a lonely don trying to divert himself with the works of Johnson on Christmas Day.

All these volumes of Johnson are now out of circulation, stored with the other college treasures in the Muniment Room. Like them, the memory of Johnson's presence in Sidney has faded. A well-placed plaque and an appropriate annual ceremony (though surely not a drink-till-dawn 'Sunday party') might one day restore to College history some of the afterglow of Johnson's remarkable visit, when Sidney added its mite to Cambridge literary history.

William Chafy and the Architectural Transformation of Sidney Sussex College, 1813–37

PETER SALT

Introduction

C.W. Scott-Giles, in his *Short History* of Sidney Sussex College, entitled his account of the College in the nineteenth century 'Transformation Scene'.[1] The first act in that transformation was the architectural refurbishment of the College in the 1820s and 1830s, during the mastership of William Chafy (1813–43) (Plate 9). In those decades, the Elizabethan brickwork of Hall Court, the slightly later but similar work of Sir Francis Clerke's range, and the then relatively new chapel (designed by James Essex) all disappeared beneath a coat of stucco; the present gateway and the stone-faced tower above it were built and the College received its existing pinnacles and crow-stepped gables – all in intended imitation of the original architecture, albeit to modern eyes not a particularly faithful imitation (compare Plates 8a and 8b). Initial proposals for this refurbishment were obtained from Charles Humfrey in 1820, but the work was carried out (more extensively than at first envisaged) in two phases during 1822–3 and 1831–7, to designs by Jeffry Wyatville.[2] These were not, however, the only building works during Chafy's mastership, which also saw changes to the Master's Lodge and garden, and revenue-earning building activity in the form of the construction of Sidney Place and of the rebuilding of the north side of Sussex Street and of part of Sidney Street. I have written elsewhere on the refurbishment of the College buildings to the designs of Wyatville.[3] The aim of this paper is to

---

[1] C.W. Scott-Giles, *Sidney Sussex College: A Short History* (rev. edn, Cambridge, 1975), chap. 8.
[2] Jeffry Wyatt was licensed to use the name Wyatville by royal warrant dated 6 November 1824, although in practice he used the longer name from August 1824 – at Sidney, there are drawings signed with the longer name dated 22 October 1824: Derek Linstrum, *Sir Jeffry Wyatville: Architect to the King* (Oxford, 1972), pp. 48, 221; Sidney Sussex College Muniment Room, 'Plans and Drawings of Sidney Sussex College by Jeffry Wyatt, 1821–1833' (hereafter: Wv), C1–11. For simplicity, and in order to distinguish Sir Jeffry from other members of his family, he is henceforth identified as 'Wyatville' throughout this paper.
[3] Peter Salt, 'Wyatville's Remodelling and Refurbishment of Sidney Sussex College, 1820–1837', *Proceedings of the Cambridge Antiquarian Society*, 81 (1992), 115–55. Material

discuss more fully the particular contribution of the Master to the conception and execution of College building enterprises during this period. The opportunity will be taken to discuss in detail those projects with which Wyatville was not involved, which were mentioned only in passing in the earlier paper.

1. *Chafy and the Origins of the Refurbishment of the College Buildings*

College records of the early nineteenth century provide no account of internal debate, and no other sources which directly reveal the collegiate decision-making process have come to light. However, Chafy's position in the College was a powerful one. Like other contemporary heads of house, he held both the mastership and the bursarship. Chafy's view of magisterial and bursarial authority is probably reflected in his opposition to the attempts of the Fellows of Christ's to appeal against the conduct of their Master and Bursar: Chafy was said to have taken the view 'that it was *merely* a dispute about the Bursar's expenditure; . . . that the Bursar was the best judge of expenditure . . .'.[4] Furthermore, Sidney was a small college – the early nineteenth-century establishment included only twelve Fellows; since some fellowships were kept vacant and many Fellows did not reside, meetings were small. The decision in 1820 to refurbish the Hall range was made by a meeting of the Master and six Fellows.[5] Meetings in 1831 and 1832, at which it was decided to implement the second phase of Wyatville's works, were better attended (by eight and seven Fellows respectively), but Chafy still provided an important element of continuity – only three Fellows were at all three meetings.[6] Finally, although there is little direct evidence for Chafy's style of management

from this paper is reproduced here by kind permission of the editor of the *Proceedings*. All those whose assistance is acknowledged in the earlier paper have indirectly helped in the composition of this one, but I am particularly grateful to Nicholas Rogers for his continuing help in identifying relevant material in the College Archives; I am also grateful to the staff of the other libraries and record repositories whose holdings are cited, and to Mr T.S. Wyatt of Sidney Sussex College, who read a typescript of this paper and drew my attention to some useful references. For the layout of the College see the plan opposite p. 3 above.

[4] Henry Gunning, *Reminiscences of the university, town and county of Cambridge from the year 1780*, 2 vols (London, 1854), II, 257–8 (my italics).

[5] Sidney Sussex College Muniment Room, Masters' Records (hereafter: MR.), 2 ('Acta Collegii Dominae Franciscae Sidney Sussex', 1637–1863), p. 205. For vacant fellowships at Sidney, see Salt, 'Wyatville', pp. 150, 152; manuscript annotations in a Cambridge University Library copy of Henry Gunning, *The Poll for the Election of a Representative in Parliament for the University of Cambridge . . . 26th and 27th November, 1822* (Cambridge, 1822), pp. 35, 37 (Cam.c.822.11) suggest that, of the six Fellows who voted, only two (the Dean and the Tutor) were resident; the Fellows who did not vote are unlikely to have been resident at the time. Only two Sidney Fellows, again the Dean and the Tutor, had voted in the poll for election of the University Librarian the previous March, suggesting that then, too, they were the only Fellows in residence: John Smith, *The Poll for the Election of Librarian of the University of Cambridge* (Cambridge, [1822]), p. 19.

[6] MR.2, pp. 219, 221.

in College, there is evidence of Chafy's behaviour in other contexts which suggests that Chafy would have pursued his aims in College with determination, and with little respect for the opinions of others.

Certainly it appears that Chafy found little difficulty in expressing his views forcefully, whatever the circumstances. When a boundary wall between the College and adjoining property was, in Chafy's view, inadequately constructed, he was said by one witness to have expressed his displeasure by kicking it down twice.[7] Chafy was, however, especially forthright when he believed that established authority – his own or others' – was under attack. Henry Gunning, esquire bedell of the University during Chafy's mastership, recalled how, as Vice-Chancellor, Chafy opposed a motion by the Chancellor, the Duke of Gloucester, for an address to both houses of parliament to promote the abolition of the slave trade. Chafy described the motion as 'a censure' of Lord Liverpool's ministry, which Chafy 'supported'; furthermore, he expressed his opposition (at a meeting in the vestry of Great St Mary's) 'so loudly and so vehemently, that the parishioners (who had in leaving the church to pass the vestry-door) crowded together in order to learn the cause of this uproar'.[8] In 1821, at a county meeting held to consider a resolution that 'a reduction of taxation and the redress of other grievances could not be expected without a complete and effectual reform of the representation of the people' and that 'the rights of the Queen ought to be fully acknowledged', Chafy seconded a motion that the resolution was 'useless, ill-timed and inexpedient'.[9] In 1834, a solicitor who had entered the College in an attempt to deliver a letter to Chafy's son, and a Fellow Commoner from Jesus College who was accompanying him, found themselves locked into the College and placed in the charge of the constable on Chafy's orders when they declined to give their names to him. According to the solicitor, Chafy's tone was 'loud and imperious', and the Master thrust 'out his tongue at him'; the solicitor 'could hardly describe how unhandsome and offensive it was'.[10]

Chafy's often obstinate conservatism and authoritarianism appear to have derived from a fear that attacks on established authority might imply the onset of revolution. In a sermon on the death of George IV, Chafy recalled how, at the beginning of the regency, 'principles, subversive of our most revered and venerable institutions, had been insidiously instilled into the minds of the ignorant and unenlightened'.[11] Such fears were widespread at the time.[12] Nonetheless, Chafy

---

[7] MR.116 (misc. papers relating to Chafy's mastership), 3/16.

[8] Gunning, *Reminiscences*, II, 289–90.

[9] C.H. Cooper and J.W. Cooper (compilers), *Annals of Cambridge*, 5 vols (Cambridge, 1842–1908), IV, 530–1.

[10] *The Times* (17 Mar. 1834), p. 6c–d.

[11] William Chafy, *A Sermon Preached before the University of Cambridge in Great St Mary's Church on . . . July 15, 1830: being the Day of the Funeral of . . . King George the Fourth* (Cambridge, 1830), p. 10.

[12] Cf. Cambridge Corporation's address to the Regent in November 1819, with its reference to 'infidel and revolutionary frenzy': Cooper, *Annals*, IV, 525. For the social and political

often found himself isolated and ineffectual. When he insisted on putting the address on the slave trade to the vote in the Senate, only one M.A. voted with him.[13] His action in detaining the two visitors to the College had a humiliating outcome: Chafy was successfully sued for false imprisonment. When the case was heard at Cambridge Assizes in 1834 it excited, according to *The Times*, 'the most intense interest in the town, County and University'; the diarist, Romilly, recorded that the judge 'summed up very strongly against Chafy' and that the jury gave 'what they meant for heavy damages'.[14] As early as 1803 Chafy spoke of how the righteous might become victimized; he perhaps had himself in mind when he lamented in a sermon that 'the iron dart of persecution, envenomed with the poison of malice, ceases not to wound and lacerate those amongst us who are most eminent for piety and virtue'.[15] It is conceivable that, in Sidney too, Chafy's strong opinions met resistance. It is certainly the case that Masters were not always autocrats within their colleges; at Trinity, where the Seniority which constituted College meetings was, like the fellowship of Sidney, a small body, the Master, Christopher Wordsworth, was unable to get the College to accept his building proposals at the first attempt, and had to wait until the changed membership of the Seniority produced a majority in his favour.[16] At Sidney, the likelihood of conflict between Chafy and the fellowship would have been increased by the fact that Chafy had obtained the mastership despite, rather than because of, the desires of the Fellows. When he was first a candidate, in 1807, he attracted only his own vote and was declared by several Fellows to be an unsuitable candidate; he became Master in 1813 only when the Visitor 'declared that Mr Chafy ought to have been chosen' after the disqualification of the Fellows' choice on the ground that he had never been a Fellow.[17]

There are, indeed, signs that, in the 1830s, Chafy's opinions did not dominate

---

instability of the period as it affected the Cambridge area in particular, see M.J. Murphy, *Cambridge Newspapers and Opinion, 1780–1850* (Cambridge, 1977), pp. 58–9, 65–6.

[13] Gunning, *Reminiscences*, II, 291–2. Many University Tories favoured the anti-slavery cause, which, indeed, helps to explain Gloucester's election as Chancellor: J.P.C. Roach, 'The University of Cambridge', in idem (ed.), *The Victoria History of the Counties of England: A History of Cambridgeshire and the Isle of Ely*, III: *The City and University of Cambridge* (London, 1959) (hereafter: *VCH*, III), p. 236; D.A. Winstanley, *Early Victorian Cambridge* (1940; reprinted Cambridge, 1955), p. 98.

[14] *The Times* (17 Mar. 1834), p. 6d; J.P.T. Bury (ed.), *Romilly's Cambridge Diary, 1832–42* (Cambridge, 1967), p. 51.

[15] William Chafy, *A Sermon Preached at the Parish-church of Gillingham . . . on . . . July the 31st 1803 on Occasion of the United Exertions . . . Called Forth by His Majesty Against the Threatened Invasion* (London, 1803), p. 11.

[16] Winstanley, *Early Victorian Cambridge*, pp. 61–3.

[17] Ibid., p. 9 and n. 2; Gunning, *Reminiscences*, II, 286–7. Winstanley accuses Gunning of being confused (*Early Victorian Cambridge*, p. 16 n. 3), but Winstanley seems not to recognise that Gunning is referring here to the 1813 election. The 'advertisement' in *The Times* (19 Oct. 1813), p. 3e, recording Chafy's unanimous election, presumably records the College's proceedings following the Visitor's decision.

the College, but similar sources for the early and mid-1820s (when the refurbishment of the College was being planned) suggest consensus between Chafy and the Fellows, and especially between Chafy and the College officers, who were most likely to be in residence.[18] Furthermore, there is much to suggest that Chafy's opinions were pivotal in the decision to refurbish the College. He evidently possessed a powerful sense of his social position and a desire to enhance it – things which, it will be suggested, gave him a particular interest in the College buildings. Chafy was, as he put it in his obituary of his father, 'descended from an ancient and respectable family in the county of Dorset'. The Master's father was a youngest son without inherited means who was for a while a Fellow of Sidney and subsequently became a minor Canon of Canterbury Cathedral. However, he married a relative who was an heiress and, although the future Master entered Corpus in 1796 as a sizar, his father was able to build up some landed income and apparently to obtain a grant to bear arms in 1823.[19] While the Master followed a clerical career, obtaining a curacy at Gillingham, as well as a fellowship at Sidney, before becoming Master, he also succeeded in adding to his father's lands. By 1834 he could be described as 'a man of considerable wealth'; at his death, according to his obituary in the *Gentleman's Magazine*, he left 'property far surpassing in amount even the expectations of those most intimately

---

[18] Two Fellows (including, strikingly, the Tutor, Heaviside) signed the 1834 petition in favour of admitting dissenters to degrees – something which Chafy can scarcely have favoured. The same two Fellows voted for the alternative candidate to the one favoured by Chafy in the 1836 election for Public Orator; one of them, Saunders, had voted for the Reform candidates in the 1831 election for the University's MPs. This can be compared with the consensus amongst the Sidney voters in the 1822 election for University Librarian and with the absence of any votes by Fellows for the candidate considered to hold Whig principles in the 1822 by-election for a University representative; in that election and in the 1826 general election all the College officers who voted cast their votes in the same way as Chafy. The only Sidney signatory of the 1822 representation against the heads' claim to nominate candidates for the Professorship of Mineralogy was the Mathematical Lecturer, John Hind; although he joined the fellowship (and also became a Tutor) in 1823–4, he remained only briefly, and had left by 1825 (for Chafy's probable involvement with the heads' claim, see n. 60). These comments are based on: Smith, *Poll for Election of Librarian*, p. 19; Gunning's poll books for the other elections mentioned; Henry Gunning, *The King v. the Vice-Chancellor of Cambridge . . .* (Cambridge, 1824), pp. 2–5; *Cambridge Chronicle* (28 Mar. 1834); the Sidney entry in the *Cambridge University Calendar* for the appropriate years; biographies of parliamentary candidates in Michael Stenton and Stephen Lees, *Who's Who of British Members of Parliament*, 4 vols (Hassocks, 1976–81), I; G.E. C[ockayne], *The Complete Peerage*, ed. Vicary Gibbs et al., 13 vols in 14 (London, 1910–40) and R.G. Thorne (ed.), *The History of Parliament: the House of Commons, 1790–1820*, 5 vols (London, 1986).

[19] J.A. Venn, *Alumni Cantabrigienses, Part 2: 1752–1900*, 6 vols (Cambridge, 1940–54), I, 549; W.K.W. Chafy, *Gesta Chaforum* (privately printed, 1910), pp. 95, 80–82, 86, 88, 93; the Chafy lineage is traced back to a John Chafy of Sherborne, buried in 1558, in L.G. Pine (ed.), *Burke's Genealogical and Heraldic History of the Landed Gentry* (17th edn, London, 1952), p. 403.

acquainted with his affairs'.[20] With the growth of the Chafy estates went increasingly exalted connections: Chafy's father had been a domestic chaplain to the fourth and fifth Earls Cowper, and Chafy's sister married into the peerage; Chafy himself married a co-heiress of John Westwood of Chatteris, sometime High Sheriff of Cambridgeshire and Huntingdonshire.[21] It is striking that, whereas the future Master and his father had entered their respective colleges as sizars, and had been 'reading men' as undergraduates, the Master's son, William Westwood Chafy, entered Sidney as a Fellow Commoner and (though he managed to win College prizes in non-mathematical subjects) took no degree – presumably there was no expectation that he would need to follow his father and grandfather into a clerical career.[22] Rather, he was able, after his marriage to a daughter of the Bishop of Cork, to live the life of a gentleman, renting the hall at Conington, west of Cambridge, and earning the epithet 'the Foxhunter'.[23] Having established his son as a gentleman, Chafy seems to have distanced himself from his own more precarious origins; according to G.M. Edwards, although Chafy had been a sizar as an undergraduate, as Master he discouraged poor men from entering the College.[24] Indeed, Chafy was occasionally ridiculed for possessing social pretensions, as well as for his political conservatism. After a newspaper had carried a report that the heads of the colleges had joined the Mayor and Corporation of Cambridge in presenting an address to the Duke of York congratulating him on a speech in favour of Catholic emancipation, a friend of Gunning's wrote to the paper in imitation of Chafy's style (and using Chafy's name) a letter which discounted the report. Not only was Chafy made to deplore

---

[20] Leslie Stephen and Sidney Lee (eds), *Dictionary of National Biography*, 22 vols (1885–1900; reprinted London, 1908–9) (hereafter: *DNB*), III, 1345; Chafy, *Gesta*, pp. 182, 186, 199; *The Times* (17 Mar. 1834), p. 6c; *The Gentleman's Magazine*, new series, 20 (1843), 214. Chafy's landholding may have contributed to the fact that, by 1823, he was named as a Justice of the Peace for Cambridgeshire, a position then shared by six other heads of house: Public Record Office (hereafter: PRO), Assize Indictment Files, ASSI 35/263/6.

[21] Chafy, *Gesta*, pp. 84, 86, 87, 178–81.

[22] Venn, *Alumni, Part 2*, I, 549; *Cambridge University Calendar* (1827), pp. 331–2. The Master and his father were both placed among the *senior optimes* in the Mathematical Tripos: J.R. Tanner (ed.), *The Historical Register of the University of Cambridge . . . to the year 1910* (Cambridge, 1917), pp. 452, 469.

[23] Chafy, *Gesta*, pp. 295, 317–18. His voluminous hunting records are preserved in the College. Pine (ed.), *Burke's Gentry*, p. 403 describes him as 'of Feltwell Place, Norfolk and 3 Brunswick Terrace, Brighton'. It is not clear if the move to Feltwell involved purchasing a seat outright. The next generation purchased Rous Lench Court in Worcestershire, where the family remained until 1926: Peter Reid, *Burke's and Savills Guide to Country Houses*, II (London, 1980), 226. The Master's son may have been forced to move away from the Cambridge area by his failure, in a libel suit, to refute an accusation of 'crimen infandum in propriam uxorem': M.E. Bury and J.D. Pickles (eds), *Romilly's Cambridge Diary, 1842–1847*, Cambridgeshire Records Society, 10 (Cambridge, 1994), 145, 202.

[24] G.M. Edwards, *Sidney Sussex College* (London, 1899), p. 222. Edwards, who became a Fellow in Sidney in 1881, cited no source, and may have been drawing on College tradition.

Catholic emancipation (as did many in Cambridge); he was also made to express the view that 'the Heads of Colleges . . . could not of course have mixed themselves up with the Corporation. They have uniformly and pointedly kept themselves aloof from that body, not deeming it consistent with the dignity of their office, and the character they bear in the University, to connect themselves in any way with a body like the Corporation.' In a further false letter, disclaiming authorship of the first, Chafy was made to admit, with scarcely diminished hauteur, to living 'in the decent habits of occasional and courteous cordiality' with the Corporation.[25]

Chafy's social connections were no doubt consolidated by the lavish entertainment for which he was to gain a reputation. According to his grandson, he revived 'The Family', a select dining club, whose members were leading figures in the University establishment.[26] Chafy was renowned for keeping a fine cellar; Gunning believed that Chafy's 'covetousness (which in many respects was almost inconceivable) did not extend to his entertainments, which were always on a costly scale; and I believe nothing pleased him better than to provide the most choice wines that could be procured, and to see them freely taken'.[27] Chafy also offered a measure of public support for the Court. It is notable that the only publications by Chafy in the Cambridge University Library and British Library catalogues are sermons given on occasions of political significance: one, given at Gillingham in 1803, 'on Occasion of the United Exertions . . . Called Forth by His Majesty Against the Threatened Invasion', and the other preached by Chafy as Vice-Chancellor in Cambridge on the day of George IV's funeral. In the former sermon Chafy chose to 'pass by the virtues which adorn the private life of our much beloved Monarch' in order to remind his audience of how much even 'the poorest of my countrymen' benefited from the political and social status quo in England – and how much they stood to lose, therefore, through any invasion from revolutionary France. The latter sermon opined that George IV 'lived beloved and revered by all classes of his people, and . . . descends into the grave amidst the general lamentation of the nation, with scarcely a single instance of disaffection to his person or government'.[28] It has already been seen, in Chafy's

---

[25] Gunning, *Reminiscences*, II, 352–8. For petitions from the Senate, the Corporation and the inhabitants of Cambridge against Catholic emancipation (the last unsuccessfully opposed by Gunning), see Cooper, *Annals*, IV, 546, 560.

[26] Chafy, *Gesta*, pp. 292, 328. Chafy's rôle is not apparent from other sources; the Family's historian speaks of a gap in references to it between 1795 and 1834, with the exception of a reference in 1819. Chafy was, however, certainly a member from 1834 to his death. The club was said in 1819 to have originated 'in attachment to the fallen Stuarts', but to have 'long since become a mere dinner-party every fortnight': S.C. Roberts, *The Family: the History of a Dining Club* (Cambridge, 1963), pp. 6–7. Cf. Winstanley, *Early Victorian Cambridge*, pp. 398–9.

[27] Gunning, *Reminiscences*, II, 369–70; cf. Cambridge University Library, Additional MS 6810 (Romilly's Diary for 1829), 13 Dec. 1829; for the size of Chafy's cellar, see Chafy, *Gesta*, p. 328.

[28] *Sermon Preached at Gillingham*, quotations from pp. 15, 17; *Sermon Preached before the University*, quotation from p. 15.

handling of the affair of the address against the slave trade, that he felt no compunction about bringing his political views into University affairs; indeed, his willingness to entertain a conflict between himself as Vice-Chancellor and the Duke of Gloucester as Chancellor (of which Gunning much disapproved) probably reflected the fact that Gloucester's election as Chancellor had been opposed by 'the Court'.[29] By whatever means, Chafy had by the 1810s built up sufficient connections at Court to obtain his appointment in 1814 as a Royal Chaplain (to George III) – a position to which he was reappointed under George IV, William IV and Victoria.[30]

It is clear that one of Chafy's concerns as Master was to provide an appropriate setting for the entertainments that were integral with his social and political position. Much effort was devoted to making the Master's Lodge both more fashionable and more convenient. The bringing of modern convenience to ancient fabrics was, indeed, a feature of early nineteenth-century architectural activity, and, in particular, of the career of Wyatville, the principal architect employed at Sidney – Wyatville added corridors at Windsor Castle, for example.[31] Dr Cocke has observed that it was difficult in the later eighteenth century to take a purely romantic preservationist view of old buildings without better arrangements than then existed for heating and lighting them;[32] the situation can have been no different in Chafy's time. Chafy obtained permission, at the start of his mastership, to make a new entrance to the Master's Lodge from the ante-chapel. There is no record of how the Lodge was entered before Wyatville's alterations; most probably there was a staircase in the south-east corner of Hall Court, where a recently discovered print, published by Mason in 1822, shows an external door. However, it is evident from Wyatville's later comments that the arrangements were unsatisfactory; Wyatville referred to 'the need for going up and down' in order to reach at least some parts of the Lodge.[33] Chafy's aim in 1813 may even have been to provide the Lodge with a formal approach from the east, so that

---

[29] See above. Gunning, *Reminiscences*, II, 274, 293–4; *DNB*, XXI, 349. Dr Jonathan Parry kindly drew my attention to Gloucester's evangelical sympathies, which may well have heightened tension between him and Chafy, since the evangelicals' co-operation with dissenters offended many Cambridge dons: F.K. Brown, *Fathers of the Victorians: The Age of Wilberforce* (Cambridge, 1961), pp. 301–7, 314–15, 360; Roach, 'University', p. 237.

[30] *DNB*, III, 1345. Chafy also received the degree of Doctor of Divinity by royal mandate in the month following his election as Master. However, of twenty-four of Chafy's contemporaries or near contemporaries as head of house who did not hold the degree of D.D. prior to their election, twenty obtained the degree of D.D. in the year of their election or in one of the two following years, and in fifteen of these cases (including Chafy's two immediate predecessors as Master of Sidney) Venn notes that the degree was awarded by royal mandate (*Alumni, Part 2*); it would appear, therefore, that this was a privilege generally available to heads of house.

[31] Linstrum, *Wyatville*, pp. 38, 181, 182.

[32] Thomas Cocke, 'James Essex, 1722–1784', in Roderick Brown (ed.), *The Architectural Outsiders* (London, 1985), pp. 101–2.

[33] Wv/AA7. The 1822 print is reproduced as Colour Plate III in the present volume.

visitors could approach the Lodge without passing through the College. Though nothing was in fact done in 1813, the idea of a formal eastern approach to the Lodge may again have been entertained around 1820, when Wyatville proposed forming a carriage entrance from Jesus Lane. This suggestion was partly followed up, since, when the eighteenth-century gateway was removed from the front of the College, it was re-erected at the point where Wyatville had suggested providing 'a College like gateway' into the Master's drive, but it is not clear whether the new drive was actually built, and the main entrance to the Lodge continued to be from the west.[34] However, the arrangements there were radically improved in the 1820s. A new entrance to the Master's Lodge from Hall Court, and a new staircase for the Lodge, were features both of Humfrey's unexecuted 1820 refurbishment proposals and of the first phase of Wyatville's works.[35] Furthermore, Chafy had meanwhile proceeded to improve the Lodge in other ways, obtaining permission to throw two rooms together so as to form a drawing room. Chafy was permitted to take down the old wainscoting and to replace it with wallpaper, probably making the room lighter, as well as more fashionable, in the process.[36] It is evident that the conversion also involved forming french windows on the east elevation, leading on to an iron balcony overlooking the garden (roughly at the position of the existing balcony later formed by Wyatville) – Chafy evidently shared the desire for a close link between indoors and outdoors which influenced contemporary country house design.[37] The room must have been particularly attractive when it was lit from the west as well as from the east – although it appears that the new fireplace was inadequately supported, something which had to be remedied in Wyatville's works.[38] In fact, Wyatville's works also deprived the room of its western windows, which were blocked by the considerable extension to the Lodge which formed part of the first phase of work, providing the Master with a new library and additional bedroom accommodation.[39]

Chafy's activities were not confined to the interior of the Lodge. At some point before 1820, he obtained a scheme for remodelling the Master's Garden.[40]

---

[34] Wv/A1. There was an entrance to the Lodge from the garden at the north end of the Chapel/Library range, according to a turn-of-the-century photograph in Cambridgeshire Libraries, Cambridgeshire Collection (E.Si.J7, 19728). The entrance would have been close to the back stairs of the Lodge and a long way from Wyatville's staircase leading to the main reception rooms; it was probably a private or service entrance, therefore, the predecessor of the existing entrance to the Lodge in the passage between Chapel and South Courts.
[35] Wv/G1; Wv/AA6–7.
[36] MR.2, pp. 180, 181.
[37] Compare Wyatville's survey (Wv/A2) with Harraden's depiction of 1799 (Richard Harraden, *Picturesque views of Cambridge* (Cambridge, 1800), part II, plate XVII) and with Baldrey's view of 1809 (published on the University Almanack for that year). Cf. Mark Girouard, *Life in the English Country House* (New Haven, 1978), pp. 218–20.
[38] Wv/AA7.
[39] Wv/B2–4, 12 and 27–33 are the plans for this work.
[40] Sidney Sussex College Muniment Room (hereafter: SSM), Plans 1/1.

Custance's map of 1798 shows that the Master's Garden then retained a formal layout, somewhat simpler than the late seventeenth-century arrangement shown by Loggan, but still sharply separated from the paddock to the east.[41] The plan prepared for Chafy incorporated the paddock into the layout of the garden.[42] The motivation of the scheme may have been partly to substitute for areas of the Master's garden lost to building, including the construction of Sidney Place, discussed below. However, the scheme also had the effect of moving the focus of the garden northwards, perhaps with the intention of improving the view from the new drawing-room balcony. Rhododendrons were to be planted near to the Lodge, and, with the proposed areas of evergreens and ferns, suggest a plant-collector's garden of the type then coming into fashion.[43] Chafy was certainly an enthusiast for horticulture: he was elected a Fellow of the Royal Horticultural Society in 1821 and became a member of the newly formed Cambridge Horticultural Society in 1824; his interest in horticultural improvement caught the attention of the local press.[44] Since the layout shown in the proposals drawn up for Chafy features in Wyatville's drawings of the site, it appears that some, at least, of the proposed work had been carried out by 1820.[45]

These labours on the Lodge and its gardens enjoyed their apotheosis in 1835, on the occasion of the Marquess Camden's first visit to Cambridge as Chancellor of the University, in order to confer honorary degrees on the Duke of Wellington and others. The Chancellor was a guest at Trinity Master's Lodge, and held a levée there; at Sidney Lodge, the Archbishop of Canterbury was a guest, and, later in the day, he too held a levée, at which Chafy acted as chamberlain. The occasion was well attended but, in the possibly biased eyes of a Fellow of Trinity, Chafy had not overcome the basic limitations of the Lodge; Romilly reported that 'the place is not half so well calculated as Trinity Lodge for such a state occasion: and I hear that from the smallness of the room the effect of the spectacle was not nearly so striking as at Lord Camden's Levee'. The 'Déjeuner in Sidney Gardens' which followed, and which continued while Lord Camden dined with the

---

[41] Custance's plan is included in the portfolio of plans published as vol. II of J. Willis Clark and Arthur Gray, *Old Plans of Cambridge, 1574 to 1798* . . ., 2 vols (Cambridge, 1921).

[42] Presumably this layout, as well as the proposed planting scheme, was new, and does not reflect changes made between 1798 and 1813.

[43] Though the most notable period of nineteenth-century plant collecting, and the heights of enthusiasm for rhododendron cultivation, occurred after 1820, there are earlier instances of this type of garden, roughly contemporary with the plan for Sidney: Miles Hadfield, *A History of British Gardening* (3rd edn, London, 1979), pp. 259–60, 275, 278–82, 322–9; Laurence Fleming and Alan Gore, *The English Garden* (London, 1979), pp. 170, 186; Anthony Huxley, *An Illustrated History of Gardening* (rev. edn, London, 1983), pp. 290–1.

[44] Chafy, *Gesta*, pp. 184, 188, 209.

[45] Wv/A1. R.G. Baker's *New Map of the University and Town of Cambridge* (1830) confirms that the major change shown in the pre-1820 plan – the integration of the paddock and the garden – had taken place, although it shows that some aspects of the pre-1820 scheme had been changed, either during execution or as a result of subsequent alterations.

Vice-Chancellor in Jesus, appears, however, to have been an unqualified success: Romilly found it 'very elegant ... The place was very tastefully fitted up: a great festoon of different coloured flowers exhibited CAMDEN: ... There was a band and lamps &c. to make a sort of Vauxhall at night and then the world danced.'[46]

Chafy's interest in the refurbishment of the College would have sprung not only from a desire to provide an appropriate setting for his social career, but also from aesthetic sensibilities. Indeed, at the time, a knowledge of architecture was an attribute of a gentleman. Howard Colvin has suggested that, in eighteenth-century Oxford, the architectural interests of the increasingly genteel members of college governing bodies led them to undertake monumental buildings without the support of outside benefactors and often in the face of financial difficulties.[47] Similar influences may have been at work in early nineteenth-century Sidney. Though Chafy's first love may have been for horticulture, he showed just the kind of 'gentlemanly' interest in scenery and in architecture which would help to explain the decision to improve the College aesthetically. He undertook tours to the Lake District in 1811, to Scotland in 1812, and to Wales in 1824 or later, and his accounts of the scenery are peppered with the vocabulary of fashionable early nineteenth-century romantic taste: the scenery was frequently deemed to be 'sublime', even to be 'sublimely awful' or to show 'awful sublimity'; 'horror and beauty' could be linked.[48] Architecture – often assessed in the early nineteenth century, like scenery, for its romantic qualities – also fell under Chafy's notice. Although he never mentioned in his journals the names of architects whose buildings he visited or admired, and although he could commit the blunder of describing pillars supporting Gothic arches as 'Corinthian',[49] Chafy nonetheless reported on some buildings with great enthusiasm. The Pelham Mausoleum at Brocklesby, designed by Wyatville's uncle, James, was, Chafy thought, a 'superb building ... well deserving a journey of ten times the distance we went to see it'.[50] The buildings which Chafy admired suggest no preference for particular styles or periods – they extended from medieval Gothic to early nineteenth-century Gothic revival, from late seventeenth-century classicism to early nineteenth-century neo-classicism.[51] However, in this eclecticism, Chafy's taste was perhaps no other than typical of the 1820s;[52] furthermore, communicating with Chafy regarding details of the Chapel front in 1833, Wyatville could compliment

---

[46] Bury (ed.), *Romilly's Diary, 1832–42*, pp. 81–3; Cooper, *Annals*, IV, 591; Gunning, *Reminiscences*, II, 370.

[47] H.M. Colvin, 'Architecture', in L.S. Sutherland and L.G. Mitchell (eds), *The History of the University of Oxford*, V (Oxford, 1986), 842–3.

[48] Chafy, *Gesta*, pp. 130, 140, 160, 169, 142–3, 144–5, 124, 162, 189–92.

[49] Ibid., p. 131.

[50] Ibid., pp. 106–7; Howard Colvin, *A Biographical Dictionary of British Architects, 1600–1840* (London, 1978), p. 952.

[51] Chafy, *Gesta*, pp. 105, 111 (medieval Gothic), 131, 145, 171 (Gothic revival), 132, 176 (late seventeenth and early eighteenth-century classical), 106–7, 132 (neo-classical).

[52] Cf. J.M. Crook, *The Dilemma of Style* (London, 1987), chap. 1 and especially pp. 34–5.

the Master on his knowledge of architecture, sending an explanatory drawing and notes, but insisting that 'the questions were such that your own genius would easily answer'.[53] The contribution of Chafy's aesthetic interests to the shaping of the project should not be discounted, therefore.

Furthermore, Chafy would have found in Sidney, as it stood at the start of his mastership, much to suggest the need for aesthetic improvements. One early nineteenth-century commentator claimed that the College resembled, before the works of the 1820s and 1830s, 'a misshapen and unsightly house'.[54] Much survived of the original buildings, and architecture of their period – no longer purely Gothic but, on the other hand, not fully adapted to classical ideals – was viewed with interest and sympathy in the early nineteenth century; it was seen to offer scope for evoking historical associations and for creating a 'picturesque' outline, without sacrificing domestic convenience.[55] Yet, in contemporary eyes, the College suffered from the dual disability of having lost much of its original decorative detail and of being faced in red brick which, by the early nineteenth century, had long been regarded as an undignified building material – indeed Sidney's combination of stone with red brick may have seemed particularly uncouth.[56]

Chafy's motives in furthering the refurbishment of the College were not, however, purely selfish. Account must be taken of the fact that the picture of Chafy painted by Gunning and Romilly was not painted by men sympathetic either to Chafy's politics or to his position in the University. Chafy was not alone in bringing politics into University affairs; rather, he was Master at a time when the University was highly politicized.[57] While Chafy was deeply conservative, Gunning and Romilly were more sympathetic to reform; Chafy and Gunning had, indeed, clashed in public over the resolution in favour of parliamentary reform proposed at the 1821 county meeting.[58] Authoritarian action such as Chafy's detention of the two men who refused to give their names in College, although not altogether indefensible, was likely to offend liberal principles, and it appears that Gunning's son assisted in the prosecution of Chafy.[59] Furthermore,

---

[53] Wv/L6.

[54] J. and H.S. Storer, *Cantabrigia Illustrata* (Cambridge, 1835), p. 27.

[55] Christopher Hussey, *English Country Houses: Late Georgian, 1800–1840* (London, 1958), pp. 13, 18; Linstrum, *Wyatville*, p. 53.

[56] On the loss of original detail, and the early nineteenth-century attitude to red brick, see Salt, 'Wyatville', pp. 137–9 and works there cited.

[57] Winstanley, *Early Victorian Cambridge*, p. 97; cf. Bury (ed.), *Romilly's Diary, 1832–42*, pp. 8, 93, 117.

[58] Cooper, *Annals*, IV, 531; see also n. 25. For Romilly's whiggery, see Bury (ed.), *Romilly's Diary, 1832–42*, p. vii.

[59] Only the more conservative of the local papers, the *Cambridge Chronicle* (21 Mar. 1834), gave space to the arguments for the defence (that the Jesus Fellow Commoner, as a junior member, should have given his name and College to any senior member who asked for them, and that the solicitor was pursuing the case for the sake of the costs), or mentioned that,

the powers of the heads of house, which Chafy may have been conspicuous in supporting, were particularly resented by the reformers.[60] It is not surprising, therefore, that Gunning's picture of Chafy was unbalanced. As Scott-Giles pointed out, while Gunning remarked on Chafy's 'covetousness', Chafy in fact paid for the refacing of the College Chapel and bequeathed £1000 to the College to set up an advowson fund, as well as leaving a large number of books to the College library.[61] He also gave 100 guineas towards the reconstruction of the University Library – among heads of house, only the Master of Trinity gave more, and several heads do not appear on Cooper's list of those who subscribed more than fifty pounds.[62] Chafy may have been a reactionary, but he evidently had the interests of the College and University, as he perceived them, as well as of himself and his family, at heart. Under Chafy's mastership, the College at least kept pace with educational developments in the University as a whole, where the gradual decline in the dominance of mathematics in undergraduate education was marked by the introduction of the 'previous examination' in classics and divinity in 1822. A College prize in classics, awarded on the basis of a College examination, had been added to the existing mathematical prizes as early as 1777, but a prize for divinity, awarded on the basis of a College examination, is first mentioned in the *University Calendar* for 1832.[63] Chafy had been Tutor from 1807–13 and College Lecturer from 1807–9 (when he became Steward), so it might be expected that he would have taken an interest in these developments, or even promoted them. Indeed, during Chafy's mastership the College added to its complement of one Tutor and two Lecturers (of whom one was not a Fellow) by appointing a second Tutor in 1824 and either a second Tutor or a third Lecturer regularly from 1829. However, in practice, during the 1830s, one Fellow often filled two posts, so that, on average, an increased involvement of the fellowship in teaching did not result from the changes during Chafy's mastership.[64] Our

---

according to some witnesses, the solicitor, as well as Chafy, had been 'very indignant'; cf. *Huntingdon, Bedford and Peterborough Gazette and Cambridge and Hertford Independent Press* (15 Mar. 1834); *The Times* (17 Mar. 1834), p. 6c–d; *DNB*, VIII, 787.

[60] Winstanley, *Early Victorian Cambridge*, pp. 29–30, 35–6, 41–2, citing Mrs Stair Douglas, *The Life and Selections from the Correspondence of William Whewell, D.D. . . .* (London, 1881), p. 76, which has been taken to imply that Chafy was instrumental in the heads' claim to nominate to the Professorship of Mineralogy: cf. J.W. Clark and T.M. Hughes, *The Life and Letters of the Reverend Adam Sedgwick*, 2 vols (Cambridge, 1890), I, 236–45. At the very least, Whewell regarded Chafy as an archetype of the heads' conservatism. Gunning's dislike of the position taken by the heads over the appointment of the Professor of Mineralogy is apparent from his preface to his report of *The King v. the Vice-Chancellor of Cambridge*.

[61] Scott-Giles, *Sidney*, p. 91; Chafy, *Gesta*, p. 327. Regarding advowsons, see below.

[62] Cooper, *Annals*, IV, 613n. An advertisement prefacing Chafy's *Sermon Preached before the University* states that profits from sales ('if any') would be given to Addenbrooke's Hospital – but perhaps such public charity could be regarded as self-serving.

[63] Winstanley, *Early Victorian Cambridge*, p. 68; MR.4 (Memoranda of College Meetings, 1776–91), ff. 3r, 17r–18r; *Cambridge University Calendar* (1832), entry for Sidney.

[64] *Cambridge University Calendar*, entries for Sidney in Calendars for years 1801–40. As

judgment on Chafy's interest in scholarship and education might be very different if it were possible to identify the books which he bequeathed to the College. However, it remains the case that the surviving direct evidence links Chafy much more closely with the development of the College as an institution than with the development of its educational rôle. Chafy probably saw his duty to maintain and enhance the College as an institution as an end in itself – much as the proprietor of a landed estate might view his duty towards his family. Hence Chafy's concern (shared by earlier Masters) with increasing the small number of advowsons owned by the College (advowsons formed part of the College's endowment and provided preferment for Fellows who wished to leave the College; most did so, at a relatively early stage in their careers, not least because College statutes forbade Fellows to marry).[65] To Chafy and to his contemporaries, the architectural standing of the College probably also seemed to be an important aspect of its general reputation (and therefore of its institutional standing), especially at a time when many other colleges were building. By the time that the second phase of work at Sidney was being considered, in 1824, major building projects in the Gothic revival style were under way at Trinity, Corpus Christi and King's Colleges, and work began on St John's New Court shortly afterwards; while this building boom was prompted above all by accommodation problems, the interest which was taken in the appearance of these new buildings is shown by their depiction, alongside older work, in the collections of engravings of Cambridge architecture then in vogue.[66] It was, indeed, said in 1827 that Corpus 'has lately claimed a pre-eminence in the University for its new buildings'.[67]

It can hardly be suggested, however, that the transformation of Sidney was entirely due to Chafy.[68] Instrumental, too, was the financial windfall which the College received from the opening of additional coal mines on the estates left to it by the will of Samuel Taylor of Dudley. Taylor had required that the College apply the income from his bequest to the creation of a fellowship in Mathematics,

---

noted above, Chafy had doubled as both Lecturer and Tutor from 1807–9, but such doubling up appears to have been exceptional until the 1830s.

[65] John Gascoigne, 'Mathematics and Meritocracy: the Emergence of the Cambridge Mathematical Tripos', *Social Studies of Science*, 14 (1984), 562–3; *The Cambridge Guide, or a Description of the University and Town of Cambridge* . . . (new edn, Cambridge, [1830]), pp. 15–16. At the time, Sidney controlled six livings (fewer than all but three Colleges, one of which was the newly founded Downing): 'A Trinity Man' [J.M.F. Wright], *Alma Mater*, 2 vols (London, 1827), II, 169–202. For earlier Masters' contributions to the purchase of advowsons, see R.H.D. Mayall, 'Sidney Sussex College', in *VCH*, III, 482–3.

[66] Royal Commission on Historical Monuments: England, *An Inventory of the Historical Monuments in the City of Cambridge*, 1 vol. in 2 (London, 1959), p. lxxxiv; Robert Willis and John Willis Clark, *The Architectural History of the University of Cambridge*, 3 vols (Cambridge, 1886), I, pp. cxvii–cxxix. On the growing number of undergraduates, and the desire to provide College rooms for them, see Salt, 'Wyatville', p. 126.

[67] Wright, *Alma Mater*, I, 109.

[68] This paragraph, and the following one, summarize the argument of Salt, 'Wyatville', pp. 119–27.

although the statutory requirement that Fellows study divinity meant that it had to be converted to a Lectureship. If minerals were found on the land, however, the additional income resulting was to be used to fund Mathematical Scholarships – a Mathematical Exhibition had already been created in 1792 using income from the Taylor bequest.[69] The size of the windfall created by the further discoveries of coal was, however, such as to prompt the College to consider diverting some of the money to other purposes[70] – initial thoughts seem to have been to use part of the money to purchase ecclesiastical livings for the College. Since Chafy later established an advowson fund by his own bequest, it may be suspected that this plan was one which the Master himself favoured. In the event, however, the College obtained permission by Acts of Parliament to divert some of the newly increased income from the Taylor estates towards building. This was ostensibly in order to improve the facilities for the Mathematical Lecturer and in order to provide accommodation for the new Taylor Scholars; in the event the building works of the 1820s and 1830s were much more extensive than these needs required. Equally, the College seems to have realised from the start that the Taylor moneys could pay only part of the cost – it cannot, therefore, categorically be said that the Taylor money was used for purposes without direct connection with mathematics, although there is no doubt that the Taylor legacy facilitated a much more wide-ranging transformation.

Furthermore, the transformation was made necessary by other factors apart from Chafy's desire to improve the Lodge, and apart from the desire to improve the College's aesthetic profile, for which Chafy probably provided much of the inspiration. Numbers of undergraduates were increasing throughout Cambridge at the time; Sidney's share in that increase was very small, but this, as well as the impending creation of the Mathematical Scholarships, may have prompted the enlargement of the attics of the east-west ranges of Hall Court, and of Sir Francis Clerke's range, in order to provide additional accommodation there. Above all, the structural condition of the College was poor. The range containing the Hall and Master's Lodge had insufficient cross-walls to tie the west and east façades together and the weight of the roof was gradually forcing the walls out of true – it is clear that this process had been under way for a long time, and had already caused the Hall walls to lean by the mid-eighteenth century. Humfrey thought that this range was near to collapse. The decay of the brickwork, also noted by Humfrey, was probably apparent throughout the original buildings.

In explaining the College's building activity in the 1820s and 1830s, all these

---

[69] The 1792 Exhibition probably did rest on the income from mineral extraction, *pace* my earlier statement (Salt, 'Wyatville', p. 121), since coal-mines are shown on a survey of the Dudley estates dated 1767: SSM, MS 104.

[70] PRO, Chancery Orders and Decrees, C.33/709, f. 498v shows that the mines were sold on forty-year leases for a total of £39,750, payable in instalments over the period to 1832. Lord Dudley's offer of £18,250, cited in Salt, 'Wyatville', p. 119, was presumably for only some of the minerals which had been discovered on the estate.

factors must, therefore, be set alongside Chafy's influence. It is fairly certain, however, that Chafy was instrumental in the selection of Wyatville as architect for the improvements of the 1820s and 1830s. Wyatville, a leading architect who enjoyed royal patronage from 1824,[71] was an architect of strikingly different character and standing from those previously employed by the College, who were local men. The College's eighteenth-century improvements had been designed by Sir James Burrough, Master of Caius and an amateur (albeit a distinguished one), and by his pupil, James Essex.[72] Humfrey, from whom the College obtained the designs for the new houses in Sussex Street and to whom it first turned for proposals for the College proper in 1820, was also a Cambridge architect and, indeed, a well known figure in Cambridge society: his father appears to have provided the College with an estimate for building a summer house to Essex's designs in 1775.[73] Other colleges employed the more prestigious William Wilkins in the early 1820s, but he had close links with Cambridge.[74] Wyatville, by contrast, had no obvious connection with Cambridge before his employment at Sidney. G.M. Edwards first suggested that Chafy's involvement might explain the otherwise unexpected appointment of Wyatville; he pointed out that 'Wyatville ... was the architect employed at Windsor Castle' and suggested that he 'would on that account commend himself to Dr Chafy, Chaplain to the King'.[75] Unfortunately, the chronology of the situation does not entirely support Edwards' suggestion, since the invitation to Wyatville to work for the King, which came as a surprise to the architect, was not made until 1823–4, three years after he had made his earliest drawings for Sidney. However, attendance at Court as a royal chaplain presumably did bring Chafy into contact with some of Wyatville's aristocratic patrons, one of whom, the Duke of Devonshire, recommended Wyatville to the King; a similar recommendation to Chafy may well account for Wyatville being considered as a potential architect at Sidney.[76] When Wyatville came to be considered, some aspects of his prior experience would presumably have counted in his favour – although his work had been on houses rather than

---

[71] Colvin, *Dictionary*, pp. 959–63; Linstrum, *Wyatville*, p. 31 and *passim*.
[72] Colvin, *Dictionary*, pp. 168–70, 297–300; Thomas Cocke, *The Ingenious Mr Essex, Architect* (Cambridge: Fitzwilliam Museum, 1984); idem, 'James Essex'.
[73] SSM, Box 36 (documents relating to Sussex Street properties), Articles of agreement with Thomas Nutter, 27 May 1825; Colvin, *Dictionary*, pp. 438–9; Willis and Clark, *Architectural History*, II, 750. For the part played in Cambridge political and social life by Humfrey and his family, see Cooper, *Annals*, IV, 513, 599, 614; Bury (ed.), *Romilly's Diary, 1832–42*, e.g. pp. 11, 136.
[74] Colvin, *Dictionary*, pp. 893–6; R.W. Liscombe, *William Wilkins, 1778–1839* (Cambridge, 1980).
[75] Edwards, *Sidney*, p. 220.
[76] Linstrum, *Wyatville*, pp. 39, 163. Cf. the reference in one of Wyatville's letters to Chafy's intention to be in London 'to attend the Drawing Room': MR.116/1/12. The chronological difficulties with Edwards' suggestion were first noticed by Royston Lambert, 'Our Gothic Revival', *The Bull and the Porcupine: Sidney Sussex College Magazine* (1959), pp. 2, 4.

on educational institutions, it had included the adaptation to nineteenth-century requirements of two country houses of similar date to the College, Longleat and Wollaton.[77]

2. *Building for Revenue: Sidney Place and Sidney and Sussex Streets*

In contrast to the concern for aesthetics and dignity which shaped the refurbishment of the College itself, the first of the revenue-earning building projects of Chafy's mastership was starkly utilitarian, to a degree which soon became an embarrassment. In 1817 a College meeting agreed to sell part of the College stock which was appropriated 'for the sole use and Benefit of the Master', and to authorise Chafy to spend the proceeds 'in erecting some Tenements and Buildings on the College Ground, belonging to the Master, the Rents and Profits of which shall be appropriated to the Master'.[78] Since the Master was the beneficiary of this scheme, it is reasonable to assume that Chafy was its instigator. The result was Sidney Place: four cottages built at the eastern extremity of the Master's Garden, on what had formerly been a kitchen garden. The cottages were double-fronted, but the buildings behind this façade constituted a lean-to against a high window-less wall which formed the eastern boundary of the Master's Garden – although small lean-tos built by 1846 on the College side of the wall appear to have been part of the cottages, these stood on College ground and were allowed to remain 'only as a temporary convenience and may be removed at the pleasure of the society'.[79] Nonetheless, the houses attracted tenants who were in business in their own right: in 1830 one of them was occupied by a coal and corn merchant, although another business carried on in Sidney Place, that of 'bird-stuffer . . . (and practical ornithologist and entomologist)', was possibly somewhat less salubrious.[80]

By the early 1840s, the setting of Sidney Place had been radically changed by the construction of Malcolm Street on Jesus College land immediately to the east of the Sidney boundary. The leases of the Malcolm Street houses contained elaborately worded restrictions on carrying out various trades, and on the residence of 'any lewd or disorderly person', likely to cause a nuisance and thus to reduce the dignity of the new street.[81] Indeed, a Sidney College order of 1846

---

[77] Ibid., p. 4.
[78] MR.2, p. 193.
[79] Ibid., 14 Mar. 1846; Willis and Clark, *Architectural History*, II, 750. Lean-tos corresponding to those shown in the 1846 plan still stood in the late 1960s: SSM, PH.B, Photograph album recording the construction and opening of Blundell Court.
[80] Pigot and Co's *National Commercial Directory . . . Bedfordshire, Huntingdonshire, Cambridgeshire, Lincolnshire, Northamptonshire* (1830; reprinted Castle Rising, 1992) (hereafter: *1830 Directory*), pp. 24, 25.
[81] B.D. T[ill], 'James Webster, Builder', *Chanticlere (Jesus College Magazine)*, 148 (1948), 13, 15.

noted that, since the construction of Malcolm Street, the 'respectability of the neighbourhood' has been 'improved; and complaints have been made to the Master that certain appurtenances of Sidney Place and the entrance thereto, viz: a dark passage out of King Street, are highly offensive and objectionable: It seems necessary for the credit of the College and the respectability of the neighbourhood to make some alterations', which were duly authorized. Phelps, then Master, noted that 'when the cottages, which are miserable buildings, fall into decay, it is certain' that the gardens, which originally faced the west side of property in King Street, but which now adjoined Malcolm Street, 'may be more profitably and respectably employed'.[82] Presumably Phelps had it in mind to build larger houses on the street edge, in continuation of the Malcolm Street terrace. In the event, Sidney Place survived until the construction of Blundell Court in the late 1960s.

Both the construction of Malcolm Street and Phelps' attitude to the opportunities which it created were examples of the 'general spirit of improvement' which a contemporary guidebook noted had 'lately displayed itself' in Cambridge.[83] Indeed, in Sidney and Sussex Streets, the College had itself been engaged in changes of just this kind during the 1810s and 1820s. Here, as in Malcolm Street and elsewhere, the 'spirit of improvement' manifested itself in speculative building, and was a response to Cambridge's early nineteenth-century economic buoyancy. James Losh, who had been an undergraduate in the 1780s, commented on the 'thriving condition' of the town when he returned in 1822; while the general economic conditions of the early nineteenth century may have contributed to this, he was probably right to attribute it in part to the economic stimulus and need for lodgings created by the contemporary expansion in undergraduate numbers.[84] As in developments carried out by other Cambridge colleges, the building in Sidney and Sussex Streets was undertaken by means of building leases whereby plots were leased, usually with an initial rent-free period, on condition that the lessee built on the site in accord with a specified plan. Uniform terraces might thus result from the activities of several individual master builders under a single ground landlord who did not himself have to provide capital – an important consideration for Sidney.[85]

---

[82] MR.2, 14 Mar. 1846. Baker's 1830 map shows that access to the cottages was via a passage from King Street making two ninety-degree turns before running in front of the cottages, separating them from gardens or yards to the east.

[83] Quoted in Bury (ed.), *Romilly's Diary, 1832–42*, p. x. The source is not identified.

[84] R. Robson, 'A Visit to Cambridge, 1822', *Cambridge Review*, 81 (1960), 629; H.M. Cam, 'The City of Cambridge', in *VCH*, III, 98. Chalklin speaks of a 'post-war housing boom' in the country at large, arising from circumstances propitious to building after 1818, although there was much regional variation: C.W. Chalklin, *The Provincial Towns of Georgian England* (London, 1974), pp. 292–3, 301.

[85] On the procedure in general, see John Summerson, *Georgian London* (3rd edn, London, 1978), pp. 39–40, 76–9; Chalklin, *Provincial Towns*, parts 2–3. Lessees might be master builders (most commonly bricklayers or carpenters) who sub-contracted the other trades involved, or might be from outside the building trade, in which case they would contract

Sidney's early nineteenth-century development mostly replaced existing buildings; it covered the north side of Sussex Street (then often regarded as an extension of Walls Lane or King Street, although sometimes called Little Walls Lane), and the east side of Sidney Street between the College and the corner of Sussex Street. It appears from early maps that this part of the site of the dissolved Franciscan Friary had been built up before the site was ceded to the new College by Trinity, although Custance's map shows that part of the Sussex Street frontage was occupied by College offices, and a small part of the Master's Garden apparently extended as far as the north side of Sussex Street until the 1820s.[86] The form of the original buildings is not clear – it is likely that they had been rebuilt at least once before the early nineteenth century. There are signs, however, that, in the early nineteenth century, the existing buildings were in poor condition. One lessee was required to spend at least £80 on repairs within the first two years of his lease when he took over one of the Sidney Street houses in 1809; at least one of the houses in Sussex Street had been sub-divided.[87] Cambridge's older houses were not looked upon with universal affection in the early nineteenth century: the contemporary guidebook writer thought that many of the houses were 'old, ill-built, and crowded closely together'; this contributed to his impression that 'the general appearance of the town' was 'certainly below what might be expected'.[88] The Sidney Street house closest to the College was to be wholly rebuilt under a lease of 1806; the plan and elevation accompanying the lease suggest that this may have been the first step in remodelling the area: the house was to be given a three-bay brick façade, albeit still only of two storeys with the attic under

the work to a master builder or to individual craftsmen. For contemporary use of building leases by Jesus College in the development of New Square, and by Peterhouse in Tennis Court Road, and for some suggestion of the increased income following development on such leases, see Royal Commission on Historical Monuments, *Cambridge*, pp. 362, 357, and p. xcvi. For the difficulties which Sidney (and other colleges) found in financing building work, see Salt, 'Wyatville', pp. 148–55.

[86] See the maps and bird's-eye views in Clark and Gray, *Old Plans of Cambridge*, II. The view from Thomas Fuller's history of 1634 shows the north side of Sussex Street fully built up, but this is probably an error, since Loggan and (later) Custance show the southern extremity of the Master's Garden extending to the street edge in the same way as Hamond's view of 1592. It appears that part, but not all, of the gap was filled at the end of the eighteenth and beginning of the nineteenth centuries: SSM, Box 36: Leases to William Peace, 7 June 1802 and 8 Apr. 1815.

[87] SSM, Box 35 (documents relating to Sidney Street properties), Lease to William Swann, 14 June 1809; Box 36, Lease to Elizabeth Halls, 28 Nov. 1817. The sum to be spent on repairs can be compared with the £300 which it was stipulated should be spent on the reconstruction of one of the adjoining houses: SSM, Box 35, Lease to Samuel Luccock, 27 Dec. 1806. 'House' is here used as a convenient description of the buildings, although it is clear that trades were carried on in many of them, in addition to their being used as residential accommodation.

[88] Bury (ed.), *Romilly's Diary, 1832–42*, p. x.

a mansard roof visible from the street.[89] In 1818 the next two houses to the south were let to Samuel Harris, bricklayer, on condition that he rebuilt them within the next two years.[90] Presumably the houses now nos. 28–9 Sidney Street resulted, their three-storey brick façades, with the roof concealed behind a parapet, being a stage more imposing than the façade of the 1806 house. The College quickly decided to extend the idea of grouping sites together to its logical conclusion. A College meeting of April 1819 agreed that 'the Master and resident Fellows [might] . . . make such Arrangements as they may deem expedient for the Improvement of their Houses and other Property in Sidney and Kings Street'.[91] In November 1820 the three un-rebuilt tenements in Sidney Street and all of the north side of Sussex Street (up to the 'Bushel and Strike' public house at its eastern end, which was not on College property) were let to Harris and to William Savage, carpenter, on condition that, within three years, they rebuilt the houses in Sidney Street so as to match those already rebuilt, and those in Sussex Street in accordance with plans by Charles Humfrey; the College undertook that it would, on completion of the houses, let them for forty years to Harris and Savage or to such as they should nominate. Humfrey had proposed nine houses in Sussex Street – the College decided, with a view (no doubt) to maximizing profit, that a space intended to be left vacant should be filled with a tenth house and that adjoining houses should be enlarged so as to fill another vacant space.[92] Preserving the College's privacy was, however, also a consideration, as it had been in Sidney Place: the houses were to have no windows on the rear elevations that could overlook College property.[93]

Though, as will be explained below, the redevelopment took much longer to complete than had been planned, the financial gains must have been considerable in the long run. An advertisement of 1825 claimed that 'the improvements [which have] already taken place, and which are going on . . ., render this property invaluable'.[94] The annual rents on the Sussex Street houses may have doubled and a consideration of £680 was taken when the first completed house in Sussex Street

---

[89] SSM, Box 35, Lease to Samuel Luccock, 27 Dec. 1806. The site in question is now no. 30 Sidney Street, occupied by Messrs Galloway and Porter. If the house was rebuilt in or after 1806 in accord with the lease, then it would appear to have been rebuilt again later in the nineteenth century.

[90] SSM, Box 35, Leases to Samuel Harris, 5 Aug. 1818. This appears to have been a building agreement of the type described above, although Harris was paid directly by the College for the improvement resulting from his digging a cellar to one of the houses and there are other payments to Harris for unspecified brickwork about this time: MR.44 (Bursar's General Account, 1808–1828), pp. 185, 191, 201, 207.

[91] MR.2, p. 201.

[92] These arrangements are recited in PRO, Chancery Proceedings 1800–42, C.13/841/37 and in SSM, Box 36, Agreement with Nutter, 1825.

[93] PRO, C.13/841/37. Photographs confirm the absence of upper floor windows facing towards the College on the more easterly houses: SSM, PH.B, Sussex street packet.

[94] *Cambridge Chronicle* (17 June 1825).

was let for forty years; in 1840 a fine of £135 was taken for effectively extending the lease of the corner house for fifteen years.[95] Since the four easternmost houses in Sussex Street stood on ground belonging to the Master, his own income was increased, as well as that of the College.[96] The prestige of the street was no doubt increased too: the western end was widened;[97] a uniform three-storey frontage was created, with matching shop windows at ground-floor level;[98] the clause forbidding tenants to use their property 'for a Melting house for Tallow or making Candles or other offensive business' which features in Sidney Street leases at least from the 1790s was included in Sussex Street leases after (and only after) rebuilding.[99]

If Wyatville had had his way, the rebuilding in Sidney and Sussex Streets would not have been the only building going on in the 1820s with a view to increasing revenue. Wyatville suggested, on his plan of the College site dated March 1821, the construction of houses or shops along the Jesus Lane boundary which 'would add to the Income of the College'.[100] Once more, these were designed so as not to overlook the College, something which Wyatville proposed to achieve by the use of minute internal courtyards. The College did not proceed with the scheme, perhaps not least because of the difficulties accompanying the work in Sussex Street. The way in which Wyatville worded his suggestion implies that he had not drawn up the proposal at the instigation of the College (or of Chafy in particular), but was putting it forward as a speculation of his own. Equally, Chafy may have had little to do with the origins of the Sussex Street scheme, which

---

[95] Rents in Sussex Street before rebuilding varied, and, of course, the frontages of the earlier buildings may have been more varied (and narrower) than those of the new houses. See SSM, Box 36, Leases to William Peace, 7 June 1802 and 8 Apr. 1815; to Elizabeth Halls, 28 Nov. 1817. For considerations and fines, see MR.116/4/7 (which implies that a substantial part of the income from the property was taken in fines); MR.56 (Bursar's General Account, 1829–1856), p. 191; cf. SSM, Box 35, Lease to James Dimmock, 28 Dec. 1840.
[96] MR.44, p. 290. As noted above, this ground was originally part of the Master's Garden, but had partly been built upon already.
[97] SSM, Box 36, Agreement with Nutter, 1825. This had not been part of the original plan, it seems, and involved Savage in redrawing the plan and elevation of the houses: PRO, C.13/2654/Bays vs. Sidney Sussex College.
[98] Some of the original shop-windows survived until demolition in the 1930s (Plate 10).
[99] SSM, Box 35, Leases to Joseph Gifford, 21 Oct. 1793; to William Swann, 14 June 1809; Box 36, Leases to William Peace, 7 June 1802 and 8 Apr. 1815; to Elizabeth Halls, 28 Nov. 1817; to James Nutter, junior, 18 Jul. 1825; to James Howell, 19 Oct. 1826. It appears that 'Sussex Street' became established as the name of the street in the 1820s, though this may have had less to do with the street's improved image than with the renaming of the 'Three Hawks' public house as 'The Duke of Sussex', which was probably a compliment to George III's Whig son (who often visited Cambridge in the 1820s), and therefore something which may have brought little pleasure to Chafy. MR.44, p. 306; MR.66 (College account book, 1818–1862), Audit for Michaelmas 1828; Cockayne, *Complete Peerage*, XII, part 1, pp. 535–6; Cooper, *Annals*, IV, 522–59.
[100] Wv/A1.

appears to have evolved from earlier piecemeal rebuilding. When Harris received his first two building leases for the future 28–9 Sidney Street he was to submit his plans for building to the Master (only), rather than to the Master and Fellows[101] – this tells us less, however, of Chafy's personal rôle in the instigation of the rebuilding than of his personal rôle in its execution.

3. *Chafy and the Execution of the Building Projects*

Chafy was, as has been seen, Bursar as well as Master, and he noted that it was his 'Duty' as Bursar 'to superintend all the Repairs and Alterations of the College'.[102] It was said that, during Savage's lease, Chafy visited the site of the Sussex Street houses two or three times a day when he was at home ('which was generally two or three times a week'); he 'gave directions about everything'.[103] Furthermore, it was alleged, during a dispute with Henry Westmacott, the contractor for the first phase of Wyatville's scheme, that Chafy had given orders to the contractor directly, without going through Wyatville.[104]

Indeed, it is likely that Chafy was partly responsible for the prolonged dispute between the College and Westmacott. Westmacott was a son of Richard Westmacott, the elder, sculptor, and a younger brother of the more distinguished Sir Richard.[105] Chafy was evidently discontented with the progress of the works by January 1823, when he wished to withhold an interim payment to the contractor which Wyatville held to be due.[106] Wyatville remarked that 'the direct cause for complaint as to delay has arisen from the first error of the Contractor in stating his notion of finishing the work in half the time that it would require to do it well', although the contractor later claimed to have lost time because he had been unable to work by candle-light, perhaps reflecting a fear of fire on the part of the College, which had been the object of arson attacks in 1812–13.[107] It was, however, ostensibly over the sums due to Westmacott that major difficulties arose, Westmacott claiming that works carried out over and above those contracted for entitled him to a payment of £3683 17s 0d, in addition to the £5000 due to him under the contract; amongst the matters involved were not only additional repairs, but a decision to use stone ashlar, rather than Roman cement, on the back wall of the new Hall porch – it was some of this additional work that Westmacott claimed had been carried out on Chafy's direct instructions, rather than on orders

---

[101] SSM, Box 35, Leases to Samuel Harris, 5 Aug. 1818.
[102] MR.116/3/15.
[103] *Huntingdon . . . Gazette and Cambridge . . . Independent Press* (15 Mar. 1823) (copy at MR.116/3/17).
[104] MR.116/2/1.
[105] Linstrum, *Wyatville*, p. 233. Discovery of the draft contract has confirmed Dr Linstrum's identification: Salt, 'Wyatville', p. 145 n. 183.
[106] MR.116/1/21.
[107] Ibid., 22; MR.116/2/6; Scott-Giles, *Sidney*, pp. 93–4; Wright, *Alma Mater*, I, 106.

made by or through Wyatville. Reporting to Chafy the sum which Westmacott claimed to have spent, the College's solicitor, Robert Gee, resorted to triple exclamation marks;[108] the College, supported by Wyatville, argued that all the work carried out had been covered by agreements between Wyatville and Westmacott and that, since a number of items specified in the original contract had been omitted by mutual agreement, the additional sum due was only £269.[109] At issue seem to have been not only the cost of the work carried out, but also whether some work had been done at all: respecting the contractor's claim regarding 'Braces for Buttresses', the College's solicitor made a note that the clerk of works was to be called upon 'to prove that there are none'.[110] When, in October 1823, Westmacott refused to accept the payment of the £5000 due under the contract, with the addition of £269, as a final settlement, the College determined that the matter should be referred to Wyatville's arbitration, in accord with the contract.[111] At more or less the same time, however, Westmacott commenced an action against Chafy in King's Bench; this suit was referred by the court to arbitration in March 1824.[112] The award was issued only in May 1827, after further heated disputes; Gee's letters refer to 'a stormy sitting' and to 'a rather warm altercation' between counsel for the two parties.[113] Uncertainty as to the outcome of the suit prompted the College to hold a fellowship open in 1825 so as to ensure that money would be available to meet any award and any legal costs; in the event, the College was obliged to pay £430 8s 11d over and above the £5269 which Wyatville had initially argued was due, and costs were divided between the parties – the expenditure detailed in the Bursar's account, including lawyers' fees and expenses of witnesses, amounted to £666 15s 2d, almost a quarter of the College's annual rental income.[114] It comes as no surprise to find different contractors employed on the later stages of the work – of these one, Edward Lapidge, also practised as an architect, and was already known to Chafy, who had recommended him as a possible architect for buildings at the University botanic gardens in 1830;[115] the others seem to have been minor figures, chosen, perhaps, in the hope of avoiding the kind of clash which had arisen between Chafy and Westmacott.[116]

Over-spending was perhaps inevitable in a restoration project where the extent

---

[108] MR.116/2/1, 6. Gee was presumably the attorney of Bene't Street, Cambridge, who was father of Walter Gee, sometime Fellow of the College: MR.116/2/5, 12; Venn, *Alumni, Part 2*, III, 30.
[109] MR.116/2/33.
[110] Ibid., 3.
[111] MR.7 (Minutes of proceedings of College Meetings, 1813–1854), 29 Oct. 1823.
[112] MR.116/2/33.
[113] Ibid., 7, 11.
[114] MR.2, p. 212; MR.116/2/2; MR.44, pp. 281, '320' [numbered in error for p. 321], 327, 329; Salt, 'Wyatville', p. 119.
[115] MR.56, p. 40; Colvin, *Dictionary*, p. 506; Chafy, *Gesta*, p. 209.
[116] The other contractors were William Quinser and one Peck; see Salt, 'Wyatville', p. 148 for details.

of the repairs necessary could not always be ascertained until work had begun. Matters disputed with Westmacott included the escalating cost of repairing the windows on the south end of the Master's Lodge, and the additional depth to which foundations had been dug.[117] There is no record of Westmacott having worked in Cambridge before, and Wyatville believed that he was anxious 'to execute the works for the chances of gaining connections at Cambridge'; Westmacott evidently allowed for less work to be done than did rival bidders for the contract and it may be that Westmacott's anxiety to obtain the contract led him to underestimate the work needed in order to put in the lowest bid. It is also evident that the College placed pressure on Westmacott to reduce his estimate.[118] However, it is likely that the protracted and bitter nature of the dispute with Westmacott also owed something to Chafy's inability to negotiate. The conviction of his own rectitude apparent in his behaviour in College and in the University, together with the care in financial matters implied by Gunning,[119] appear to have resulted in repeated collisions with those employed by the College. In the course of the dispute over Westmacott's contract, Chafy quarrelled not only with Westmacott, but also with most of the others involved. Gee, the College's solicitor, was criticized by Chafy for not giving 'immediate attention' to the dispute with Westmacott; he received from the Master an 'intimation that, if I could not attend to it, some one else should'.[120] One Charles Muss, employed to paint the arms in the window of the Master's dining room, found that he had offended Chafy in seeking payment for some extra-contractual work agreed directly with the Master.[121] James Parke, the arbitrator appointed by the King's Bench, had to defend himself against complaints of delays in proceedings (although these were made in the name of the College, rather than by Chafy personally). Parke told the Master that 'I have no power of being more expeditious than the parties choose that I shall be, and if they omit to bring forward their own case, or to urge on that of their opponents, the blame is with them, and not with me'; these protests did not, however, prevent Chafy from forwarding a further letter from the College 'earnestly' soliciting Parke 'to bring the Business to as speedy a Termination, as his own pressing Engagements will permit'.[122]

Relations between Wyatville and Chafy also went through periods of difficulty. When the dispute erupted with Westmacott in January 1823, Wyatville evidently felt some initial sympathy for the contractor, signing a certificate entitling him

---

[117] MR.116/2/33, 7, 8, 1. Cf. the unexpected necessity, in the second phase, completely to replace the oriel windows at the west ends of the wings: Salt, 'Wyatville', p. 127.
[118] MR.116/2/13; MR.116/1/18.
[119] See above.
[120] MR.116/2/5.
[121] Ibid., 14–15.
[122] Ibid., 16–17. For Parke, a barrister who had been a Fellow of Trinity and who would be raised to the King's Bench in 1828, see Edward Foss, *A Biographical Dictionary of the Judges of England* (London, 1870), pp. 497–8.

to an interim payment against Chafy's wishes and informing Chafy that it was 'perhaps proper to state that whenever the contractor calls for any explanation respecting the works I am under the necessity of hearing his complaints against you'; 'I fear', Wyatville concluded, 'that you [Chafy] have made up your mind to quarrel with me, or is all ... to be attributed to your "being much out of Temper" as your letter states?'[123] Nonetheless, even this letter is marked by a straightforwardness on Wyatville's part which perhaps rested on a close acquaintance. Wyatville's son had been admitted to the College at the end of 1821,[124] and Wyatville felt able in 1822 to ask that a pupil of his who was unable to continue in the architectural profession, but who had 'a fair expectation of a small living', might be admitted to the College as a pensioner.[125] The tension evident in early 1823 was certainly resolved by October of that year, when Wyatville wrote to Chafy to thank him for 'so readily liquidating my account' and for 'the gratifying expressions respecting my conduct and the effect of the works performed'.[126] When the dispute with Westmacott became an argument over the sum due, Wyatville supported the College's position.[127] Chafy's relationship with Wyatville had indeed become cordial by the 1830s – Wyatville was a guest in the Master's Lodge for a week at the time of Lord Camden's first visit to the University as Chancellor.[128] Wyatville was felt to lack social grace (he had a broad accent and tended to dwell on financial matters in his conversation), but his intimacy with both George IV and William IV no doubt did something to compensate for this in Chafy's eyes.[129]

Not only did Chafy and Wyatville end on good terms; the tension between Chafy and Parke evident in 1826 did not prevent Parke also being Chafy's guest on the occasion of Lord Camden's visit.[130] Nonetheless, disputes also marked the construction of the new houses in Sidney and Sussex Streets, and Chafy found himself sued by the lessee, William Savage, who had bought out Harris's interest following the latter's bankruptcy in 1821.[131] The dispute, which was heard at Cambridge Assizes in Lent 1823, centred, like that with Westmacott, on additional work done, beyond that originally agreed, in this case on the boundary wall between the new houses and the Master's garden – apparently there had been frequent changes of plan, prompting Savage to declare that 'there has been so many alterations that I'll build as I like, for all the Master, the Fellows and the Devil'. Judgment was given against Chafy, seemingly on the ground that the

---

[123] MR.116/1/21–2.
[124] Venn, *Alumni, Part 2*, VI, 601; cf. MR.116/1/17.
[125] MR.116/1/20.
[126] Ibid., 26.
[127] MR.116/2/29, 1.
[128] Chafy, *Gesta*, pp. 239–40; for the festivities in Sidney on this occasion, see above.
[129] Linstrum, *Wyatville*, pp. 49, 42–5.
[130] Gunning, *Reminiscences*, II, 370.
[131] PRO, C.13/841/37.

disputed works had not formed part of the contract and had been carried out for the 'private accommodation of the Master'.[132] However, around April 1823, when the first house was completed, the College refused to lease it to the party nominated by Savage (as it was required to do by the original agreement with Harris and Savage). The ground for refusing the lease was that the house had not been built according to contract, although the College did not dispute Savage's claim that the house was substantially built and objected principally to the insertion of windows on the rear elevation.[133] Rather than grant a lease to Savage's nominee, the College began an action for arrears of rent. Savage, who had stopped work, commenced a suit in Chancery with the aim of compelling the College to grant a lease of the completed house, and obtained an injunction obliging the College to desist from legal proceedings elsewhere. However, the College persuaded the Court that this injunction should be conditional on Savage paying his arrears within three months.[134] This Savage was unable to do, since he was prevented from letting even the one completed house, and could therefore raise no income from the scheme. Consequently he was evicted and he shortly joined Harris, his erstwhile partner, in bankruptcy.[135]

The partially built houses were soon said to be 'going rapidly to decay'.[136] In January 1825 the solicitors of Savage's assignee suggested that the case be put to arbitration, but, although at least some of the matters in dispute were laid before an arbitrator during 1827,[137] the College meanwhile proceeded to find a new tenant to complete the scheme. In May 1825 the whole site was assigned by the College to Thomas Nutter, brewer, who had made an earlier attempt to secure Savage's interest and who now undertook to complete the development;[138] the

---

[132] *Cambridge Chronicle* (21 Mar. 1823) (copy at MR.116/3/18); *Huntingdon ... Gazette and Cambridge ... Independent Press* (15 Mar. 1823); MR.116/3/15; MR.116/4/6. Chafy did not deny that he had made a separate agreement for Harris to do work on College property at the same time as the work on the houses; it is not surprising that this caused confusion and dispute: cf. MR.44, p. 229.

[133] SSM, Box 36, Agreement with Nutter, 1825; MR.116/4/9; PRO, C.13/841/37. Savage claimed that the College's surveyor had not objected to the windows and blamed the College for withholding the original plans.

[134] PRO, C.13/2654/Bays vs. College; C.33/720, ff. 1v, 85r, 333v. Savage had not defended the suit for arrears of rent: *Huntingdon ... Gazette and Cambridge ... Independent Press* (2 Aug. 1823); however, the Chancery injunction would have prevented the College actually recovering the sum which had been adjudged to be due, and from evicting Savage from the site.

[135] MR.116/4/9.

[136] PRO, C.13/841/37.

[137] MR.116/4/9. The College's London solicitors thought it 'very doubtful whether the Plaintiff will ... be entitled to any compensation', implying that little would be achieved by arbitration. For arbitration in 1827, see MR.116/3/16.

[138] SSM, Box 36, Agreement with Nutter, 1825. Nutter's business was in Bridge Street; he was presumably the 'Thomas Nutter ... common brewer' who was a son of James Nutter (died 1829), and a member of the family of millers and corn traders which at the time owned

College agreed to oppose any claim to the site which Savage or his assigns might make, an undertaking which involved inconclusive litigation in Chancery at least until 1832.[139] The agreement with Nutter provided that he could sell the four partly completed houses and the vacant sites to others before completion, and he put all except the completed house up for auction in twelve lots in June 1825. The purchasers of at least three of the lots were interested in taking forty year leases under which they would complete the buildings themselves, and the College re-let these sites on further building leases in accord with the agreement with Nutter. The remaining sites were apparently sub-let by Nutter, singly or in pairs (or, in one case, as a group of three): six of them were let to building tradesmen, who probably acted as master builders of these houses; the tenants of the remaining four may have supervised construction themselves, or employed master builders to complete the houses on their behalfs.[140] Of these houses, most, if not perhaps all, appear to have been completed, and re-leased by the College

the King's and Bishop's Mills near Silver Street bridge: Pigot and Co's *London and Provincial New Commercial Directory for 1823–4* (n. pl., [1823]), pp. 165–6; Cambridgeshire Record Office, Miscellaneous legal documents, 132/T.360; cf. F.A. Reeve, *Victorian and Edwardian Cambridge from Old Photographs* (London, 1971), fig. 80; Faith Packard, *Our Family History* ... (privately printed, 1989), pp. 69–74, which provides a family tree but omits Thomas.

[139] Savage's assignee, George Henry Bays (a Cambridge attorney who styled himself 'gentleman' and who also had a residence in Bedfordshire), was unsuccessful in applying for an injunction to stop the lease of the site to Nutter. Despite this, and despite the attempt at arbitration, Bays kept the suit alive until 1829–30, when he abandoned an attempt to revive it after it had been dismissed on account of his failure to prosecute. Instead he began a new suit, naming various tenants of the site as defendants, as well as the College, but this seems to have lapsed when the defendants put in a plea that Bays was acting without the necessary consent of Savage's creditors and of the Court for Relief of Insolvent Debtors. *1830 Directory*, p. 23; PRO, C.13/2654/Bays vs. College; C.33/736, f. 1712v; C.33/796, f. 1919r–v; C.33/825, f. 482v; C.33/828, f. 1855r–v, the final order to be located, dates from June 1832 and relates to the College's attempts to recover costs. Inspection of the indexes to Chancery Orders and Decrees for 1832–7 (PRO, IND.10699/63–71) revealed no further proceedings. For the ease with which plaintiffs could harass defendants by prolonging Chancery suits without seriously prosecuting them, see Sir William Holdsworth, *A History of English Law*, IX (3rd edn, London, 1944), 351–2.

[140] Advertisement in *Cambridge Chronicle* (17 June 1825); SSM, Box 35, Lease to John Bicheno, 18 Jul. 1825; Box 36, Leases to James Dimmock and to James Nutter, junior, 18 Jul. 1825 ('James Nutter, junior' may have been Thomas's eldest brother, or he may have been a more distant relative; the existence of the latter is suggested by the fact that both a 'James Nutter' and a 'James Nutter, junior' witnessed a marriage at Great Shelford in December 1829, after the death of Thomas's father: Cambridgeshire Record Office, T.P.R. Layng's transcript of the Parish Register of St Mary's Church, Great Shelford, p. 179); PRO, C.13/2654/Bays vs. College. Some of the statements in Bays' Chancery bill conflict with documents in the College archives, and one needs to bear in mind Bentham's dictum that 'under the name of a [Chancery] *bill*, a volume of notorious lies' might be promulgated: Holdsworth, *History of English Law*, IX, 339. However, while several of those whom Bays lists as purchasers at the auction do not appear as tenants in the College records, he supplies so much detail that it is improbable that his account of the outcome of the sale is altogether

to new tenants, by the end of 1828.[141] Ultimately, Nutter retained a long-term interest only in the house completed by Savage, and in two others; at least two (and probably all) of these properties were sub-let by Nutter, the first becoming the 'Three Hawks' public house, shortly renamed the 'Duke of Sussex'.[142] With regard to the other houses, Nutter was a middle-man who relieved the College of the trouble of finding individual tenants, and of the risk of not finding them.

Redevelopment had therefore taken at least eight years instead of the intended three; furthermore, litigation continued for some four years after the completion of building, although the College arguably escaped lightly from Chancery, since suits lasting twenty or thirty years were not unknown in this period.[143] Nonetheless, the College had not only lost rental income but had by 1825 become liable for nearly £400 in legal fees and damages to Savage – a sum which it might not have been easy to raise had not Nutter been prepared (and able) to purchase his lease of the completed house, together with his tenure of the rest of the site and buildings (such as they were), with a down payment of £945 which compensated the College for its losses in the Savage affair.[144]

There is no doubt that a personal antipathy had developed between Chafy and Savage, and this must have contributed to the protracted disputes over the scheme. Some observers appear to have felt that Savage was being victimized: the proceedings at Cambridge Assizes were interrupted by a 'display of popular feeling' against Chafy.[145] However, if personal antipathy did exist, it was probably

---

a fabrication. Hence the inference that some of the purchasers at the auction obtained sub-leases from Nutter.
[141] MR.66, Audit for Michaelmas 1828, shows the houses on College ground let to new tenants. The houses on the Master's ground do not appear in the College accounts. Counterpart leases show that one was re-let in 1826, another in 1828. A third was not re-let until 1831, though the lessee was Nutter himself, and, since he already had tenure under the 1825 agreement, he may have been slow to obtain a new lease; no counterpart lease of the fourth house has been located: SSM, Box 36, Leases to James Howell, 19 Oct. 1826; to James Cribble, 6 Feb. 1828 (lease of four houses, one of them on the Master's ground) and to Thomas Nutter, 28 Feb. 1831.
[142] MR.66, Audit for Michaelmas 1828; SSM, Box 36, Lease to Thomas Nutter, 28 Feb. 1831; ibid., 'Three Hawks' packet, lease to same, 27 May 1825. The four houses leased by James Cribble, who was a Huntingdon grocer, were presumably also sub-let; for these and for Nutter's sub-tenants, see: SSM, Box 36, Lease to James Cribble, 6 Feb. 1828; *1830 Directory*, p. 28. The 'Three Hawks' had previously occupied one of the three houses in Sidney Street included in the development: SSM, Box 36, Agreement with Nutter, 1825.
[143] It was partly on his experience of Chancery in the late 1820s that Dickens drew in *Bleak House*: W.S. Holdsworth, *Charles Dickens as a Legal Historian* (New Haven, 1928), pp. 79, 105; John Butt and Kathleen Tillotson, *Dickens at Work* (London, 1957), pp. 185–6, 200.
[144] The College's losses in the Savage affair up to 1825 are listed and compared with the value of what was conveyed to Nutter in MR.116/4/7; cf. MR.44, p. 290. Although the College was awarded costs in Chancery, these apparently related only to part of the suit, and it is not clear if the College ever succeeded in recovering them: see n. 139.
[145] *Huntingdon . . . Gazette and Cambridge . . . Independent Press* (22 Mar. 1823) (copy at MR.116/3/19).

not entirely a product of Chafy's obstinacy, since it is apparent that Chafy had met his match in Savage. One observer suggested that Savage's behaviour matched his name, and it was alleged that he had threatened the Master with a trowel, declaring that, if Chafy demolished the disputed wall again, 'I will make a corpse of you'.[146] Furthermore, while it appears that the College became determined to end Savage's control of the site,[147] it had good reasons for doing so, since Savage was clearly in severe financial difficulties by 1823: he became liable to pay rent equivalent to that of the completed houses after the first year of the lease, yet he had completed only one house at the end of the second year. While the presence of windows which were not part of the plan may have constituted a legal ground for the College to refuse to lease the completed house, it does not appear that this was in fact of serious concern to the College, which did not require Nutter to alter the house when he took it over. Rather, the College admitted in its answer to Savage in Chancery that it had declined to lease the completed house to Savage's nominee because it believed that Savage – who had yet to pay any rent – was 'in desperate circumstances and utterly unable to perform' the building agreement. Indeed, Savage was accused of planning to demolish what he had built in order to recover the cost of the materials.[148] Since the College was in no position to inject capital into the scheme, it had little choice but to seek to eject Savage from the site and to re-let it to tenants with adequate capital.

Nor is it likely that undue pressure on Harris and Savage from Chafy and the College was responsible for the builders' financial problems. It is true that the agreement with Harris and Savage assured them of control of the site for only three years, whereas Nutter's tenure was, at forty years, the longest that the College could legally grant. However, it was not unusual for a landlord to withhold a long lease until the buildings had been completed to his satisfaction. Furthermore, Nutter was, like Harris and Savage, obliged to complete the buildings within three years, without the one-year rent-free period which Harris and Savage had enjoyed. Nonetheless, Nutter secured the completion of most (and possibly of all) of the houses within the stipulated three years and did so without falling seriously behind with his rent.[149] In fact, the successive bankruptcies of Harris and Savage may have owed less to the terms offered by the College than to the instability of the building trade. Master builders were notorious in the Georgian period for the frequency with which they got into financial difficulties. In

---

[146] MR.116/3/8, 16.

[147] Cf. the accusation that Chafy had sabotaged Savage's attempts in 1822 to sell his interest to others, saying that the College 'intended to take the premises away from . . . Savage immediately' (C.13/2654/Bays vs. College), although Savage's lack of success probably also derived from the brevity of the period which his lease still had to run.

[148] PRO, C.13/841/37; SSM, Box 36, Agreement with Nutter, 1825.

[149] Chalklin, *Provincial towns*, pp. 64, 70–1; MR.44, pp. 306, 330, 337. Though it is possible that two of the houses were not completed by 1828 (see n. 141), it appears that the College retained confidence in Nutter's ability to complete the agreement in reasonable time – there is no sign of proceedings against him for failure to fulfil it.

London, at least, they often operated with minimal capital, depending on bartering labour on others' projects for labour on their own and on being able to sell houses on leased sites quickly, before they became liable to pay ground rent to the landlord. Such arrangements were obviously vulnerable, even in a period when building costs were low; as Chalklin observes, the fact that credit was becoming easier to obtain around 1820 may have tempted master builders to borrow excessively.[150] Indeed, the arrangement with Nutter may have succeeded, where that with Savage failed, because, under Nutter, the project was handled as a number of small enterprises, separately financed, rather than as one large one.[151]

Conclusion

It cannot be suggested that Chafy was either popular or generally respected. Feeling against him was apparent not only during the 1823 Assize trial against Savage, but also at the 1834 Assize trial of Chafy for false imprisonment, when the statement of the prosecution's case was accompanied by 'some expressions of applause'.[152] Yet, as a head of house, he was part of a group whose rôle in the government of the University was viewed with hostility; furthermore, aspects of the University's rights and privileges were viewed with hostility by townsmen.[153] In these circumstances, the most affable of men might have found it difficult to achieve popularity. It would be unwise, therefore, to attribute too much of the friction surrounding the College's building activities in the 1820s to Chafy's personality, rather than to the uncertainties which attach to restoring old buildings, on the one hand, and to speculative building, on the other hand. Equally, the transformation of the College in the 1820s and 1830s could not have taken place without the financial windfall created by the opening of new mines on the Taylor estates; the work was also a response to the decayed state of the existing buildings and perhaps partly, too, a response to increased student numbers. Yet Chafy's stamp is clear, in the extent and variety of the work done in and around the Master's Lodge and in the refacing of the Chapel, which he financed. Almost certainly, and most significantly, Chafy's ambition for the College and for himself (the two cannot, perhaps, be separated) led to the employment of Wyatville; Chafy thus played a signal part in giving to Hall and Chapel Courts their current

---

[150] Summerson, *Georgian London*, pp. 77–8; Chalklin, *Provincial towns*, pp. 292–3, 296; for building costs in Cambridge in particular, cf. Willis and Clark, *Architectural History*, II, 302. However, it should be noted that, in proceedings relating to Savage's insolvency, he was described as a victualler, as well as a carpenter and builder (MR.116/4/4); his financial problems may therefore have had their root in activities outside the building trade.

[151] That Savage himself saw the solution as being to break the development up into small units is suggested by his decision to market his interest as several lots when he attempted to sell it in 1822: Advertisement in *Cambridge Chronicle* (7 June 1822).

[152] *The Times* (17 Mar. 1834), p. 6d.

[153] Winstanley, *Early Victorian Cambridge*, pp. 122–30.

appearance. Wyatville's Roman cement did not prove to be particularly durable, and, by the end of the nineteenth century, was no longer admired; some of it was removed in an attempt to 'restore' the buildings as early as 1890.[154] However, most of Wyatville's work has itself since been restored,[155] and Chafy's mark on the College seems likely to be a permanent one.

---

[154] Some of Wyatville's stucco was removed from part of the north façade of Hall Court at the time of the construction of Cloister Court. Remaining parts on that front were removed in 1934, with a view 'so far as is possible' to restoring the 'original design'; Royal Commission on Historical Monuments, *Cambridge*, pp. 207–8; Wv/D28; *Sidney Sussex College Annual* (1931), p. 13; ibid. (1934), p. 13.

[155] Scott-Giles, *Sidney*, p. 123. Stucco was replaced by stone on the west front of the Chapel in the 1950s – formerly, only the centre-piece was stone-faced – but Wyatville's design was copied: Nicholas Taylor and Philip Booth, *Cambridge New Architecture* (3rd edn, London, 1970), p. 47. Cf. the removal of early nineteenth-century stucco from Magdalene College's First Court in the 1950s in order to expose original brickwork: Peter Cunich, David Hoyle, Eamon Duffy and Ronald Hyam, *A History of Magdalene College, Cambridge, 1428–1988* (Cambridge, 1994), p. 253.

The Growth of Cleethorpes and the Prosperity of Sidney, 1616–1968

R. W. AMBLER and ALAN DOWLING

Sidney Sussex's interest in Cleethorpes dated back to the second decade of the seventeenth century, but the estate assumed a particular degree of importance in the College's history in the second half of the nineteenth century when its farmlands began to be leased out for building. This new source of income provided the financial means by which the College was able to respond to change both internally and within the University, offsetting the diminishing returns of agricultural estates from the 1870s. The management of the changes at Cleethorpes also provides an example of the way in which the particular priorities and needs of a collegiate body were worked out within the context of urban growth and, on part of the estate, the development of a seaside resort.

The College bought the manor of Itterby in 1616 for £1400 using part of the Blundell bequest. Itterby (Map 1) was a township in the parish of Clee on the mouth of the Humber in north-east Lincolnshire. In the seventeenth century Clee's neighbour, the borough of Grimsby, was said to be 'a little poor town, not a quarter so great as heretofore', but its growth from the middle of the nineteenth century was to have as important an influence on the College's estate as the contemporaneous metamorphosis of the parish's coastal hamlets into the seaside resort of Cleethorpes.[1]

At the time of the 1616 purchase Clee was a parish of some 3,500 acres, nearly half common coastal meadow and grazing land, supporting a population of some three hundred inhabitants who lived in the village of Clee and four hamlets: Itterby and Oole (the 'thorpes' of Clee or 'Cleethorpes'), Thrunscoe also on the coast and Weelsby inland (Map 1).[2] There were 20 College tenants at Michaelmas 1618: 7 renting property in both Clee and its thorpes, 10 in Itterby and another

---

[1] Sidney Sussex College, Cambridge, Archives (hereafter SSC), 4/4, Indenture of bargain and sale of the manor of Itterby; *The Diary of Abraham de la Pryme, the Yorkshire Antiquary*, ed. Charles Jackson (Surtees Society, vol. LIV, Durham, 1870), p. 153.
[2] Frank Baker, *The Story of Cleethorpes and the Contribution of Methodism over Two Hundred Years* (Cleethorpes, 1953), p. 138; SSC 18/37; R.W. Ambler, 'The Historical Development of Grimsby and Cleethorpes', in *Humber Perspectives: a region through the ages*, ed. S. Ellis and D.R. Crowther (Hull, 1990), pp. 229–30; *Farmers and Fishermen: the probate inventories of the ancient parish of Clee, south Humberside, 1536–1742*, ed. R.W. Ambler and B. and L.

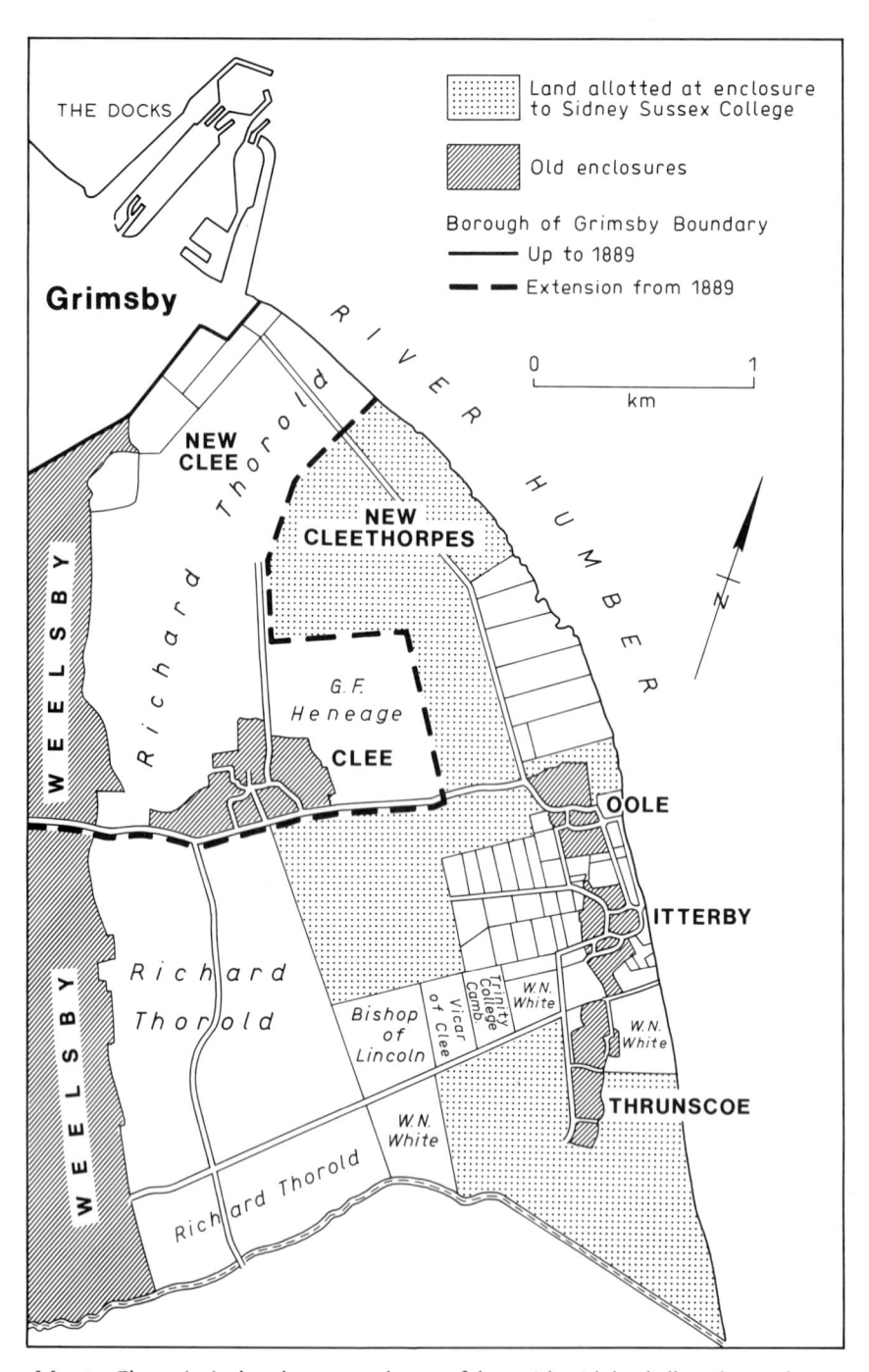

Map 1. Clee: principal settlements and areas of the parish with land allotted at enclosure to Sidney Sussex College and other main landowners.

3 in Thrunscoe and Oole. Although there was some gradual consolidation of holdings, their number and size remained basically unchanged for some two hundred years. There is no evidence for any substantial degree of innovation or development in farming practices over the same period – a reflection of the generally stagnant condition of the agrarian economy of the Lincolnshire marshland in the period. A 1662 terrier has details of the largest of Sidney's farms with its 50 acres of arable land, 20 acres of meadow and 10 of pasture as well as the right of grazing cows and oxen on the West Field. This arrangement reflected the balance of local agriculture, although there were also houses and cottages belonging to the College without any land as well as one with only meadow and grazing rights.[3]

The College gained few particular benefits from the estate's position on the coast, and at least eighteen and a half acres of its arable land and about three acres of pasture were said to have been 'wasted by the sea' in the course of the seventeenth century. Clee fishermen had been sea-going into the sixteenth century but by 1616 their operations were largely confined to the use of nets and traps near the shore. They tended to be poor, and although the establishment of an oyster fishery in the eighteenth century was a new phase in the parish's maritime history, it was not one which added directly to the value of the Sidney estate.[4] The first half-year's rents from the College's newly acquired Clee property were £41 7s 11½d and they remained at this level throughout the seventeenth and into the eighteenth century – initially some 20 per cent of its total income, but just under 11 per cent by the 1640s when the College's income had increased to total just over £380 a half year.[5]

Increases in the number of livestock and in the size of arable holdings among Clee farmers in the first four decades of the eighteenth century were not reflected in the College's rents. Its tenants usually held their land on 21-year leases and it was only in 1773 that income from Clee moved up to £64 0s 7½d a half year, raising the proportion it contributed to the College's income to 12.5 per cent. This proportion continued to increase and reached nearly 30 per cent in the years following the Napoleonic Wars, falling back to 13.6 per cent by 1840.[6]

Watkinson (Hull, 1987) pp. 1–3, 8; *Protestation Returns 1641–42 – Lincolnshire*, ed. W.F. Webster (Nottingham, 1984), p. 52.
[3] SSC, Masters' Records (hereafter MR) ff. 147–8, 364–5; *Farmers and Fishermen*, p. 14; Joan Thirsk, *English Peasant Farming. The Agrarian History of Lincolnshire from Tudor to Recent Times* (London, 1957), p. 146; SSC 3/6, Terrier of College Lands in Clee and Cleethorpes; SSC 27/5, Terrier of Lands held by David Field, 1734.
[4] Ambler, 'Historical Development of Grimsby and Cleethorpes', p. 233; *Farmers and Fishermen*, pp. 20, 22–4; Baker, *Story of Cleethorpes*, p. 10.
[5] G.M. Edwards, *Sidney Sussex College* (London, 1899), p. 229; SSC, MR 61, ff. 147–8, 155, 345–7.
[6] *Farmers and Fishermen*, pp. 16–20, 21; SSC, MR 62, ff. 368–9; SSC, MR 66, Lady Day 1818 and 1819; SSC, Bursar's General Accounts (hereafter BGA), Lady Day and Michaelmas, 1840.

Table 1: Population of Clee and Cleethorpes

	1801	1811	1821	1831	1841	1851	1861
Clee with Weelsby	103	115	154	177	199	195	325
Cleethorpes with Thrunscoe	284	375	406	497	803	839	1,230

Source: *Census Reports*, 1801–1961

The rent increase of 1773 came towards the end of a period of constrained reparation and reconstruction of the College's fabric. Its archives also show that there was some tidying of the material connected with Clee estate in the middle of the century, but it was one new lease which provided the increased income. This lease was not associated with any radical changes on the estate itself. The new lessees were, like some of the other tenants, absentees who sub-let to resident local farmers, and both parties were subject to restrictive covenants imposed by the College on their farming practices. The increases of the nineteenth century were part of a general rent rise rather than the result of any active College policy.[7]

The rent increase of 1773 may have been made in expectation of an enclosure of the open fields and common lands of Clee, but the tardiness of its landowners and farmers to embark on improvements was exemplified by their attitude in this matter. There were four attempts to initiate enclosures between 1770 and 1821 which came to nothing, and an enclosure act was not passed until 1841. When the award came in 1846 the College, as the second largest landowner in the parish, was allotted some 748 acres. This was 34.3 per cent of the total acreage of which 603 acres were in the old 'thorpes' of Clee – Itterby and Oole – together with Thrunscoe, making the College the dominant landowner in these townships with 57.2 per cent of their total area. Although the next largest owners there had only 136 and 115 acres each, Sidney's control was weakened by the division of the rest of the land between forty-nine others, many of whom had only very small holdings[8] (Map 1).

---

[7] C.W. Scott-Giles, *Sidney Sussex College: A Short History* (Cambridge, 1975), pp. 75–8; SSC, MR 39, ff. 619–22; SSC 27/11, Map of Clee and Thrunscoe and various terriers.

[8] Thirsk, *English Peasant Farming*, pp. 237–8; SSC 18, Copy of Mrs Prowse's letter, 17

Table 1: Population of Clee and Cleethorpes (contd)

1871	1881	1891	1901	1911	1921	1931	1951	1961
2,058	11,620	18,755[1]						
1,768	2,840	4,306	12,578	21,417	28,155[2]	28,621[3]	29,557[3]	32,700[3]

[1] Parts of the ancient parish of Clee, including the village of Clee, the New Clee development and Weelsby, were incorporated into Grimsby under the 1889 Grimsby Extension Act. The population of the area was thenceforth enumerated with that of Grimsby.
[2] Extended 1922 and 1927 to include adjacent parts of the parish of Humberston and Weelsby.
[3] Population of Cleethorpes Urban District and Civil Parish.

After enclosure the College tenancies were rationalised, giving 3 farms of 271, 173 and 101 acres, 3 smaller tenancies of between 30 and 40 acres each and 14 cottage holdings, some with workshops (such as the carpenter's shop together with 18 perches of land let to Richard Chapman at an annual rent of 30 shillings). In 1850 the estate brought in just over £887 a year, some 16 per cent of the College's total income (Table 2).[9] Enclosure was costly. As well as the general charges which the College shared proportionately with other landowners, there was the need to provide new farm buildings and to hedge, fence, ditch and drain its land. In March 1844 the College's local agent, the Grimsby solicitor William Heaford Daubney, advertised for tenders to erect a new brick-built farmhouse and buildings. To meet these costs, the College raised a mortgage of £3,000 in 1844 at 4 per cent interest, used increased rent income from Clee and sold some of its seafront property by auction. Whatever its gains from enclosure, the College's attitude to what remained of the small peasantry of the parish was tempered by paternalism. It was agreed that Widow Wright, an old tenant at Cleethorpes, should be allowed three or four acres of land for the rest of her life at a low rent 'by way of compensation for being deprived of her holding when the inclosure took place'.[10]

February 1770; *Lincoln Rutland and Stamford Mercury* (hereafter *LRSM*), 13 September, 6 and 13 December 1811, 2 September 1814, 14 September 1821; 5 Victoria, 1842, An Act for Enclosing Lands in the Parish of Clee, in the County of Lincoln; South Humberside Area Record Office (hereafter SHARO), 1/920/1, Clee Enclosure Award, 1846.
[9] SSC, BGA, Lady Day and Michaelmas, 1850.
[10] Humberside Leisure Services (hereafter HLS), Grimsby Library, Skelton Collection 1844/30, 66, 84; SSC, Memoranda of College Matters, 16 October 1843, 5 and 12 February, 18 June, 19 October 1844, 31 January, 4 April 1845; Baker, *Story of Cleethorpes*, pp. 90–91.

Table 2. Sidney Sussex College Annual Income 1840–1914

1 YEAR	2 INCOME FROM CLEETHORPES	3 TOTAL COLLEGE INCOME	4 COLUMN 2 AS PERCENTAGE OF COLUMN 3
	£	£	%
1840	609	4,492	13.6
1850	887	5,525	16.0
1860	1,427	6,036	23.6
1870	1,893	8,234	23.0
1880	2,101	8,418	25.0
1890	2,159	7,361	29.3
1900	5,590	11,161	50.1
1910	8,170	14,528	56.2
1914	8,563	14,912	57.4

Source: Sidney Sussex College Bursar's General Accounts, 1840–1914.

In common with that of many Lincolnshire towns and villages, the population of Clee nearly doubled during the first half of the nineteenth century; but after 1851 its growth diverged dramatically from that of its rural neighbours (Table 1). This was the result of housing development in the north-east corner of the parish stimulated by the rapid growth of Grimsby which began to spread out of its ancient boundaries into those of its neighbour. This area, which became known as 'New Clee', was incorporated with the village of Clee into the borough of Grimsby in 1889. As New Clee became built up to its boundaries, the spread of housing reached the College's lands, leading to their development as 'New Cleethorpes' (Map 1). While New Cleethorpes grew because of its proximity to Grimsby's docks, providing space for terraced housing in which to house the people who worked there (Plate 11a), the separate older settlements of Cleethorpes developed as a seaside resort. The population of both parts – new and old – of what had from the 1870s been known as Cleethorpes expanded rapidly with a threefold increase in the 1890s but slowing down from 1921. The land which separated them finally became built over in the twentieth century (Table 1 and Map 2).[11]

Old Cleethorpes had become a small sea-bathing resort by the 1790s, said by the Hon. John Byng to be 'the best of the Lincolnshire bathing shops'. In the early nineteenth century it was seen as 'the most eligible and agreeable bathing-place on the Lincolnshire coast'. The land which the College sold there in 1844

---

[11] Baker, *Story of Cleethorpes*, p. 131; Ambler, 'Historical Development of Grimsby and Cleethorpes', p. 241.

to meet the cost of enclosure was divided into building lots with a sea frontage. High Cliff Terrace which was built on it was 'a splendid pile of buildings, containing seven houses, fit for the reception of large families' with 'a full view of the sea', but a seasonal 'influx of respectable families' was not enough to sustain large-scale growth. The extension of the Manchester, Sheffield and Lincolnshire Railway Company to Grimsby in 1848 increased the number of day trippers and the range of places from which visitors came, but the Company's lack of interest in extending into Cleethorpes, together with opposition over its proposed route, delayed the building of a branch line to the coast until 1863.[12]

A railway extension, passing the new Grimsby docks, had the potential to open up Cleethorpes for residential development and would present

> very favourable opportunities to those gentlemen who transact business at the new dock works having their family residences at Cleethorpes, which will then be brought within a few minutes run of the town of Grimsby, and by which they will be enabled to come in the morning and return in the evening in less time than would be requisite for walking from one end of the town to the other.[13]

The College appears to have been well aware of these opportunities and responded with relative alacrity. It initiated a private parliamentary bill which freed it from traditional constraints on the ways in which it was able to exploit its lands, particularly the limitation of building leases to 40 years. Robert Phelps, the Master, giving evidence during proceedings on the bill, said that the estate would 'be much increased in value if it could be leased on terms of 99-years' while the local agent William Heaford Daubney stated that he had been 'several times applied to for land belonging to the college for building purposes'. There were references in the Sidney Sussex College Estate Act, which received royal assent in June 1853, to both what was seen as the potential created by the seaside development of Cleethorpes and to that of the newly enclosed land in what was to become New Cleethorpes. Cleethorpes had long been 'a bathing place of considerable resort' and there had been a 'great increase in the number of visitors ... in the summer season' bringing 'a demand for increased accommodation and for land ... for building purposes'. The proximity of College land to Grimsby had also 'contributed to render the said estate eligible for the purposes of building and of forming brick-yards and accommodation grounds'. It was less explicit in

---

[12] R.W. Ambler, 'Cleethorpes: the development of an East Coast Resort', in *Ports and Resorts in the Regions*, ed. E.M. Sigsworth (Hull (1981)), pp. 179–82; *The Torrington Diaries containing the Tours through England and Wales of the Hon. John Byng (later Fifth Baron Torrington) between the years 1781 and 1794*, ed. C. Bruyn Adams, vol. 2 (London, 1935), pp. 387–9; HLS, Skelton Collection, 1844/15 and 66; Edward Dobson, *A Guide and Directory of Cleethorpes* (Cleethorpes, 1850), p. 13.

[13] *LRSM*, 23 June 1854.

its appreciation of the potential of Cleethorpes for the type of suburban development envisaged by the propagandists for a railway extension.[14]

Sidney Sussex's Act not only enabled the College to grant 99 year building leases, but also to provide a framework for development by marking out roads and plots as well as setting aside sites for churches, churchyards and parsonage houses. Lessees were to be required to enter into covenants to keep their property in good repair, to pay their yearly rents and to give up the buildings they had erected in good order at the termination of the lease. The College could also raise the sum of £10,000 for the improvement of the estate which was to be repaid out of rents. This initiative, a contrast to what had hitherto tended to be a rather passive attitude to the Clee property, anticipated the provisions of the Universities and Colleges Estates Act of 1858 which gave some further relaxation of the conditions under which colleges could develop their estates.[15]

The College's assiduity brought it few immediate benefits, although the local market in building land became more lively in Cleethorpes after enclosure. The number of houses increased from 159 in 1841 to 198 in 1851 and to 287 by 1861, but the divided landownership of the resort brought competition from other landlords selling freehold land. The College's leases were less attractive, and only 734 square yards were let on its old enclosures between 1853 and 1857. This was divided into 2 plots with ground rents of 1 shilling and 9 pence a square yard respectively. For 31 years after 1854 only 27 individuals took building land from the College, most of whom were local men with a plot each. These fish merchants and retailers demonstrated, even if their numbers did not fulfil, the potential of Cleethorpes for suburban development, and a syndicate which included a smack owner, 2 fishermen and 2 fish merchants took 15 building plots in 1874. Only Robert Stainton, a house steward from Stoneleigh in Warwickshire and Thomas Fisher, a Birmingham solicitor, came from outside the immediate neighbourhood.[16]

Initially, the pace of development was also slow in New Cleethorpes, and the College was dependent on the exhaustion of building land in New Clee to provide the impetus for opening up its own estate. While cheaper leases had been available in Grimsby, it was the geographical position of land rather than its price which ultimately determined when it was leased for building. The College's plans for New Cleethorpes were most immediately affected by the neighbouring estate of

---

[14] House of Lords Record Office, Proceedings of Committees on Estate Bills, Session 1852–52, ff. 1–6; 16–17 Victoria ch. 1, 1853, Sidney Sussex College Estate Act.

[15] Sidney Sussex Estate Act; 21–22 Victoria ch. 44, 1858, The Universities and Colleges Estates Act; P.J. Aspinall, 'Speculative Builders and the Development of Cleethorpes, 1850–1900', *Lincolnshire History and Archaeology*, 11 (1976), 45–6.

[16] Anne J. Kay, 'The Development of Housing in Cleethorpes, 1876–1901', unpublished long essay, University of Hull Certificate in Regional and Local History (1982), p. 5; *Grimsby News* (hereafter *GN*), 7 July 1882; *Grimsby Gazette*, 2 May 1854, 14 March 1856, 17 April 1857; Aspinall, 'Speculative Builders', p. 46.

the Thorolds, later Grant Thorolds (Map 1). This estate is poorly documented and has been subject to demolition and redevelopment, but the visual evidence shows that its proximity to Grimsby's docks meant that its land in New Clee was the first to be taken for building after that within the boundaries of Grimsby had been filled. However, not content to wait for the spread of building to come to the College estate, Daubney persisted in his efforts to let it. In 1876 he proposed that a road should be built along the New Clee boundary between the College and Grant Thorold estates which would enable the College to 'let off a great deal of land'. It was, he reported, an area where 'buildings are extending in all directions'. The road, which became the present day Park Street, was completed as a joint venture between the two owners; but the College's powerlessness to influence the speed of development can be seen in the way it had to wait until the mid 1880s before there was any return from its investment (Map 2). Daubney summed up the position in a letter to Dr Phelps in 1885:

> With regard to the land near to Grimsby everything has been done that can be done towards leasing it. Mr. Thorold's land being nearer to Grimsby is of course preferred. He has now exhausted his frontage, and the college may reasonably expect to get on with theirs.[17]

When the Grant Thorold land had been taken up the College began, over three decades after it had been passed, to benefit from its Estate Act. Building began on the frontage of the road between Cleethorpes and Grimsby which had been laid out at enclosure, but which was now 'exhausted' on the Grant Thorold estate. In the summer of 1886 two local builders, Joshua Loughton and John Garton Pickering, applied to the Local Board of Health for permission to build 8 and 2 houses respectively immediately inside the boundary of the College's property. They leased the land for 99 years from 3 December 1886 at an annual ground rent of 3 pence a square yard. Pickering, with William Garton Pickering, took more land in 1887 and began to build on Park Street 7 years after its completion. Here the ground rent was 2½ pence a square yard. Smaller plots were also leased to other builders and new side roads began to be constructed.[18]

The cost of preparing land for building by constructing roads and drains as well as the administrative expenses of leasing were met by the College: between £30,000 and £40,000 was spent in this way in New Cleethorpes in the two decades from 1887. This was raised by mortgages such as the £4,845 which the University Life Assurance Society advanced on the Cleethorpes estate in 1894. Expenditure was controlled by providing roads in stages as land was opened up for building. Three streets were extended and a new one opened in New

---

[17] Aspinall, 'Speculative Builders', p. 46; SSC, Cleethorpes Correspondence (hereafter Corr.), W.H. Daubney to R. Phelps, 16 May 1876, 27 February 1884, 13 October 1885.
[18] Aspinall, 'Speculative Builders', p. 46; SHARO, 53/600/1/1, Cleethorpes Urban Sanitary Authority, Building Plan Register, 1876–1895, nos. 202, 207, 240, 241; SSC Leases, 1886–1893, f. 187.

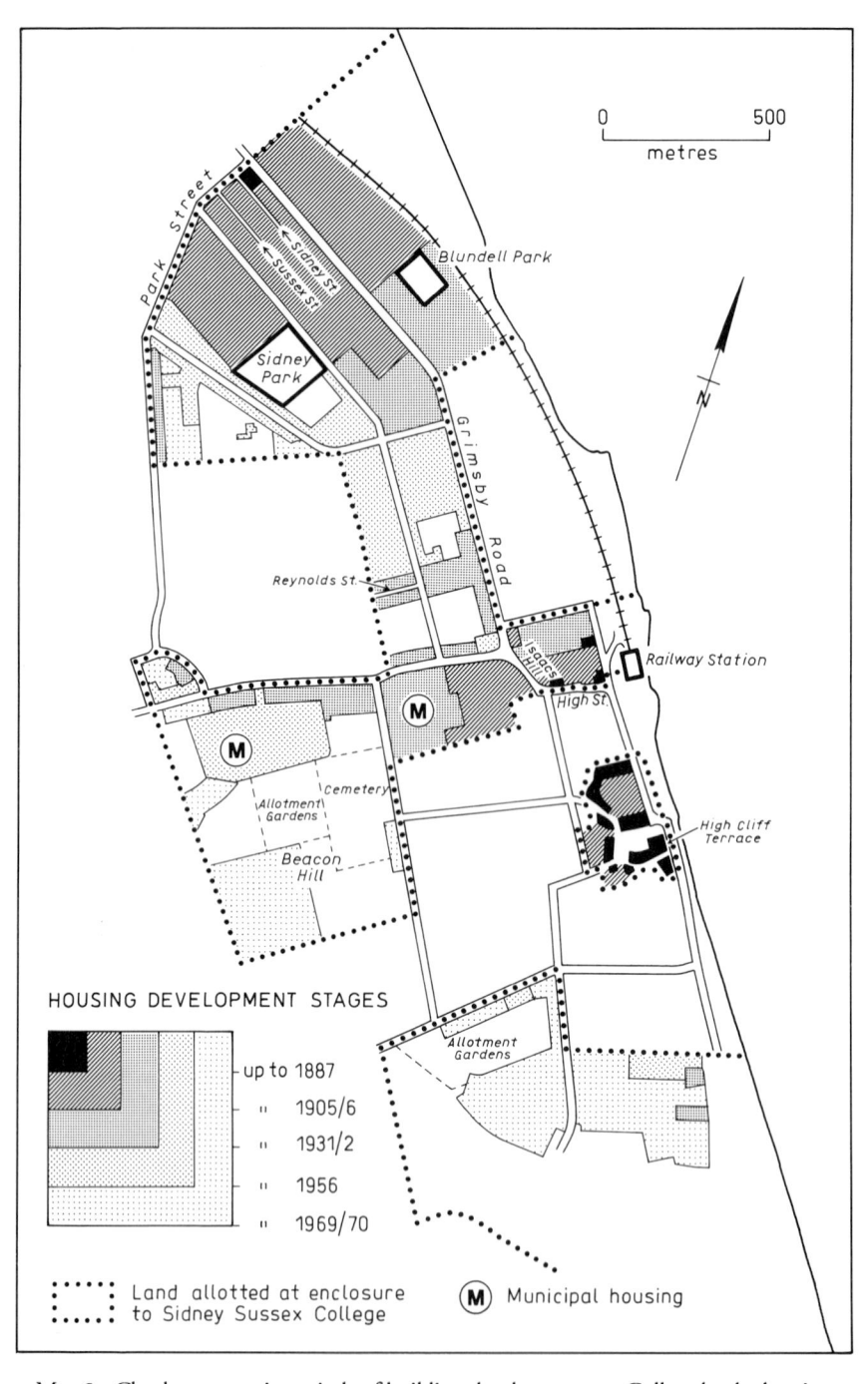

Map 2. Cleethorpes: main periods of building development on College lands showing places mentioned specifically in the text.

Cleethorpes in 1893, bringing a further 67,392 square yards of land – nearly 14 acres – into use. There was, according to Daubney, 'a steady demand'. The outlay would be £3,851 but an estimated annual rental of £792 1s 1d would yield a gross return of 20.6 per cent while the capital could be raised on mortgages at 3.5 per cent.[19]

The College also began to benefit from the growth of old Cleethorpes. In the mid 1890s 3 acres of land in the area of the High Street and the railway station (Map 2) were leased to local builders who met the cost of road construction in return for reduced ground rents. There were also some freehold sales and nearly 2 acres of land were sold to a local businessman for £2,200, while an acre of land along Cleethorpes High Street was sold at an average price of 5 shillings a square yard. This was a case where the return to the College was a direct result of the development of Cleethorpes as a resort, since the land was used for three-storey buildings incorporating shops for holiday-makers. In 1883 the College had received £289 11s 2d from ground rents in central Cleethorpes, but it was New Cleethorpes which still provided the largest part of its income from the Clee estate, where leasehold land produced £777 5s 0d by 1890. A typical house in the area occupied a plot of approximately 150 to 200 square yards and had 3 bedrooms, a parlour, kitchen and scullery with its own water closet or box privy. It was terraced with a small front garden overlooked by a bay window. There was also access to its rear yard or garden via a narrow road or footway. Larger houses, terraced or semi-detached, were built on the main thoroughfares such as Grimsby Road.[20]

The majority of ground rents on College lands settled at between 3 pence and 3½ pence a square yard in the 1890s, but however much this had fallen back from the few more highly priced leases of the 1850s and 1860s, the effect on College finances of large scale development was dramatic (Table 2). Agricultural depression meant that the College had to give reductions on farm rents and its income from this source declined: there were arrears of £567 10s 0d at Michaelmas 1890 on its other Lincolnshire estate at Saleby. Total College income fell from £8,418 6s 7½d in 1880 to £7,361 14s 9d by 1890 and the extra £58 which the Clee estate brought in by this date did nothing to compensate, although the percentage it contributed to income rose from just under 25 per cent to just over 29 per cent in the same period. By 1900 the College's income from Clee, at £5,590

---

[19] Aspinall, 'Speculative Builders', p.46; SSC, Corr. 1875–1909, T. Lamming, Specification of Materials to be used in constructing [roads] . . . May 1894; SSC, Minutes of College Meetings (hereafter Minutes), 1876–1895, 14 October 1893, 13 October 1894.
[20] SHARO, 51/1/8, Cleethorpes Urban District Council (hereafter CUDC), Minutes, 1894–1896, 12 and 19 June 1895, 15 October 1896; SSC, Corr. 1875–1909, C. Smith to F.H. Neville, 18 August 1896; SSC, Minutes, 5 October 1895, 23 April 1896; SSC, Leases etc. 1894–1898, f. 343; SSC, BGA, Lady Day and Michaelmas 1883 and 1890; SSC, Leases 1886–1893, no. 91.

4s 4d, had reached 50 per cent of an increasing total and was 57.4 per cent by 1914 when it reached £8,563 15s 2d.[21]

The increased income from the Clee estate came at an opportune time in the College's affairs. Plans had already been made to build a new residential wing when the aged Master, Dr Robert Phelps, died in January 1890. The means to achieve the development of the College were therefore beginning to come to hand when Charles Smith, a reformer, succeeded him. As the number of undergraduates in residence increased from about 50 to 72 by 1901 and to 91 by 1910 the College was able to grow in step with the rest of the University. It was not a totally uninterrupted process and the fortunes of the Clee estate remained a crucial influence on it. Moreover, just as the management of College affairs began to assume a new style, so the increased commercial significance of its Clee property meant that the approaches, attitudes and relationships which were appropriate for agricultural property became less relevant. This was epitomised in the decision of W.H. Daubney to stop holding the annual dinner for College tenants:

> I found a great difficulty in making selections out of the great number of tenants without creating dissatisfaction and it was not possible to treat the little holders and the leaseholders in the same way as the agricultural tenants, for whom the dinner was originally instituted, that I thought it better to abandon the dinner altogether.[22]

The abandonment of the tenants' annual dinner did not mean that the College's paternalistic approach had ended. This continued to be expressed in ways which were more appropriate to new conditions and brought a more active and continuous involvement in the affairs of the estate. The terms of the building leases increased the control the College exercised over the living conditions of much larger numbers of people, but a clear sense of its obligations as a landlord informed the management of the property. The College had provided regular support for the work of the National School in Cleethorpes, and when a new church was built for the resort it gave £525 towards the building fund. It also gave the site for a church in New Cleethorpes and 12 acres of land for the recreation ground which was to become Sidney Park. The College's influence and interest were confirmed by the way it stamped its mark on local topography through the policy of naming streets and roads after people and places connected with the College, beginning with Sidney and Sussex Streets. The names were chosen in the College and passed to its agent, Daubney.[23]

---

[21] Aspinall, 'Speculative Builders', p. 47; SSC, BGA, Lady Day and Michaelmas 1880–1890, 1900–1901.

[22] Scott-Giles, *Sidney Sussex College*, pp. 106–7; C.N.L. Brooke, *A History of the University of Cambridge*, vol. IV, 1870–1900 (Cambridge, 1993), pp. 593–4; Parliamentary Papers, 1922, (Cmd. 1588), Royal Commission on the Universities of Oxford and Cambridge, Report, p. 27; SSC, Corr. 1895–1909, W.H. Daubney to F.H. Neville, 7 April 1890.

[23] Baker, *Story of Cleethorpes*, p. 113; SSC, Minutes, 21 November 1863, 30 May 1868;

While its support for the Church of England can be seen as part of a continuing tradition of clerical paternalism, the provision of facilities for recreation also enhanced amenities on the College's estate (although the land for Sidney Park was given at the request of the local council). The 1853 Estate Act limited the College's power to give land free of charge, and other public needs were met by sale, although sometimes at below market price. The Burial Board purchased eight acres of land from the College for £1,400 in 1875 to be used for a cemetery extension, and the site of the first board school was sold for £1,250 an acre in 1895. The price of the land for new council offices, which was in fact used for a technical institute, was reduced to £818 an acre. Support for the Church of England did not extend to the prohibition of nonconformity, and both the Wesleyan and United Methodists requested and were offered sites for chapels. The College sold land to the trustees of a set of cottage homes erected to mark the Coronation of Edward VII, but then met the cost of two of the cottages, so fulfilling charitable obligations to the local community without breaking the prohibition on making gifts of land.[24]

The Estate Act had given the College powers to include specific conditions and covenants in its leases, most of which were directed at maintaining the fabric of the estate. They continued to be an important influence on the character of Cleethorpes and were regularly used in the College's leases after 1886. Buildings had to be kept in good repair with their exterior woodwork and iron work repainted every three years, no extensions were to be built without the College's consent, while lessees were to flag the footpaths in front of buildings and build brick walls to separate gardens. These conditions were upheld by reserving the right to enter and repossess buildings if the terms of the leases were infringed.[25]

While the conditions and covenants imposed by the College preserved the fabric and general appearance of its estate, the length and detail of those which aimed to control nuisances impinged on the personal behaviour of lessees. Commercial buildings such as slaughterhouses, blacksmiths' workshops and beershops 'or any other manufactory' could not be erected; the keeping of 'hogs, boars, sows, pigs or other offensive beast' was forbidden and tenants could not 'harbour, lodge or permit to dwell therein any lewd or disorderly person' or allow anything 'which shall or may grow to the annoyance, grievance, disturbance or damage of the Lessors or Lessees or tenants in the neighbourhood'. Later covenants were extended to prohibit the sale of any intoxicating liquor, as well as fish-curing houses, smoke-houses and fried-fish shops. None the less, over seven

---

Grimsby Observer, 7 September 1898, 5 January 1900; *GN*, 6 January 1899; SSC, Minutes, 29 January 1900; SSC, Corr. 1875–1909, W.H. Daubney to R. Phelps, 1 November 1889.
[24] Sidney Sussex College Estate Act; SHARO, 51/1/8, CUDC, Minutes, 1894–1896, 12 June 1895, 14 January and 13 May 1896; SSC, Minutes, 12 June 1896, 3 June and 4 November 1897, 28 January 1909; SSC, Corr. 1875–1909, C. Smith to A. Bates, 14 May 1896; *GN*, 12 January 1904.
[25] Sidney Sussex College Estate Act; SSC, Leases etc. 1894–1898, pp. 1–6.

acres of land were sold in 1899 on the Grimsby Road for £8,181 as the site of an hotel and of Grimsby Town football ground – Blundell Park – while the estate had a hundred retail shops by 1914.[26]

The building byelaws adopted by the Cleethorpes Local Board in 1875 were an additional influence on the ambience of the estate. The relationship between the local authority and the College was to become increasingly important in the twentieth century as their policies for the development of Cleethorpes became interdependent, maintaining the College's influence on the shaping of the town's distinctive identity. This was an important factor in resistance to attempts by the borough of Grimsby to extend its boundaries further; proposals which involved all the College's New Cleethorpes development. As the College joined what had in 1894 become the Cleethorpes Urban District in its opposition to the scheme, it emphasised the particular character of its estate. At the enquiry into Grimsby's proposals (which were rejected in 1908) the College's counsel stated with some confidence that:

> no one can go through that area [New Cleethorpes] without seeing it is well laid out, that the streets have been well planned, and that it is a thoroughly well-developed and well-administered district, I venture to think, superior in character, in the width of the streets, and the fore courts of the houses, to the adjacent parts of Grimsby.[27]

A large part of the enquiry was concerned with sanitary and drainage provision in Grimsby and Cleethorpes. Cleethorpes pointed to its better record in this respect, but the question of drainage had become crucial to the College's plans to develop its estate further while the inadequacy of the existing sewerage system meant that more building on some of its land in both the north and south parts of the town was impossible. Until new works were undertaken there was a brake on building both in Cleethorpes in general and on College land in particular. The Council passed plans for 395 new houses in the Urban District in 1907, but the number dropped to 187 in 1909, while there were only 48 houses in the course of erection in 1910 compared with 104 in 1908. The College was affected particularly and the number of houses planned for its land dropped from 192 in 1907 to 67 in 1908, and fluctuated between 40 and 96 each year from 1909 to 1914.[28]

The £8,170 13s 7d it received from its Clee estate was just over 56 per cent of

---

[26] SSC, Leases etc. 1894–1898, pp. 1–6, 1906–1926, p. 4; SSC, Minutes, 19 June 1899, 9 March 1900.
[27] SHARO, 51/90/1, Cleethorpes with Thrunscoe Local Board of Health, Byelaws as to the Level, Width, etc., of New Streets and Sewerage thereof, etc., 1875; SSC, Minutes, 11 October 1907; Local Government Board Enquiry, County Borough of Grimsby Incorporation Scheme, 1908, p. 385.
[28] *GN*, 10 April and 13 November 1908; SHARO, 51/20/4–5, Cleethorpes and Thrunscoe Urban District Council, General Orders, IV, 1910 and V, 1911.

Sidney's income by 1910, making it a significant influence in College affairs. The decision to postpone the extra wing needed to complete the New Court (now Cloister Court) until the new drainage scheme at Cleethorpes was underway in 1911 is a measure of this. Yet despite the check on building in Cleethorpes towards the end of the period, the annual revenue yielded by the estate there increased by some 36 per cent in the ten years up to 1910 and was to grow by just under 5 per cent by 1914 (Table 2).[29]

Delays in the northern part of the College estate were in part compensated for by leasing land for building on the higher ground at the entrance to the central resort area known as Isaacs Hill Applications were made to build 113 houses there from 1897 until 1902 with a further 222 in the three years from 1903 to 1905. There was greater variety in the type of housing in this area, fulfilling the potential of the resort for suburban development, although terraces similar to those in New Cleethorpes were built in the resort. The College also began to consider the possibility of leasing its land to the south of Cleethorpes in the area of the former township of Thrunscoe, although here again drainage was a problem. The need for coastal protection with the added possibility of enhancing the resort's amenities meant that the interests of the College and the local authority were again complementary. After some initial bargaining over conditions and price in 1901 the College sold the Council some thirty acres of sandy coastal dunes. These were used to create a recreation area and to build a bathing pool and boating lake in the 1920s. The sale was conditional on the council completing sea defences, which made it possible in 1905 for the College to lay out two roads. The outcome was described by a local newspaper as 'a mutual bargain': 'The development of the college estate would follow if the improvement was carried out. It would enrich the College and Council also.'[30]

The first house on the Thrunscoe estate was a large villa built for a local fishing magnate, but the land was low lying and its further use limited by inadequate drainage and sewerage. As had been the case with the seafront property at Cleethorpes in the middle of the nineteenth century, other landowners with more favourably placed property were able to develop their land, some of it freehold, before the College. The proposal to complete the College's New Court could not be undertaken until there was more land available for leasing in Cleethorpes, but although work on the drainage and sewerage scheme was completed in 1916, the new wing was never built. None the less, the Cleethorpes estate had made a major contribution to the finances and development of Sidney Sussex College between 1887 and 1914. Total net expenditure on laying out roads and drainage in Cleethorpes had been £45,587 in the period, of which £36,606 had been raised

---

[29] SSC, Minutes, 18 June, 8 September and 31 December 1909, 27 May 1911; SHARO, 51/20/5, Cleethorpes and Thrunscoe Urban District Council, General Orders, V, 1911.
[30] SHARO, 53/600/1/2–3, CUDC, Building Plan Registers, 1895–1901, 1902–1914; Baker, *Story of Cleethorpes*, p. 151; SSC, Minutes, 14 October 1905; *GN*, 15 November 1901.

by mortgages, while income from the estate had totalled £150,866, of which £123,428 was in ground rents.[31]

After the First World War the Cleethorpes ground rents continued to be important. The local agent emphasised that the College 'was not out to squeeze the last penny but were only asking for a reasonable return on their outlay', although the ground rents still gave a good return. It was estimated in 1929 that an expenditure of £1,800 on extending Reynolds Street would produce an annual return of £250 based on ground rents of 5 pence a square yard while in the 1930s the College Bursar said that its ground rents were 'one of the best forms of investment'. The development of New Cleethorpes was practically completed as the newly drained lands to the west of Grimsby Road were built over. The general layout of the area broke away from the grid-iron pattern of terraces which had previously been characteristic of College development. Semi-detached houses and short terraces were built on a more varied road system and on wider plots with larger gardens. Bathrooms and indoor sanitation became the norm.[32]

In 1919, Cleethorpes UDC had become involved in the provision of housing, and it approached the College which sold 13 acres of land for £3,250 on which to build 134 houses. The creation of the town's first municipal housing estate marked the beginning of a change in the provision of the housing in Cleethorpes. Immediately after the Second World War the College again sold land for housing to what was by now the borough of Cleethorpes, this time 17½ acres for £8,000 (Map 2). The College continued to extend its leasehold estate with a large-scale development for owner-occupied housing in the Beacon Hill area (Map 2) and the return on its investment remained healthy: £45,763 spent on roads and preparation with annual ground rents of £3,766 or just over 8 per cent.[33]

Beacon Hill was to be the College's last major piece of leasehold development in Cleethorpes. Land in Thrunscoe had begun to be sold for freehold housing from the 1950s and in a report presented to the College meeting in 1959, the Estates Bursar, Mr J.F.Q. Switzer, demonstrated the declining value of ground rents as an investment in an inflationary economy. This applied particularly to those from before 1914. A limited scheme to sell them as freehold to the College's

---

[31] SHARO, 51/1/12, Cleethorpes and Thrunscoe Urban District Council Minutes, 1906–1907, 16 May 1906; SHARO, 56/601, Cleethorpes Building Plans, nos. 763C, 792, 800C, 828C; SSC, Minutes, 18 June, 8 September, 31 December 1909, 19 January 1910, 27 May, 8 June, 23 November 1911, 3 December 1912, 27 March and 16 June 1913.

[32] SSC, Cleethorpes Boxfile: 'Cleethorpes Roadmaking 1927–1940, 1946–1955', H. Mountain to A.H. Davenport, 14 February 1929 and W.S. Willis to A.H. Davenport, 15 February 1929; Cleethorpes Boxfile, 'F. Higgins to 2 December 1930, Bates and Mountain to 26 January 1934', A.H. Davenport to Bates and Mountain, 16 May 1933; SHARO, D/53/220, Charter of Incorporation Inquiry, Reports and Papers of Cleethorpes UDC Engineer.

[33] SHARO, 51/1/20, CUDC, Minutes 1919–1920, Housing and Town Planning Committee, 9 October 1919; SHARO, 51/1/20, CUDC, Minutes, 1919–1920, 18 February 1920; SSC, Minutes, 1941–1953, 7 April 1946; SSC, Minutes, 1960–1964, 3 June 1964.

tenants was begun in 1963, and before the end of the year was extended to all the leases from this period. In the next few years the College disengaged itself from most of its estates, investing the proceeds from the sales on the Stock Exchange. In 1964 it was decided to sell all its farms, its Cleethorpes building land and all its Cleethorpes leases. By May 1968, the proceeds from this were £763,949, although the College still had 3,740 of its original 5,199 Cleethorpes leases on its hands. These were sold *en bloc* by the end of the year.[34]

One of the last pieces of College property in the town was 26 acres of council allotments. This final link from an association of just over 350 years was representative of its last and most significant period. For a century the interests of the College and the successive local authorities of Cleethorpes had been intertwined. Their relationship, although mutually beneficial, had been one of more than mere utility. It had contributed to the creation of an urban community, the distinctive characteristics of which can be understood by reference to this relationship: in itself an example of the particular role of a corporate landowner in urban development.

---

[34] SSC, 'Cleethorpes Leasehold Estate: report presented to College Meeting' by J.F.Q. Switzer, 15 July 1959; SSC, 'Report on College Estates' by J.F.Q. Switzer, May 1968, p.3 and Table II; SSC, Minutes, 1960–1964, 6 and 26 June 1962, 6 February and 16 October 1963, 11 November 1964; SSC, Minutes, 1965–1968, 16 October 1968.

The Sidney College Laboratory

A. L. GREER

1. *Introduction*

The period of the Sidney Laboratory, 1860 to 1908, spans the emergence and growth to respectability of the natural sciences at Cambridge. Viewed from today, the concept of significant laboratory activity in a college is a strange one, yet in this period a handful of colleges set up laboratories which played a significant rôle in teaching and research. The history and context of these laboratories, why they came into and fell out of use, are outlined in Sections 2 and 3. Sections 4 to 6 deal with the history of the laboratory at Sidney Sussex, focusing on the metallurgical researches of Heycock and Neville, whose work arguably made this the most distinguished of the college laboratories at Cambridge. The fabric and some aspects of the functioning of the laboratory are described in Sections 7 and 8, and finally Section 9 treats the relationship between the laboratory and the growing Cambridge Scientific Instrument Company.

2. *Early Problems of the Natural Sciences at Cambridge*

For Cambridge University the nineteenth century was a period of reform,[1] promoted both by powerful figures within such as William Whewell,[2] and by external scrutiny by a series of Royal Commissions. That reform was necessary there was no doubt. The only University teaching officers were the professors who were few and often grossly neglected their duties. The small endowments supporting many of the chairs made it difficult for professors, even had they wished, to devote their full energies to the University. Teaching in the colleges was in an equally bad state. The college lecturers were poorly paid, and most posts were restricted to men in holy orders. The more able people often preferred to take positions in the public schools rather than fellowships. Many students recorded that the college lectures were of little use, not providing even the minimum necessary instruction. As the century progressed a more academic

---

[1] A compact discussion of Cambridge in this period can be found in J.P.C. Roach (ed.), *A History of the County of Cambridge and the Isle of Ely*, Vol. 3: *The City and University of Cambridge* (hereafter Roach) (Oxford, 1959), pp. 235–265.
[2] Master of Trinity College from 1841 to 1866.

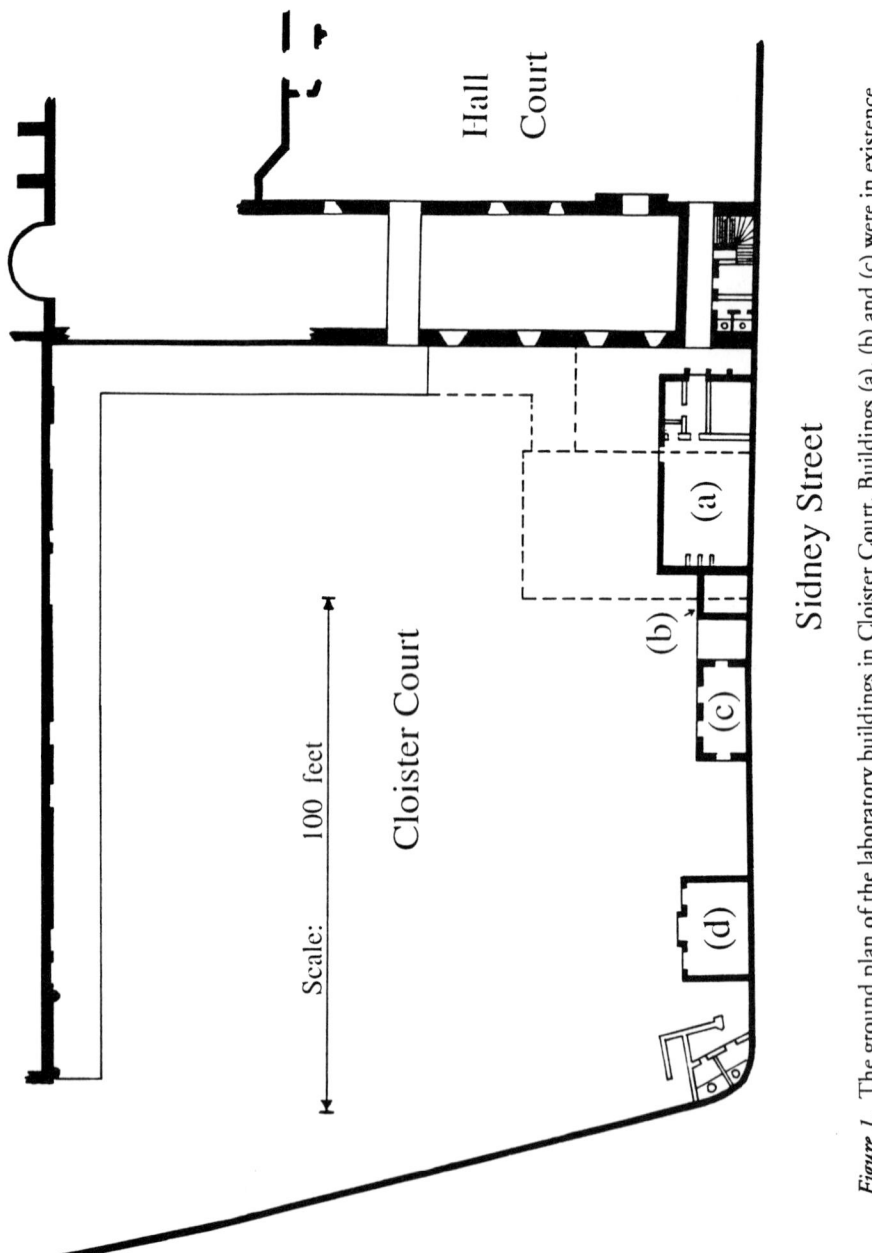

Figure 1. The ground plan of the laboratory buildings in Cloister Court. Buildings (a), (b) and (c) were in existence by the 1880s and building (d) was built before 1895. The dashed lines are the outline of a lecture-room building planned in 1909 to replace the laboratory.

outlook prevailed, and among the students competition for honours became more intense. Given the state of college teaching, it was natural that private tuition or 'coaching' should become prominent. At its height, coaching could cost a student as much as the total of all his other expenses in Cambridge,[3] and it was the sole support of a significant number of teachers. In addition, some college fellows took on coaching to augment meagre stipends. As we shall see, some of the characters associated with the Sidney Laboratory were active and successful coaches.

For the natural sciences, in the early nineteenth century Cambridge (and Oxford) lagged far behind universities in continental Europe, and in due course also behind other British institutions. Progress was made with the founding of the Cambridge Philosophical Society 'for the purpose of promoting scientific enquiry' in 1819 and the inauguration of the Natural Sciences Tripos, first examined in 1851. Yet professors' lectures in the natural sciences were often attended more by senior members dabbling in new fields than by undergraduates. The lectures themselves were sometimes directed more at the general public and less at providing rigorous instruction. Even when the Natural Sciences Tripos came into existence, it was natural that the students did not pay it too much attention, for it was to be nine years before the Tripos would be considered sufficient to permit a student to proceed to the B.A. degree. Further discouragements were the lack of college teaching (even worse than usual in the new subjects) and the lack of scholarships and exhibitions. In addition there was an almost total lack of suitable teaching and laboratory facilities.

Starting in the 1820s, a series of University Syndicates had reported on the lack of public rooms.[4] In 1828 Whewell (anonymously) wrote a lengthy statement on the state of affairs in the natural sciences, yet little was done. In 1853 a Syndicate started to plan the development of what today is known as the New Museums Site. By the end of the year they reported in detail on the need for new facilities, given the current problems particularly in the sciences:

> ... the actual accommodation afforded in the shape of museums, laboratories, and other apartments, as well as of apparatus and assistants, all which are necessary for the successful prosecution and teaching of these various subjects is miserably deficient ...

The recommendations for new buildings and alterations were well received, but the University had only about £5,000 available out of the estimated cost of over £23,000. After much argument over the estimates and revised plans, ground for the new buildings was finally broken in 1863 and they were essentially complete by 1865. Even then the provision was at the minimum level and clearly

---

[3] Roach, p. 246.
[4] The developments outlined in this paragraph are described in detail in R. Willis and J.W. Clark, *The Architectural History of the University of Cambridge and of the Colleges of Cambridge and Eton*, 4 vols (Cambridge, 1886) (hereafter Willis and Clark), vol. 3, pp. 145–181.

soon to be outgrown. Given the late and inadequate response of the University, particularly with regard to practical teaching, there was clearly a strong need for laboratories in those colleges wishing to promote the natural sciences.

The colleges were resistant to seeing any diversion of their income to the University to alleviate its financial weakness. The Royal Commission report of 1852 estimated total annual income of the colleges as £185,000, compared to £18,000 (£10,000 of which was for special subjects) for the University.[5] Robert Phelps, Master of Sidney from 1843 to 1890, and Vice-Chancellor of the University in 1844-45 and 1847-48, featured prominently in defence of the colleges. As Vice-Chancellor he supported a broadening of the teaching at Cambridge into such areas as the natural sciences. Unfortunately for him the Commissioners ultimately recommended that this would best be achieved by the provision of scientific laboratories in the University, funded by contributions from the colleges. So strongly did Phelps oppose college contributions that he refused to co-operate with the Commissioners, who in their 1873 report recorded: 'We regret to state that Sidney Sussex College, Cambridge, failed to give the required information. The Fellows of the college indeed expressed their willingness that the information should be given, but as the Master discharges the duties of Bursar, and has the college accounts books in his custody, the Fellows had not the means which would enable them to make the necessary returns.'[6] Phelps may have felt that the laboratory at Sidney, expanding during his long mastership, was quite adequate support for the natural sciences at Cambridge.

3. *College Laboratories*[7]

The first recorded laboratory in Cambridge was established for Francis Vigani, who in 1702 became the first Professor of Chemistry (Cambridge thus having the oldest continuously occupied chair of chemistry in Great Britain). Bentley, the Master of Trinity, provided an 'elegant Chymical laboratory',[8] but this arrangement did not survive Vigani's death. In 1782, Isaac Milner, Jacksonian Professor, was permitted by Queens' College to set up a laboratory[9] in some college buildings to the west of the Cam. Laboratories such as these reflected the ability of colleges to respond to the requirements of well motivated individuals;

---

[5] *Report of Commissioners appointed to enquire into the State, Discipline, Studies, and Revenues of the University and Colleges of Cambridge* (1852–3), pp. 138, 197.
[6] *Report of Commissioners appointed to enquire into the Property and Income of the Universities of Oxford and Cambridge and of the Colleges and Halls therein* (1873).
[7] The history of the laboratories in Cambridge has been outlined in F.G. Mann, 'The Place of Chemistry – II. At Cambridge', *Proc. Chemical Soc.* (July 1957) (hereafter Mann), 190–193.
[8] *The Historical Register of the University of Cambridge . . . to 1910*, edited by J.R. Tanner (Cambridge, 1917), p. 247.
[9] Willis and Clark, vol. 3, p. 153.

they did not form part of a continuous provision for teaching or research. That started with St John's College. George Downing Liveing, admitted to St John's in 1845, graduated Eleventh Wrangler in 1850, and obtained a First Class in the inaugural Natural Sciences Tripos of 1851. In 1852 he started the first course in practical chemistry for medical students. This was given in 'a primitive laboratory fitted up in a cottage in Corn Exchange St.'[10] This was clearly inadequate and when in the next year St John's appointed Liveing to a college lectureship in Natural Science, a laboratory was built in the college for his use. This building had five rooms in all and was erected at a cost of £511. The facilities were such that Liveing was able to base his work there, even after his election to the Professorship of Chemistry in 1861. As Liveing records, this was very important for him:[11]

> The College built me the chemical laboratory, which was the first seed sown towards the growth of a large chemical school. When I vacated my fellowship by marrying, I vacated, of course, my lectureship as well, and the charge of the Chemical Laboratory. The College, however, created a new post for me: it made me Director of the Laboratory and, what is more, helped me materially by paying me a salary . . . When I became professor the College again helped me – they continued me in my last post because there was no other laboratory in which I could give instruction in practical work.

Liveing was indefatigable in his efforts to set up a fully equipped University chemical laboratory. The laboratory at St John's enabled him to resist the offers of inadequate accommodation from the University authorities and to continue his pressure for better facilities. Finally his efforts were successful and in 1888 the new University Chemical Laboratory on Pembroke Street opened, 'then one of the finest in the kingdom'.[12] The St John's laboratory continued in use after Liveing had moved to his new University laboratory, but by 1922 it had been demolished to make way for a new bath-house.

Sidney is second in the list of colleges with laboratories. The originator was J.C.W. Ellis, who had attended Liveing's classes at St John's and served with Liveing on the 1862 Syndicate which had finally succeeded in making some progress on the New Museums Site. As will be detailed below, the Sidney laboratory was set up in 1860, fell into disuse in 1908 and was substantially destroyed in 1910.

The Sidney laboratory was followed by others at Gonville and Caius, Girton,

---

[10] J.A. Venn, *Alumni Cantabrigienses, Part II, from 1752 to 1900* (Cambridge, 1951) (hereafter Venn), vol. 4, p. 183.
[11] *Eagle* (St John's College), vol. 42, no. 185.
[12] Venn, vol. 4, p. 183. (The building still stands, on the New Museums Site at the corner of Pembroke Street and Free School Lane. The main entrance is from Pembroke Street and the building incorporates the Heycock lecture theatre. Externally the only alteration is the addition of two extra stories where part of the original roof was destroyed by fire in the 1960s.)

Newnham and, finally, Downing. The main purpose of the college laboratories was the teaching of students reading for the Natural Sciences Tripos. The opening of the Cavendish Laboratory in 1874 absorbed the physics laboratory teaching, so the college laboratories became associated almost exclusively with chemistry. The teaching included not only training in experimental techniques, but also lectures combined with practical demonstrations. The laboratories tended to specialise;[13] Girton students in 1926-28, for example, took practical classes in organic and inorganic chemistry in the College, but in physical chemistry in the University Laboratory. Students from one college could for some courses be taught in the laboratory of another college. At St John's the students (in 1911-13) could choose to take practical organic chemistry in the College or the University. The laboratories were also used for private courses given by coaches; for example, Heycock (Section 5) gave very popular courses in the Downing laboratory.

In addition to their teaching function, some of the laboratories were also home to significant research efforts, the two most distinguished being Sidney and Caius. The Caius laboratory opened in 1873. From 1877 the Praelector in charge was Pattison Muir, and the laboratory closed when he retired in 1908. The closure coincided with that of the Sidney laboratory on the retirement of Neville. The decision to close the laboratories appears to have been linked to the great increase in University provision of laboratory space (for both teaching and research) brought about by the 1907 extension of the University Chemical Laboratory along Pembroke Street. The most significant work in the Sidney laboratory is described in Section 5. At Caius, space was made available for an active researcher under unusual circumstances.[14] The Jacksonian Professor of Natural Experimental Philosophy, James (later Sir James) Dewar, appointed a German-trained organic chemist, Ruhemann, as Demonstrator in the University Chemical Laboratory. The two quarrelled and Dewar obtained the Vice-Chancellor's permission to dismiss Ruhemann, who subsequently appealed and was reinstated. However, Dewar excluded Ruhemann from the University Laboratory. In due course Ruhemann's work was widely recognised and he was appointed a University Lecturer, still excluded from the University Laboratory! Thus it was that Ruhemann, who effectively initiated modern research in organic chemistry at Cambridge, did his distinguished work in a college laboratory. When the Caius laboratory closed he was able to return to the University Chemical Laboratory, Dewar by then being largely absentee, based in London.[15]

---

[13] The details here are from Mann, p. 191.

[14] Mann, p. 192; A.J. Berry and E.A. Moelwyn-Hughes, 'Chemistry at Cambridge from 1901 to 1910', *Proc. Chemical Soc.* (December 1963) (hereafter Berry and Moelwyn-Hughes), p. 358.

[15] Appointed to the Cambridge chair in 1875, Dewar had since 1877 also held the Fullerian Chair of Chemistry at the Royal Institution, where he found the experimental facilities much better. He is best known for his work on the liquefaction of gases and the Dewar flask; he features in this article again in connection with Figure 2.

The Girton laboratory, opened in 1877, was used mainly for teaching, and long after the other College laboratories had closed it was maintained on the insistence of Miss M.B. Thomas that organic chemistry be taught in the College and not in the University laboratories. The laboratory finally closed in 1935 on Miss Thomas' retirement. The Newnham laboratory was under the charge of Miss I. Freund, from its opening in 1879 to its closure in 1912. The Downing laboratory was started in the 1890s (an odd timing, given the advent of significant University facilities), and closed in 1920.

Before the next and subsequent sections turn to focus on the Sidney Laboratory, a brief comparison with Oxford will serve to put the development of college laboratories in a wider context.[16] In the mid-nineteenth century Oxford saw the emergence of the natural sciences in parallel with developments in Cambridge. However, Oxford acted much more quickly and effectively to provide accommodation. The University Museum, built between 1855 and 1860, provided facilities for chemistry, experimental philosophy, mineralogy, geology, medicine and anatomy. With the establishment of the Clarendon Laboratory for physics in 1868, six years before the opening of the Cavendish in Cambridge, Oxford must have seemed well prepared to outdo its rival. That just the reverse happened appears to have been largely the result of two bad appointments. In physics R.B. Clifton, Professor of Experimental Philosophy from 1865 until 1915, and in chemistry W. Odling, Wayneflete Professor from 1872 until 1912, seem not only to have avoided making distinguished contributions, but also to have impeded the development of their subjects. Odling in particular considered it beneath the dignity of a professor to appear in the laboratory, and the University Chemistry Department produced almost no published work for the forty years of his tenure. In this period of stagnation, much of the teaching and essentially all of the research facilities in chemistry at Oxford were provided in college laboratories, at Magdalen (founded 1848), Balliol and Trinity (1852 and 1897), Christ Church (1866), Queen's (1900) and Jesus (1908). Activities in the college laboratories were co-ordinated, but by 1922 not much had improved in the University Laboratories at Oxford, so that the Royal Commission remarked:[17]

> There can be no doubt that the Teaching of Chemistry in a number of small College Laboratories is less economical and in some respects less effective than centralised teaching in the larger Laboratories of the University. At Cambridge it has been found advisable gradually to abolish the College laboratories altogether, and to concentrate the practical instruction entirely in the University Laboratories . . . it appears to us that all the practical instruction in Chemistry and Physics should, as in other subjects, be supplied in large and well-organised Laboratories belonging to the University.

[16] The general context of college laboratories at Oxford, and the Balliol-Trinity Laboratory in particular, are covered by T. Smith, in *Balliol Studies*, edited by J. Prest (London, 1982), Chapter 8, pp. 185–224.
[17] *Report of Royal Commission on Oxford and Cambridge Universities* (1922), p. 145.

But the University could not provide the required facilities, with the result that the reorganisation of 1923 assigned the College laboratories to the new University Departments, an arrangement not remotely approached at Cambridge. The last college laboratory in Oxford closed in 1941 when new University buildings finally became available.

4. *Early Days of the Sidney Laboratory*

In 1723 Sidney Sussex College received a bequest which was to have a large effect on the future direction of the College. Samuel Taylor of Dudley bequeathed a property with an annual income of £60 to establish a Mathematical Fellowship. He also directed that 'if any money should thereafter be raised out of the estate from any coal or other mine upon it' the additional monies were to be used for the maintenance of students in mathematics. Taylor, who had entered the College as a student in 1688, considered mathematics to be 'a Study very useful and beneficial to the public interest and national good; which sort of Study, in the Time of his being a Student . . . was, as far as he did observe, much neglected'.[18] Under the Statutes of the College at that time, Fellows of Sidney had to devote themselves to divinity, and permission had to be obtained to convert the fellowship into a lectureship, which was duly established in 1738. Two of the Taylor Lecturers, Ellis and Neville, feature prominently in the history of the Sidney Laboratory. By the beginning of the next century Taylor's hint of greater wealth materialised. In 1818 and 1823 the College was empowered by Acts of Parliament to use the proceeds of a mining lease for various purposes, including the spending of £8,500 on building and fitting out a Taylor Mathematical Library, founding additional Taylor Exhibitions and providing extra rooms for the Exhibitioners. The Taylor monies went to support not just mathematics as now understood, but a range of natural sciences. In the early nineteenth century mathematics at Cambridge was taken to include subjects such as mechanics, optics and astronomy, but at Sidney, at least as indicated by library purchases, geology, biology and chemistry were also considered worthy of support.[19] When the College Statutes were revised in 1881, it was noted that of the twenty-four Scholars in the College, twelve were to receive their support from the Taylor Endowment and these were to be proficient in mathematics or natural sciences.[20]

The application of the Taylor Endowment to set up a laboratory was due to John Clough Williams Ellis[21] ; he entered Sidney in 1853, and three years later he graduated Third Wrangler and was elected to a fellowship. He was appointed

---

[18] *Acts of Parliament, Private* (printed), 58 George III, c.39, pp. 693–5.
[19] S.P. Salt, 'Wyatville's Remodelling and Refurbishment of Sidney Sussex College, 1820–1837', *Proc. Camb. Antiquarian Soc.*, 81 (1992), 121–22.
[20] C.W. Scott-Giles, *Sidney Sussex College. A Short History* (Cambridge, 1975), pp. 100–101.
[21] Venn, vol. 2, p. 410.

Taylor Lecturer, and in 1859 became Tutor. He was succeeded as Taylor Lecturer by John Rundle Cornish (later Bishop of St German's).[22] According to Cornish,[23] 'Ellis and I took up, I fear somewhat superficially, many subjects, attending the Professors' lectures on Chemistry, Geology, Anatomy, Mechanism, History and some others'. Ellis, 'though he never professed to be a Chemist', had a keen interest in the subject and in 1860,[24] as he records:[25] 'I got the College to allow me to make a chemical laboratory at Sidney, the only other College laboratory being at St John's.' The laboratory was 'started in some ground-floor rooms, but as the complaint of fumes was made in rooms above, possibly to disguise a fear of explosions, the Sidney laboratory was moved to a separate building'. Cornish more sympathetically records that the original set of rooms 'afterwards had to be replaced by one unconnected with the College buildings, owing to the piteous complaints of those near in regard to smells'.

In Sidney, Ellis and Cornish were not alone in their interest in the sciences. They were joined by the Dean of the College, Robert Machray (later Archbishop of Rupertsland, and Primate of All Canada).[26] The three men were close friends, who breakfasted in each others' rooms for four years prior to Machray's departure for Canada in 1865. Ellis's memoirs give a sense (perhaps we might say smell!) of the early amateur work at Sidney:

> We used occasionally to try some simple experiments. Once in Bishop St. German's rooms we started an experiment, a fine india rubber was carrying hydrogen to our experimental retort. We suddenly discovered that the tube was on fire and the fire stealing up to the explosive mixture. We used to accuse Machray of rushing into Cornish's bedroom and bolting the door – this was possibly unjust – we I think dived under the table as the safest place waiting in agony for the coming explosion to blow the College to atoms. Finding nothing happened we naturally accused each other of abject cowardice.

It can hardly be a surprise that other Sidney Fellows wished the laboratory to have its own separate building!

Whatever Ellis's approach to chemical experiments, he revived Sidney's academic fortunes. In his seventeen years as Tutor, the personality of Ellis and the teaching in the College attracted students. In the 1862 edition of *The Student's Guide to the University of Cambridge*, Sidney announced that in addition to the

---

[22] Venn, vol. 2, p. 139.
[23] *Sidney Sussex College Annual*, 1913.
[24] *Minutes of College Meetings* (hereafter *Minutes*), *vol. 1854–1876*, in Sidney Sussex College Muniment Room (hereafter SSM), 23 March 1860: 'Also agreed that a room be assigned for a Taylor Chemical Laboratory to be fitted up with all requisite fixtures and apparatus, the rent of the room and all expenses connected with it to be defrayed out of the Taylor Fund.'
[25] J.C.W. Ellis, *Memoirs*, unpublished manuscript in possession of Mr W. Ellis, photocopy in SSM.
[26] Venn, vol. 4, p. 267.

laboratory it had a library entirely devoted to scientific works, and that it proposed shortly to establish 'a course in subjects connected with Natural Sciences'. Of the twelve Junior Taylor Scholarships several would be for the encouragement of Natural Sciences, and an annual College examination would be held in Chemistry, Electricity and General Physics with a prize of £20. At this time no other college advertised awards or provision of facilities for Natural Sciences. In the same year, 1862, the first Sidney student enrolled in Natural Sciences and the next year he obtained a First Class in the Tripos.

For some time it had been felt that college teaching could be improved by having inter-collegiate lectures. In 1873 the Royal Commission on Scientific Instruction[27] noted that some progress had been made in this direction. In particular, Trinity, St John's and Sidney were providing inter-collegiate teaching in Natural Sciences. That Sidney had this level of prominence, linked with the dominant colleges, can be largely attributed to the particular nature of the Taylor Bequest and the energy of Ellis.[28] By 1873, Neville was already a Fellow of Sidney and the work in the laboratory itself was about to become much more professional and distinguished.

5. The Work of Heycock and Neville

The Sidney Laboratory is known to the outside world above all for the work of Charles Thomas Heycock and Francis Henry Neville (Plate 12[29]). Their joint research spanned thirty years and resulted in some twenty-five papers on which the Laboratory was given as their address. Their work was the best of its kind at the time, and in some ways has not been bettered since. It made a very significant contribution to the development of scientific metallurgy, and led directly to the founding of the Department of Metallurgy in the University. The accurate measurement of temperature was central to their work, and in this they were greatly aided by Ernest Howard Griffiths.

Neville (1847–1915) entered Sidney in 1867.[30] He graduated in mathematics (Fifteenth Wrangler) in 1871 and in the same year was admitted to a fellowship.

---

[27] *Third Report of Royal Commission on Scientific Instruction and the Advancement of Science* (1873).

[28] The prominence of Sidney in the natural sciences at this time is one reason why Dorothy L. Sayers in *Unpopular Opinions* (London, 1946) concludes that it was the college of Sherlock Holmes. She estimates the date of his matriculation to be October 1871; this is between the matriculation dates of Heycock and Neville, the most prominent workers in the College laboratory (Section 5).

[29] The photograph of Heycock is reproduced from one presented to the Department of Metallurgy by Heycock's widow in 1931. The photograph of Neville is reproduced from the Fellows' photograph album in Sidney Sussex College. Neville was the donor of the album itself.

[30] Venn, vol. 4, p. 528.

He was Taylor Lecturer in Natural Sciences, and in 1880 took over the management of the Sidney Laboratory, a responsibility which he kept for twenty-eight years until his retirement. He was also Bursar from 1890 to 1896, a period when his researches with Heycock were particularly active. Neville was a man of wide reading and interests, an authority on Italian history, interested in metaphysical speculations, an admirable talker and a graceful after-dinner speaker. His friends and pupils presented a portrait of him[31] to the College. Of this it was written 'though it does justice to the dignity and intellectual strength of its subject, it fails to give any hint of the fire and vivacity which were characteristic of Mr Neville at his best'.[32]

Heycock (1858–1931) entered King's College in 1877.[33] Previously he had attended lectures by Liveing and Dewar, and in the summer of 1876 had worked in the Cavendish Laboratory on a spectroscopy problem inspired by Liveing's course. This early research led to Heycock's first publication[34] later the same year. Heycock graduated with a First Class in the Natural Sciences Tripos in 1881, and from then until his election to a fellowship at King's in 1895, Heycock made his living very successfully as a coach in chemistry, physics and mineralogy.[35] He was the first Goldsmiths' Reader in Metallurgy in the University, remaining in that post from 1908 until his retirement in 1928. According to the Head of the University Chemical Laboratory:[36]

> Heycock was an excellent lecturer; his whimsical mode of addressing a class sustained an interest in inorganic chemistry during a period when that subject seemed in danger of eclipse by the rapid advance of organic chemistry. He had few equals as a teacher in the laboratory; his deliberate method of working and his sarcastic denunciation of slovenliness inspired respect and awakened the spirit of emulation.

His keenest outside interest was in the Volunteers (forerunner of the Territorial Army). By 1895 he was Lieutenant-Colonel of the Cambridgeshire Regiment,

---

[31] The College has two portraits of Neville: this one by Charles Shannon, and an earlier, less sombre one by W. Hammond Smith (son of the Master of the College, Charles Smith (see Section 6)).
[32] *Sidney Sussex College Annual*, 1915.
[33] Venn, vol. 3, p. 352; *The Cambridge Review*, 52 (1931), 484 (June 10).
[34] The work was with an undergraduate, Arthur Clayden: C.T. Heycock and A.W. Clayden, 'The Spectra of Indium', *Philosophical Magazine*, November 1876, pp. 1–2.
[35] Heycock's coaching records from the 'October Term' 1883 to the Long Vacation 1908 are in the Heycock Archive in the Department of Materials Science and Metallurgy (hereafter Heycock Archive). His coaching was of students reading Natural Sciences and Mechanical Sciences, but above all Medical Sciences. He did a flourishing trade with many colleges, but took very few students from Sidney. Perhaps the Sidney men were coached by Griffiths, or their teaching by Neville was such that they did not feel the need of coaching.
[36] Sir William Jackson Pope writing in his obituary of Heycock, *Proc. Royal Soc. London*, Ser. A, 135 (1932), *Obit. Not.* p. i.

and he served with distinction in the 1914–18 war, being mentioned in the Secretary of State's lists. In 1917 he was recalled to work on mustard gas. In 1921 he was appointed Deputy Lieutenant for Cambridgeshire.

Griffiths,[37] first educated at Owens College, Manchester, was admitted to Sidney in 1870, and obtained a pass degree four years later. After graduation he established himself as a coach, and also undertook some research in the Sidney Laboratory and at a laboratory in his own home. His research, and his book *The Thermal Measurement of Energy*, became very widely recognised. He was elected a Fellow of Sidney in 1897, and subsequently became Vice-Chancellor of the University of Wales and Principal and Professor of Experimental Philosophy in the University College of South Wales and Monmouthshire. Another of his books was *Lyra Fumosa*, a set of his songs, well known to many undergraduates.[38] He was noted for his 'vigorous personality and his social gifts'.[39]

Griffiths and Heycock established a coaching partnership, and it was through Griffiths that Heycock made contact with Neville, who gave him the opportunity to undertake some research in the Sidney Laboratory. Their collaboration comprised the greater part of Heycock's total output and all of Neville's. Until Neville's death in 1915 all of their publications were on the subjects of their common interest, and in nearly all of these works they were joint authors.

The first paper of Heycock and Neville appeared in 1884, on the determination of the molecular weight of ozone by the diffusion method.[40] From that point on, however, their interests focused on metallic alloys. The depression of the freezing point of a liquid with increasing concentration of solute had been demonstrated by Raoult and analysed by Van't Hoff in terms of the molecular weight of the solute. Heycock and Neville wished to test these ideas for the simplest case, namely solutions of one element in another. They succeeded in verifying the main points using dilute solutions of other metals in liquid tin. In 1891 there appeared a classic paper on alloys of gold and cadmium in tin.[41] At that time studies on alloys of any kind were unusual, studies of three-component alloys very much so. Heycock and Neville could have had no idea that this ternary system would some eight decades later become of interest for making electrical connections to the semiconductor gallium arsenide. In the course of modern researches their data

---

[37] Venn, vol. 3, p. 155; *Obit. Notices Fellows Royal Soc.*, 1 (1932–35), 15; *The Cambridge Review*, 53 (1932), 235 (April 22).
[38] Both lyrics and music by Griffiths, written for the Sidney smoking concerts, then a popular form of undergraduate entertainment.
[39] *Sidney Sussex College Annual*, 1921.
[40] C.T. Heycock and F.H. Neville, 'On a Simplified Form of Apparatus for Determining the Density of Ozone', *Proc. Camb. Phil. Soc.*, 5 (1884), 207–210.
[41] C.T. Heycock and F.H. Neville, 'On the Freezing Points of Triple Alloys of Gold, Cadmium, and Tin', *Trans. Chem. Soc.* (1891), 936–966.

have received renewed attention. Thus a paper of 1985[42] from the GEC Research Laboratories notes:

> interpreting the data of Heycock and Neville with the hindsight that 100 years allows, it is possible to present some idea of the equilibria in the tin-rich corner of the gold-cadmium-tin system. This contribution is therefore a further tribute to the meticulous experimental work of Heycock and Neville. It is a rare circumstance that allows analysis of 19th century data to shed light on the current knowledge base ... modern work would be hard pressed to achieve comparable precision of measurements to those of Heycock and Neville in 1891.

Heycock and Neville noticed an anomaly in the freezing-point depression and correctly deduced that the formation of a compound of gold and cadmium was lowering the amount of these elements in solution. Later they isolated this compound, AuCd, and their work (particularly Neville's erudite reviews)[43] contributed significantly to the acceptance that stoichiometric compounds could be formed between metals. Although such intermetallic compounds are now known to be common,[44] chemists in the nineteenth century were inclined to discount the idea as it was not in accord with standard views of valence.

So far the tin-rich alloys studied by Heycock and Neville had remained within the range of the mercury thermometers, but they were interested to extend their work to alloys with higher melting-points. The advent of reliable platinum resistance thermometers enabled them to do this, and in this area the assistance of Griffiths was crucial. The impact of this work can be gauged against the degree of ignorance at that time about high-temperature behaviour. The value for the melting-point of antimony, for example, was accepted to be 432°C. Heycock and Neville determined it to be 629.5°C (the currently accepted value is 630.5°C). Subsequent papers dealt with the freezing-points of alloys of silver, gold, copper and zinc.

A major departure from the work on freezing and thermometry was the pioneering investigation of the internal structure of alloys. Less than two years after Röntgen's discovery of X-rays, Heycock was able to demonstrate to the Royal Institution[45] that radiography of alloys could reveal the arrangement of phases inside alloys and that the arrangement could be related to stages by which the solidification progressed during cooling. The solidification stages were revealed

---

[42] A. Prince, 'An Interpretation of the Work of Heycock and Neville on Au-Cd-Sn Ternary Alloys', *Zeitschrift für Metallkunde*, 76 (1985), 162–169.
[43] F.H. Neville, 'On the Chemical Nature of Alloys', *Science Progress*, 4 (1895), 1–11, and 'Report on the Chemical Compounds Contained in Alloys', *Brit. Assoc. Adv. Science Report*, Sect. B (1900), 1–20.
[44] Neville's review of 1900 lists 37 intermetallic compounds. By 1920 about 300 were known, and today about 25,000. They are the focus of very active current research in a number of areas, notably on materials resistant to high temperatures.
[45] Friday Evening Discourse on 2 April 1897, 'Metallic Alloys and the Theory of Solution'.

in 'cooling curves' – plots of temperature as a function of time. This work, well before the discovery of X-ray diffraction (1912), was based on the differential absorption of X-rays passing through thin plates cut from solidified ingots. Such a technique, though very powerful, was clearly inconvenient; Heycock and Neville soon abandoned it in favour of the examination of polished and etched surfaces by reflected light microscopy, the technique known today as optical metallography. This had originated with Sorby's studies of irons and steels at Sheffield in the 1860s, but appears to have been first practised in Cambridge by Ewing and Rosenhain, whose 1899 Bakerian Lecture to the Royal Society is a landmark in the understanding of the deformation of metals.[46] Heycock and Neville supplied alloy samples to Ewing and Rosenhain and were obviously influenced by the latter's work, adopting 'photomicrography' as their main technique for structural analysis and thanking Ewing and Rosenhain for advice and the loan of apparatus.[47]

In their paper of 1900 on gold-aluminium[47] Heycock and Neville made their first reference to J.W. Gibbs's Phase Rule, which was to provide the theoretical underpinning so far lacking. The Rule provides the basis for understanding the number of phases which can co-exist in equilibrium, and is of great use in plotting phase equilibrium diagrams.[48] Gibbs's great work on the Phase Rule was published in 1876 in the *Transactions of the Connecticut Academy of Sciences* and had lain largely unnoticed, and was certainly not promoted by Gibbs himself. It was Professor H.W. Bakhuis Roozeboom, Van't Hoff's successor at the University of Amsterdam, who performed the great service of interpreting Gibbs's work and applying it to heterogeneous equilibria. Also in 1900 Bakhuis Roozeboom published his seminal study of the application of the Phase Rule to the iron-carbon system, and in 1901 Neville initiated correspondence with him in order to develop an interpretation of Heycock and Neville's new results on copper-tin.[49] With all the necessary experimental techniques and the underlying theory at their disposal, Heycock and Neville were equipped to make their greatest contribution – the study of the copper-tin alloys presented in the 1903 Bakerian Lecture to the Royal Society.[50] This monumental paper, containing no fewer than 101 photomicrographs, was the first comprehensive study of the phase equilibria in

---

[46] J.A. Ewing and W. Rosenhain, 'The Crystalline Structure of Metals', *Phil. Trans. Roy. Soc. London*, Ser. A 193 (1900), 353–375, and ibid., 195 (1901), 279–301.

[47] C.T. Heycock and F.H. Neville, 'Gold-Aluminium Alloys', *Phil. Trans. Roy. Soc. London*, Ser. A, 194 (1900), 201–232.

[48] These diagrams are a cornerstone of metallurgy, being essential to the understanding and control of the constitution of alloys. Heycock and Neville were among the first to plot the diagrams in a form sufficiently comprehensive to be recognizable to a present-day metallurgist.

[49] Bakhuis Roozeboom's letters survive: see D. Stockdale, *Metal Progress*, June 1946, 1183–1187.

[50] C.T. Heycock and F.H. Neville, 'On the Constitution of the Copper-Tin Series of Alloys', *Phil. Trans. Roy. Soc. London*, Ser. A, 202 (1903), 1–69.

a non-ferrous alloy, and can without exaggeration be considered the foundation of modern studies of phase equilibria and microstructure in alloys. Work in this field remains active today, in a form which would be recognisable to Heycock and Neville, though now incorporating crystal structure determination, analyses on finer length scales and computer fitting of the Gibbs functions.

The work on gold had led to contact with the company of Johnson and Matthey. The company had lent the considerable quantities of gold used[51] and provided free assaying to Heycock and Neville. In addition George Matthey had chaired the Discourse at the Royal Institution at which Heycock had presented his X-ray results. Heycock thus developed a link with the Worshipful Company of Goldsmiths, in which Matthey was prominent, being on its Court and having served as Prime Warden (1872 and 1894). It appears that Matthey played a major part in persuading the Company in 1908 to endow a Readership in Metallurgy for Heycock. The Company also made monies available to the University Chemical Laboratory for the refitting of some existing rooms for teaching and research in the subject.

The next joint paper by Heycock and Neville was also their last. It was published in 1914, the slowing in their work since 1903 presumably being related to Neville's retirement, the closure of the Sidney Laboratory, Heycock's appointment as Reader, the setting up of the Goldsmiths' Metallurgical Laboratory, and the loss of research records in 1910 (Section 6). The work was on aluminium-gold alloys, and had not gone according to plan, Heycock and Neville noting that: 'as the experiments consume a great deal of labour and time, we are not likely to complete the work for at least another year';[52] at the time of Neville's death in 1915 the work was still not completed.

After Neville's death, Heycock published only a few papers, devoting his energies to the direction and expansion of the Goldsmiths' Metallurgical Laboratory within the University Chemistry Department. Rosenhain, the foremost scientific metallurgist of the age, remarked in 1922 that 'the school of metallurgical activity which produced years ago the classical partnership of Heycock and Neville had been rejuvenated' in Heycock's laboratory'.[53] This was to lead to the founding of the Chair of Metallurgy in 1932 and the development of an independent department.[54]

Heycock and Neville worked so closely together that it is hard to distinguish

---

[51] This excellent arrangement, under which samples are given to the company after use and the gold recovered from them, continues in the Department of Materials Science and Metallurgy today – though with rather smaller quantities than the kilogrammes used by Heycock and Neville.

[52] C.T. Heycock and F.H. Neville, 'Dilute Solutions of Aluminium in Gold', *Phil. Trans. Roy. Soc. London*, Ser. A, 214 (1914), 267–276.

[53] Discussion at the Institute of Metals Meeting, Swansea, 1922, in *J. Inst. Metals*, 28 (1922), 291.

[54] Originally the Department of Metallurgy, then the Department of Metallurgy and Materials Science, and currently the Department of Materials Science and Metallurgy!

their individual contributions. However, it seems that Heycock was the gifted experimentalist, and Neville the theorist. Of the two, Heycock is the more prominent, partly because of the accident of alphabetical precedence, but also because he lived for a further sixteen years in which the fruits of their joint labours were to become more apparent. Heycock himself remarked of Neville that it would be impossible to find 'a more modest man, or one who had less push, in the worldly sense'.[55] Yet in strictly scientific matters it was often Neville who took the lead.

Reading Heycock's and Neville's series of papers it is possible to see the subject of physical metallurgy taking shape. This naturally involved an evolution of the language: at the outset we read of *body*, *freezing-point curve* and *melting-point curve*. By the end these terms have been replaced by the more precise ones introduced by Gibbs and Bakhuis Roozeboom and still in use: *phase*, *liquidus* and *solidus*. Heycock's and Neville's contribution to the subject is today undoubted.[56] Recognition came in their own lifetimes also. Heycock was elected a Fellow of the Royal Society in 1895, Neville in 1897. In 1900 the British Association for the Advancement of Science appointed a Committee to Investigate the Nature of Alloys; the members were Neville (as Chairman and Secretary), Heycock and Griffiths – a remarkably closely knit group, all directly linked to the Sidney Laboratory. Neville contributed the article on 'Alloys' to the *Encyclopædia Britannica*. In 1920, on the basis of his work with Neville, Heycock was awarded the Davy Medal of the Royal Society, and in the same year served as President of the Chemical Section of the British Association for the Advancement of Science.

Workers in a small college laboratory might be supposed to be rather isolated from the scientific mainstream. Yet for Heycock and Neville this was certainly not the case. They were prominent in Cambridge[57] and (as noted above) recognised at the national level. In addition, Neville in particular was active in international correspondence with the leading men of the time, including Le Châtelier on the subject of intermetallic compounds and Bakhuis Roozeboom on the Phase Rule. Neville's international outlook may in part be attributable to his facility with languages – he was fluent in French, German and Italian – though the correspondence with Bakhuis Roozeboom was conducted in English (albeit slightly fractured on the latter's part).

---

[55] Heycock's obituary of Neville, in *Nature*, 95 (1915), 432.

[56] The development of the subject, and Heycock's and Neville's rôle are discussed in C.S. Smith, *A History of Metallography: The Development of Ideas on the Structure of Metals before 1890* (Cambridge, Mass., 1988), Chapter 16. See also L.B. Hunt, 'Heycock and Neville: The Great Partnership in the Early Years of Physical Metallurgy', *Metallurgist and Materials Technologist*, July 1980, 392–394.

[57] In addition to their links with Ewing and Rosenhain already noted, Heycock and Neville were in close scientific contact with Sir G.G. Stokes (Lucasian Professor of Mathematics), and featured in presentations given to the Cambridge University Chemical Club in the years 1901–1910 (Berry and Moelwyn-Hughes, p. 359).

A significant indication that Heycock and Neville were in the scientific mainstream is the speed with which they took up ideas. Their rapid adoption of X-rays for micrography has already been mentioned, as has the timely correspondence with Bakhuis Roozeboom. Further examples relate to the key area of thermometry. Guillaume's great work *Traité pratique de la thermométrie de précision* was published in 1889, but Heycock and Neville were already using his methods in a paper appearing in print the next year. And results of Le Châtelier published in 1895 were being disputed by Heycock and Neville in a paper published in the same year. This pace would not be out of place today.

6. *The End of the Laboratory*

Neville resigned from the Taylor Lectureship in 1908 and subsequently moved from Cambridge to Letchworth. He set up a laboratory in his new home there. In the same year Heycock took up the new position of Goldsmiths' Reader in Metallurgy in the University Chemical Laboratory and experimental facilities were established in rooms assigned to him there. The College decided to close the laboratory and 'to present to the University Laboratory the chemical apparatus etc. – exclusive of the platinum and mercury[58] – now in the College Laboratory'.[59] The value of this apparatus was estimated as £50. The closure of the laboratory was not for want of manpower, for Neville's successor as Taylor Lecturer was the very active Fearnsides, who had assisted Neville's researches (Section 8); rather, it reflected the improvement in the University laboratories. By 1909 thought was being given to the redevelopment of the laboratory site. Plans were drawn up for a new building in the position shown by the dashed line in Figure 1. With no further need for a laboratory the intention was to provide a lecture room, but the plan was abandoned.[60] Though the laboratory was out of use after the academical year 1907–08, much valuable material remained stored in the building. On 11 June 1910 (Saturday) revelry in College got out of hand and much of this material was lost when it was carried out to fuel a Bump Supper bonfire in Cloister Court.

The 'May' races of 1910 received wide coverage in the press. There was a consensus that the rowing had been mediocre, but that the celebrations following had been spectacular. The *Daily News* (London) reported:

> The last night of the races at Cambridge is always one on which students are allowed a little freedom, but yesterday's scenes were of a much more riotous character than usual. The bill for the damage will be a very long one. At most Colleges the evening passed off without much damage being done, but a different tale was told at Sidney College. The bonfire was a most gigantic

---

[58] 'thermometers' has presumably been omitted at this point.
[59] *Minutes, vol. 1907–1919*, 20 May 1908 and 15 June 1908.
[60] *Minutes, vol. 1907–1919*, 3 March 1909 and 18 June 1909; architect's drawings (uncatalogued) SSM.

affair, and was kept going from soon after nine o'clock till two o'clock this morning. When the fuel which had been provided ran short, rooms were raided and furniture sacrificed ... Everything which would burn was rushed off to the fire.[61]

The *Cambridge Daily News* took the line that 'youth will have its fling' and it considered that, while the celebrations had been 'an astounding success', the reports of damage had been exaggerated. It thought the damage no worse than usual, and seems to have been particularly incensed at the suggestion in a London paper that 'conservatories' had been demolished. Under the headlines 'Bump Celebrations, Lively Scenes in College Grounds, Enthusiasm and Fireworks', it reported that there had been fireworks on Midsummer Common, and that afterwards:

> ... the crowd dispersed homeward, or in search of similar amusement. This was found at the Sidney Street end of Jesus Lane where the Sidney men were celebrating an unusual experience of three bumps.[62] Despite statements of enormous damage there is little sign at Sidney this (Monday) morning, of the 'trampled flower beds laid waste' or the 'demolished conservatories' ... The 'conservatories' certainly did receive considerable attention from a few strayed revellers in white flannels, dress shirts and college and boating blazers. The 'conservatories' happen to be the glass covered roof of a passage which runs alongside the high wall bounding Sidney Street. When the fun was at its height one or two daring spirits clamboured (sic) along the top of the wall and smashed every pane of glass within reach.[63] Thus were the 'conservatories demolished'. It is however strongly denied at the College that 'everything inflammable was consumed'. Altogether, the college which has suddenly been thrown into such a blaze of publicity in the London Press is bearing up remarkably well.[64]

Books and papers from the laboratory were burned on the bonfire, and it is possible that further material was damaged the next day by heavy rain coming in through the broken skylights of the laboratory. There is no doubt about the great loss suffered by Heycock and Neville. Laboratory notes and photographic negatives were destroyed. They tried to reconstruct as much as they could, being forced to reproduce micrographs from old prints. Their research on aluminium-gold was greatly delayed.

The College appears not to have been greatly concerned. While celebrations

---

[61] Article dated Sunday 12 June, appearing in the *Daily News* (London), Monday 13 June 1910.
[62] The celebrations were on the fourth day of the races. Sidney had bumped Queens' on the first day, Trinity Hall II on the second day and Lady Margaret II on the third day, and had rowed over on the fourth day.
[63] As will be described in Section 7, the laboratory had skylights and a glazed addition.
[64] *Cambridge Daily News*, Monday 13 June 1910.

on the same evening at Emmanuel 'in which the famous lake . . . is said to have played a prominent part'[65] led to several students being sent down, there was no such action at Sidney. The *College Annual*,[66] in the style of such publications, merely records: 'A Bump Supper was given, in honour of our three bumps . . . and permission was kindly given for a bonfire in New Court.[67] Speeches were made during the supper by the Master, the Tutor and the Dean.'

On 23 June the Master of Sidney, Charles Smith, wrote to Heycock, the entire body of the letter being:

> At a College Meeting held on June 20, I was directed to write to you, on behalf of the Governing Body, to say that we all very greatly regretted that valuable books and papers belonging to you and Neville had been burnt in College on June 11.

Heycock, however, considered the matter to be more than a one-sentence affair. It has been recounted that years later he was still refusing Sidney students entry to his lectures or laboratory classes. The records show that it was not until 1914 that Sidney students were again enrolled for his metallurgy courses.

7. *The Buildings*

Ellis's original laboratory was on the ground floor of H staircase in Chapel Court. This was adjacent to a set of latrines which were at the end of the Chapel (at the time shorter than at present);[68] perhaps it was felt that all the bad smells should be in one place. The 'separate building' set up sometime after 1870 was presumably on the site which continued to be occupied by the laboratory for the next thirty, or more, years, piecemeal development taking place over that time. The site, to the north of Hall Court on the Sidney Street perimeter, is shown in Figure 1; it was then part of the Fellows' Garden, but later it became Cloister Court. While the details of the early laboratory are not known, the main features of its development can be established. Figure 1 is based on ground plans of the 1880s and 1895.[69] In 1880 the buildings labelled here as (a), (b) and (c) were standing; by 1895 building (d) had been added. The main building, (a), was entered

---

[65] Ibid.
[66] *Sidney Sussex College Annual*, 1910.
[67] This is now known as Cloister Court. Bonfires of this kind were a regular feature of Bump Supper celebrations in this period.
[68] These details are from a plan, dated 1870, in SSM, showing proposed alterations to the Master's stable yard, in the area of what is now the southern end of the chapel and South Court.
[69] The 1880s plan is in Willis and Clark, vol. 2, p. 730, fig. 3. The 1895 plan, in SSM, was drawn up as part of a survey of drainage in the College necessitated by the new town system dividing ordinary storm water from sewage. The survey was commissioned by F. H. Neville as Bursar.

through a doorway directly at the end of the A staircase passageway. The state of the laboratory towards the end of its life is fortunately recorded in a series of photographs, two of which are shown in Plate 13.[70] Building (a) contained the main laboratory shown in Plate 13a. This room was lit by skylights and in its north wall had a fume cupboard (central in the photograph) venting to a chimney. Plate 13b shows building (a) adjacent to the North range of Hall Court. The skylights and the chimney can be clearly seen. Also seen are buildings (b) and (c). Building (d) lies out of the photograph, to the right. The laboratory in which Heycock and Neville worked has been variously described by later writers as 'primitive', 'temporary' and 'wooden'. However, the photographs show instead a substantial range of buildings, undistinguished certainly, and rather resembling a row of potting sheds (contemporary students referred to the 'shooting gallery', and as seen in Section 6 a newspaper mistook the buildings for conservatories), but providing very adequate working facilities. Presumably the College did not intend these to be permanent additions to its range of buildings, but they were nonetheless solidly constructed in brick.

The interior view in Plate 13a gives a good impression of how the laboratory was equipped – reagents and Bunsen burners being particularly evident. The overall impression is of a rather well equipped laboratory, aimed mainly at practical teaching in chemistry. There is nothing in Plate 13a or in the other photographs taken at the same time of the metallurgical equipment which would have been used for the research of Heycock and Neville. This would have included furnaces, crucibles, pyrometers and associated electrical equipment, the boiling apparatus for pyrometer calibration, polishing wheels and a photomicroscope. Perhaps this equipment was in building (d).

8. *Work in the Laboratory*

Finance for the building and equipping of the laboratory came from the College. The account books refer to the 'Taylor Laboratory' and show that its costs were borne mainly by the Taylor Endowment. In the 1860s building expenses amounted to some £100.[71] In addition an annual rent of £14 was levied on the Taylor Endowment and credited to the general College account.[72] There was

---

[70] The photographs were given to Sidney Sussex College by the Rev. Dr L.E. Browne, see *Sidney Sussex College Annual*, 1990. The date is there stated as 1909, but the photographs must have been taken prior to the removal of the equipment from the laboratory in 1908. The complete set of photographs can be found in SSM, together with annotations by the present author; there are external views of buildings (a), (b), (c) and (d), and interior views of buildings (a) and (c).

[71] Mr Taylor's Mathematical Lectureship Account, SSM; see entries for 13 Nov. 1860, 20 Nov. 1866, May 1867, and 1 October 1869.

[72] Bursar's General Accounts 1856–1875, M.R. 57, SSM, for example, p. 160. This transfer from the Taylor Endowment was overlooked for up to three years and then paid in one sum.

additional expenditure on assistant staff, who came from a variety of backgrounds in the College, from porters to undergraduates.[73] Against these expenses there was the income from fees which came both from colleges[74] and from individuals. In the 1880s a typical annual fee income was about £20, representing payments from two colleges for provision of facilities mainly in the Michaelmas and Lent terms;[75] this income could be used directly: 'Agreed that Mr Neville be authorized to expend the money he receives for laboratory fees on apparatus at his discretion, keeping an account of the same.'[76] It is not clear to what extent the provision of equipment for teaching sufficed to serve the research efforts in the Laboratory. However, at least from 1895 Heycock's and Neville's increasingly prominent research attracted support from the Royal Society and the British Association.

Throughout its life, the bulk of the work in the laboratory must have been the standard experiments used for teaching purposes. Figure 2[77] from lecture notes of Heycock on organic chemistry shows a typical experiment of the period, in this case for the preparation of acetylene. Organic chemistry at this time was changing its emphasis from analysis to synthesis. The laboratory was also used for the entrance examinations in practical chemistry. C.T.R. Wilson records that his examination was conducted by F.H. Neville.[78]

In this section we concentrate not on the teaching experiments of the kind shown in Figure 2, but on the research work of Heycock and Neville, about which much is known from their scientific papers and laboratory notebooks. The use of mercury thermometers restricted their early work to metals and alloys of rather low melting-point. The most important thermometers came from 'Mr Hicks of

---

The rent appears to have been discontinued after the 1860s. This annual rent for the laboratory was approximately equal to six months' rent of one of the College houses in Sussex Street or six months salary for the Under Porter at the time.

[73] In respect of a period of about two months work it was agreed 'that the Junior Porter H. W. Johnson receive in addition to his present wages £6 out of the Taylor Fund . . . for his services in the Taylor Laboratory' (*Minutes, vol. 1876–1895*, 20 May 1880). Also, 'agreed that Johnston, an undergraduate, shall receive for Michaelmas last £10 a year from the Taylor Fund and £42 a year from the College for his service in the laboratory, thus making his salary equal to £1 a week' (*Minutes, vol. 1876–1895*, 4 December 1884).

[74] Downing, Emmanuel and Christ's Colleges are mentioned in *Master and Tutor Settlements 1875–1890*, M.R. 29D, SSM.

[75] *Master and Tutor Settlements 1875–1890*, M.R. 29D, SSM, for example entries for 1875, LD 1881, LD 1890.

[76] *Minutes, vol. 1876–1895*, 19 March 1886.

[77] From a notebook in the Heycock Archive 'Lecture Notes, Prof. Dewar, Lent Term 1877'. The hand-written notes are from the lecture of Thursday 6 February; Heycock did not matriculate until October of that year.

[78] Despite holding a B.Sc., Wilson had never done any practical chemistry. Neville told him to make what he could of the examination, and Wilson was admitted. *Notes Records Royal Soc. London*, 14 (1960), 163–73.

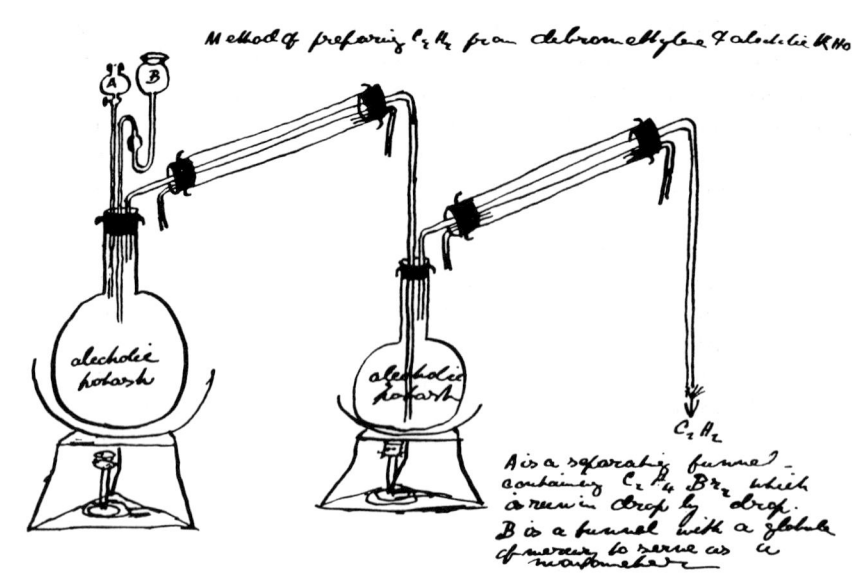

Figure 2. A page from Heycock's lecture notes of 1877, before his matriculation as an undergraduate. The experiment is the production of acetylene from dibromethylene and alcoholic potash.

Hatton Garden'.[79] The practical difficulties, compared to thermometry today, were large. Hicks supplied fifteen thermometers in total, each covering a range of just 28°, with 4° overlap between adjacent thermometers in the set. The total measurable temperature range was 0°C to 325°C. Each of these thermometers had a stem two feet in length. Using this rather unwieldy set, Heycock and Neville could measure temperatures to an accuracy of 0.01°C. Since the thermometers were used for long periods at elevated temperatures, there was a problem with a drift in the zero. This was countered by treating first in boiling mercury or boiling sulphur for eighteen days, a procedure which would strike fear into a University Safety Officer today.[80] Heycock and Neville seemed well pleased with these thermometers, recording that thermometer no. 10 (210°C to 237°C), between 8 August 1889 and 1 March 1890, 'was used for several hundred experiments, and was kept nearly daily for two months continuously plunged in molten tin for seven or eight hours, a treatment which will be admitted was somewhat severe'.[81] Hicks calibrated his thermometers by complete immersion. For Hey-

---

[79] C.T. Heycock and F.H. Neville, 'On the Molecular Weights of Metals when in Solution', *Jour. Chemical Soc.*, 57 (1890), 656–661.

[80] C.T. Heycock and F.H. Neville, 'On the Lowering of the Freezing Points of Cadmium, Bismuth, and Lead When Alloyed with Other Metals', *Trans. Chemical Soc.* (1892), 888–914.

[81] This particular thermometer, and many of its siblings, still exist in the Heycock Archive,

cock and Neville, complete immersion of a two-foot thermometer in a crucible of molten alloy was quite impractical, and indeed the scale could not have been read had immersion been possible. They immersed only the bulbs of the thermometers, leaving the stems exposed. Under these conditions of use, a thorough recalibration was necessary, and this was effected using a platinum (Pt) resistance thermometer, thus introducing Heycock and Neville to this instrument.

They subsequently used platinum resistance thermometry as their main technique to determine the melting-points of a wide range of metals and salts. The platinum resistance thermometers were, albeit for different reasons, like the mercury thermometers prone to drift. For six months, Heycock and Neville carefully recorded the sequence of experiments performed in order that the drift of the thermometer could be monitored. This record is now of interest for the working pattern which it reveals. In 1894–95, experiments were performed on all of the following dates:[82]

> July: 2–6, 8–16, 29, 30
> August: 1–7, 9–13, 15–17, 19, 20
> September: 17–20, 23–29
> October: 1–3, 7–9, 15
> November: none
> December: 9–13, 16–22, 24–28
> January: 9

A heating experiment in this sequence could have lasted for up to three days (without interruption), but a more typical period was two to six hours. Most of the work seems to have been performed around the middle of the day, the earliest recorded measurement being at about 10 a.m. and the latest at about 6.30 p.m. This seems rather at variance with the comment of Pope in his obituary of Heycock: 'The major part of Heycock and Neville's work was carried out in a small laboratory in Sidney Sussex College and, owing to the many other duties which fell upon the two partners, much of it had to be done late at night and in the early hours of the morning.' What is indisputable is that teaching did reduce the time available for research; in the middle of what was a well devised sequence of experiments, the dates quoted above show a large gap in October and November, presumably coinciding with the pressures of term. Pope adds that 'It may seem surprising that such a quantity of data of enduring value could be

---

together with other thermometers with larger ranges from German, French, and other English manufacturers.
[82] C.T. Heycock and F.H. Neville, 'On the Determination of High Temperatures by Means of Platinum-Resistance Pyrometers', *Trans. Chemical Soc.* (1895), 160–199.

collected under such conditions; but both men were enthusiasts, both possessed an exquisite sense of technique and both were meticulous in their striving after accuracy.' Their enthusiasm is certainly demonstrated by the continuation of the sequence of experiments through Christmas. One can but hope that some seasonal cheer was brought to the work by its being on one of the three gifts of the Magi – gold, up to 1.2 kg of it, was being used for freezing-point determinations.

Heycock and Neville employed a number of assistants in their research, and the training provided by this must be counted as a major contribution of the laboratory, in addition to the teaching of undergraduates. Among those thanked for their assistance are: Miss Field (Newnham College), Miss Marshall (Girton College), C.T.R. Wilson, W.G. Fearnsides, F.E.E. Lamplough (Trinity College) and G.M. Clark. While a number of these had prominent careers,[83] we turn attention to just two. The most distinguished of them all is Charles Thomas Rees Wilson,[84] who, after graduating from Owens College Manchester, entered Sidney Sussex in 1888 and obtained a First Class in the Natural Sciences Tripos of 1892. While an undergraduate, shortage of money was among the factors inducing him to take up employment in the Sidney Laboratory. He assisted Heycock and Neville with their work on thallium alloys. After graduation he made a living for some years by demonstrating in the Cavendish Laboratory, assisting Ruhemann's chemical research in the Caius laboratory and coaching. In due course Wilson was to become Jacksonian Professor of Natural Philosophy at Cambridge, and to win the Nobel Prize in Physics in 1927 for his development of the cloud chamber. Fearnsides[85] was admitted to the College in 1897, obtained a First Class in the Natural Sciences Tripos (1901), was elected a Fellow (1904) and succeeded Neville as the Taylor Lecturer in Natural Sciences. He subsequently became Professor of Geology and Dean of the Faculty of Pure Science at Sheffield. He furnishes an example that the laboratory assistants provided more than just pairs of hands. Heycock and Neville give him the credit for a significant insight in their Bakerian Lecture work; as a geologist, Fearnsides identified twinning in some of their samples by analogy with feldspars.[86]

---

[83] Lamplough went on to make further metallurgical contributions as a University Assistant Demonstrator in Heycock's laboratory. Clark had a distinguished career in engineering, ultimately becoming President of the Institute of Engineers of South Africa.
[84] Venn, vol. 6, p. 517. *Notes Records Royal Soc. London*, 14 (1960), 163–73.
[85] Venn, vol. 2, p. 472.
[86] The work in the Sidney Laboratory led to one of Fearnsides' own lines of research – 'Structural Analogies between Alloys and Igneous Rocks', presented to the Cambridge University Chemical Club in the early 1900s (Berry and Moelwyn-Hughes, p. 359).

9. *The Cambridge Scientific Instrument Company*[87]

A close link developed between the Sidney laboratory and the Cambridge Scientific Instrument Company.[88] Griffiths in the Sidney laboratory and H.L. Callendar in the Cavendish Laboratory worked, at first separately and later together, to develop platinum resistance thermometry into a reliable technique. Callendar overcame the difficulties in Siemens' earlier design and in 1891 granted sole manufacturing rights to the Cambridge Scientific Instrument Company, then newly under the sole control of Horace Darwin.[89] Heycock and Neville were very interested in the new technique because of its potential for measuring higher temperatures than were possible with mercury thermometers. They obtained resistance thermometers from the Company, but they found that the turns of platinum wire around the central glass former gave recurrent problems because of movement and electrical shorting. Griffiths was well aware of this defect and it is reported that during some lecturing a solution occurred to him; he cut out a model from a postcard and sent it to Horace Darwin. The Griffiths construction, with a cruciform former of mica plates with serrated edges, became standard in the Company's thermometers (Figure 3). Griffiths and Callendar can be given credit for making the platinum resistance thermometer into a widely used reliable instrument. Their papers of 1887 and 1891, presented to the Royal Society,[90] were central in reversing the previous bad reputation of the instrument. In 1893 the Company's catalogue stated: 'In the absence of Mr Callendar as Professor of Physics in the McGill University in Montreal, Canada, each instrument will, before it is issued, be tested under Mr Griffiths' supervision in his laboratory at Cambridge and he will supply a form showing the corrections, if any, that have to be supplied to each instrument.' This laboratory was in the garden of Griffiths' home,[91] for in 1891 he had ceased work in the Sidney Laboratory, finding that his measurements were affected by vibration from the traffic in Sidney Street, a problem which may lend extra meaning to his lines in *A Song of Sidney Sussex*:

> Then seek a little College just beside a busy street;
> Its name is Sidney Sussex, and you'll find it hard to beat.

---

[87] Much of the material in this section is from: M. J.G. Cattermole and A.F. Wolfe, *Horace Darwin's Shop: A History of the Cambridge Scientific Instrument Company 1878 to 1968* (Bristol, 1987).

[88] The company had its origins in a workshop set up in 1877 in the Department of Mechanism, and in its early days was most closely associated with research on physiology, then making great progress under Michael (later Sir Michael) Foster.

[89] Horace Darwin (1851 to 1928) was the ninth of the ten children of Charles Darwin and the youngest of the seven to survive into adulthood.

[90] H.L. Callendar and E.H. Griffiths, *Phil. Trans. Roy. Soc. London*, Ser. A (1887), 161; ibid. (1891), 119.

[91] At 12 Parkside, a popular spot it seems, for Neville resided at 15 Parkside.

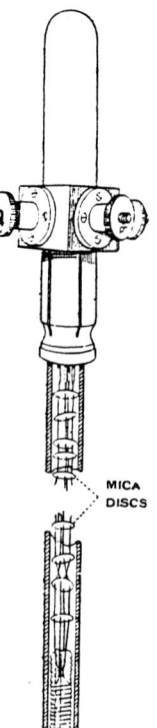

Figure 3. A platinum-resistance thermometer, as made by the Cambridge Scientific Instrument Company and used by Heycock and Neville. Near the bottom can be seen the cruciform arrangement of mica plates devised by Griffiths.[82]

Griffiths' link with the Company was close. When in 1895 it became a limited liability company, he was one of the few shareholders not a member of the Darwin family.

Heycock and Neville seemed less perturbed by the vibration and used the thermometers with great precision. They took care to improve on Griffiths' adjustments, describing how they dismantled the thermometers and corrected the length of the fine platinum wire to within 0.1%. Their work was crucial in establishing the platinum resistance thermometer as the instrument of choice for accurate measurement in physical and chemical laboratories. In this they may have been too successful and have exerted too strong an influence on the Cambridge Scientific Instrument Company. Though Le Châtelier had shown in 1886 that high temperatures could be measured accurately using thermocouples, the company remained convinced that the resistance thermometer was superior for standard laboratory work, and was abnormally late (1902) in introducing thermocouples into its product range. The superiority of the resistance thermometer, even for routine measurements, was still being expounded forcefully by Heycock in 1911, though the discussion of his paper suggests that he was rather behind the times.[92]

Heycock and Neville used not only the company's thermometers but also other instruments. They record that

> The pressure regulator we have used was designed by Mr. Horace Darwin, and supplied by the Cambridge Scientific Instrument Company. Careful measurements have shown that this regulator controls the very great variations of gas pressure we have in Cambridge, passing, as they do, from a minimum of about 1¾ inches to a maximum of about 3 inches; it also overcomes the changes of pressure produced by conducting other furnace operations simultaneously in the laboratory.[93]

10. *Reflections*

The general history of the college laboratories at Cambridge, in which Sidney Sussex was so prominent, reveals some tensions between the University and the colleges which are echoed still today. It is clear that the capability of the colleges for independent action permitted a fast response to the rapidly developing needs of a new subject; as a result, the college laboratories played an important rôle in teaching and research for some decades. At Sidney Sussex Heycock and Neville showed that world-class research was possible in a small but well equipped College laboratory. Their work shows a fast pace in a scientific world much smaller than today, but with the principal players in good communication with each other. The work in the Sidney Laboratory also contributed to the emergence of close links between the University and local 'high-technology' industry. In all it can be concluded that the commitment of the College to the natural sciences produced impressive results.[94]

---

[92] C.T. Heycock, 'Measurement of High Temperatures', *Jour. Soc. Chemical Industry*, 30 (1911), 3–16.
[93] C.T. Heycock and F.H. Neville, 'Röntgen Ray Photography Applied to Alloys', *Trans. Chemical Soc.* (1898), 714–723.
[94] The author is especially grateful to Mr T.S. Wyatt for his assistance with the preparation of this article. His thanks are also due to: Mr R.C. Andrew, Prof. D.E.D. Beales and Mr S.P. Salt, of Sidney Sussex College; Prof. P.J. Herley, sometime Visiting Fellow of Sidney Sussex College; Mr N. Rogers, Archivist, Sidney Sussex College; Dr A. Prince, formerly of the General Electric Company Ltd; Dr D. Agar of Newnham College; and Dr J.P. Chilton and Dr I.M. Hutchings of the Department of Materials Science and Metallurgy in the University of Cambridge.

George Ralph Mines (1886–1914) and the Electrophysiology of Sudden Cardiac Death

REGIS A. DE SILVA

The present state of knowledge in human physiology owes a great deal to the Cambridge men who worked in its physiological laboratories in the latter part of the last century and well into the present. Spearheaded by Michael Foster, these young physiologists contributed to the understanding of processes in nervous, muscle and cardiac physiology.[1] Among the most promising of these young men was George Ralph Mines, whose career spanned only a decade at Cambridge. Shortly after leaving Cambridge to assume the Professorship of Physiology at McGill University in Montreal in 1914, Mines was found dead in his laboratory at the age of twenty-eight.

Mines's Family and his Work at Cambridge

Mines was born in Bath on 13 May 1886, the son of H.R. Mines, HM Inspector of Schools, and Alice G. Ward.[2] His early education was at Bath College. After his family moved to King's Lynn when he was quite young, he went to the local grammar school. He entered Sidney Sussex College at the age of eighteen as an exhibitioner in 1904. Under F.H. Neville's guidance he gained a First Class in both parts of the Natural Sciences Tripos. In 1908 Mines received the University's Allen Scholarship, and in 1909 he was awarded the Walsingham Medal and elected to a fellowship at Sidney Sussex. That same year, he married Miss Marjorie Rolfe of Newnham College, the daughter of the Rev. and Mrs G.W. Rolfe; her father was then Vicar of Swanton Novers, Norfolk. Marjorie was a poet who was drawn to the group of young men around Rupert Brooke whose fates were emblematic of the tragic and romantic aspects of the *belle époque*. Many of these

---

[1] G. Geison, *Michael Foster and the Cambridge School of Physiology* (Princeton, 1978).
   I wish to thank Professor D.E.D. Beales, Sir Andrew Huxley, and Nicholas Rogers of Cambridge University, England, and Mrs June Schachter of the Osler Library, McGill University, Montreal, Canada. The late Anatole Mines of Cambridge, England and the late Professor F.C. MacIntosh of McGill University also contributed to my researches.
[2] Most of this paragraph is based on the obituary of G.R. Mines in *Sidney Sussex College Annual* (Cambridge, 1915), with some assistance from McGill University archives.

men, including Brooke, died in the Great War of 1914–1918, and Marjorie's work is included in a book of poetry by these Cambridge poets. Mines himself had a strong artistic bent and, being extremely gifted at the piano, had seriously considered a career in music before turning to physiology. Pictures taken at the time show him to have been a serious, handsome young man with dark hair, full lips and a saturnine aspect, who dressed with a certain elegance.

His literary tastes extended to Anatole France, who enjoyed a rather mixed reputation at the time, and he expressed the wish that his third child, if a son, should be named after the author. When a daughter was born to him posthumously in 1915 and christened by the future Master of Sidney, G.A. Weekes, she was nonetheless named Anatole at her aunt's suggestion in deference to her late father's wishes.[3] Anatole, who became a professional viola player, was Mines's last surviving offspring. She died in 1993 at the age of seventy-eight.

Mines was elected to the Physiological Society in 1910 at the same time as A.V. Hill. In 1911 Mines won the Gedge Prize and was subsequently appointed Assistant Demonstrator in the Physiological Laboratory at Cambridge. Besides his teaching function as demonstrator, he taught a physiology course at Newnham, and there met Dorothy Dale (no relative of Sir Henry Dale) in 1910 while she was a second-year student. She helped him with his experimental work until 1914 and they published many of their researches together.[4] The research he did while at Cambridge was published largely in the *Journal of Physiology*, whose pages reveal the remarkable productivity both of the Physiological Laboratory and of Mines himself during this period. He published in this journal two papers jointly with other scientists in the volume for 1907–8, the year after his graduation, and nine more papers over his own name between 1908 and 1914. He kept company in these volumes with several authors who have passed into the annals of contemporary science: Langley, Adrian, Hill, Starling, Bayliss, Sherrington and (Thomas) Lewis.

Some idea of Mines's high level of scientific activity and almost restless energy can be gathered from his movements during the two years before he left for Canada in 1914. In the summer of 1912, he and Dorothy Dale worked for ten weeks in the Marine Biological Laboratory in Plymouth. Mines also worked at the Zoological Station in Naples, probably in 1912, and at a laboratory in Roscoff in Brittany in August 1913. It was at Roscoff that Mines did the experiments leading to the important discovery of the vulnerable period of the ventricle which would be published posthumously the following year. From 2–6 September 1913, he took part in the Ninth International Congress of Physiology at Groningen, presenting a paper on his work done at Roscoff entitled 'Functional Analysis of Cardiac Muscle (With Demonstration, Projection and Cinématografic (*sic*) Projection)'.[5] In early 1914 he was acting as assistant to Professor T.G. Brodie in

---

[3] Personal communication from Anatole Mines.
[4] Archives, McGill University.
[5] Archives, McGill University.

his laboratory at the University of Toronto. He travelled to Montreal to lecture at McGill, and then left for England at the end of spring via Boston. He arrived in Cambridge in time for the dedication ceremony and official opening of the new Physiological Laboratory in June 1914. At this time the Professor of Physiology was J.N. Langley and the department was made up of W. Gaskell, E.D. Adrian, A.V. Hill, K. Lucas, F.G. Hopkins, W.B. Hardy, H.K. Anderson and W.M. Fletcher.

After the dedication, Mines returned to Canada a second time for the commencement of the fall term at McGill with his wife and his two children, a girl of four and a boy of two and a half years. They found a home in the Travancore Apartments on Cedar Avenue in Montreal and lived there until his death three months later. His wife, who was pregnant at the time, moved back to Cambridge, where Anatole was eventually born. Marjorie Mines subsequently remarried and moved to Sussex, living until the mid-1960s. Anatole was brought up by Mines's sister, who had married Reginald Hackforth, Fellow of Sidney Sussex and later Professor of Ancient Philosophy at Cambridge.

Appointment at McGill University

It was because of the great shortage of qualified men in physiology in Canada that Mines had been asked to act as assistant to Professor T.G. Brodie at the University of Toronto during the winter of 1913–1914. Brodie himself was one of the many British scientists who staffed the Canadian medical schools in the early part of this century.[6] While he was at Toronto, Mines came to the attention of the faculty at McGill where the post of Professor of Physiology had been vacant for some time.[7] J.G. Adami, the Professor of Pathology at McGill, was put in charge of the search for a new Professor. Mines was invited to Montreal to lecture there, and the McGill faculty was suitably impressed by the young physiologist. There was an exchange of letters between Montreal, Toronto and Cambridge before and after Mines's visit to McGill to ascertain his suitability for the position of Professor of Physiology. Before he returned to Cambridge in the summer of 1914, Mines was contacted by Principal William Peterson of McGill University and offered the Chair of Physiology. Mines demurred, in large part because the salary offered of $3,000 was insufficient to support a wife and two young children. After an exchange of letters with the Principal, he accepted the position and hurried back to England after spending a couple of days in Boston. It is clear from the letters exchanged between Cambridge, McGill and Toronto that, though Mines was barely twenty-eight at the time, he had already made his mark on physiology and had established himself as an important figure at Cambridge. The high regard his colleagues had for him is evident in the glowing letters with

[6] Obituary of T.G. Brodie in *Canadian Medical Association Journal*, 6 (1916), 953–956.
[7] The evidence for this paragraph is to be found in McGill University Archives.

unstinting praise for Mines and his scientific work that were written to Adami by Langley, Gaskell and Lucas of the Physiological Laboratory at Cambridge. Lucas, in his letter to Adami, regretted that he could not accept the appointment himself, but warmly endorsed Mines as a superior candidate for the position. It is apparent that the Dean and the faculty at McGill thought highly of their newest professor, since Mines was asked to give the Founder's Day oration in October 1914, barely two months after his arrival in Montreal.

Experimental Work in Physiology: The Discovery of the Vulnerable Period

Mines had a great facility for making his own equipment and devices for his experiments, and he provided drawings and photographs of this equipment in the papers he published. For some of his experiments, he constructed a teak box with a roller-and-drum mechanism which held bromide paper for photographing electrocardiograms while studying the actions of electrolytes and other influences on the heart.[8] Mines reported a novel method of recording the contraction of the frog heart, by photographing it at fifteen frames per second on motion film, and a sequence of eighteen still photographs of this experiment was published in the same paper.[9] His younger daughter, Anatole Mines, had in her possession a machine he had constructed and modified to record the progress of an experiment, which he called a 'chrondictaphone'. Mines published an account of this machine in German under the title 'Das Chrondiktaphon' in 1914.[10] Sometime in the 1970s, Anatole asked a physiologist (or physicist) from the Cavendish Laboratory to look at it as it was still in the basement at her home in Selwyn Gardens. Unfortunately, he advised her it was useless and it was destroyed.[11] Additionally, Mines was a very good draughtsman and he made freehand drawings of his equipment and of electrocardiograms from tracings he took during his experiments, in order to economise on labour and costs of publication.

Mines's research methods were innovative and involved the meticulous measurement of diffusion of metallic ions through colloids, and of both elapsed time and electrocardiographic intervals during his experiments. He was aided by A.V. Hill in the mathematical analysis of some of his early experiments. Hill, who was then a Fellow of Trinity, was already making his own brilliant career in muscle mechanics. Though he was an excellent mathematician and had done his Tripos in Mathematics before switching to physiology, Hill himself was not inclined towards studying the electrocardiogram. Later, he came to know Willem Ein-

---

[8] G.R. Mines, 'On Functional Analysis by the Action of Electrolytes', *Journal of Physiology*, 46 (1913), 188–235.

[9] G.R. Mines, 'Further Experiments on the Action of the Vagus on the Electrogram of the Frog's Heart', *Journal of Physiology*, 47 (1914), 419–430.

[10] 'Das Chrondiktaphon', *Zeitschrift für biologische Technik und Methodik*, Band 3, no. 6, 1914.

[11] Anatole Mines, personal communication.

thoven personally, and enjoyed his hospitality at his home at Leyden, as he later wrote in an obituary in *Nature* in 1927.[12] Einthoven, of course, won the Nobel Prize in Medicine in 1924 for developing the electrocardiogram as a standard clinical tool. Though Mines's own work consisted primarily of investigating the generation of arrhythmias using Einthoven's invention, it is not known whether Mines met the great man.

Reviewing the work Mines did over eighty years ago, a modern cardiologist is struck by the contemporary ring of the language contained in the papers he published between 1908 and 1914. Given the paucity of sophisticated equipment that was available at the time, the keenness of his observations, the scientific content of his work and the series of stochastic deductions Mines made are all quite remarkable. His electrophysiological studies included the effects of the vagus and of various elements such as barium, calcium and potassium on the electrocardiogram, the effect of strophanthin and Munchi arrow poison on the heart.[13] Mines also provided recognition of arrhythmias such as 'reciprocating rhythm' of the heart.[14] This concept, which is still used in clinical cardiology, was first recognized in the frog heart and was subsequently described in humans by A.N. Drury – also from the Cambridge school – in 1924.[15] It is, however, two other important contributions to cardiac electrophysiology which have endured which will be described briefly here.

The first concept that Mines advanced was a description of circular movement of an impulse which explains how re-entrant rhythms are generated in excitable tissue.[16] Briefly stated, when a wave of excitation is set up in a circular ring of muscle, the 'head' catches up with the 'tail' of the wave very quickly before repolarization can take place, so that the wave is extinguished. In abnormal tissue, conduction is slowed, so that there is time for tissue to repolarize between the slowly moving 'head' and the 'tail' of the wave. The circulating wavefront does not die out, but is sustained by virtue of conductive tissue being always available for excitation in advance of the 'head'. He found that the best way to distinguish between spontaneous series of beats and a wave of excitation which continues to circulate because there is always excitable tissue ahead of it, was the new method of cinematography. He made a film of this type of experiment, possibly the first use of moving pictures for this purpose, and demonstrated it in Groningen.[17]

---

[12] Obituary of W. Einthoven in *Nature*, 123 (1927), 591–92.
[13] E.g. 'On the Munchi Arrow Poison and Strophanthin', *Journal of Physiology*, 37 (1908), 37–45; 'Action of Rare Earths on Frog's Heart', *ibid.*, 40 (1910), 327–46; 'On the Replacement of Calcium in Certain Neuro-Muscular Mechanisms by Allied Substances', *ibid.*, 42 (1911), 251–66.
[14] See n. 8 above.
[15] A.N. Drury, 'Paroxysmal Tachycardia of Atrioventricular Nodal Origin Exhibiting Retrograde Heart-Block and Reciprocal Rhythm', *Heart*, 11 (1924), 405–411.
[16] G.R. Mines, 'On Dynamic Equilibrium in the Heart', *Journal of Physiology*, 46 (1913), 349–383.
[17] McGill University archives.

While working in Brodie's laboratory in Toronto in March 1914, he did similar experiments with cut rings of canine ventricular muscle and filmed the results again. Unfortunately, the fate of these films is presently unknown. In an article which he published in the *Journal of Physiology* in 1913 elaborating on the concept of re-entry, he provided a classical diagram which explains this concept. This diagram is still used unchanged to explain this mechanism to students of electrocardiography.[18] Mines made an additional discovery during the course of these experiments: section of the ring instantly stopped the circulating waveform. Today, this experiment forms the basis for surgical sectioning or radio-frequency ablation of bundle branches in the conduction system of the heart, or of abnormal pathways responsible for recurrent re-entrant arrhythmias.

Mines's second major contribution was also his most important discovery. It was published posthumously in 1914 in the *Transactions of the Royal Society of Canada* in a paper entitled 'On Circulating Excitations in Heart Muscles and their Possible Relation to Tachycardia and Fibrillation'.[19] The paper was presented by Professor T.G. Brodie for publication by the Royal Society of Canada, and a footnote indicates that the proofs were read by him 'owing to the sudden death of the Author'. The material for this signal paper was obtained during a relatively short stay in 1913 at the Station Biologique, Roscoff, France, under the patronage of Professor Yves Delage. Mines could not have realized the importance of this work and the impact it would have on the development of electrophysiology, the understanding of sudden cardiac death and the development of technology for the electrical termination of cardiac arrhythmias in the latter half of the century.

There was much interest at that time in the mechanisms of ventricular fibrillation, the essential arrhythmic mechanism for sudden death. This rhythm disturbance, which was produced by subjecting the heart to electrical shocks, had been considered largely as an experimental curiosity after its discovery by Ludwig and Hoffa in 1850 in Leipzig. It was another British physiologist, John Alexander MacWilliam of the University of Aberdeen, who advanced the hypothesis in 1889 that ventricular fibrillation was the primary mechanism of sudden death in humans.[20] The commonest method of inducing fibrillation was by the application of electrical shocks to the heart via an induction coil. Mines's innovation in studying the onset of fibrillation was to modify the method by applying *single* shocks of brief duration to the rabbit heart via platinum electrodes, and by *timing* them at various periods during the cardiac cycle. By so doing, he found that the delivery of shocks during the refractory period of the ventricle produced no response but that, if properly timed during electrical diastole of the heart, fibrillation could be induced. He also made two other important observations:

---

[18] See n. 16 above.

[19] *Transactions of the Royal Society of Canada*, 8 (1914) (ser. 3), 43–52.

[20] R.A. de Silva, 'John MacWilliam, Evolutionary Biology and Sudden Cardiac Death', *Journal of the American College of Cardiology*, 14 (1989) 1843–1849; J.A. MacWilliam, 'Cardiac Failure and Sudden Death', *British Medical Journal*, 1 (1889), 6–8.

that fibrillation was never transmitted back to the ventricles, and that it was often non-sustained in the rabbit heart. The ingenuity of these experiments lies in the innovation that Mines introduced in carrying out these demonstrations. In the absence of present-day devices for studying the vulnerability of the heart to fibrillation, the timing of the delivered shock was recorded mechanically; the beating of the heart was measured by connecting the cardiac apex to a kymograph, rather than by using electrical timing devices coupled to the electrocardiogram. Mines did, however, record the electrocardiogram, using an Einthoven galvanometer to record the onset of fibrillation.

The importance of Mines's discovery lies in the fact that it identified for the first time a narrow zone fixed within electrical diastole during which the heart was extremely vulnerable to fibrillation. An external stimulus, or a stimulus generated from within the heart, if properly timed to fall within this zone, could trigger a fatal arrhythmia and cause sudden death. This discovery has spurred three generations of scientists to study the factors which cause death by disruption of what Mines called 'the dynamic equilibrium of the heart'. Later researchers who were experimenting with use of electrical discharge across the thorax did not realize that, if discharged during the vulnerable period, it might provoke ventricular fibrillation, as described by Mines in 1914. Astonishing though it may now seem, this realization came belatedly, and it was not until 1961 that Lown and his co-workers incorporated a timing device to avoid this hazardous complication of using electrical energy to terminate cardiac arrhythmias.[21]

Another important application of this discovery in contemporary cardiology is the deliberate provocation of ventricular tachycardia by discharging an impulse during the vulnerable period to test the heart for electrical instability. This form of electrophysiological testing of the heart is used to evaluate patients clinically when they are at high risk of sudden death from ventricular fibrillation. Such patients include those who have been resuscitated from this otherwise fatal arrhythmia, or those patients who have sustained recurrent ventricular tachycardia. Once baseline testing is performed, the patient is treated with a suitable antiarrhythmic drug, or combination of drugs, and re-tested electrically to determine whether the arrhythmia is still provoked. Failure to induce arrhythmia generally indicates that drug treatment has successfully suppressed the arrhythmia and that sudden death is unlikely to occur.

Topographical mapping of the heart using modifications of this method of electrical testing is also used for radio-frequency ablation and electrosurgery in the termination of arrhythmias due to re-entrant pathways and arrhythmogenic foci in the heart.

---

[21] B. Lown, R. Amarasingham and J. Neuman, 'New Method for Terminating Cardiac Arrhythmias – Use of Synchronised Capacitor Discharge', *Journal of the American Medical Association*, 182 (1961), 548–551.

Death of Mines and his Place in History

On the cold Saturday evening of 7 November 1914, the night janitor entered Mines's laboratory and found him lying unconscious with equipment attached to him, evidently for the recording of the breathing actions of his body.[22] On the left forearm were two linear incisions, made presumably to infuse a solution. The alarm was raised and he was taken immediately to the Royal Victoria Hospital, where he regained consciousness briefly. However, shortly before midnight, he developed seizures and died without regaining consciousness. An autopsy, which included examination of all the abdominal and thoracic viscera and the brain, was performed, but no final clinical diagnosis was given.[23] The presumption was that death resulted from self-experimentation. In his tribute following his death, Principal Peterson of McGill University said 'he was one of the most distinguished of the younger group of scientists at Cambridge'. The Dean of Medicine, Dr H.S. Birkett, said the tragic death of Mines was a great loss to the world. On 9 November at 3.00 pm a funeral service was held at the chapel of the Royal Victoria Hospital, and the Rev. Arthur French officiated. Professor T.G. Brodie, who was Mines's last superior, was present and represented the Toronto faculty.

What is perhaps most surprising about Mines's place in medical history today is that, despite his early success, after his death he was all but forgotten. This is especially so because the concept of the vulnerable period of the ventricle is a vital cornerstone of cardiac electrophysiology and one with which all cardiologists are very familiar. However, few clinicians and scientists know that Mines discovered this key property of the heart. Other than an occasional and passing reference to his posthumously published paper reporting this discovery, his name is almost never mentioned in the literature. The circumstances of his death are virtually unknown outside the Physiology Department at McGill, and there is no comprehensive review of his life or work. The classic 1964 treatise, *A History of Electrocardiography* by Burch and De Pasquale, acknowledges Mines's work on circulating rhythms and reciprocal rhythm.[24] In the 1970s David Rytand at Stanford obtained some biographical information from Dorothy (Dale) Thacker and published a brief biographical note in a long article on re-entrant mechanisms in atrial flutter.[25] In 1983 Arthur Winfree made reference to Mines in an article in the *Scientific American* and, like Rytand, acknowledged his major contributions to cardiac electrophysiology and described the unfortunate circumstances of his

---

[22] For this paragraph see *Montreal Gazette*, Monday 9 November 1914.
[23] Autopsy report, G.R. Mines, Royal Victoria Hospital, Montreal, Canada, 7 November 1914.
[24] G.E. Burch and N.P. De Pasquale, *A History of Electrocardiography* (San Francisco, 1990), pp. 153, 256.
[25] D.A. Rytand, 'The Circus Movement (Entrapped Circuit Wave) Hypothesis and Atrial Flutter', *Annals of Internal Medicine*, 65 (1966), 125–159.

death.[26] Soon afterwards, the McGill Department, in recognition of his seminal contribution, commemorated him in a conference on electrophysiology.

Mines is mentioned in Harvey Cushing's magisterial prize-winning biography of Sir William Osler, as one of the members of the Physiological Laboratory when it was opened in 1914.[27] Osler had travelled up to Cambridge in early June of 1914 from Oxford, where he was Regius Professor of Medicine. It was an occasion not to be missed, for it was the culmination of Michael Foster's efforts since 1870 to create what has since then been famously known as the Cambridge School of Physiology. In fact, Osler gave up an important commemoration in honour of Roger Bacon at his own university after having served on the executive committee to prepare for the Oxford celebration. The new laboratory was opened by Prince Arthur of Connaught, but had already been in full operation by then for some time. Demonstrations were arranged for the opening by Langley, Mines, Miss Dale, R.A. Peters, A.V. Hill, W.H.R. Rivers, J. Barcroft (with C.G. Douglas of Oxford), W. Fletcher, W.B. Hardy, Keith Lucas and many others. Mines hurried back to Cambridge from Toronto via Montreal and Boston for the opening, before formally accepting the position at McGill. It is likely that Osler and Mines met on this occasion, as Osler had previously attended McGill as a medical student and had been Professor of Medicine at McGill. Though there is no known record of such a meeting, Mines, having accepted the position of Professor of Physiology at the same university, would probably have indicated to Osler his intention to leave for Montreal in the next several weeks. By a curious coincidence, Osler had only five days earlier, on 4 June, been at Bath, Mines's birthplace, for the opening of the Pathological Laboratory in that town. It will be remembered that this was a time of great tumult and excitement in Europe. Only twelve days before the opening of the Physiological Laboratory, on 28 May, a fanatical Serbian student had thrown a bomb at the Archduke Franz Ferdinand and his consort, killing both, an event that led to the outbreak of the Great War that autumn. Of those members of Langley's group present at the opening, Mines would leave the laboratory for Canada and die five months later, Keith Lucas would be killed flying after the war erupted, and A.V. Hill would leave Cambridge temporarily to apply his mathematical skills to improving the ballistics of navy and anti-aircraft guns.

At the time of Mines's death in November 1914, Britain was already at war with Germany, but the United States was not. In London, three days after Mines's death, Sir William Osler, who was then Regius Professor of Medicine at Oxford (having previously been Professor of Medicine at both Johns Hopkins and McGill) gave an interview to the *New York Times* on the American point of view about the war. In his opinion, the Americans would have to take up the task of guarding the world's freedom. In the light of contemporary geopolitics and

---

[26] A. Winfree, 'Sudden Cardiac Death: A Problem in Topology', *Scientific American*, 148 (May 1983), 144–161.
[27] H. Cushing, *The Life of Sir William Osler* (Oxford, 1925), vol. II, pp. 413–414.

renewed problems in Sarajevo, it is interesting to note that Osler was espousing the concept that the United States had a role in preserving world peace and freedom. It will be remembered that Osler, though resident in the United Kingdom, and previously in the United States, was actually a Canadian 'who was considered to be qualified to speak on these questions'.[28] It is unknown if the possibility of war breaking out in Europe played a role in Mines leaving for Canada with his young family.

Mines's last piece of writing was his address to the McGill Faculty on Founder's Day, which he was privileged to give on 6 October 1914, almost exactly a month before he died.[29] In this address, he makes an important allusion which was to portend his death. It was a fairly long address, scholarly in its sweep and very thoughtful and philosophical for a man who was only twenty-eight at the time. Mines, in describing the pursuit of experimental physiology, quotes two examples of self-experimentation by physiologists. He remarks on Head's experiments at the London Hospital involving severing nerves in his arm to study skin sensation. Additionally, he cites studies on digestion by Cannon and Washburn at Harvard, in which the latter swallowed a stomach tube. It would seem that, by the time of his arrival at McGill, Mines had decided that the time had come for human experimentation in his own field. It was to have, as we have seen, fatal consequences.

Mines lies buried atop Mont Royal in a grave marked only by a very low headstone. On brushing away the snow, the visitor learns from the granite marker that this forgotten young stranger from Cambridge died in the course of self-experimentation. One remembers the short life of this remarkable man and the contribution he made to understanding the deadly swiftness of death. And one recalls the closing lines of 'The Death of a Stranger' by another Cambridge man, the poet Thom Gunn:

> They buried him upon the road in sight
> Of houses: he would have no ghost.
>   Already from his gravestone
>   Sprung flowers ignorant of frost
> He had no ghost. Now no one fears the night.[30]

Mines deserves the credit for being the first to cast light on the exact physiological mechanism which causes ventricular fibrillation and sudden death. Cardiac arrest has since become the single most important cause of mortality in the Western Hemisphere. Cardiac electrophysiology and the technology of

---

[28] *Montreal Gazette*, 10 November 1914.
[29] G.R. Mines, 'Science and Individuality', address given at McGill University, 6 October 1914, Osler Library of Medicine Archives, McGill University.
[30] Thom Gunn, 'The Death of a Stranger' in *The Cambridge Mind: Ninety Years of the Cambridge Review 1879–1969*, ed. W. Janeway and S. Schama (Boston and Toronto, 1970), p. 288.

resuscitation have made prodigious strides since Mines's original discovery, and in large measure because of it. An analysis of Mines's work also demonstrates the beginning of the application of quantitative methods to electrophysiological research at a time when biomedical technology was still in its infancy. The discovery of the vulnerable period will remain one of those few timeless discoveries in science.

The New Chapel of Sidney Sussex College, Cambridge

C. S. B. PYKE

Sidney's neo-Baroque chapel, built between 1912 and 1923, is both architecturally unique and unique among the college chapels of Oxford and Cambridge in so unequivocally insisting on High Church attributes: the stone high altar with its six Italian candles, the altar painting from Catholic Venice, the statues of St Francis and St George. Each generation of members of the Christian Union has found it a stumbling-block, and recent Chaplains have struggled against the stream to give it a more ecumenical character. Sidney men and women often ask how the College could have become for a time so closely identified with High Church Anglicanism. Unfortunately, the written evidence is sparse, consisting mainly of laconic entries in the minutes of the Governing Body and the reminiscences of Tom Knox-Shaw, Fellow from 1909 and Master from 1945 to 1957.[1] However, the story can be supplemented to some extent by reference to developments in other colleges, in the town and in the Church more generally.

What can be safely asserted is that the decision of Sidney's Governing Body to have work begin upon a new chapel in 1912 marked the culmination of a long-standing recognition that its predecessor was inadequate, not least for practical reasons. A photograph illustrates the point: stone-paved and panelled in varnished deal, the old chapel, if not the smallest in the University, was manifestly too small for a college which had expanded and which still hoped to maintain the illusion of the college at prayer.[2] Indeed, although it should be acknowledged that the comparably small Chapel of Trinity Hall did not receive similar treatment, in the case of Sidney it is significant that the designs for the new Chapel were not the first to be considered. Already in 1896 Sidney had commissioned J.L. Pearson to draw up plans for an eastward- rather than (as in the old and present chapels) southward-oriented chapel, to be built between Cloister Court and Jesus Lane, which might 'by its beauty attest the importance

---

[1] T. Knox-Shaw, *Reminiscences* (Cambridge, 1974). For the architecture of the new chapel, see T.H. Lyon, 'The Chapel of Sidney Sussex College, England', *The Architectural Forum*, 39 (1918), 91–96; and L.A. Powys, 'Sidney Sussex College, Cambridge, Chapel, designed by T.H. Lyon', *The Architectural Review*, 55 (1924), 100–101.
[2] See Plate 16a.

the College attaches to Divine Worship'. At the tercentenary celebrations of that year an appeal was made for funds to build the new Chapel.[3] Pearson, the architect of Truro Cathedral, had already designed New (Cloister) Court for the College, and this commission may be seen as a natural corollary of that successful scheme (see Plate 15).

Although Pearson's plans were never implemented for lack of the requisite funds, the College's choice of a noted Gothic revivalist and the designs themselves indicate that the Governing Body was very conscious of the alterations which had taken place in other college chapels during the preceding half century.[4] On 13 November 1895 the Rev. J.A. Robinson, Norrisian Professor of Divinity and Lady Margaret Preacher, could write that 'at least 10 of our 17 older colleges have done much of late to beautify the sanctuaries of their common life'.[5] These alterations had been inspired by the Cambridge Camden Society and later 'ecclesiological' proponents of the Gothic Revival such as the Cambridge Architectural Society, who had attempted to revive the ornamentation of the medieval Church as the legitimate style of church construction and restoration. Such 'beautification' might take the form of the stained-glass windows executed by Morris and Company in Jesus Chapel from 1866 to 1878 or the interior decoration completed by Bodley in the new chapel of Queens' between 1889 and 1891. Pearson's 1896 plans for a new chapel at Sidney, therefore, which include a raised altar with reredos, sedilia, stalls and organ – all of which were favoured by ecclesiologists – would have been thoroughly consistent with the Victorian embellishment of other college chapels and thus relatively uncontroversial.

In this context, it may also be noted that the commission to Pearson came from the Governing Body as a whole rather than merely from individuals, such as the Rev. G.A. Weekes and the Rev. J.W. Hicks, with pronounced High-Church sympathies. Indeed, although in the 1840s and 1850s the adoption of the aesthetics of the pre-Reformation Church had been a matter of ecclesiastical controversy in that ecclesiologists such as Neale encouraged a return of 'sacramentality' in church architecture which seemed to have Roman Catholic overtones, by the 1890s ecclesiology was more an indicator of aesthetic values than of a particular theological position within the Church of England. Further, as in the Victorians' acceptance of 'fully choral' services, the desire for 'dignity', decorum and grandeur and the conviction of superiority to all preceding ages were important considerations in encouraging Governing Bodies such as Sidney's to authorise expenditure in 'improving' their chapels. The *Magdalene College Magazine* of 1901, for example, commenting on Comper's adornment of the east

---

[3] The Archbishop of Rupertsland (Fellow of the College), 24 June 1896, *The Pheon*, 1896; *Sermon and Speeches at the Tercentenary Commemoration* (privately printed, Cambridge, 1896) (SSCMR).
[4] See D. Robinson and S. Wildman, *Morris and Company in Cambridge* (Cambridge, 1980).
[5] *The Guardian*, 13 November 1895.

end of the Chapel, reported that 'The Chapel . . . is assuming an aspect which cannot fail to give pleasure to all who see it . . . Old members of the College will doubtless be glad to hear how the focus . . . of our common life has received added beauty and brightness.'[6] If, however, such factors partly explain the decision of Sidney's Governing Body to rebuild the Chapel, they do not explain the adoption of a much more controversial design in 1912.

More fundamental to an understanding of how Sidney came to be so closely identified with High-Church Anglicanism is the transformation which the religious essence of the University underwent as a result of the alteration of the law and College statutes which took place in the 1870s and 1880s and the admission of Dissenters as full members in 1871. Until the Universities Tests Act of 1871 all Fellows were clergy and unmarried, and in principle undergraduates were Anglican. This piece of legislation is therefore crucial to the development of college chapels, for the abolition of such legal requirements in part contributed to and in part reflected the emergence of an increasingly secular institution and a secular profession of university teaching and scholarship; the foundation of Selwyn College, for example, 'on the broad but definite basis of the Church of England' was explicitly a counter to such a development.[7] It is arguable that the phenomenon of governing bodies in which Fellows in holy orders by no means constituted a majority enhanced the role of deans and chaplains and in practice gave them more opportunity to conduct chapel services according to their own persuasions. This was a development which conceivably favoured innovation as opposed to conservatism and was particularly important in the case of Sidney.

Thus, in Sidney, the statutes of 1882 removed the requirement for the Master or any of the Fellows to be in holy orders. Further, the Chapel was placed under the authority of the Dean and Chaplain as opposed to the Governing Body. This separation of 'sacred' and 'secular' incidentally reflected the Tractarian wish to minimise the established position of the Church of England. The 'Tractarian' or Oxford Movement had gained momentum in the 1830s in part as a protest against the perceived threat to the established Church of England posed by a reforming Whig government. By claiming, for example, that the commission of the Church of England derived not from the state but from the Apostles, the movement identified itself with a High Church or 'Catholic' position which seemed increasingly to imply a controversial revival of Catholic ritual. Controversial, because ceremonial was 'Catholicism' at its most conspicuous. But by the time of Sidney's commission to Pearson in 1896, there existed a well-organised High Church 'party' within the Church of England which had successfully defied

---

[6] *Magdalene College Magazine* (1901), pp. 145–6.
[7] W.O. Chadwick, *Selwyn College, 1882–1973*, pp. 2–3 and passim. The Anglican identity of Selwyn was reinforced by the statutes of 1913, which effectively limited the terms of the original Charter of 1882. For general religious developments in the University, see S. Rothblatt, *The Revolution of the Dons: Cambridge and Society in Victorian England* (Cambridge, 1965) and A.J. Engel, *From Clergyman to Don* (Oxford, 1983).

the attempt on the part of the state to legislate against 'ritualist' innovations through the Public Worship Regulation Act in 1874.

It is these developments which suggest how Sidney Chapel came to be identified with High Church Anglicanism at least twenty years before the new chapel was begun. Knox-Shaw gives a telling clue when he emphasised the importance of Sidney's statute of 1882, which enabled, for example, an Eastern Orthodox Mass to be celebrated without the need to obtain the approval of the Governing Body.[8] Two key figures in the introduction of High Church teaching and practice into Sidney Chapel were J.W. Hicks, Dean from 1887 to 1890, and G.A. Weekes, Chaplain from 1893 to 1895. A notable chemist and author of *Inorganic Chemistry* (1877), Hicks also served as Examining Chaplain to Edward King, who as Bishop of Lincoln was tried by the Archbishop of Canterbury in 1890 for alleged ceremonial illegalities. As Vicar of St Mary the Less in Cambridge from 1887 to 1892, Hicks developed the Tractarianism of Guillemard his predecessor, particularly in affirming the Catholic doctrine of the Real Presence of Christ in the Eucharist and in expounding the sacramental teaching of St Augustine, Keble and Pusey. The Altar Book used by Hicks in Sidney Chapel, significantly entitled *The Priest to the Altar, or Aids to the Devout Celebration of Holy Communion, Chiefly after the Ancient English Use of Sarum*, contains handwritten insertions from the Latin Canon of the Mass, including the reference to 'Papa nostro' – 'our Pope', together with additions to the Calendar in memory of High Church figures such as John Keble and Sister Theodora of St Margaret's East Grinstead, the religious community for women established amidst great controversy by the hymnologist and ecclesiologist J.M. Neale (1818–1866) in 1855.[9]

Indeed, in an era of ecumenism as well as secularism, it is easy to underestimate the controversy which anything deemed 'popish' aroused among many Protestant Anglicans in the nineteenth century. Indeed, whereas the label 'High Church' has come to imply the use of incense, private confession to a priest, statues of Saints, Marian devotion and the keeping of the Reserved Sacrament in a church, in the nineteenth century it meant very much less. The Protestant mentality of Victorian England, which demonised Mary Tudor, Jesuits, the Spanish Armada and James II and had more recently denounced the establishment of a Roman Catholic hierarchy in England in 1850, viewed surpliced choirs, clerical vestments and fully choral services with suspicion, even though by 1939 these were to be adopted in much of the middle ground of the Church of England. What is therefore unusual about Sidney is not merely the controversial innovations introduced by Hicks and Weekes, but the fact that Sidney seems an exception to the general experience of the Oxford and Cambridge colleges which, compared to the town churches, were seen as slow in accepting ceremonial 'Catholicism';

---

[8] Knox-Shaw, p. 8.
[9] Hicks was elected Fellow of the College in 1874. See unpublished sermons and Altar Book (SSC Muniments Room).

even Pusey and Keble had celebrated at the north rather than the east end of the altar in scarf and hood rather than in clerical Eucharistic vestments. This was confirmed by the experience of J.W. Reynolds, Fellow of Sidney from 1909 to 1915, who on going up to Trinity College, Cambridge, in 1902 encountered no altar lights, no ablutions after the blessing, and north-end celebration.[10] Given that the Church Association's list of twenty 'Romanising' clergymen in Cambridge in 1902 does not include Sidney among its three college chaplains,[11] it appears that Sidney had not adopted extreme Catholic ritual at this stage, at least not on a regular basis. Nevertheless, by the time of Hicks's elevation to the see of Bloemfontein in 1892 the chapel had become identified with High Church Anglicanism and the new chapel of 1912 to 1923 may thus be seen as the logical outcome of this development.

Of course, one must not exaggerate the extent to which a dean or chaplain was free to pursue his own inclinations independently of the Governing Body, particularly if the introduction of such ceremonial involved expense. As has been observed, Pearson's plans could not be executed for financial reasons and even Eric Milner-White, Dean of King's College from 1918 to 1941, who was able to persuade a predominantly agnostic and in some cases anticlerical Governing Body to authorise expenditure on fitting out the two north-westernmost chapels as chantries and on medieval stained glass, sometimes had to seek additional vestments from private sources.[12] Similarly, Sidney's elaborate sets of Eucharistic vestments seem to have been acquired piecemeal and from a variety of sources after 1900.

Sidney's High Church orientation may thus be seen to have arisen partly from the development whereby the everyday conduct of worship in the chapels came to be controlled more directly by deans and chaplains, particularly those of High-Church opinions. This, however, can be more specifically related to the phenomenon of lay Masters, who would presumably be less likely than their clerical predecessors to interfere in the organisation of the college chapels. Charles Smith was the first lay Master of Sidney from 1890 to 1918. His predecessor, the Rev. R. Phelps, died on 11 January 1890 after a tenure of forty-seven years; and at once, it seems, it was possible to make changes in the Chapel. Phelps was Bursar as well as Master and is known to have obstructed change in general, especially the building of Cloister Court. Evidence suggests that his death was a watershed for Sidney Chapel. On 7 April 1890 the College Council 'agreed to pay for the hire of an harmonium and for books necessary for a musical service in the College

---

[10] E.A.L. Donaldson, *Reminiscences of J.W. Reynolds*, typescript (1920?), p. 20 (SSCMR).
[11] The Church Association's *Ritualist Clergy List* (London, 1902) mentions Child at Emmanuel, Swain at King's and Johns at Queens'.
[12] D. Wilkinson, *Eric Milner-White: A Memoir* (Cambridge, 1963), p. 18. In chapel matters Milner was 'more and more given his head. If he was not given it he took it.' See S. Gaselee (?) to Eric Milner-White, 8 October 1935 (Eric Milner-White papers, King's College, Cambridge), in which he offers two ornate chasubles and a cope.

Chapel';[13] in March 1895 came the announcement that 'a regularly organised choir is to be raised from men in the College',[14] followed a year later by the commission to Pearson. A comparison may be made with Corpus Christi. Perowne, Master from 1879 to 1906, was keen to uphold the image of an Evangelical seminary, and his opinions found expression in the austerity of the chapel: a bare altar table and a brass eagle placed prominently in the centre of the aisle.[15] Under Caldwell, the first lay Master, from 1906 to 1916, Holy Communion was introduced every Sunday in Full Term and, with the hanging of curtains on each side of the altar, the lectern was moved to the side of the chapel, thus no longer obscuring the view of the altar. The fundamental point, however, is that such changes were initiated by the liberal Anglo-Catholic Dean, Pearce.[16] Indeed, that a real enhancement of the influence of deans and chaplains had taken place is indicated by Spens, who became Master of Corpus in 1927 and stipulated that changes in chapel worship ultimately required the sanction of the Governing Body, although in practice as a lay Anglo-Catholic he preferred to oversee the minutiae of chapel liturgy personally.[17] Of course, in the case of Sidney it should be acknowledged that the College experienced a clerical Master of decidedly Anglo-Catholic opinions from 1918 to 1945 in Weekes, who had been instrumental in developing Sidney's High Church Anglicanism as a Fellow from 1894 and who as Master attended chapel and encouraged the appointment of Anglo-Catholic Fellows. His successor Knox-Shaw lived in College from 1905 to 1957 except during the First World War, and attended Matins, Communion and Evensong daily, although he was never ordained.

The desire to rebuild Sidney's Chapel was related to the Universities Tests Act in another respect. That piece of legislation stipulated that 'Morning and Evening Prayer, according to the order of the Book of Common Prayer, shall continue to be used daily as heretofore in the Chapel of every College subsisting at the time of the passing of the Act'. This requirement, together with the decline of compulsory chapel – a separate and more gradual development – created a dilemma whereby services must by law continue but attendance was no longer guaranteed. On 8 December 1911 the *Guardian* observed: 'The discipline of different colleges already differs considerably. It is undeniable that in those colleges where the compulsion has ceased or is almost formal chapel attendance has become noticeably small, though opinion is divided . . . as to whether it is better to have the willing few than to risk alienating those who are restive under coercion.'[18] The decline of compulsory chapel was already under way in some

---

[13] Minutes of College Council (SSCMR).
[14] *The Pheon*, March 1895.
[15] See H.P. Stokes, *Corpus Christi* (Cambridge, c.1898), plate VII and J.P.T. Bury, *Corpus Christi College: The College's Chapels and Patterns of Worship, 1352–1972* (Cambridge, 1976).
[16] E.W. Pearce, Dean of Corpus Christi College from 1901 to 1914.
[17] I am indebted here to the reminiscences of the Rev. Geoffrey Styler and the Rev. Canon James Owen.
[18] *The Guardian*, 8 December 1911.

colleges before the First World War and in many cases did not survive it. Sidney abolished fines for non-attendance on 21 May 1867, which was unusually early compared to other colleges. Indeed, in a sermon in Great St Mary's in 1915, Fitzpatrick, referring to the pre-War situation, stated that, as a result of decreased attendance, chapels must work out 'how their services may be modified so as best to meet the spiritual needs of the whole body'.[19] Thus, the dilemma effectively presented new opportunities. In 1913, *Comment and Criticism* indicated that services were sometimes criticised as 'mid-Victorian', that there was 'a demand for services expressing the religious sense in a less conventional form', and that there was 'room for experiment', citing the new Chapel begun in 1912 and Sunday Eucharist at Sidney Sussex as examples.[20] Sidney's new Chapel was thus partly conceived as a practical means of evangelising the undergraduate who was no longer obliged to attend chapel worship.

These were the opinions of the pre-1914 Cambridge liberal Anglo-Catholic journal to which several Sidney Fellows such as the Rev. A.H. McNeile, Fellow from 1897 and Dean from 1905 to 1917, had contributed, and they indicate some of the thinking behind the decision to rebuild the chapel. In 1916, Pearce, as Master of Corpus, wrote from personal experience that the decline of compulsory chapel had 'restored to the Dean his functions as a priest of the Church, with proper pastoral duties to perform', as opposed merely to the exercise of disciplinary coercion.[21] Further, it is significant that the revived musical tradition in Sidney and in many of the college chapels received an impetus from the disappearance of compulsory chapel; voluntary attendance was deemed to be more likely at a service invigorated by music. E.W. Naylor, who went up to Emmanuel in 1884, recorded that the Chapel services were dull and musically lifeless, 'reading interspersed with half-hearted grumblings and chants and hymns, sung by the undergraduates'.[22] From 1898 Naylor gradually introduced fully musical services, and the formal termination of obligatory chapel in the 1920s was significantly followed by the award of choral exhibitions to help maintain an undergraduate choir. Sidney's revived musical tradition in the 1890s has already been placed in the context of the first lay Master and a collegiate desire for decorum. Thus, in 1895, Robinson, whilst regretting 'the slowness with which the great revival of the beauty of external worship makes its way into college chapels', declared: 'No one . . . who was an undergraduate fifteen or twenty years ago can fail to see a real difference . . . and to mark a growth . . . of the devotional spirit in our college services.'[23] Further, developments in musicology, such as the Victorian interest in

---

[19] *Cambridge Review*, 20 January 1915, p. 148.
[20] *Comment and Criticism*, vol. II no. 2 (June 1913), pp. 33, 39 (Cambridge University Library).
[21] E.W. Pearce, 'The Opportunities of the Church of England within the Colleges', in J. Plowden-Wardlaw (ed.), *Religious Reconstruction after the War: A Cambridge Programme* (Cambridge, 1916), p. 78.
[22] Quoted in F. Stubbings, *History of Emmanuel College Chapel* (Cambridge, 1987), p. 25.
[23] *The Guardian*, 13 November 1895.

plainsong, might also enhance the introduction of 'Catholic' liturgy. From 1929 in King's College Chapel, for example, Boris Ord was keener to introduce the music of Byrd and John IV of Portugal than Mann, his predecessor as organist; such musical forms by Catholic composers neatly reflected Milner-White's predilection for elaborate celebrations of the Eucharist. Plainsong was certainly introduced into Sidney Chapel, initially in the form of Stainer's version of Marbecke,[24a] but the little evidence available suggests that at least until 1955 the range and quality of music there remained limited. Indeed, the organ of Sidney's new Chapel was, according to Knox-Shaw, reluctantly bought, the chapel designs not having contemplated such a thing, conceivably because of a plainsong cult. Knox-Shaw himself certainly disliked organs, thinking them usually too noisy and their players a nuisance to the clergy.

The decline of compulsory chapel and the dilemma thereby presented also partially stimulated the introduction of a weekly Sunday Eucharist in college chapels; such a development could be said to reflect the 'Catholic' aspiration of regular sacramental Communion. In this respect Sidney, given its early association with High Church ideology, was pioneering if not unique. As early as 1872 the two Deans of King's College had written to the resident Fellows that 'As the central act of our worship', the 10 a.m. Communion service 'ought . . . to take a more proper place so as to impress the congregation with the obligation laid on all Christians to share in it'.[24] Further, in 1912, Reynolds, with Sidney and the college chapels in mind, had observed, with some exaggeration: 'The old compulsory Matins Religion is futile and dead. At Trinity (1902 to 1905) the chapel was crowded, . . . then chapels were made more optional and Sunday Matins dropped to a very small number. Now the voluntary choral celebration . . . is becoming the popular thing.'[25] Thus, in 1850 a freshman of Corpus could write: 'The term divided a few nights since, so we have the Sacrament in our Chapel on Sunday', whereas in 1916 the Master of the same College stated: 'The one service upon which one has to concentrate one's energies is the Holy Communion . . . We must keep it as simple in character as will appeal to all shades of opinion', whilst suggesting the possibility of a second celebration 'of a more ornate character'.[26] Indeed, as in the case of musical services, the partial displacement of Matins by Holy Communion represented a development which by 1939 had affected the Church of England at large, the centrality of the Eucharist being expressed in the 1930s in the 'parish communion' service.[27] Thus, by 1933 Sidney, King's, Caius, Trinity, Pembroke, St Catharine's and Selwyn had also introduced a daily

---

[24] Round letter to the resident Fellows from W.R. Churton and A.A. Leigh, 8 November 1872 (Chapel File, King's College Archives).
[24a] *The Pheon*, Tercentenary Edition, 14 February 1896.
[25] Donaldson, p. 22.
[26] Pearce, p. 80.
[27] See A.G. Herbert (ed.), *The Parish Communion* (London, 1937).

Eucharist.[28] However, Sidney's Roman Catholic vestments purchased after 1924 indicate that the new Chapel was intended, at least by some, as a fitting vehicle for Catholic Eucharistic worship based upon the English Missal rather than as a response to wider developments within the Church of England. The liturgy as well as the design were to be controversial.

As has been observed, although there were practical considerations behind the decision to rebuild the chapel, its design may be considered a veritable statement of High Church Anglicanism. The sanctuary windows in honour of the Passion and of the Blessed Sacrament, the circular panels over the Lady Chapel arches, symbolic of the sacrament of the altar, and the windows of the Lady Chapel, presented by the Sanctae Trinitatis Confraternitas – a 'Confraternity of the Holy Trinity' composed of University Fellows and undergraduates and devoted to supporting Catholic services[29] – and depicting the imagery of the Litany of Loreto, constitute the essential Anglo-Catholic paraphernalia as it had developed over the preceding sixty years. It is perhaps significant that the Baroque exuberance of the Chapel is reminiscent of the publications of the Society of SS. Peter and Paul, the propaganda machine of the triumphalist Anglo-Catholic Congresses of 1920, 1923, 1928, and 1933, to which B.T.D. Smith, Dean of Sidney from 1919, was to contribute in the 1920s.[30] Further, Sidney's choice of T.H. Lyon as architect is itself indicative of churchmanship: Lyon's Anglo-Catholic faith was to find expression in a significant proportion of 'Anglo-Catholic' ecclesiastical alterations in Cambridge between 1918 and 1939, most notably in the erection and adornment of a Lady Chapel on the site of a former Chantry chapel at Little St Mary's in 1931. The influence of those of Anglo-Catholic sympathies within the Governing Body of Sidney at the time when work upon the new chapel was begun in 1912 – Weekes, who was President of the Sanctae Trinitatis Confraternitas from 1906 to 1914, Knox-Shaw, Reynolds, Reginald Hackforth,[31] and McNeile,[32] for example – was decisive, not least because three-quarters of the capital cost was provided by the Fellows themselves and it had been cost which had prevented the realisation of Pearson's plans in 1896. It should be acknowledged, however, that the Chapel was completed only in 1923 after further fundraising, for which its completion was presented as a memorial to members of the College killed in the First World War. Indeed, for some churchmen, the horrors of the war had exposed the need for a more dynamic and vigorous form of Christianity within the Church of England and thus effectively

---

[28] W.J. Sparrow-Simpson, *The Contribution of Cambridge to the Anglo-Catholic Revival*, (London, 1933), p. 27.
[29] See C.G. Griffinhoofe, *The Story of STC* (Cambridge, 1915).
[30] See B.T.D. Smith, *The Resurrection of Christ*, The Anglo-Catholic Congress Books, VI (London, 1923). Smith was Chaplain of St John's from 1915 to 1919.
[31] R. Hackforth, Fellow of the College from 1912 to 1957.
[32] Fellow of the College from 1897 to 1933. One of Gore's Examining Chaplains and Chaplain to the (Cambridge) House of Mercy.

legitimated some Anglo-Catholic practices. In the case of Sidney's new Chapel, however, to obtain the requisite funds ultimately demanded a wider basis of appeal than churchmanship: the loyalties of alumni in general made possible the completion of an Anglo-Catholic design.

Indeed, the process whereby the Anglo-Catholic Movement, which had from its origins as the Oxford Movement in the 1830s been fraught with controversy, became an acceptable component of the Church of England effectively began in 1906 with the conclusion of the Royal Commission on Ecclesiastical Discipline:

> The law of public worship in the Church of England is too narrow for the religious life of the present generation. It needlessly condemns much which a great section of Church people, including many of her most devoted members, value ... Modern thought and feeling are characterised by a care for ceremonial, a sense of dignity in worship, and an appreciation of the continuity of the Church, which were not similarly felt at the time when the law took its present shape.[33]

Further, the widespread bereavement as a result of the First World War was effectively to legitimate prayers for the dead, which had been modified almost out of existence in the Prayer Books of 1552 and 1662 on account of their association with the Roman Catholic doctrine of purgatory.

Whilst such developments might suggest that the new Chapel was intended and able to be inclusive, it does seem that those Fellows who were instrumental in its execution conceived of it in rather ambitious terms. Knox-Shaw, for example, saw its completion as inaugurating Sidney as a High Church seminary. Before the Universities Tests Act of 1871 not only were undergraduates in principle Anglican, but in effect a high percentage of those attending chapel became clergy. In the context of the decline of compulsory chapel and the admission of Dissenters as full members in 1871, Knox-Shaw was doubtless concerned to encourage undergraduates towards Tractarian Theological Colleges such as Ely and to attract Fellows of Anglo-Catholic sympathies by means of an explicitly Anglo-Catholic College Chapel. This is reflected not only in the unusual degree of applause accorded to ordinands in the College publication *Pheon* and in the ordinations which, unusually for college chapels at that time, took place in the Chapel from 1914,[34] but also in the appointments of Anglo-Catholics after the First World War, particularly E.J. Passant in 1919 and B.T.D Smith as Dean in the same year. Smith in particular would seem to have been ideally suited to spreading the name of Sidney as a centre of Anglo-Catholic worship, collaborating with Milner-White in 1920 to produce *Cambridge Offices and Orisons*, an

---

[33] *Royal Commission on Ecclesiastical Discipline, Evidence*, (London, 1906), pp. 383–85.
[34] See *Sidney Sussex College Annual*, passim. I am particularly indebted to the reminiscences of the Rt Rev. Kenneth Riches, College Chaplain from 1936 to 1942, and of Sir Austin Robinson, Fellow from 1931 to 1993.

anthology of medieval liturgies.³⁵ In their grandiose conception of the chapel, Weekes and Knox-Shaw were possibly motivated by the dearth of valuable advowsons possessed by the College as means of promoting College members. Most of the older Colleges had many more livings over the country as a whole than Sidney, and Jesus College could also present Fellows to St Clement's and All Saints' in Cambridge, whilst Peterhouse's advowsons included that of Little St Mary's.³⁶ This consideration conceivably explains Knox-Shaw's exalted view of the purpose of the Chapel. A final consideration behind Sidney's new Chapel was the need to respond to a vigorous intellectual attach upon Christianity in the form of Frazer's *Golden Bough* and Moore's *Principia Ethica* (1903), which represented the apogee of a militant agnosticism in the University before 1914: 'No freshman could be in the University a week without being aware of it: if he came from a Christian house and school he would soon have to give an answer for his faith.'³⁷ Sidney's new Chapel was thus an emphatic statement of faith in the minds of the Governing Body.

The success of closely identifying the Chapel with High Church Anglicanism seems to have been equivocal. In 1916, Pearce, as Master of Corpus, wrote from personal experience: 'A College . . . will contain men of every possible shade of opinion as regards teaching and ritual, and those in authority will have to be careful not to exercise undue influence in any direction as regards ritual.'³⁸ Spens, his successor, similarly decided that vestments, for example, would prove divisive, notwithstanding his own High Church Anglicanism, and he would select the music according to what he called the 'political or public opinion view'. Visitors were asked in advance not to genuflect. In Sidney, not only might undergraduates accustomed to public-school worship be alienated by the explicitly High-Church tone of chapel worship, but a more fundamental problem was posed by the loss of faith suffered by Passant, Hackforth and, most disastrously, Smith, necessitating the appointment of a chaplain in 1929. In a somewhat lighter vein, Reynolds founded a Confraternitas Historica in 1910 whose constitution was amusingly drawn from the terminology of ancient Rome and the late-medieval Catholic Church.³⁹

By 1939, however, the grandiose intentions behind the new chapel seemed to have lost their impetus. Sidney continued to act as a focus for the activities of Anglo-Catholic undergraduates such as the Sanctae Trinitatis Confraternitas,

---

[35] Passant was elected Fellow of the College in 1919. For Smith, see *A Little Guide to Eucharistic Worship* (Cambridge, 1920) and (with E. Milner-White) *Cambridge Offices and Orisons* (Cambridge, 1920).

[36] Note, however, that recorded discussion of appointments to advowsons on the part of Governing Bodies yields scant evidence of concern about churchmanship.

[37] E.G. Selwyn, 'The Outlook for English Theology', *Theology*, January 1940, p. 6.

[38] Pearce, p. 90.

[39] The author delivered this paper to Reynolds's 'Confrat.' as Princeps on Ash Wednesday 1992.

whose public image, as satirised by Shane Leslie, was that of a small group which 'gathered in each other's rooms to sing Compline over a whiff of incense',[40] as well as of the Oratory of the Good Shepherd, a confraternity of priests and laymen which acquired a Cambridge house in 1920 and which was a visible and popular institution in Cambridge during the inter-war period.[41] Indeed, the Oratory adopted the Cambridge Mission to Fruitpickers at Wisbech in 1922, which was to attract about a hundred undergraduates from various colleges during the Long Vacation. It appears, however, that the thoroughly Catholic tone of the chapel alienated non-High Churchmen to a greater degree than in other College chapels where less controversial elements of Catholic ceremonial were employed. If, for example, an undergraduate might object to the 'uncongregational' nature of the liturgy of King's College Chapel, Milner-White, whose Service of Nine Lessons and Carols was first broadcast in 1928 and 'subsequently listened to by innumerable infidels on the radio',[42] was more generally the subject of lighthearted satire:

> Eric Milner-White
> Looks well by candle-light;
> That's why
> We have our service High.[43]

Similarly, whereas J.B. Atkins, on going up to Pembroke in 1889, observed that the more Evangelical undergraduates refused to bow and turn eastwards towards the Altar during the Creed,[44] this constituted a single objection to an otherwise acceptable act of worship. Thus, college chaplains of different shades of churchmanship were able to employ a regular and uncomplicated celebration of the Eucharist, supplemented by a surpliced choir and the widely acceptable *Hymns Ancient and Modern*, as a practical and uncontroversial means of 'meeting the spiritual needs of the whole body'. The unique design of Sidney Chapel as well as the style of its worship and the introduction of the more Catholic *English Hymnal* in this century made its services less generally acceptable, and it is difficult to avoid the conclusion that, by 1939, the optimism and elaborate vision which had conceived the chapel had been overtaken by practical failure and anticlimax.

But it is the uniqueness of Sidney's Chapel among the college chapels of Oxford and Cambridge which renders it worthy of serious study. Its confident design involved considerable capital expenditure. Seen in the context of the demise both of the Anglican monopoly of University entrance and scholarship and of compulsory chapel, it represents a practical and ambitious attempt to meet the challenge of pluralism and ultimately secularism. It was conceived and designed

---

[40] S. Leslie, *The Cantab* (London, 1926), p. 117.
[41] See G. Tibbatts, *The Oratory of the Good Shepherd: The First Seventy Years* (Windsor, 1988) and H.R.T. Brandreth, *History of the O.G.S.* (Cambridge, 1958).
[42] T.E.B. Howarth, *Cambridge Between Two Wars* (London, 1978), p. 48.
[43] *The Basileon*, 28 November 1933.
[44] J.B. Atkins, *Incidents and Reflections* (London, 1947), p. 49.

in the form of an emphatic statement of the vitality of the Catholic faith, ironically in the chapel of a post-Reformation college. Worship was to be supported by sympathetic Fellows and was intended to evangelise the undergraduate with the beauty of holiness. It is these considerations which lie behind Sidney Chapel and do something to explain both its success and its failure.

INDEX

Abbreviations: B Benefactor of Sidney; C Chaplain of Sidney; F Fellow of Sidney; HF Honorary Fellow of Sidney; M Master of Sidney; b. born; d. died; m. member of Sidney

Abbot's Langley, Manor of, 82
Abingdon Abbey, 10
Abington, Dorothy, 82n.
Abington, Thomas, 82n.
Acton, 1st Lord (historian), 129f.
Adami, J.G., 225f.
Adams, Charles Francis, 97
Addenbrooke's Hospital, Cambridge, 157
Adrian, E.D., 1st Lord (Chancellor), 224
Afflighem, Franco of, *see* Franco of Afflighem
Agnellus of Pisa, St, 25
Agricola, Rodolphus, 82n.
Albemarle, Christopher Monck, 2nd Duke of (Chancellor), 120
Albertus Magnus, 84
Aldrich, Francis (M), 79
Alençon, François, Duc d', 39
All Souls College, Oxford, 10, 114, 143
America, British Colonies in North, 89–104
Anderson, H.K., 225
Andrewes, Lancelot, 82n.
Annual, Sidney Sussex College, 213
Aristotle, 80, 115
Armstrong, Sir Thomas, 107
Arthur, Prince, of Connaught, 231
Ascham, Roger, 8
Atkins, J.B., 246
Atkinson, John, 48
Aubrey, John, 77
Augustine, St, 238
Ausonius, 70
Avila, St Teresa of, *see* Teresa of Avila, St

Bacon, Roger, 4, 231
Bagington Manor, Warwickshire, 52f.
Baker, R.G. (map of Cambridge, 1830), 162

Balderston, Dr John, Master of Emmanuel, 124
Balliol College, Oxford, 201
Banos, Théophile de, 55
Barclay, John, 82
Barcroft, J., 231
Barbara, St, 25
Barrington, Cambs., 49
Basset, John, 114
Basset, Joshua (M), 77, 111–130
Bates, Dr George, 105f.
Bays, George Henry, 171n.
Bayliss, Sir William, 224
Beales, Derek (F), 105
Beauclerk, Topham, 133f., 136ff.
Beaumont, Francis, 61
Bedford, John, 1st Duke of, 38
Bedford, Lucy Russell, *née* Harington, Countess of (B), 57f., 60f., 63f., 71, 73, 80f.
Bentley, Richard, Master of Trinity, 198
Berkeley, Sir William, 91f.
Berwick, James Fitzjames, Duke of, 119
Bible, 87
Biblia Regia, 79
Bill of Rights, 126, 129
Billers, John, 123
Birkett, H.S., 230
Blastaris, Matthaeus, 84
Blundell bequest, 177
Blundell Court, Sidney Sussex College, 50, 162
Boat Club, Sidney Sussex College, 211–213
Bodleian Library, Oxford, 78, 142
Bosse, Mr (College clerk), 80f.
Bossuet, Jacques Bénigne, 129
Boston, Mass., 90f., 98, 100–103
Boswell, James, 131, 138, 142

249

INDEX

Bradshaw, John, 107
Bradwardine, Thomas, 84
Brasenose College, Oxford, 29
Brasher, Richard, 49
Braun, Georg (map of Cambridge, 1575), 9
Brodie, T.G., 224f., 228, 230
Brooke, Baron, *see* Greville, Fulke
Brooke, Rupert, 223f.
Brookes, Matthew, 95
Broughton, Hugh, 84
Browne, Dr L.E., 214
Bruno, Giordano, 55
Buchanan, George, 55
Buck, Thomas, 85
Bulstrode, Sir William, 81
Burdett, George (m), 90, 94–98
Burges, John, 67
Burghley House, 70
Burghley, Lord, 40, 58f., 70
Burke, Edmund, 142
Burnet, Gilbert, 124
Burney, Charles, 140
Burrough, Sir James, Master of Caius and architect, 160
Burroughes, Edward, 106
Burton Agnes, 46
Burton Constable, 46
Byng, John, 5th Baron Torrington, 182f.
Byrd, William, 242

Caius College, *see* Gonville and Caius College
Caldwell, R.T., Master of Corpus Christi College, 240
Callendar, H.L., 219
Calvin, Jean, 79, 82, 115
Cambridge Archaeological Unit, 27
Cambridge Architectural Society, 236
Cambridge Camden Society, 236
Cambridge Philosophical Society, 197
Cambridge Scientific Instrument Company, 195, 219ff.
Cambridge, University of, *see* University of Cambridge
Camden, 1st Marquess (Chancellor), 154f., 169
Camden, William, 55, 61
Cannon, W.B., 232
Canterbury Greyfriars, 26
Carew, Thomas, 67

Casaubon, Isaac, 82
Cassander, George, 130
Castlemaine, Earl of, 76
Cavendish Laboratory, Cambridge, 200f., 205, 218f., 226
Cecil, William, *see* Burghley, Lord
Chafy, John, 149
Chafy, William (M, B), 145–161, 165–170, 172–175
Chafy, William Westwood (m), 150
Chapel, Sidney Sussex College, 10f., 27, 31ff., 45, 51f., 145, 155, 157, 174f., 235–247
Chapel Court, Sidney Sussex College, 11, 46, 48, 153, 174, 213
Chapman, Andrew, 49
Chapman, George, 55
Charles I, 63, 73, 77, 85, 93, 105, 116
Charles II, 77, 98, 105f., 117f.
Charlett, Arthur, 116, 124
Charlton, T.M. (F), 105
Chesterfield, 1st Earl of (B), 78n.
Chesterton, Cambs., 50
Chilcott, Samuel (F), 143f.
Cholmondeley, 5th Marquess of, 78
Christ Church, Oxford, 39, 111, 125, 201
Christ's College, Cambridge, 44f., 49, 146
Cicero, 65
Clap, Captain Roger, 91
Clare College (formerly Clare Hall), Cambridge, 8, 43, 53, 90, 138
Clare, Elizabeth de, 8
Clarendon, Henry Hyde, 2nd Earl of, 112
Clark, G.M., 218
Clayden, Arthur, 205
Cleethorpes, 177–193
Cleland, James, 81
Clements (carpenter), 49
Clerke, Sir Francis (B), 46, 48, 145, 159
Clifford, Anne, Countess of Dorset, Pembroke and Montgomery, *née*, 60
Clifton, R.B., 201
Cloister Court (New Court), Sidney Sussex College, 9, 16ff., 21, 23, 25, 50, 175, 191, 196, 211ff., 235f., 239
Coke, Sir Edward, 82
Cole, William, 111, 114f.
Combe, Francis (m, B), 82f., 87
Confraternitas Historica, ix, 245
Cook, John, 106
Cornish, John Rundle (F), 203

250

INDEX

Corpus Christi College, Cambridge, 46, 75, 114, 149, 158, 240, 242, 245
Corrie, George, Master of Jesus College, 129
Cotton, Sir Robert, 81
Coulthurst, Henry William (F), 141
Cowper, 4th and 5th Earls, 150
Cracow, 84
Cranch, John, 108
Craven, Joseph (M, B), 113ff., 117, 128
Creede, Thomas, 82
Crete, 77
Crew, Nathaniel Lord, Bishop of Durham, 126
Cromwell, Henry, 94
Cromwell, Mary, 110
Cromwell, Oliver (m), Lord Protector, 93f., 100f., 103, 105–111, 119, 137, 141
Cromwell, Richard, Lord Protector, 110
Cromwell, Thomas, 29
Cruttenden, William (F), 143
Cushing, Harvey, 231
Custance, William (map of Cambridge, 1798), 153f., 163

Dale, Dorothy, 224, 230f.
Danforth, Samuel, 89
Daniel, Samuel, 55
Dark, Kenneth (m), 17, 23, 25f., 28, 34
Dartmouth, Lord, 112, 126
Darwin, Charles, 219
Darwin, Horace, 219, 221
Daubney, William Heaford, 181, 183, 185, 187ff.
Davenport, A.H. (F, Bursar), 10, 192
Davies, John, 55
Dee, John, 84
Deighton (bookseller), 143
Delage, Yves, 228
Dempster, Thomas, 80
Department of the Environment, 16
Devereux, Lady Penelope, later Lady Rich, 40
Devonshire, 6th Duke of, 160
Dewar, Sir James, 200, 205, 215
Digby, Everard, 82n.
Ditton, Cambs., 50
Döllinger, Ignaz von, 129f.
Donne, John, 55, 57, 60, 62, 81
Dorsten, Jan van, 59

Douglas, C.G., 231
Dover, Mass., 96ff.
Downing College, Cambridge, 158, 200f.
Drake, Sir Francis, 40
Drayton, Michael, 55
Drury, A.N., 227
Dryden, John, 141
Duckworth Laboratory, Cambridge, 21f.
Dudley estates, 159
Dudley, 1st Earl of, 159
Dugard, Richard (F, B), 85, 92
Dugard, William (m), 85, 87
Duns Scotus, 4, 79
Du Puy, Claudius, 107
Durham, Bishop of, *see* Crew, Nathaniel
Dyer, Edward, 55, 59
Dyer, General R.E.H., 37

Edgeworth, Maria, 108
Edmund of Cornwall, 28
Edward I, 8, 31
Edward VI, 38, 70
Edward VII, 189
Edwards, G.M. (F, B, College historian), xii, 9, 10, 150, 160
Einthoven, Willem, 226f.
Elizabeth I, 38ff., 42, 44, 56, 58, 60, 70
Ellis, John Clough Williams (F, Tutor), 199, 202, 204, 213
Elliston, Martha, 140
Elliston, William (M), 107f., 140f.
Elliston, Robert William, 108
Ely, Cambs., 49
Emmanuel College, Cambridge, 33, 45ff., 51, 87, 90, 124, 133, 135, 138ff., 142, 213, 241
Erasmus, Desiderius, 130
Essex, Walter Devereux, 1st Earl of (d. 1576), 40
Essex, James (architect), 11, 13, 23, 25ff., 29, 31ff., 145, 160
Estienne, Henri, 55
Ewing, J.A., 208, 210

Fagius, Paul, 84
Family, The (dining club), 151
Farmer, Anthony, President of Magdalen College, Oxford, 115f.
Farmer, Richard, Master of Emmanuel College, Cambridge, 133, 138ff., 142
Fauconberg, Earl, 110

INDEX

Fearnsides, W.G. (F, HF), 211
Fellows' Combination Room, Sidney Sussex College, *see* Senior Combination Room
Fellows' Garden, Sidney Sussex College, 18, 25, 28, 50, 213
Fellows' Parlour, Sidney Sussex College, 46, 48
Fenton, Geoffrey, 59
Feuillerat, Albert, 37
Finch, Heneage, 121
Fitzpatrick, T.C., President of Queens' College, 241
Fletcher, John, 61
Fletcher, W.M., 225, 231
Florio, John, 55, 59
Foster, Sir Michael, 219, 223, 231
Foxe, John, 119
France, Anatole, 224
Francis, Alban, 120ff., 124
Franciscan Friary, Cambridge, 3f., 7–33, 43ff., 50f., 75, 163
Franciscans (Grey Friars), 3–10, 13, 16, 20, 25f., 28, 32f., 44
Franco of Afflighem, 84
Fraunce, Abraham, 55
Frazer, Sir James George, 245
Freke, John, 125
Freund, Miss I., 201
Fuller, Thomas (m), 9, 13, 31ff., 43, 85, 163

Garden Court, Sidney Sussex College, 27, 50
Gaskell, W., 225f.
Gascoigne, George, 59
Gay, John, 142
Gee, Robert, 167f.
Gee, Walter (F), 167
George III, 108, 142, 152, 165
George IV, 147, 151, 169
Gibbons, John, 79
Gibbs, J.W., 208ff.
Gifford, Bishop Bonaventure, 127
Girton College, Cambridge, 199ff., 218
Gloucester, Prince William, Duke of (Chancellor), 147f., 152
Golding, Arthur, 59
Goldsmith, Oliver, 142f.
Gonville and Caius College, Cambridge, 46, 49, 112, 114, 125f., 160, 199f, 218, 242
Goodlad, Thomas (F, B), 87, 117
Goring, Sir George, Earl of Norwich (m), 79
Gother, John, 127, 129
Gothofredus, Dionysius, 81
Gower, Humphrey, 121
Gower, John, 84
Grainger, James, 132
Gray, Thomas, 141
Greene, Robert, 55, 59
Greville, Sir Fulke, Baron Brooke, 35, 37, 55, 59
Griffiths, Ernest Howard (F), 204–207, 210, 219f.
Grosseteste, Robert, 5
Grotius, Hugo, 130
Guibert, Philbert, 106
Guillaume, Charles Édouard, 211
Gunn, Thom, 232
Gunning, Henry, 146f., 149–152, 155ff., 168
Gunpowder Plot, 82, 112, 115, 119
Gunthorpe, John, Dean of Wells, 84

Habington, Thomas, *see* Abington, Thomas
Hackforth, Reginald (F), 225, 243, 245
Hakluyt, Richard, 81
Hall, Sidney Sussex College, 46–50, 137, 166
Hall Court, Sidney Sussex College, 11, 17f., 25f., 46, 49, 145f., 152f., 159, 174f., 213f.
Halley, Edmund, 122
Hamond, John (map of Cambridge, 1592), 11, 27, 163
Hardy, W.B., 225, 231
Harington, Lady Anne (B), 80
Harington, Sir John (writer and translator), 55, 60
Harington, Sir John (1st Baron Harington of Exton (1603), d. 1613, B, executor of the Foundress), 43ff., 47ff., 52f., 79, 87
Harington of Exton, 2nd Baron (d. 1614, B), 76, 80f.
Harington, Lucy, *see* Bedford, Countess of,
Harraden, Richard, 153
Harris, Samuel, 164, 166, 169f., 173

INDEX

Harrison, Colonel Thomas, 106
Harrison, Thomas (m), 90–94
Hart, Sir John (B), 79
Harvey, Gabriel, 55, 59
Harvey, William, 77
Haslingfield, Cambs., 49
Hawkins, Sir John, 143
Head, Sir Henry, 232
Heaviside, James (F), 149n.
Hebrew literature, 84
Hedley (lessee of land on Sidney site), 11
Henry III, 5ff., 31, 44
Henry VI, 29
Henry VIII, 8, 29, 31, 44, 82
Henry, Prince of Wales (d. 1612), 80
Herbert, George, 55, 72
Herbert, William, *see* Pembroke, 3rd Earl of,
Hey, Richard (F), 140f.
Heycock, Charles Thomas (F), 195, 199f., 204–221
Hicks, J.W. (F), 236, 238f.
Hill, A.V., 224, 226, 231
Hind, John (F), 149n.
Hobson, Thomas (carrier), 51, 80f.
Hoffa, A.J., 226
Holberg, Ludvig, 142
Holinshed, Ralph, 59
Hollis, Thomas, 137
Holmes, Sherlock, 204
Hopkins, F.G., 225
Horace, 65, 70
Hoskins, John, 55
Houghton Hall, Norfolk, 78
Hügel, Baron Anatole von, 130
Huguenots, 119
Hulsius, Levinus, 81
Humfrey, Charles, 145, 153, 159f., 164
Hunter, Christopher (F), 141
Huntingdon, 3rd Earl of (d. 1595), 59
Hurd, Richard, 138
Hus, Jan, 79
Hutchinson, Ann, 101

Ireton, Henry, 107
Irvine, J. Murray (C), 10

James I and VI, 37, 44, 60f., 69f., 73, 82, 106
James II and VII, 100, 107, 111–129, 238

Jeffreys of Wem, George, 1st Baron, Lord Chief Justice, 122f.
Jenner, David (F), 117
Jennings, Thomas (B), 79f.
Jesus College, Cambridge, 112, 129, 147, 155, 161, 163, 236, 245
Jesus College, Oxford, 201
Jesus Lane, 9f., 17, 21, 23, 153, 165, 212, 235
Jewish properties in Cambridge, 5, 7, 31
John IV, King of Portugal, 242
Johnson and Matthey, 209
Johnson, James (M, B), 113, 117, 127
Johnson, Samuel, 131–144
Johnston, Nathaniel, 113
Jonson, Ben, 55, 61–74
Juvenal, 70

Keble, John, 239
Kent, Henry Gray, Earl of (B, executor of the Foundress), 43f., 47f., 52f.
Kenyon, John (historian), 125
King, Edward, Bishop of Lincoln, 238
King's College, Cambridge, 10, 49, 84, 90, 122, 138, 158, 205, 239, 242, 246
King's Ditch, 7, 9f., 17, 26–30, 32, 44, 46, 50f.
King Street, 162ff.
Kirk, John, 108
Knox-Shaw, Thomas (M, B), 27, 235, 238, 240, 242–245
Kyd, Thomas, 55, 61

Laboratory, Sidney Sussex College, 195–221
Lamb, Mary Ellen, 58
Lamplough, F.E.E., 218
Lancaster, John of, *see* Duke of Bedford
Langley, J.N., 224ff., 231
Languet, Hubert, 39, 55
Lapidge, Edward, 167
Lash, Nicholas, 130
Laud, William, Archbishop of Canterbury, 90, 95ff.
Laughton, John, 116, 124
Le Châtelier, Henri, 210f., 220
Leibniz, Gottfried Wilhelm, 129f.
Leicester, Robert Dudley, Earl of, 36, 40, 42, 56, 58f.
Leiden, University of, *see* University of Leiden

253

INDEX

Leland, John, 8
Le Quien, Michel, 128
Leslie, Shane, 246
Lettice, John (F), 131–135, 138–143
Leveson, Edward, 82n.
Levet, Robert, 132, 135
Lewis, C.S., 36f., 41
Lewis, Thomas, 224
Leycester, George, 133, 135, 138f.
Library, Sidney Sussex College, 51, 75–88, 141, 143f., 157f., 202
Lindenbrog, Erpold, 78
Liveing, George Downing, 199, 205
Liverpool, 2nd Earl of, Prime Minister, 147
Locke, John, 125
Loe, Richard, 49
Loggan, David, 9, 17, 21, 45, 47, 50f., 75, 154, 163
Longleat House, 70, 161
Lort, Dr Michael, 135, 138
Losh, James, 162
Louis XIV, 119
Lown, B., 229
Lublin, 84
Lucas, Keith, 225f., 231
Ludolph of Saxony, 80
Ludwig, K.F.W., 228
Luther, Martin, 79, 115
Lyon, Thomas Henry (architect), 243
Lyons, Sir John, Master of Trinity Hall, 130

Macaulay, Catharine, 137
Macedo, Francisco de Santo Agostinho, 86f.
McGill University, Montreal, 223, 225f., 230ff.
Machray, Robert, Archbishop of Rupertsland (F), 228, 235f.
McNeile, A.H. (F), 241, 243
MacWilliam, John Alexander, 228
Madingley, Cambs., 7, 9, 32, 44
Magdalen College, Oxford, 115f., 124, 201
Magdalene College, Cambridge, 47, 50, 75, 120, 126, 141, 175, 236f.
Maier, Michael, 82
Malcolm Street, 10, 161f.
Mann, A.H., 242
Marlowe, Christopher, 61
Marotti, Arthur, 57
Martial, 65, 70
Martyn, Thomas (F), 140f.

Marvell, Andrew, 71f.
Mary I, 238
Mason, W. (aquatint of 1822), 152
Massachusetts, 93, 95f., 99–103
Massey, John, 111
Master's Garden, Sidney Sussex College, 26, 50, 75, 145, 153f., 161, 163, 165, 169
Master's Lodge, Sidney Sussex College, 26f., 45–48, 51, 76, 115, 127, 145, 152ff., 159, 168f., 174
Mather, Cotton, 101
Matthey, George, 209
Matthews (plasterer), 49, 51
Matthews, Edmund (F), 87n., 113, 116, 121
Melanchthon, Philipp, 39, 115
Meres, Francis, 55
Merton College, Oxford, 28
Micklethwaite, Paul (F, B), 76, 78, 83
Milner, Isaac, 198
Milner-White, Eric, 239, 242, 244, 246
Milton, John, 85, 135, 141
Mines, Anatole, 224ff.
Mines, George Ralph (F), 223–233
Mines, Marjorie, *see* Rolfe, Marjorie
Minshull, Richard (M), 111
Molyneux, Emery, 76
Monmouth, Duke of, 118, 122
Montagu, Sir Edward (m, B), 79
Montagu, James (M, B), 43ff., 47–53, 78, 81f., 87
Montagu House, Sidney Sussex College, 10, 27
Montagu, Roger (B), 84
Moore, G.E., 245
Moorer, Humphrey (F), 79
Moorman, J.R.H. (historian), 16
Morrice, Roger, 115, 124
Morris, William, 236
Moxon, George (m), 90, 98ff.
Moxon, Joseph, 125
Muir, Pattison, 200
Munby, Julian, 28
Music in the College Chapel, 238–42, 246
Muss, Charles, 168

Nashe, Thomas, 55
Nathan ben Jehiel, 84
Naylor, E.W., 241
Neale, J.M., 236, 238

INDEX

Nevile, Thomas, 45
Neville, Francis Henry (F), 130, 188, 195, 200, 202, 204–221, 223
Newcastle, Margaret Cavendish, Duchess of, 85
New College, Oxford, 106
New England, 89f., 95–104
Newman, John Henry, Cardinal, 129f.
Newnham College, Cambridge, 200f., 218, 224
Newton, Alderman Samuel, 127
Newton, Sir Isaac, 111, 113, 122ff., 126
Newton, Peter, 20
Nottingham, University of, *see* University of Nottingham
Noutch, M.R., 46
Nutter, James, 171
Nutter, Thomas, 170–174

Oakham School, 132f.
Occo, Adolphus, 81
Ockham, William of, 5
Odling, W., 201
Opechancanough, Chief, 92
Opsimathes, Johannes, 82n.
Ord, Boris, 242
Organ in College Chapel, 236, 242
Osler, Sir William, 231f.
Oughtred, William, 76
Ovid, 132
Oxenham, Henry, 129f.
Oxford, 3–8, 13f., 16, 20, 23–26, 28f., 39, 114, 142, 155
Oxford Archaeological Unit, 28
Oxford Movement, 237, 244
Oxford, University of, *see* University of Oxford

Palfrey, George (m), 87
Paris, 5, 39, 128
Parke, James, 168f.
Parsons, Hugh, 99
Passant, E.J. (F, HF), 244f.
Patin, Dr Charles, 107
Pattison, William (m), 141
Peachell, Dr John, Master of Magdalene College, 120–124, 126
Pearce, E.W., 240f., 245
Pearson, J.L., 17, 235ff., 239f., 243
Peck, William, 51
Pemberton, Sir Francis, 121

Pembroke College, Cambridge, 90, 114, 138, 242, 246
Pembroke, Henry Herbert, 2nd Earl of, 36, 56
Pembroke, Mary Herbert (*née* Sidney), Countess of, 39, 56–60
Pembroke, Philip Herbert, 4th Earl of, 60
Pembroke, William Herbert, 3rd Earl of, 56, 60f., 70
Penn, William, 125
Penshurst Place, 38f., 41, 67–74
Pepys, Samuel, 120f.
Percy, Thomas, 132, 138f.
Perne, Andrew, 81
Perowne, E.H., Master of Corpus Christi College, 240
Peterborough, 49
Peterhouse, Cambridge, 138, 163, 245
Peters, Hugh, 106
Peters, R.A., 231
Peterson, William, 225, 230
Phelps, Robert (M), 162, 183, 188f., 198, 239
Pheon, The, 244
Phillipps, Samuel (m), 143
Pilkington, John, 84
Plantin, Christopher, 79
Plasterer, John, 49
Plumb, Sir John (J.H.) (historian), 78
Plutarch, 133
Pocklington, Dr John (m), 79
Powell, William Samuel, Master of St John's, 107f.
Pride, Thomas, 107
Pringle, Gordon (m), 31
Prüss, Johann, 79
Pseudo-Dionysius, 82n.
Pusey, E.B., 239
Pynchon, William, 99f.

Queens' College, Cambridge, 48f., 138, 198, 236
Queen's College, Oxford, 201
Quinser, William, 167
Quintilian, 65

Raleigh, Sir Walter, 55
Ramsey Abbey, 50
Ramus, Petrus, 87
Raoult, François Marie, 206
Reach, Cambs., 50

255

INDEX

Rewley Abbey, Oxford, 3, 28f.
Reynolds, J.W. (F), 239, 242f., 245
Reynolds, Sir Joshua, 108, 142
Rhodes, Robert (F), 79
Rich, Robert, 3rd Baron (later Earl of Warwick), 40
Riches, Kenneth (C, HF), Bishop of Lincoln, 244n.
Richard, Earl of Cornwall, 20
Ringler, William, 37
Rivers, W.H.R., 231
Robinson, J. A., 236, 241
Robinson Sir Austin (F, B), xii, 244
Rochester, Laurence Hyde, 1st Earl of (d. 1711), 112
Rogers, Nicholas, xii
Rolfe, Marjorie, 223ff.
Roman remains on Sidney site, 21, 23, 30
Romilly, Joseph, 148n, 150n., 151n., 154ff., 160n., 163n.
Röntgen, Wilhelm Konrad von, 207,
Roozeboom, H.W. Bakhuis, 208, 210f.
Rosenhain, W., 208ff.
Rottenwode, John, 84n.
Royal Society, 208, 210, 215
Rudolf II, Holy Roman Emperor, 39
Ruhemann, S., 200, 218
Russell, Samuel Thomas, 108
Rutland, Elizabeth Manners (née Sidney), Countess of, 60, 63, 65f.
Ruusbroec, Jan van, 83

St Catharine's College, Cambridge, 49, 138, 242
St Giles' Church, 23
St John's College, Cambridge, 45, 48, 78, 107, 121, 158, 199f., 203f., 243
St Mary the Great, Church of (Great St Mary's), 31, 134, 147, 241
St Mary the Less, Church of (Little St Mary's), 238, 243, 245
St Mary's College, Oxford, 29
Saleby Manor, 53, 187
Salem, Mass., 95f.,
Salisbury, Robert Cecil, 1st Earl of, 61, 63, 66, 72n.
Salmasius, Claudius, 85, 87
Saunders, James (F), 149n.
Savage, William, 164ff., 169–74
Sawtry, Cambs., 50
Sayers, Dorothy L., 204

Sclater, Edward, 114
Scot, John (the elder), 77
Scott-Giles, C.W. (m, College historian), xii, 9, 131, 145, 157
Scotus, Duns, *see* Duns Scotus
Selwyn College, Cambridge, 237, 242
Seneca, 65, 67
Senior Combination Room, Sidney Sussex College, 18, 23, 142
Shakespeare, William, 55f., 60ff., 138
Shannon, Charles, 205n.
Sharp, Dr John, 134, 139
Shenstone, William, 138
Sherrington, Sir Charles, 224
Sidney, Algernon, xi
Sidney, Elizabeth, *see* Rutland, Countess of,
Sidney, Lady Frances, Countess of Sussex (Foundress of Sidney Sussex College), 11, 31, 43f., 47, 49, 52f., 55, 58f., 79
Sidney, Frances, wife of Sir Philip, née Walsingham, 40
Sidney, Sir Henry, 38f., 42, 69
Sidney, Mary (mother of Sir Philip), 59
Sidney, Mary, *see* Pembroke, Countess of,
Sidney, Sir Philip, 35–42, 55–62, 65, 70, 74
Sidney, Robert, Viscount Lisle and Earl of Leicester, 70
Sidney, Sir William, 38
Sidney Place, 145, 154, 161f., 164
Sidney Street, 10f., 16, 23, 27, 145, 161–165, 169, 211f., 219
Sidney Sussex College buildings, *see* under individual buildings and under Blundell Court, Chapel Court, Cloister Court, Hall Court
Simon, John, 49f.,
Simons, Ralph (Rodolph) (architect), 33, 45f., 48f., 51ff.
Smail, R.C. (F), xii
Smart, Christopher, 131, 136
Smith, B.T.D. (F, B), 243ff.
Smith, Charles (M), 188, 205, 213, 239
Smith, Sir Thomas, 82n.
Smith, W. Hammond (m), 205n.
Smith, William, 84n.
Sorby, H.C., 208
South Court, Sidney Sussex College, 153, 213
Southgate, Richard, 108
Spanish Armada, 38, 119, 238

256

INDEX

Spence, Edward, 112
Spencer, John, 1st Earl, 136
Spens, Sir Will, Master of Corpus Christi College, 240, 245
Spenser, Edmund, 55, 57, 59
Sprat, Thomas, 124, 126
Starling, E.H., 224
Stephens, Edward, 127f.
Sterne, Laurence, 136
Stevens, Captain (of Rotherhithe), 77
Stokes, Sir George, Bart., 210
Stow, John, 59
Streyzius, Georg, 82n.
Suarez, Francisco, 80
Sussex, Thomas Radcliffe, 3rd Earl of, husband of Lady Frances Sidney, 58f.
Sussex Street (*see* also Walls Lane), 27, 51, 145, 160–166, 169, 215
Switzer, J.F.Q. (F, Bursar), 192f.

Tasso, Torquato, 83
Taylor, Samuel (of Dudley) (m, B), 158f., 174, 202
Taylor Endowment, Sidney Sussex College, 158f., 202ff., 214f.
Taylor Mathematical Library, Sidney Sussex College, 202
Tercentenary celebrations, Sidney Sussex College, 236
Teresa of Avila, St, 83
Thacker, Dorothy, *see* Dale, Dorothy
Theodora, Sister, 238
Thetford Ware, 21
Thomas, Miss M.B., 201
Thompson, William, 126
Thomson, David (M), 105
Thornely, John W.A. (F, Senior Tutor), 105
Thorpe, Richard, 49
Thynne, Sir John, 70
Titelmann, Franz, 87n.
Toletus, Franciscus, 87
Trinity College, Cambridge, 9–12, 29–32, 43ff., 48–52, 78, 111, 115, 133ff., 138f., 148, 154, 157f., 163, 168, 204, 218, 226, 239, 242
Trinity College, Dublin, 94
Trinity College, Oxford, 82, 133, 201
Trinity Hall, Cambridge, 78, 130, 138, 235
Truro Cathedral, 236
Turner, Baptist Noel, 132–138
Turner, Francis, Bishop of Ely, 121

Twining, Thomas (F), 140f.
Tyndall, William, 79
Tyrconnel, Earl of, 119

Uffenbach, Zacharias Conrad von, 75ff., 107
University of Amsterdam, 208
University of Cambridge, 7–10, 25, 31, 43f., 77, 87, 118, 120–123, 125, 130f., 142f., 147f., 151f., 154–158, 168, 174, 177, 188, 195, 197–201, 204f., 209, 211, 221, 223, 231, 237, 245
University of Leiden, 76
University Library, Cambridge, 142, 146, 151, 157
University of Nottingham, 81
University of Oxford, 77, 116, 121, 124, 131, 197, 201f., 231, 235, 246

Valkenburg, Beatrice van, 20
Van't Hoff, J.H., 206, 208
Vasquez, Gabriel, 80
Vatican Library, 78
Vaughan, George, 101
Victoria, Queen, 152
Vigani, Francis, 198
Virginia, 89–93

Wadham College, Oxford, 43
Wake, William, Archbishop of Canterbury, 128
Waldstein, Zdenkonius, Baron, 47
Walker, Thomas (F), 118
Wallace, Malcolm, 36f., 40
Walls Lane (*see also* Sussex Street), 13, 31, 51, 163
Walpole, Colonel Robert, 78
Walsingham, Norfolk (Franciscan house), 3f., 13f., 16, 25ff.
Walsingham, Frances, *see* Sidney, Frances
Walsingham, Sir Francis, 40
Ward, Samuel (M, B), 79n., 84f.
Warkworth Castle, 27
Warwick, Ambrose Dudley, 2nd Earl of, 40, 59
Warwick, Anne, Countess of, 59
Washburn, E.W., 232
Waymouth, John, 81 and n.
Weekes, G.A. (M, B), 224, 236, 238, 240, 243ff.
Wellington, 1st Duke of, 154

257

INDEX

Westmacott, Henry, 166–169
Westmacott, Sir Richard, 166
Westmacott, Richard, father of Sir Richard and of Henry, 166
Westminster Abbey, 53
Westwood, John, 150
Wheelwright, John (m), 90, 100–103
Whewell, William, Master of Trinity, 157, 195, 197
Whitaker, William, 80
Whitgift, John, Archbishop of Canterbury, 11, 43f.
Whitney, Geoffrey, 55, 59
Wigge, Gilbert, 48
Wilkins, William (architect), 160
Wilkinson, Dr H.N.S., 105
Wilkinson, Josiah Henry, 108
William of Orange, 'the Silent', 39
William III, 107, 111, 117, 126
William IV, 152, 169
Willmer, William (m), 80
Wilson, C.T.R. (F, HF), 215, 218
Wilton House, 59f.
Windsor Castle, 152, 160
Winthrop, Adam, 93
Winthrop, John, 93, 96–99, 102
Woburn Abbey, 80
Wolfe, General James, 37
Wollaton House, 161
Wood, Anthony, 114
Woodcock, John, 99
Woolston, Thomas (F), 117
Worcestre, William, 25
Wordsworth, Christopher, Master of Trinity, 148
Wren, Matthew, Bishop of Norwich, 95
Wroth, Lady Mary, *née* Sidney, 60f.
Wyatt, James (architect), 155
Wyatt, Jeffry, *see* Wyatville
Wyatville, Sir Jeffry (architect), 17f., 23, 145f., 152–156, 160, 165–169, 174f.

Yarmouth, Great, 95
York, Frederick, Duke of, son of George III, 150
Young, John (F), 80
Young, Patrick, 82

Zabarella, Jacopo, 87
Zanchius, Hieronymus, 79